DEMOCRATIC THEORY

DEMOCRATIC THEORY

by Giovanni Sartori

UNIVERSITY OF FLORENCE

Based on the author's translation of
Democrazia e definizione (2nd edition),
Il Mulino, Bologna, 1958

GREENWOOD PRESS, PUBLISHERS
WESTPORT, CONNECTICUT

Library of Congress Cataloging in Publication Data

Sartori, Giovanni, 1924–
   Democratic theory.

   Original ed. issued as Waynebook no. 6.
   Bibliography: p.
   1. Democracy. I. Title.
[JC423.S273 1973]   320.5'1   72-8241
ISBN 0-8371-6545-8

JC
423
.S273
1976

Originally published in 1962 by Wayne State University Press, Detroit

Reprinted with the permission of Wayne State Unviersity Press

Reprinted by Greenwood Press,
a division of Williamhouse-Regency Inc.

First Greenwood Reprinting 1973
Second Greenwood Reprinting 1976

Library of Congress Catalog Card Number 72-8241

ISBN 0-8371-6545-8

Printed in the United States of America

*It is our way of using the words
"democracy" and "democratic
government" that brings about the
greatest confusion. Unless these
words are clearly defined and their
definition agreed upon, people will
live in an inextricable confusion
of ideas, much to the advantage of
demagogues and despots.*

TOCQUEVILLE

Preface
To the American Edition

THIS BOOK MAY give a somewhat disconcerting impression to an American audience. For it is one thing to address an audience which is already convinced, and another to address one which is not. And my *Democratic Theory* has been conceived in the latter perspective, among other reasons because I live in a frontier zone of the West—a country in which more than 40 per cent of the electorate vote for parties which do not, in truth, want democracy. Perhaps this fact also helps to explain why this book relies heavily on argument, why I am laying a good deal of emphasis on explanation, and on the kind of explanation which leads to theory construction.

Theory, to be sure, is not at this moment in great favor. As Hans Morgenthau recently observed, "Theory, being by definition useless for practical purposes, was assigned an honorific but ineffectual position." And not only has it been assigned a secondary role but, still worse, the word theory, at least in politics, is often not even honorific. Economic theory sounds all right, but political theory has a dubious ring, as if it were akin to ideological rationalization. This seemed to me, however, all the more reason for giving to this book, somewhat polemically, the title it bears. For I am not in agreement with those who underestimate the practical impact of theory, and much less with those who view it with suspicion.

I understand, however, that to speak of theory might lead to some ambiguity. It would only be fair, therefore, if I were asked what I mean when I use this term, and furthermore what the relationship is between my approach and that of the political philosopher or the political scientist. Since I answer these questions in the course of the book (Chapter 9) I will only say at this point that I have not bothered much about how my theory ought to be classified. My first purpose has been to fill a gap, handling my subject matter in a way that might be useful and needed.

This is not to say that I speak of theory just for the sake of polemics and that I attach no definite meaning to the term. There are reasons for my choice of the title *Democratic Theory:* the main one being that I wish to stress from the very outset my concern with the ideas and/or ideals that produce and preserve a democratic system. And theory is traditionally associated with this concern, which seems to me all the more important in view of the growing tendency to think of ideas as the product of something else, or to reduce them to something else. In this light my book would appear to deal with the ideology of democracy. But I happen to dislike the word ideology very much.

The reasons for this particular antipathy will be given at the end (in Chapter 18), but it is worth making the point here. To use a certain term instead of another one is not at all unimportant, and one of my concerns throughout the whole text is to oppose the attitude expressed in remarks like "No matter what term we use," or "We need not quarrel about terminology," or "You can choose whatever name you prefer." Of course our quarrels are not about words although it would be more accurate to say that our quarrels *ought not* to be merely about words. However, this is not a sufficient reason for not quarrelling *also* about them. Granted that we are not fighting *for* words, we are certainly fighting *by means of* words, and this implies that words are an essential issue in our discussions (as I stress in Chapter 17). To "capture" a word such as democracy—that is, a word which has favorable emotive properties—is per se to assure oneself of a formidable position of strength. And to "surrender" to a word with negative associations—to accept for instance the term ideology as the proper label for all that we say in political matters—is in itself to start off with a handicap.

So I attach great importance to terminology and hence to definitions. This does not imply in the least that I take a nominalistic stand (as evidenced in Chapter 10). My recommendation is simply not to forget that all our problems have to be solved via the use of words. Likewise my concern with definitions does not mean that I follow the line of present-day conventionalism. Nowadays there is a growing tendency to dispose of all controversy by saying: "It is just a matter of definition." This is not at all my position. To say that everything depends on the definition we adopt, and to stop there, is to utter a platitude, when it is not an alibi for intellectual inertia. Thus the attention which I pay to definitions only means that we should not overlook the fact that if people happen to be democratic, hyper-democratic or anti-democratic, this is evidently connected with a mental yardstick and conditioned by the idea of democracy that they have in mind. It also means, in particular, that when we have to deal with cases of mental confusion it is helpful to attack the problem from its verbal end. It does not mean in the least that definitions are a panacea.

Another reason for having chosen the title *Democratic Theory* is that it is a traditional label for the so-called fundamental issues, which, in my view, remain fundamental even if a number of scholars apparently consider them obsolete. Nowadays, books on politics deal with two quite different things: politics as approached in political science, and politics as it is lived, thought about and perceived by the people involved. Now, I see no reason for going in the first direction to the detriment of the second. I mean that both approaches are just as necessary and that they are not mutually exclusive, whereas some scholars tend to substitute the first approach for the second, thereby confusing the position of the "observer" with the situation of the "actor."

What has been said until now as an explanation of my title, is also—I believe—a sufficient clue to the contents of the book. Chapter 1 will give an outline of how it is conceived and organized; and the opening chapter of the second part (Chapter 10) will discuss in a somewhat technical fashion the query raised in the first chapter. However, as a rule, I have rarely dealt with technicalities in a technical way. Almost always I try to use plain language, preferring the simpler to the more sophisticated expression. At times I also dwell on questions which may seem quite obvious and elementary; but that a notion is obvious does not mean that it does not merit attention, and what is elementary must not for this reason be ignored.

A final point ought perhaps to be raised. American literature on democracy is impressive, in quantity as well as in quality. Why, then, have a book on democracy translated into English? I will not repeat with Mill and Bagehot that "on all great subjects much remains to be said." Let me just answer that the problems and their priority appear different when seen—as I see them—from the very fringe of the democratic hemisphere. On the other hand, our thinking is inevitably—although in different degrees—ethnocentric and culture-bound, because our ability to see beyond the world we live in is confined to the languages we know. Hence, translations are useful, at least in principle, because they allow us to travel abroad. Whether my *Democratic Theory* may be useful is not, however, for me to say.

To pass from the why to the how of this translation, the present volume is based on the 1958 second Italian edition of my book, the first edition of which was published in 1957. I have found it necessary to make the changes that the different audience seemed to demand. For example, many issues which are violently controversial in the rational democracies are not even discussed in the United States: and therefore in this connection I have cut many passages. On the other hand, some familiar points which can be explained *en passant* to the Italian reader are not at all familiar elsewhere, and therefore I have had to expand and particularize in places. I have also added some topics which do not arouse interest in my country, but which are relevant in the English-speaking countries, and in this connection two new chapters have been written for this edition. Finally, some very troublesome translation problems concerning terms which have no satisfactory equivalents in English compelled me to rephrase an unexpected number of paragraphs. And, of course, the references have been brought up to date. On the whole, then, this edition has been thoroughly revised.

This does not imply that I am presenting an entirely new book. In the present enlarged American edition, the structure and the main content of the original text remain unaltered. To overhaul the volume excessively would have taken away—I feel—one of the reasons for translating it, namely, to offer, as far as possible, a broad picture, inclusive of another quite different democratic world with problems and mental patterns of its own.

It is pleasant to be able to publicly record my thanks to Victor A. Rapport, Dean for International Studies, Wayne State University, who recommended my book for translation, and to Armand De Gaetano, Professor of Italian and Spanish, Wayne State University, who kindly consented to translate the entire footnote matter and to consult the original sources in English, French, and Spanish of references in Italian translations of those foreign works cited. I am particularly grateful to Mrs Ita Kanter, editor, for the understanding and capable editing, and to Harold A. Basilius, Director, Wayne State University Press, for the patience with which he has attended the completion of the book. Last but not least, I am especially indebted to Professor Raphael Zariski, University of Nebraska, for his friendly assistance in checking the translated manuscript and for his precious advice on innumerable thorny points. It goes without saying that the responsibility for injections of Italian terminology and for stylistic deviations are to be attributed solely to my own obstination.

G. S.

University of Florence
November 4, 1961

Contents

Part Two: The Evidence
(*An historical appraisal*)

Part One

The Argument
A Logical Appraisal

"Our ideas are our spectacles."
  (Alain, *Le Citoyen contre les Pouvoirs*)

"In a democratic whole we must make a
distinction between three diverse elements:
1) a *reality,* that is, rapid circulation of
elites; 2) a *desire,* that is, equality . . .
3) an *illusion,* that is, direct government
of the masses."
  —F. Burzio, *Attualità e Essenza del Liberalismo*

Chapter I

What Is Democracy?
The Quest for a Definition

> *"In the case of a word like democracy*
> *not only is there no agreed definition but*
> *the attempt to make one is resisted from all*
> *sides. . . . The defenders of any kind of regime*
> *claim that it is a democracy, and fear that*
> *they might have to stop using the word if it*
> *were tied down to any one meaning."*
>
> —G. Orwell †

1. Descriptive and Prescriptive Meaning

IN A SOMEWHAT paradoxical vein, democracy could be defined as a highflown name for something which does not exist. Of course, this statement is provocative, and it would be more tactful to say that democracy is a misleading term for what it claims to designate. Although this way of putting it may still sound somewhat unfair, I believe that it gives us a clue to the difficulties of our problem.

If defining democracy merely signifies giving the meaning of the word, the problem is quickly solved, for all that is required is some knowledge of Greek. Literally, democracy means "power of the people" that the power belongs to the people. But here we have simply solved a terminological problem. Our explanation is nothing more than a "word-word definition" that renders in a known language the meaning of a term coming from another language.[1] And

3

the problem of defining democracy is much more complicated than that. When we use the term, it clearly *stands for* something. The question is not only: What does the word mean? but also: What is the thing? And when we try to answer this latter query, we discover that the thing does not correspond to the word. We discover, that is, that there is little resemblance between the facts and the label, between our findings and the name. So although "democracy" has a precise literal meaning this does not really help us to understand what an actual democracy is.

How can we remedy this? At first glance, the solution seems simple enough. If observation reveals that the term democracy is misleading, why don't we start giving things more fitting labels? If the name is not right, why not look for a proper one? In the real world, R. A. Dahl has pointed out, democracies are "polyarchies." [2] If this is so, why not call them that?

But the solution is not so simple. That a name is misleading for descriptive purposes does not mean that it has to be replaced. For "democracy" is exactly the label that we need for the prescriptive purpose. And this purpose is just as important. A democratic system is established as a result of deontological pressures.[3] What democracy *is* cannot be separated from what democracy *should* be. A democracy exists only insofar as its ideals and values bring it into being. No doubt, any political system is sustained by imperatives and value goals. But perhaps a democracy needs them more than any other. For in a democracy the tension between fact and value reaches the highest point, since no other ideal is farther from the reality in which it has to operate. And this is why we need the name democracy. Notwithstanding the disadvantage that it gives no information about the real world, it helps to keep ever before us the ideal—what democracy ought to be.

The term democracy, then, has not only a descriptive or denotative function, but also a normative and a persuasive function. Consequently the problem of defining democracy is twofold, requiring both a descriptive and a prescriptive definition.[4] One cannot exist without the other and, at the same time, one cannot be replaced by the other. So, to avoid starting out on the wrong foot we must keep in mind three points: first, that a firm distinction has to be made between the *ought* and the *is* of democracy; second, that this distinction must not be misunderstood, because, clearly, ideals and reality interact (without its ideals a democracy cannot materialize and, conversely, without a basis of fact the democratic prescription is self-denying); third, that although complementary, the prescriptive and the descriptive definitions of democracy must not be confused, because the democratic ideal does not define the democratic reality, and vice versa, a real democracy is not, and cannot be, the same as an ideal one.

2. Behavior and Definitions

The foregoing, we must admit, is quite complicated. Yet we should try to make it simple, since an essential condition for the survival of a democratic system is the intelligibility of the idea of democracy. While democracy is more complex and intricate than any other political form, paradoxically enough it may not survive if its principles and mechanisms are not within the intellectual reach of the average man. A democracy requires that what is complex be simplified, and what is intricate be untangled, for, in the final analysis, our political behavior depends on our idea of what democracy is, can be, and should be. When we declare, for instance, that a political system is "more" democratic or "less" democratic, our evaluation clearly depends on what we think of as being a true democracy. Likewise, when one says, "This is not democratic," or "Here there is no democracy," both our judgment and our behavior are related to a definition. And if we define democracy unrealistically, we will find ourselves rejecting all real democracies.

So, if democracy is incorrectly defined, we are in danger of refusing something we have not properly identified, and getting in exchange something we would not want at all. Of course, definitions are no panacea, and it would be absurd to say that all our difficulties come from semantic malpractices.[5] My argument is that in the final analysis the existence of democracies depends, other things being equal, on the popularization of the idea of democracy, in the sense that a clear understanding of what democracy is about is a major condition (although not the only one) for behaving democratically. For wrong ideas about democracy make a democracy go wrong.

5

It goes without saying that the general public is not articulate enough to be able to offer a definition. It reacts to an image of democracy, just as it gives its votes to the image rather than the policy of a party. Yet these images are the reflection and echo of conclusions arrived at in the sphere of critical thinking and have been molded by definitions. Therefore, it will be more rewarding to explore the problem of democracy at the articulate level of reactions to definitions than at the derived and inarticulate level of reactions to the image, provided that we keep in mind that that which at the critical level is a definite idea, at the inarticulate level becomes an indefinite picture. My contention, then, is that definitions are important because they are responsible, in the last analysis, for our image of democracy. Of course, what I consider important somebody else may not. This is to be expected. However, there are two objections which cannot be ignored; one concerns principle and the other practice.

The first objection is expressed in the old saying: *Omnis definitio est periculosa*. Certain writers make such a point of repeating the statement, "It is dangerous to define," that at times one wonders whether defining might not be especially dangerous for their own thinking. But I am ready to agree that avoiding definitions cannot always be explained away as a form of self-protection, and that the warning of the Latin adage is sound when it is addressed to those scholars who conceive of definitions as a means of freezing language. If this is agreed, I frankly see no danger in conveying clearly and explicitly to our audience the meaning or meanings of the term democracy, and our reasons for choosing them. And not only do I find nothing dangerous in this procedure, but further I insist that a concern with definitions is particularly important in the case of democracy. For democracy is government by consent, and consent, in the long run, is the product of what an electorate believes a democracy to be; it depends on the sort of democracy the voters deem to be true.

The second objection will not deny that my concern may be justified in theory, but will point out that in practice things seem to work out well enough. After all—it may be said—government by consent has managed to survive successfully for quite a while, and there is no sign that it will not continue. But let me reply that this is

6

correct for only a small number of countries. Furthermore, when formulas like "government by consent," or "government by discussion" were created, what they stood for was quite different from what they refer to now. The formulas have remained the same, but their referents have not.

If, for instance, we look at Walter Bagehot's classic account of the mid-nineteenth-century British constitution, the change that has occurred since then becomes clear. To Bagehot government by discussion meant—and actually was—a political system which operated on the assumption that the discussion was limited to those most fit to participate. The political wisdom of the English—this was Bagehot's very serious *plaisanterie*—lay in their praiseworthy "stupidity," that is, their refusal to bother about abstract principles, and their deferential attitude toward the wiser.[6] But Bagehot's account could hardly be applied to our own time. I do not mean to suggest that stupidity is no longer available, but simply that it is no longer "deferential." To paraphrase Ortega y Gasset's language, it has become contemptuous ignorance, or ignorant arrogance.[7] And it is precisely for this reason that the twentieth century is the era of the "revolt of the masses." Ortega's diagnosis of our time may be too highly colored, but we must admit that Bagehot's passive and helpful stupidity has given way to an active and even aggressive one.

Hence the problem of consent has to be taken more seriously in our time than it has ever been before. For better or worse, today there is ever less deference when people go to the ballot box. If, then, we still want government by discussion, we shall have to replace diminishing deference with increasing awareness. Instead we find that the ordinary voter's growing need for clear ideas runs parallel to the intellectuals' growing tendency to deal in elusive and obscure ideas. And this is precisely when the word democracy no longer has one generally accepted basic meaning.

3. The Age of Democratic Confusion

To put it bluntly, we are living in the age of confused democracy. It would take too long to explain how and why we have reached this unhappy stage of muddled thinking, i.e., of democratic confusion. It would also lead us far afield. Let me just indicate, therefore, the

7

two reasons for our present plight which are most closely connected with our line of argument.

A first rather obvious remark is that perhaps no key political term lends itself as easily as democracy to controversial interpretations. At the time when Louis XIV could say, "I am the State," this sentence had a precise meaning, and it was very clear what political system he referred to. But the sentence "We are the State," is, to say the least, obscure. Democracy is a troublesome label even when we compare it to terms like liberalism and socialism, which are also vague enough. If this had been a book about liberalism or socialism, to say that liberalism (or socialism) is a highflown name for something which does not exist would have been an impertinent rather than a pertinent start (although there might be a grain of truth even in that impertinence). For neither liberalism nor socialism can be as easily challenged as democracy on the grounds that there is no such thing.

However, thus far we have simply suggested that the word democracy may give more trouble than any other current political label. This is not to say that it need be more troublesome. In short, to explain our present plight we need some other reason. And with this end in mind we must consider that "democracy" has become more and more a universally honorific term. Nowadays people attach a deeply felt laudatory meaning to it. This might be considered a positive development in that it makes everybody want to be—or seem to be— democratic. But there is a negative aspect of the honorific development that cannot be neglected: that the word may triumph at the expense of clarity, and consequently at the expense of the thing.

In 1939 Eliot wrote: "When a term has become so universally sanctified, as 'democracy' now is, I begin to wonder whether it means anything, in meaning too many things." [8] At the time when Eliot was expressing his perplexity, democracy was still a despised word in many parts of the world. Today, apparently, democracy has no enemies left. In 1949 a UNESCO inquiry into ideological conflicts concerning democracy, East and West, produced a concluding statement (and the emphatic tone of its opening is worth noting): "For the first time in the history of the world, no doctrines are advanced as anti-democratic. The accusation of anti-democratic action or attitude is frequently directed against others, but practical politicians and political theorists agree in stressing the democratic element in the institutions they defend and the theories they advocate." And the committee that issued this statement could not resist the comment: "This acceptance of democracy as the highest form of political or social organization is the sign of a basic agreement in the ultimate aims of modern social and political institutions. . . ." [9] But I am not prepared to accept such an unwarranted inference. Being hopeful is one thing, being naïve is another.

Given the fact that the *name* democracy is now so sacred that nobody dares to say he is anti-democratic, it would indeed be very optimistic to conclude from this that in the second half of the twentieth century a common ideal is warming the hearts of mankind. A less optimistic observer would remark instead that never before has ideological and terminological falsification been conducted so intensively, so shrewdly, and on so large a scale. If the same word can be used to signify and dignify antithetical practices, clearly the term democracy has become even more meaningless than it seemed to Eliot in 1939. As Bertrand de Jouvenel wrote in 1945, "Discussions about democracy, arguments for and against it, are intellectually worthless because we do not know what we are talking about." [10]

Personally, I do not underestimate the importance of the unanimity with which faith in some kind of democracy is expressed by the UNESCO document, even though it is chiefly faith in the word.[11] For the words that we revere are entangling, and capture us before we are even aware of it. *Nomina numina.* Nonetheless, if we want to refute the pessimistic interpretation we must see to it that the term democracy is not emptied of all logical and descriptive meaning, that it is not reduced to a mere trap word. Everybody is in favor of democracy—but *what* democracy? If the answer were, "Anything that goes by that name," then the price of unanimity of consensus on democracy would be too high. For to believe that a political system *is* a democracy just because it *is called* a democracy, is a way of destroying democracy by means of its own name. And this may well be the final outcome if instead of stressing that different names should be used to denote different things we encourage ambiguity by applying the same label to opposite practices.

By saying this I do not mean that there are many scholars

9

today who are intentionally fostering ambiguity. Only a few would openly subscribe to the statement that democracy is any political system which declares itself to be such. Yet very little, if anything, is said to show that this is nonsense. Which means, in practice, that the above conclusion can be easily inferred not from what is said, but from what is *not* said. Take, for example, the innumerable European textbooks on constitutional government which consider it a principle of scientific accuracy to include a chapter on "progressive" democracy or "popular" democracy—that is, to list as democracies all the regimes which claim to be such. It will be argued that it is not the business of jurists to decide what a democracy is, and what the word means. That may be so, but whose business is it? The political scientist's? The political philosopher's? Surely somebody should concern himself with this problem. But very few scholars seem to do so. The political scientist passes it on to the political philosopher, and the philosopher is likely to say that he is unable to solve it. Apparently, Western culture as a whole has adopted an attitude of non-commitment.[12]

No doubt, good reasons can be given to explain this attitude. The political scientist may argue that scientific knowledge must be value-free, which seems to imply that we are not permitted to choose between different definitions because our choice would have to be based on a value preference.[13] As for the philosopher, the more recent trends in Western philosophy, like the Oxford school, are inclined to take a very conventionalistic stand, whose strict formulation can come to be that a word means only what we decide it shall mean.[14]

Although political science and political philosophy have very little in common today, and the value preoccupation is quite different from the conventionalistic argument, it is interesting to note that the two approaches have converged to such a degree that it is sometimes difficult to detect whether an author is a hyper-factualist with a strict non-evaluative position, or whether he is following the conventionalistic line, or both. The latter is presumably the case, however, when the question "How should we use the word democracy?" is given this kind of answer: "A scientist is only supposed to report on how the term is actually being used by the people who use it." I cannot enter now into a discussion of this approach. Let me just call attention to the rather startling situation that the most sophisticated expert, on one side, and the most incompetent common man, on the other, agree for once, and agree in saying that they do not know or cannot say what "democracy" means.

Perhaps one of the best illustrations of this *Zeitgeist* can be found in Maurice Cranston's clever little book on *Freedom.* Cranston comes to the typical and melancholy conclusion that the question "What is democracy?" can be given only the "provisional" answer that it is "a different doctrine in different people's minds." It would be unfair to Cranston to say that this response strikes me as being the product of intellectual escapism, since he hastens to explain that he "calls this a provisional answer because an analysis which ended there would be little more than sophistry."[15] But Cranston's analysis does end there. Now, I am ready to concede that provisional answers of the sort suggested by Cranston may still make sense when addressed to English-speaking audiences. After all, in England and in the United States, people have been practicing democracy successfully for some time, and do not really have to be told what true democracy is. They know perfectly well that true democracy is—of course—what they have at home, and they still believe that they know what it is all about, even if refined intellectuals refuse to tell them. But this is all I am willing to concede.

In principle—that is, on methodological as well as on logical grounds—my stand is that both hyper-factualism and conventionalism are more a way of avoiding than of solving problems. On practical grounds, furthermore, I wish to stress that, whereas the attitude of non-commitment—as I have called it—may be harmless where democracy is not a controversial issue, it may do harm elsewhere, and that what may not be dangerous in English becomes so in other languages. Where democracy is challenged, provisional answers will not do. From a global point of view, to say that democracy means different things in different places is not just a way of stating the obvious, it is a way of not answering at all—and we are in desperate need of answers. The fundamental values and beliefs of our civilization are at stake, and it is through definitions and the corresponding images of democracy that we are playing the game and that we are going to win or lose it, because it is through definitions, and the ideas that they convey, that we make our choices.

Perhaps it will be argued that I am offering an overly intellectual interpretation of history. It might be objected that even if intellectuals like to give provisional answers and enjoy discussing the sex of angels, their sophisticated amusements hardly affect the public at large. I do not agree, because what ordinary people think reflects, in the long run, what thinkers have previously thought. And, let me add, we should not be surprised that in this situation of intellectual paralysis the Anglo-American political model has so little appeal for the rest of the world. If anything, we should be surprised at ourselves for expecting our democratic systems to compete in the world-wide political market, while we accept the view that the word democracy can mean whatever anyone wants it to mean, the only question being, "which is to be master"—as Humpty Dumpty would say.

4. An Outline of the Difficulties

Having stressed *why* we should define democracy, let us return to the *how*. The foregoing discussion warns us that it will not be an easy task. However, it is well to face the difficulties from the outset, for we cannot overcome obstacles unless we know that they are there. Let us therefore try to single out the problems which have to be dealt with.

The basic complication seems to be—as already indicated—that the *thing* democracy is not described properly by the *word* democracy. The word tends to distract our attention from what a democracy is in the real world. And there is little we can do about it, for we can neither escape the word (we can never do without words), nor change it, saying polyarchy, instead of democracy, for instance.[16] All we can do, then, is to keep in mind that the term "democracy" only leads us to a prescriptive definition, and that we shall have to seek a descriptive definition as well. To have to deal with two definitions may seem somewhat confusing, but, as we shall see, the distinction between the descriptive *is* and the prescriptive *ought* of democracy will help us to settle a number of problems which might otherwise lead to endless, worthless disputes.

Yet, there is another question, namely: What is the connection between the *is* and the *ought*? For the connection is just as important

12

as the distinction. What *is* and what *should be* do not proceed on two parallel roads which never meet. On the contrary, they always interfere and collide with each other. So if we do not understand clearly the nature of the connection, the advantage of establishing a distinction between descriptions and prescriptions is lost, little by little, on the way. Therefore the first part of this book will deal at length, implicitly when not explicitly, with this relationship, because a misunderstanding of the connection between facts and deontology is the most serious and frequent logical and methodological error we meet with. When attention is focused exclusively on *what is,* the result is a misunderstood realism. When we place all the emphasis on *what ought to be,* we stumble into the pitfall of perfectionism.

Realism and perfectionism are, however, two sophisticated kinds of mistakes. Therefore my argument will be introduced by a criticism of the "simplistic approach," by a discussion of the most elementary and naïve type of error. As I observed at the beginning, democracy is a difficult system that has to be made easy and put within the reach of all minds. But how can this be done? Unfortunately, the usual way of making democracy simple leads us nowhere or makes for trouble. Simple-minded people are inclined to believe that once the word is explained, everything is explained. The product of this simplistic approach is what I call "etymological democracy," which I will discuss in the next chapter. For the time being let us only say that when democracy is made to seem very simple, we can be sure that we are dealing with a verbal question and that the real problems are not being faced. So let us refrain from being too simple, although we must try hard not to be needlessly abstruse.

Even though the errors of over-simplification, hyper-realism (if I may call it that), and perfectionism are the snares into which we most often fall when we discuss the problem of democracy, our difficulties do not end there. To mention some other problems that are considered in the first part, further difficulties arise from the fact that democracy conveys the idea that the governed should be the governors; and this entails distrust for leadership and elites. The denial of leadership may not be a controversial issue in the Anglo-American kind of democracy, but it certainly is a problem elsewhere, and therefore I am dealing extensively with it. Finally, there is a great deal of confusion about what democracy *is not;* and defining democracy *a contrario* is an important way of getting to what democracy *is.* Last, but not least, it is not at all clear how we should go about proving democracy, assuming there is some sense in such an undertaking. So this point is also reviewed.

These typically methodological or logical issues close the first part of my survey. And if I were a logical positivist, or if I were inclined to agree with the conventionalistic line of linguistic analysis, this would also end the volume. But this is not my platform. Therefore the book does not end at this point, and there follows a section which is concerned with the historical meaning, or content, of the word "democracy." [17]

One final point. I will be dealing with *political* democracy as opposed to so-called *economic* democracy, and with its difference from *social* democracy. Now, it should be clearly recognized from the start that political democracy is the most difficult of all democratic undertakings; that is, the one which operates under the most difficult conditions. Although democracy in the political sense represents the oldest and most persistent connotation of the idea of democracy, its long historical record only confirms that political democracy is a most disappointing realization. As a political form democracy has to reduce the manifold wills of millions of scattered people to a single authority, and this means that the conditions under which it has to work are but a remote approximation to the optimum conditions found in primary groups and small integrated communities. Between a face-to-face democracy and a large-scale democratic system, there is a yawning gap. Mankind had to suffer for more than two thousand years in order to build a bridge between the two sides. And in passing from the small democratic communities where all the people take part, to the democracy of the large numbers who cannot take part, that is, to the present nationwide democratic systems, many of the requisite conditions for an authentically democratic society are bound to disappear on the way.

As far as the realization of the ideal model is concerned, political democracy operates under the worst possible conditions; and if we still have democracy in a political sense, we cannot expect of large-scale, difficult, and cumbersome political democracy what we can expect of micro-democracies. Actually it is highly dubious whether our political macro-democracies can be correctly conceived and understood as an enlargement of some micro-prototype.

NOTES

† "Politics and the English Language" in *Selected Essays* (Baltimore, 1957), p. 149.

1. Cf. Richard Robinson, *Definition* (Oxford, 1954), esp. Chap. II: "Word-word definition correlates a word to another word, as having the same meaning. Word-thing definition correlates a word to a thing, as meaning that thing" (p. 17).

2. Robert A. Dahl, *A Preface to Democratic Theory* (Chicago, 1956), esp. pp. 63-89. Cf. also for democracy as the "real-world" approximation of democracy: R. A. Dahl and C. E. Lindblom, *Politics, Economics and Welfare* (New York, 1953), p. 43 and Chaps. X-XI *passim*.

3. Deontology means literally "discourse on what must be done," on dutifulness. The term was introduced by Bentham, who used the word deontology as a synonym for "the science of morality." In this context the word is used instead without any specific reference to ethics. It alludes in general to that dimension of our existence which is rendered linguistically in an imperative form, with such words as "must" or "should": that is, as a synonym of "prescription" and contrary to "description."

4. I use "norm" and "prescription" as synonyms, given the fact that I am not concerned here with the distinction between moral norms and prescriptions of a non-moral nature. For this point, cf. Chap. IX, 1, below.

5. As a rule I use the term "semantics" in a general sense, to refer to the study of the use and meanings of words. In the cases where the adjective "semantic" is used in a specific sense, this will be clearly indicated by the context.

6. Cf. *The English Constitution* (1867), esp. No. VIII.

7. Cf. *The Revolt of the Masses* (New York, 1932), esp. Chap. VIII.

8. T. S. Eliot, *The Ideal of a Christian Society* (London, 1939; New York, 1940), pp. 11-12.

9. *Democracy in a World of Tensions—A Symposium Prepared by UNESCO*, ed. Richard McKeon (Chicago, 1951), p. 522.

10. *Du pouvoir* (Genève, 1947), p. 338.

11. For the facts, let it be noted, are different. Out of the present-day ninety-odd nations—as J. Barents appropriately points out—less than half qualify for

15

democracy "even if we take that word in the most skeptical way and define it with the *minimum-est* minimum condition of democracy we can think of." Cf. Barents' effective brief survey in *Democracy: An Unagonized Reappraisal* (The Hague, 1958), Chap. II.

12. This attitude will be appraised in Chap. XVII, 5, below.

13. For my views in this connection, cf. G. Sartori, "Der Begriff der 'Wertfreiheit' in der politischen Wissenschaft" in *Politische Vierteljahresschrift,* I (1960), pp. 12-22.

14. This approach will be discussed in Chap. X, below.

15. Maurice Cranston, *Freedom, A New Analysis* (London, 1953), p. 113.

16. To be sure, there are some proposals in favor of change. For instance, John M. Murry, in *The Free Society* (London, 1948), suggests that "democracy" be replaced by "free society." Aside from considerations of a practical character, it seems to me that such suggestions miss the very nature of the problem.

17. Cf. Chaps. IX, X, below.

Chapter II

Etymological Democracy

> *"If we examine not the verbal definitions that most people, including dictionary-makers, give for 'democracy,' but the way in which they use the word in practical application to affairs of our time, we will discover that it does not have anything to do with self-government."*
>
> —James Burnham†

1. The Meaning of "People"

WHENEVER we ask: What is it? the first answer that comes to mind is an explanation of the word that "it" stands for. In the case of democracy, the most common way of defining is to go back to the word's etymological meaning. This is what I call etymological democracy, and in this case our definition will be: democracy is the rule of the people. However, to inquire about the original, literal meaning of a term is only the first step of an inquiry. If it ended there it would end too soon. And since most people with clear and assured ideas about democracy usually derive them from etymology, it will be useful to show that from the premise, "Democracy is the power of the people," we cannot draw definite or useful conclusions.

In the first place, what is the meaning of *demos?* Even in Greek the term was not free from ambiguity. *Demos* in the fifth century B.C. meant the Athenian community gathered in the *ekklesía.* However, even thus defined, *demos* can be reduced to *plethos,* that is, the *plenum,* the entire body; or to the *polloí,* the many; or to the *pléiones,* the majority; or to *óchlos,* the mob (this being a degenerative meaning). And the moment *demos* is translated into modern language the ambiguities increase. The Italian term *popolo,* as well as its French and German equivalents (*peuple, Volk*) convey the idea of a singular entity, whereas the English word *people* indicates a plural. In the former case we are easily led to think that *popolo* denotes an organic whole which may be expressed by an indivisible general will, whereas in the latter case to say "democracy" is like saying *polycracy,* a separable multiplicity made up of each one. (Thus it is no mere coincidence that the holistic interpretations of the concept have come from scholars thinking in German, French, or Italian.) It turns out then that our concept of "the people" cannot be reduced to less than five different interpretations:

1. people meaning an approximate plurality, just a *great many*
2. people meaning an integral plurality, *everybody*
3. people as an entity, or as an *organic whole*
4. people as a plurality expressed by an *absolute majority* principle
5. people as a plurality expressed by a *limited majority* principle

We can dismiss the first interpretation, the people understood as "the many," because it cannot be used as a criterion, and each case would require separate examination. We may also dismiss the second, the people understood as "everybody," because by this strict standard no democracy ever has or ever will exist. (When we say everybody we allow for the exclusion of minors, the disabled, or women—as is still the case in Switzerland.) But even after we have excluded the first not very usable meaning, and the second hyper-democratic interpretation of the term, we still have three meanings on the basis of which one can justify any political system whatever. From the people understood as an "organic whole" we can infer that each individual counts for nothing; from the idea that the people equals an "absolute majority" we can conclude that only the majority counts; whereas the "limited majority principle" comes to mean that even the minority counts.

If "the people" is understood in the way the romantics suggest, as an organic whole or as a kind of over-soul, it is not difficult to

18

see that this approach can justify the most tyrannical rule. In the name of the whole, each and all can be crushed one at a time. In fact, no democracy properly so called, takes "the people" in the organismic, romantic meaning of the term. In practice, democracies break up that compact entity, resort to counting, and are concerned with majorities. Behind the *Volksgeist* and *Volksseele* of the romantics, behind the slogan "all as a single one," we glimpse the justification of totalitarian autocracies, not of democracies. A people, understood as the absolute right of the majority to impose its will on the minorities, seems therefore to be the first acceptable meaning of the term (from a democratic point of view). Yet it is not quite so. Assuming that the victorious 51 per cent count for everybody and that the losing 49 per cent do not count at all, the winners are in a position to prevent the losers' return to power and the system—as we shall see later—cannot work for long. We thus come to the conclusion that only the last meaning of "people"—which, while recognizing majority rule nevertheless protects minority rights—can be regarded as the correct interpretation and a working solution.

So far so good. But this is clearly no longer an etymological explanation of "democracy." We have reached the conclusion that the notion of people fits within a democratic system only if understood in its most elusive technical meaning of requiring majority rule to be limited by minority rights. The vital question is: How can we restrict the power of those who are, in principle, fully entitled to exercise it? And this question cannot be answered by having recourse to the "will of the people" notion of democracy, since a people entitled to make decisions in accordance with a system of majority rule exercises its power *within limits* only to the extent that elements totally extraneous to the popular will come into play.

The etymologist not only cannot grasp these technicalities—he does not want to. When we are hypnotized by the word, the word becomes a fetish. I mean that the natural outlet of etymological democracy is demolatry, i.e., a great deal of talking about the people without ever actually looking at them. For demolaters never become involved in empirical research. They speak about the "real people" in order to make clear that anybody else deals only with "abstract people." But we can repeat the word *real* as often as we wish without

19

ever coming a step nearer to the facts. And no close inspection is needed to discover that the "real people"—whose latest and most illustrious champion seems to be Georges Burdeau[1]—remains a terminological counterfeit for an abstract entity which for all this is no less idealized.

Nor must we think that in speaking of the "real people" we are deeply concerned with them. Demolatry is not necessarily *demophilia,* love for the poor and the disinherited. Actually, it is striking how often making a fetish of an ideal people goes hand in hand with a contempt for real people, for actual people. Marx was certainly not a humanitarian, and from Robespierre to Stalin we have ample evidence of how easily a mystique of the ideal works out, in practice, in reverse, as a ruthless and merciless *Realpolitik.*

2. The People in Megalopolis

The analysis of the meanings of "people" implies also a problem of historical referents. When the term *demokratía* was coined, the people concerned were the *demos* of a Greek *polis,* a small, tightly knit community, operating on the spot as a collective deciding body. Now, when the etymological theory of democracy, so to speak, attempts to illustrate tangibly "Who are the people?" what it recalls is the Greek *demos,* whereas little if any attention is paid to the fact that the larger a polity becomes the less does the concept of people designate a real community, and the more does it tend to denote a logical construction, or a logical fiction.

We are no longer living in a *polis,* and it is not enough to say that we are living in a metropolis; our society is a megalopolis. That is to say that the people of the *polis,* of the medieval communes, as well as the third (and fourth) estate of the *ancien régime* no longer exist. In its tangible and corporate meaning, the concept is obsolete and, to say the least, anachronistic. With the collapse of corporative structures and of the corporate conception of life, and with the repudiation of the Thomistic principle that one's existence must conform to one's condition, "the people" has come to stand for *everybody.* And this everybody has become more and more a fluctuating and amorphous aggregate, always more a *Gesellschaft* and always less a *Gemeinschaft.*[2] In short, modern society turns out to be the opposite of that organic whole which the romantics in their euphoria and medievalist dreams had deified. Today "the people" stands for a highly unstable, atomized and normless society.[3] And this is an entirely different thing from the referents on which ancient democracy and its imitations, the medieval communes, were based.

If today we are increasingly accustomed to use "the masses" instead of "the people," [4] it is because of the profound transformation brought about by the loss of community[5] which followed the fall of the medieval order, and the drastic changes provoked by the rapid evolution of the last 150 years. The present-day world moves at such a dizzy speed that in the brief span of a lifetime we have difficulty in our old age in recognizing the world we knew as children. And in a reality that is so changeable, man has neither the time nor the means to adjust himself to it. The dynamics of our megalopolis does not seem to allow for a society linked by natural connective tissues. The primary group structure of our society has indeed become loose, and the intermediate relations of neighborhood, occupation, and association are incapable of filling the great emptiness brought about by our brave new world. The individual feels lonely, alienated and self-estranged. In a word, he is uprooted and rootless. This is why we ask so insistently for social integration, why we speak so much of the socialization of man. And this is why the proper label for our society is "mass society." [6]

So, if etymological democracy is to be brought up to date it should be called *masso-crazia* or massocracy. And it must be emphasized that a mass man and a mass people are at the antipodes of the balanced and orderly society required for a government of the people. Kornhauser, among others, has made the point very forcibly. He writes: "The psychological type characteristic of mass society provides little support for liberal democratic institutions. . . . The individual seeks to overcome the anxiety accompanying self-alienation by apathy or activism. . . . Thus the mass man is vulnerable to the appeal of mass movements which offer him a way of overcoming the pain of self-alienation. . . ." [7] An atomized society can be easily mobilized and manipulated. The mass man is isolated, exposed, and hence available. His behavior tends to be extreme behavior, in which activist modes of response and intervention in the political process are the only alternative to apathy. All in all, a mass society is open to charismatic domination and to total mobilization.[8]

Even though the concept of mass society only indicates a trend and an abstract type, we certainly have enough evidence of mass behavior and mass psychology to conclude that the etymologist constructs his edifice on a foundation that no longer exists. His *demos* was buried centuries ago. And his failure to realize it only confirms how little reality filters into his so-called real people.

3. Power "of the People and Power over" the People

Up to this point we have been speaking of the people. That is, we have been examining the most elementary aspect of our problem. For when we come to analyze the link between the concept of people and the concept of power, between *demos* and *kratos,* the difficulties increase. In fact they become insuperable for the etymological approach.

The problem of power is a question concerning not so much the titular holders as the actual wielders. Power, *de facto,* belongs to the power holders. How can the people, however understood and defined, be effective wielders of power? Clearly, the titular right to power does not solve the problem of popular sovereignty. Absolute monarchies in their struggle with the Church affirmed their independence substituting the formula *omnis potestas a Deo* with *omnis potestas a populo,* thus resorting to a democratic justification. This justification was used for instance by Marsilio da Padova, one of the first in medieval times to revive the concept of popular sovereignty, in his defense of Ludwig of Bavaria and of imperial supremacy. But if Marsilio da Padova fell back on popular sovereignty to support the Empire against the Church, the Church, particularly the Jesuits, used the same weapon to fight the absolute monarchs.[9]

The medieval doctrine aimed at bridging the gap between nominal power and the exercise of power by the *fictio* of representation, i.e., by having the titular holder of power delegate the exercise of his power to somebody else. It was indeed a fiction, since the medieval doctrine was not concerned with the fact that the representative had few or no electors. It was mostly a *praesumptio juris et de jure,* a presumption allowing of no possibility of proving the contrary. And representation without election became simply a device which legitimized monarchical absolutism in a position of permanent, irrevocable representation, belonging by hereditary right to the sovereign and his descendants.[10]

We can understand, then, the intransigent aversion that Rousseau had for the notion of representation, and the reason he reversed the formula, substituting for non-elective representation the principle of election without representation. Rousseau's democracy elects its magistrates, but does not give them the chrism of representatives. The people, for Rousseau, do not delegate their power, should not give up the exercise of power.[11] And we cannot deny that Rousseau saw where the danger lay. For as soon as we permit the exercise of power to be transferred to representatives, the parliament becomes sovereign. And in this case, power can again slip out of the hands of its nominal holder, with popular sovereignty becoming an abstract titular right that can sanction any form of slavery.

But Rousseau's solution can hardly be applied. He himself admitted that it was realizable only on a small scale, for very small republics,[12] while today we have to deal with large republics. So we cannot follow his advice and elect leaders without considering them representatives. If we did, the remedy would be worse than the disease, for if he who is elected is not regarded as the representative of those who elect him the election simply creates, per se, an absolute ruler. Thus, the head of the Catholic church is elected by the College of Cardinals but does not represent them, nor is he obliged to answer to his electors: in spite of the fact that he is elected, he is not a representative. Speaking in general, autocratic rulers have been and can be created by means of an election no less than by violence and hereditary succession.

Hence, we need both election and representation. Election, in itself, does not create a representative. It can do so only if the person elected and those who elect him consider that he is responsible to them. And even that is not sufficient, since experience has shown that unless elections take place in conditions that assure freedom, they cannot produce leaders who are responsive to the will of the voters. The history of the twentieth century has proved *ad abundantiam* that, just as representation without voters has no meaning, voting without free choice cannot result in representative government, and becomes nothing more than the people's periodic renunciation of their sovereignty. If presumed representation is fraudulent, election without choice is equally so.

In sum, modern democracies hinge on majority rule (those who obtain the most votes obtain the mandate, and those who have the most seats in parliament rule), on elective mechanisms and on representative transmission of power. This means that the section of the people who count are above all those who constitute the victorious voting majority; that as far as the actual wielding of power goes, even they count only partially; and that a series of mechanisms modifies and reduces the degree of control that is left in the hands of the governed, who are farther and farther removed from the levers of authority. It is not possible to construct a different democratic system. But once we have recognized this, our discussion shifts from the etymological democracy and the power of the people context to the techniques of constitutional democracy. In order to realize democracy, the nominal attribution of power and its actual exercise cannot remain in the same hands. And none of the instrumental, procedural, and technical means for achieving democracy as a going political system are either implied or suggested by what the word *means*.

"Power of the people," it must be noted, is simply an elliptical expression. The phrase describes the beginning of the political process, but leaves it hanging in mid-air. For power is exercised over somebody, and governing presupposes the existence of the governed. Power of the people over whom? Who are the subjects of popular sovereignty? If the formula is expanded, it reads: "democracy is the power of the people over the people." But the problem then takes on a completely different aspect, as the crucial and decisive point is the coming-back of the power, not the going. If this passage is not watched over, if in the process of transmission of power the controllers lose control over the controlled, government *over* the people is in danger of having nothing to do with government *of* the people. Therefore a literal explanation of democracy loses sight of the essential issue, namely, that he who delegates his own power can also lose it.[13]

The demolater is incapable of answering the crucial question: "How can we maintain the link between the nominal attribution and the actual exercise of power?" He fails to see that the weak point in the whole structure is in the transmission belts of power. Elections and representation are necessary instruments of democracy, but they are at the same time its Achilles' heel. Elections are not necessarily free, and therefore representation is not necessarily genuine. What are the remedies and the safeguards against such eventualities? The question can certainly be answered, but not by saying that popular sovereignty as such can take care of these problems.

The truth is that a theory of democracy consisting of nothing but the notion of the power of the people, is adequate and effective only so long as we are opposing autocratic power. Once this adversary is defeated, the problem is not simply a matter of transferring power from the monarch, he who ruled alone, to his counterpart, the people. For what changes hands in this reversal is not the actual exercise of power, but its nominal attribution. And this is the reason that the monocratic solution is easy while the polycratic is difficult. Strictly speaking, if power is really to belong to the people, any allocation of it elsewhere is inadmissible. A literal democracy can only be a stateless society. Power actually belongs to the people only as long as it is the people who really wield it, and therefore as long as it is not wielded by others, or in any other *locus imperii*. Only thus can the titular right to power and actual power remain in the same hands when monocracy is replaced by democracy.

However, if we have to wait for such a requirement to be met, the advent of democracy is in danger of indefinite postponement. Given the present dimension of a polity, the people's self-government becomes for all practical purposes more and more nominal. The people of whom we are speaking are no longer a small territorial community; they are neither few in number nor a genuine community. Today the people are the entire scattered and plural collectivity of the nation-state. Yet modern democratic States exist, they are not Erewhons, and they unquestionably deserve to be called democracies. But they exist because it was understood that the problem of how they can be established begins exactly where the etymological argument leaves off.

25

4. The Lincoln Formula

I have emphasized that whenever we judge a democracy by the standard of the etymological definition, the inadequacies that emerge lie in the definition and not in the reality. And our problems cannot be solved—as the demolater assumes—by twisting reality to fit the word. I do not wish to suggest, however, that the literal meaning of the word is unimportant. If the etymological definition does not lead us far, it does provide a start. For the phrase "the power belongs to the people," establishes a principle concerning the sources and the legitimacy of power. It means that in a democracy power is legitimate only if it is attributed from below, only if it is an emanation of the popular will—in other words, only if it is granted freely.

Considered as a theory about the sources of and the titular right to power, the literal concept of democracy indicates what we expect and require from a democratic form: namely, a free society that is not exposed to arbitrary and uncontrolled political power, nor dominated by a closed, inaccessible oligarchy. Democracy, then, exists to the degree that there is an "open society" [14] in which the relation between the governors and the governed is consistent with the principle that the State is at the service of the citizens and not the citizens of the State, that the government exists for the people, not vice versa. In short, democracy implies that society takes precedence over the State, that *demos* precedes *cracy*.

In his Gettysburg address of 1863 Lincoln characterized democracy in words that seemed to express its very spirit: "government of the people, by the people, for the people." It is symptomatic that this aphorism defies analysis and poses insoluble problems of interpretation. If we attempt to dissect the phrase "government *of* the people" all the following conjectures are possible: (i) government of the people meaning a self-governing people, a direct democracy; (ii) conversely, that the people are the object of government, that they are governed; (iii) that the government belongs to the people, whatever this "belonging" may mean; (iv) that government is chosen and guided by the people; (v) that government emanates from the people in the sense that it derives its legitimacy from the people's consent; and (vi) that the government is responsible to the people. (Let us note in passing that even the last three possible interpretations entail very different instrumentalities.) As for Lincoln's "*by* the people," it can hardly be deciphered: *by* the people in what sense? Actually, only the final phrase "government *for* the people" is not ambiguous, in that it is very likely that Lincoln meant, in the people's interest, for their benefit. However, the only clear statement contained in the formula can hardly qualify, per se, a democracy: for any government claims that its purpose is to govern for the people.

The truth is that Lincoln's words have stylistic impetus rather than logical meaning. As they stand they constitute, strictly speaking, an inexplicable proposition. But this is precisely its purpose and its value—and I am not being paradoxical, for to use "democracy" in its literal sense opens a prescriptive discourse whose very nature is to remain unfinished, to go on *ad infinitum* as well as *ad indefinitum*.

NOTES

† *The Machiavellians, Defenders of Freedom* (New York, 1943), p. 243.

1. I have reference to the last two volumes, VI and VII, of his *Traité de science politique* (Paris, 1949-1957). In Vol. IV (1952), p. 112, Burdeau observed that the attempt to recognize that which is designated as people is resented by some as sacrilege, ". . . a sacrilege because, in the Pantheon of political values, the people are cloaked by a mystery which cannot be separated from their power." In reading the volumes which followed, one suspects that Burdeau took special care not to commit that sacrilege.

2. This is F. Toennies' distinction. Cf. *Gemeinschaft und Gesellschaft* (New York, 1940). *Gesellschaft* is society understood as an external, impersonal network of business-like associations, an exterior mode of coexistence; a *Gemeinschaft* is a community in the symbiotic meaning of the term, that is, a mode of coexistence reaching a maximum of personal interpenetration, a very strong intensity of the "we." Naturally Toennies' typology connotes only two extreme ideal types. It does indicate, however, an actual trend: the passage from primary communities to secondary groups, i.e., to the merely formal organizations of an "associational society."

3. It is the relapse in dictatorial solutions that has aroused the attention of present-day scholars to this reality of the modern *demos*. Thus the literature on this subject is often to be found in studies on totalitarian regimes and/or in investigations on the sense of loneliness and the correlative "fear of freedom" of the man of today. Hannah Arendt's book. *The Origins of To-*

27

talitarianism (New York, 1951) despite its disparities, is representative of the first type of analysis (cf. esp. pp. 301-332). Representative of the second type of analysis is Erich Fromm's, *Escape from Freedom* (New York, 1941) which in the English edition (London, 1942) is entitled *The Fear of Freedom*.

4. The expression became popular in France, during the years between the Revolutions of 1830 and 1848, to refer to that part of the people which remains absent and external to the political order. Even Marx in his early writings up to 1844 spoke about masses: it was only through his contacts with French Socialism, and precisely in the *Zur Kritik der Hegelschen Rechtsphilosophie* (first published in the *Deutsch-Französische Jahrbücher*, I-II [Paris, Feb., 1844]), that he recasts the concepts of both masses and classes into the notion of proletariat. What is meant by "masses" has been well synthesized by Pierre Duclos: "The notion of the masses expresses . . . the twofold sentiment of depersonalization into uniformity, and of the exaltation of community power which tempts the man of the twentieth century." (*L'Évolution des rapports politiques depuis 1750* [Paris, 1950], p. 138). It goes without saying that the study of the mass-man is not to be confused with the earlier studies on the psychology of crowds. For an analytical classification and the additional distinctions between crowds, mobs, audiences, etc., cf. R. W. Brown, "Mass Phenomena" in *Handbook of Social Psychology,* ed. G. Lindzey (Cambridge, 1954) Vol. II, pp. 833-876.

5. "Community" today is used, often confusingly, in two different meanings: a specific one, by which community indicates intimacy, a special mode of relationship in which the individual really lives in common with his aggregate; and a generic meaning indicating a merely functionally defined unit (such as in the expressions urban community, or, even more vaguely, political community). Of course a real community is also functionally significant; but the opposite is not true, for functional significance does not imply any intimate communion. Obviously, I am using community here in its strict sense, in which a modern urban community is not a community. For valuable insights and a comprehensive panorama, cf. *Community,* ed. C. J. Friedrich (New York, 1959).

6. Still a classic work for its unsurpassed insights, is the pioneer volume of Ortega y Gasset, *La rebelión de las masas* (1930), after which I would mention the less known writing of Karl Jaspers, *Die geistige Situation der Zeit* (Leipzig, 1932), also available in the French translation, *La situation spirituelle de notre époque* (Louvain, 1951), the first part of which is devoted to a subtle analysis of the *Massenmensch* (the man of the masses). See also G. Perticone, *Studi sul regime di massa* (Torino, 1942). Of course, Freud also is relevant in the matter, for his approach has provided, as Lasswell says, "an ultramicroscope" for the social scientists. Cf. esp. his *Group Psychology and the Analysis of the Ego* (London, 1922), a work

especially dedicated to mass psychology (as the original title *Massenpsychologie* makes clear). In the approach of political science, William Kornhauser's *The Politics of Mass Society* (Glencoe, 1959) seems to be an outstanding assessment in the direction of a general theory of mass society. Consult it also for the bibliography (pp. 239-249).

7. *Ibid.*, p. 112. As for mass movements, see the effective synthesis on p. 47: "Mass movements generally have the following characteristics: their objectives are remote and extreme; they favor activist modes of intervention in the social order; they mobilize uprooted and atomized sections of the population; they lack an internal structure of independent groups." Somewhat astonishingly, the "incompatibility between the mode of political action of the masses and the postulates of democracy in the classical sense" is recognized even by Burdeau (cf. *Traité de science politique*, Vol. VI, pp. 75-79).

8. For the "charismatic" domination see Max Weber's typology in *Wirtschaft und Gesellschaft—Grundniss der Sozialökonomie*, Vol. I, Part I, Chap. III, "Die Typen der Herrschaft," and Vol. II, Part III, Chaps. IX, "Charismatismus," and X "Umbildung des Charisma." Since Weber's time, however, new features have to be added to his "control by fascination": manipulation of anxiety, hatred scapegoats, and continuous, deep ideological insemination.

9. Cf. in general: E. Crosa, *La sovranità popolare dal Medioevo alla Rivoluzione Francese* (Bocca, 1915). For Marsilio in particular: F. Battaglia, *Marsilio da Padova* (Firenze, 1928); and also *Studi raccolti nel VI centenario della morte di Marsilio da Padova* eds. A. Cecchini and N. Bobbio (Padova, 1942).

10. For the inception of the theory of representation, cf. O. Gierke, *Les Théories politiques du Moyen Age* (French trans. Paris, 1914), Chaps. VI-VII; and M. V. Clarke, *Medieval Representation and Consent* (New York, 1936). Mommsen has maintained that the principle of representation can be traced back to Antiquity, a line of interpretation followed, e.g., by J. O. A. Larsen, *Representative Government in Greek and Roman History* (Berkeley, 1955). I find this thesis rather misleading, and agree entirely with Rousseau's statement: "The idea of representation is wholly modern: it derives from feudal government. . . . In the ancient republics the term was unknown. (*"Contrat social*, III, 15). For the present terms of the problem and a more accurate analysis of the relationship between representation and elections, cf. G Sartori, "La rappresentanza politica," in *Studi politici*, IV (1957), pp. 527-613.

11. Cf. *Contrat social*, III, 15.

12. Cf. *Contrat social*, III, 1, 13, 15.

13. As Considerant wrote, with perfect Rousseaunian orthodoxy: "If the people delegates its sovereignty, it abdicates. The people do not govern themselves, they are governed. People, delegate your sovereignty! This will make your

sovereignty have a fate just the opposite of Saturn's: your sovereignty will be devoured by its daughter, the delegation." Cf. Victor Considerant, *La Solution, ou le gouvernement direct du peuple* (Paris, 1850), pp. 13-15.

14. This is K. R. Popper's formula, cf. *The Open Society and Its Enemies,* 2nd ed., Vol. II (London, 1952). Although I approve of the imagery, we must not forget the point made in this connection by Michael Polanyi, namely, that a free society is not an open society in the sense that individuals are not dedicated to a distinctive set of beliefs, quite the contrary. Cf. *The Logic of Liberty* (Chicago, 1951), *passim.*

Chapter III

The Quid Pro Quo of Political Realism

> "Politics should be realistic; Politics should be idealistic: *Two principles which are true when they complement one another, wrong when they are kept apart.*"
>
> —Bluntschli†

1. What is "Pure Politics"?

EVERYBODY KNOWS more or less what a democracy should be, but few realize what it *can* be. And this is what political realism is supposed to find out. But political realism raises a number of questions which are relevant to the problem of defining democracy, because unless we understand properly what is the role of the *verità effettuale,* or "effectual truth," as Machiavelli would say, we are in danger of replacing a one-sided approach with another, and thereby of correcting an empty verbalism with a misunderstood realism. And democracy is endangered just as much by bad idealism (perfectionism) as by bad realism.

I have purposely recalled the Machiavellian expression *verità effettuale,* because the misunderstanding of political realism can be traced back to him. Since the time of Machiavelli the realistic approach to politics has been understood in two ways which are seldom clearly

31

differentiated: as meaning that politics is politics and not something else, or as implying that political realism embodies itself par excellence in a specific type of political behavior called "pure politics." In recent times, pure politics has been rechristened *Machtpolitik,* power politics. However, no matter whether we say pure politics or *Machtpolitik,* the labels are often understood in the sense that there is a type of politics that is not committed to or by ideals, but is entirely based on force, fraud, and the ruthless use of power. And the implication seems to be that this is the kind of policy advocated, or suggested, by political realism. My contention is that to speak of "pure politics" is very misleading, and that no necessary link can be established between the realistic approach and so-called pure politics.

In truth, Machiavelli is not responsible for these misunderstandings. Nevertheless it will be useful to start from the old dispute about what Machiavelli himself said, and what his interpreters made him say. The Florentine secretary is considered the founding father of political realism inasmuch as he discussed politics as it is. He was, in effect, the first dispassionate observer of the modern age. Aristotle, by the way, was also a good observer, but there is undoubtedly a difference between Aristotle's *Politics* and Machiavelli's *Prince:* precisely the difference which explains how political realism begins with Machiavelli and not with Aristotle.[1] The difference can be briefly elucidated, in a very up-to-date fashion, by saying that Machiavelli was value-free whereas Aristotle was not.

Of course, Machiavelli was not value-free as a follower of Max Weber would be, in the modern meaning of *Wertfreiheit.* But he happened to live in a time in which the medieval idea of the *Respublica Christiana* had become meaningless, in which a new word—the word "State"—had to be invented,[2] and in which the creation of the State appeared to be the vital issue. Briefly, Machiavelli was recording the creation of the Renaissance Principalities by a new kind of Prince, whose behavior fits very well into our idea of a value-free politician. This is not to say that politics had been formerly carried on in moral terms by gentle rulers. But Cesare Borgia was a shocking and unprecedented case even for his disenchanted contemporaries and victims. Thus, without detracting from Machiavelli's intellectual stature, it can be suggested that he became a value-free observer because, or partly because, what he observed was a peculiar political value void.[3] And this helps to explain why Machiavelli is the first to state bluntly that politics does not bow to moral precepts, and thus establishes the so-called autonomy of politics.

However, in interpreting Machiavelli, it should always be kept in mind that he referred to the formation of the Renaissance Principalities, which were unique political microcosms that could hardly be compared to present-day politics and political units. For one thing, in Machiavelli's time politics and the Prince were one. It might be argued that the same applies to all tyrannical rule, but it should be noted that the tyranny with which Aristotle was already well acquainted was grounded on popular support, just like our caesaristic dictatorships. The Greek tyrant started his career as a demagogue. This can hardly be said of Cesare Borgia and men like him. I am emphasizing this point, because the situation described by Machiavelli tends to obscure an essential distinction or, at least, a distinction which has become essential to us, namely, the difference between the concrete and the abstract noun, between *the politician* and *politics*.

In our time politics is *more* than the politician. We speak of a policy as being democratic, socialist, nationalist, and so on. And this implies that no matter how powerful the modern Prince may be, he is tied to a course of action which is, as such, more powerful than his personal will. Stalin as a communist was in a position to do almost anything, but he could hardly have changed his mind about communism, even if he had wished to. So we must be careful not to equate politics with the politician. Speaking of the politician, we may well construct a typology, on the basis of which the pure politician is at one extreme and the idealistic politician at the other, meaning by this that the former is a cynical politician who despises ideals, while the other cares only about ideals and pursues them at all costs. But once having granted that we may well meet with a pure politician, or a purely idealistic politician, can we infer from this that "pure politics" and/or a wholly "idealistic politics" exist? My answer is No. However, if we refer specifically to the Machiavellian Prince, we might be tempted to answer Yes. And this is why we must be careful not to draw hasty inferences from what Machiavelli actually did say.[4]

The Florentine secretary did say that politics is not ethics. But he did not say what politics is per se. And to declare that politics is amoral, does not imply that a thing such as pure politics exists. The only inference that can be drawn from the Machiavellian premises is that politics is morally impure. We still have to find out, therefore, what politics is in itself. And on that score Machiavelli has told us nothing. He has only told us how a certain type of policy-maker behaves. But since we cannot follow the line of equating the politician with politics, we cannot deduce from the premise that the Machiavellian Prince can be classified as a pure politician, that what he embodies is pure politics.

In fact, even the pure politician, if he is shrewd, takes care not to underestimate what he regards as the impure elements that help make his policy succeed, for the true man of politics knows that ideas are forces, that ideals are weapons, and as Machiavelli himself said, even paternosters are useful bulwarks for a State. Pure politics is as unreal as its opposite, purely ideal politics. Every policy is a mixture of idealism and realism. And if either element becomes disproportionate, if too much idealism eliminates realism, or vice versa, then an essential component is missing and a policy will fail. No one has ever been able to institute successfully either a genuinely pure policy, or a wholly moral policy. They both fail for the same reason. What today goes under the name of sheer "power politics" can function only insofar as it is nourished by an *ethos*. (Let us not forget that *Machtpolitik* was founded upon the Hegelian *Sittlichkeit*, Hegel's higher form of morality.) And if this *ethos* has taken the form of bloodshed and barbarism, behind it there has been the ideal of the nation or the eschatology of class redemption. Which means that such a policy is not pure at all, for it, too, is based on ideals (even though not moral ideals). We may consider these ideals bad, but the people who accept them obviously believe in them.

There is, then, no such thing as pure politics because no man engages in political action unless he is impelled by beliefs and goals. Politics without adjectives, or pure politics, is based at one time or another on nationalism, racialism, imperialism, or simply patriotism. It is not that creeds such as these leave values out of consideration: they differ only in the values they propound. If a political creed is

34

believed in and accepted, obviously it is because values are involved, since nobody seeks ends that he considers worthless. Politics, then, even in its most brutal and cruel forms, is always *Sache,* that is, devotion to a task.

2. Power Politics and Legalitarian Politics

My suggestion is that the expression "pure politics" should be ruled out. It is either pleonastic—when it is intended to mean that politics is not ethics but just politics—or wrong. Because when pure politics is understood as an ideal-less politics, we are only speaking of a phantom that should be exorcised. And if a realistic politician advocates a pure politics of the latter sort, this only shows that he has very little knowledge about the reality of politics—that he is a bad realist.

The real distinction is not between *pure* ideal-less politics and *impure* ideal-oriented politics, but between a war-like view of politics[5] and a legalitarian view of politics. For the latter persuasion takes precedence over force, and self-interest does not allow recourse to any and all means; whereas, for the former, force precedes persuasion and might establishes right. The liberal, the democratic, and the social-democratic *forma mentis* imply a legalitarian-peaceful approach to politics; whereas nationalists, communists, and others are brought to approach politics from the war-power angle. In the first case force is kept in reserve as an *ultima ratio,* and conflict resolution is sought by means of covenants, courts, and established codes of self-restraint; in the second case force is a *prima ratio,* and conflict resolution is sought in terms of the defeat of the enemy—of the "other" looked upon as a *hostis.*

We may now return to the question: For which side does political realism contend? The usual answer is that political realism advocates power politics, and that it is usually and even necessarily opposed to the liberal-democratic approach. The answer is correct to the extent that we say "usually" and cancel the "necessarily." For it is a fact that the realistic school of politics and the democratic school have been very frequently at war with each other. Nevertheless we must not confuse frequency with necessity. Historically speaking it is quite true that the realists sneer more often than not at democratic idealism,

35

while the democrats consider realism an anti-democratic approach. But if we ask ourselves Why? we shall find that there are no real reasons, by which I mean no valid logical reasons, for pursuing a quarrel which is basically the result of a series of misunderstandings.[6]

As we have seen, the alternative is not between ideal-less or ideal-loaded politics: any policy is committed to, and activated by ideals. Therefore my answer to the question: For whom does political realism take sides? will be: In principle, for nobody. Because political realism is not what it is wrongly assumed to be. It is not a self-sufficient type of policy, something to be aligned with and opposed to the policies that we call democratic, socialist, nationalist, and so on. In this *continuum* there is no place for political realism. And this for the simple reason that political realism is just an element, an ingredient, of any and all political positions.

Any accurate descriptive proposition is a realistic proposition— which is the same as saying that realism only takes us as far as the antechamber of politics. Politics needs information, needs to know the facts; and this is what political realism provides. For the sake of everybody, not just for the sake of one side.

3. Facts and Values in B. Croce

The last fifty years of Italian history provide a cogent illustration of the fact that the division into realists and democrats is artificial, uniting those who should be divided, and dividing those who could very well be united. One of the reasons that pre-fascist democracy turned out to be so fragile when it was put to the test is that its ideals had been worn away, and that the natural supporters of liberal democracy were, though largely unintentionally, responsible for this.[7] From 1920 to 1924 many public figures with democratic and liberal feelings found themselves, almost without realizing it, in the ranks of those who were working for the destruction of liberty, so that not only were the anti-democratic ranks unnaturally inflated, but the partisans of democracy were deprived of contingents that really belonged to them.

Let us look at the case of Benedetto Croce, whom I single out not because I am interested in assigning responsibility but because he had more influence on Italian culture during the first half of this century than any other philosopher.[8] Croce always advocated *Real-politik*, and this position led him to attack mercilessly the "hypocrisy" of democracy and to fight in the breach against what he called the blandishments of the goddesses Justice and Humanity.[9] It cannot be denied that Croce's attack was justified in part. In all fairness we must admit that the ideals of pre-fascist democracy were undermined by both sides—by the bombastic rhetoric and chatter of the democrats just as much as by the equally excessive realistic anti-rhetoric of their opponents. Nationalism, futurism, and fascism thus resulted from a kind of chain reaction in which the official democrats undermined democratic beliefs no less than Croce and the official anti-democrats did in their reaction to them.

As a result, when fascism appeared nobody believed in democracy any longer, neither those who had listened to the preaching of the Socialists, nor the Catholics who preserved their traditional hostility to the secular State, nor even the believers in the *Risorgimento* tradition who ought to have been the natural and the most effective defenders of the system. Croce's case was typical. Years later he confessed that "it had never seemed to him even remotely possible that Italy could let herself be robbed of the liberty that had cost her so much and that his generation had considered a permanent acquisition." [10] Which means that, historically speaking, from 1896 to 1924 Croce was in a false position in which neither his doctrine nor his political attitude was consistent with the real "tendency of his feelings" and with his genuine "mental and moral conformation." [11] And the falseness of his position lay in the fact that instead of waving the banner of political realism within the camp of liberal-democracy—a position which would have been perfectly admissible, since Croce as a liberal never felt he had to repudiate his former realism—he used it to lead the attack against democracy. This might have been understandable in someone else, but not in Croce's case, as he belonged by tradition, instinct and "blood" in the ranks of those whom he riddled with sarcasm. And he realized it only after they had been defeated.[12]

If the case of Croce emphasizes the degree to which a misunderstanding of the nature of political realism may be responsible for the confused and inconsistent alignment of the various political groups, it consequently provides an eloquent indication of the need to review the theoretical question which is involved—namely, what is the relation between facts and values, or better, between factual truth and our value options in favor of liberalism, democracy, socialism, and so on. We are thus confronted with the fundamental problem of how to deal with what *is* and what *ought to be*.

The usual way of assessing the problem is rendered by the statement that facts and values (what *is* and what *ought to be*) interact. This is, of course, true. But as long as the statement remains in a vague dialectical form, we have made little progress. I mean that the verb "to interact" and similar dialectical expressions do not make us understand in what respect the *is* and the *ought* must be kept separate and in what respect we must never forget that the two poles are interdependent and complementary. In reference to the first question, we should not make the mistake of using a fact to refute a value, nor, vice versa, of using a deontology to reject a factual statement. In this connection the fact-finding and the value-oriented approaches have to be dealt with separately. On the other hand, in reference to the second question, we must not fall into the error of believing that the whole case can be presented either in terms of a matter-of-fact description, or conversely in terms of value prescriptions. I mean that to cover the whole field of politics we need both the facts and the ideals. Otherwise we only give half of the picture, and probably a distorted half at that. And it is only if these two preliminary points are kept in mind that we can subsequently indicate the proper "interactions."

In terms of political realism and political idealism, the bearing of what I have just said is that no polity can be expressed only realistically, or only idealistically. If we understand political realism as the search for the factual basis of politics, then the account of the realist stops just where liberalism, democracy, and socialism (to take the examples that are closest to us) begin. For liberalism, democracy, and socialism are not the fruit of a *Realpolitik* but, let us say, for symmetrical reasons, of a *Phantasiepolitik*. They are built *on* facts, but *by* phantasy. The same applies to the case of the idealist. His *Phantasiepolitik* has to take off where the facts are known, not before. Otherwise it will lead nowhere, just to Erewhon. Ideals cannot replace facts, they are superimposed on the facts.

Croce provides a good example of what happens when one does not comply with the rules indicated above. Being an idealistic philosopher he was not concerned with the distinction between *is* and *ought,* since the idealistic approach is to merge this distinction in a dialectical equivalence.[13] For Croce, the *sein* and the *sollen,* what is and what should be, just interact. As a result, the whole of his political philosophy hovers between too much realism first, and too much idealism later, between a matter-of-fact attitude which leaves no room for ideals and a subsequent attitude which leaves no room for reality.

In his first period, what we might call his anti-democratic phase, which ended in 1924, his failure to distinguish between the is and the ought made him put the first term in the place of the second. The only thing that mattered, in this phase, was politics as it really is. Instead of using the realistic approach in order to find a solution for the problems of a liberal-democratic order, he made the former the antithesis of the latter, and refuted the norms and values of democracy by adducing facts. In his next phase, Croce reversed his approach so much that his liberalism is entirely based on a moral ideal of Freedom (written with a capital). In other words, after 1924 Croce became aware of the importance of the ought dimension, of those ideals that he had previously neglected; but in doing so he went from one extreme to another. For his liberalism is formulated only in moral terms, is only an "ethical liberalism." [14] And Croce's ethical liberalism therefore remains in mid-air. It is always weakened and contradicted by a realism with which it cannot merge.

Croce maintained to the very end that politics consists of nothing but expediency, utility, and force.[15] Now, even if this may be true in point of fact, it is no longer true if we are seeking a definition, not of politics *in se* and *per se,* but of liberalism. For a political stand can be described as liberal to the degree that the fact of force is complemented by the duty to reject direct action and reduce power politics to a minimum. Hence, by characterizing all politics as *Machtpolitik* Croce continued to deny the existence of the typical *modus vivendi* of liberalism. On the other hand, in order to preserve his liberalism as a "pure moral ideal," Croce refused to taint his ideal of Freedom with the empirical techniques and instruments of the liberal State. To the very end Croce was to reject constitutionalism, and with it all the practical means of bringing the liberal idea down to earth and of translating it into reality.[16]

It follows from this that in Croce's liberalism the realistic and ethical elements are juxtaposed but not integrated. Facts and values proceed independently of each other, like a world and a superworld. What Croce attempted was to carry the political realism of his first period over to the philosophy of Freedom of his next period. This is perfectly possible, except that in Croce's case the two components of his thought are not only unassimilated but unassimilable. Thus his doctrine hovers between two positions, each of which by itself is inadequate. On the one side is power politics in the Machiavellian tradition; on the other is an extra-political ethic set in a "higher and different sphere." [17] The result of this is that his political realism conflicts with his liberalism, and on the other hand his ethical liberalism contradicts his realism. Realism and liberalism can very well co-exist, but they do not in Croce. His political philosophy is vitiated first by an excess of realism, and then by an excess of moralism. Having started from an inaccurate distinction between real and ideal, or rather by paying no attention to it, Croce never found the correct connection, i.e., a balanced unity of what is and what ought to be. In point of method, his case is an eloquent illustration of the importance of clearly assessing the relation between facts and values, and of the vital role played by this distinction.

4. The Machiavellians: Mosca, Pareto, Michels

The misunderstanding of realism can be summed up in two erroneous arguments. The first, the realistic argument, runs: "I do not believe in democracy because reality is in contradiction to it." The second is expressed in the democratic thesis which retorts: "Being a democrat, I refuse to be a realist." Both arguments are clearly mistaken.

In the first place, if we do not believe in democracy it is because we believe in different values, and not because the consideration of reality need exclude, or be in any way incompatible with, the choice of a democratic deontology. There is no contradiction in terms between a realistic approach and a democratic creed, for the good reason that realism can subsist everywhere and anywhere, *nec cubat in ulla parte.* If realism is, in itself, "assessing the facts," then there can be democratic, just as there is undemocratic, realism. In the first case we relate our findings to democratic values, and in the second to other values. It follows from this that it is illogical to maintain that we do not believe in democracy *because* the facts disprove it. This "because" does not demonstrate anything.

Vice versa, it is equally illogical to reject a realistic approach because its factual reports seem to be in conflict with democratic beliefs, as if democracy ought not to take into account the actual conditions in which it has to operate. The only way to refute realism is to adduce different and contrasting facts. But there is no sense in contesting the validity of the realistic approach because we do not wish to face disagreeable facts and to be told how the world really runs.

In principle we might be willing to agree to this *mise à point,* but in practice we seldom behave accordingly. Let us consider, for instance, the case of the so-called modern Machiavellians: Mosca, Pareto and Michels.[18] They are classified as anti-democratic authors, and no doubt they did not believe in democracy, although for quite different reasons and to differing extents. The question, however, is: Were they anti-democratic because they were realists? Many critics seem to imply that this is the case. I would say, instead, that the anti-democratic development of their theories corresponds to the less realistic aspect of their work, and more precisely to those parts that have been infiltrated by their value preferences. On the other hand, insofar as they actually were realists, they were not in favor of or against anybody; they were just trying, more or less successfully, to make accurate predictions on the grounds of factual analysis.

Gaetano Mosca's law of the "political class" (not of the ruling class) is undoubtedly vague, as his basic concept is much too loose. Furthermore, many pages of his *Elements of Political Science*[19] bear the stamp of the time in which they were written (the first volume having been published in 1896). Yet, Mosca's intuition is either valid or invalid, and it makes little sense, in my opinion, to argue whether it is fascist or anti-fascist. If political classes are found in all political systems, then Mosca was right, although their role, composition and circulation will have to be better specified. If we think instead that

41

Mosca was wrong, we shall have to ascertain that in some given political systems there is nothing resembling what Mosca understood by a political class. And this is the only correct way to pose the problem. As for Michels' "iron law of oligarchy," I concede that it is open to wide criticism in that Michels drew from it a series of unwarranted inferences. However, this does not mean that we are entitled to brush aside his law as being anti-democratic. His law of oligarchy must be tested, to begin with, on the same grounds on which it was built—on a fact-finding basis. And the same applies to Pareto. He unquestionably disliked democracy (more than Mosca); but this can be used as a charge against his scientific work only to the extent that we can show that, under the solemn cover of a "pure science," Pareto was only smuggling in his deep and polemical pessimism.[20]

This does not mean that we should pay no attention to the fact that Mosca, Pareto, and Michels happened to be very critical of democracy. I am just saying that their realism and their anti-democratic beliefs must be dealt with separately, as they were not against democracy *because* this attitude is in any way a logical outgrowth of realism. The proof is that Mosca remained a realist but became a liberal [21] paralleling Croce's experience. Pareto died too soon, in 1923, and thus we cannot know what would have been his long-run reaction to fascism (which, in 1923, had not yet taken on the outright form of a dictatorship).[22] As for Michels, he was a disappointed socialist. In principle he favored democracy but having discovered that socialist parties were not democratic parties he reached the conclusion that democracy was impossible. So Michels was able to align himself even with fascism—disillusion is an erratic state of mind. Not so Croce the philosopher, or Gaetano Mosca the professor of constitutional law. Neither of them felt himself bound by his realism to approve an illiberal system. And rightly so.

Rightly so because genuine realism is not committed to values, being the step in the cognitive process that precedes our value choices. Briefly, inasmuch as we are *only* realists, we are neutral. And it is especially important that the theory of democracy should recognize this. Democracy is not safeguarded by issuing excommunications and creating taboos. I mean that democrats have nothing to lose but

42

an inferiority complex and much to gain if they will rid themselves of the fear of realism. For even the democratic ideal has its own political realism. Or, I ought to say, it should have. I use "should" because, even though my assertion is obvious enough, our democracies (I am referring particularly to those in continental Europe) are endangered by a serious internal imbalance in that they lack democratic realism. And to the extent that they lack it they help to produce a situation in which the realists are made to join the anti-democratic ranks.

5. Realism versus Rationalism

If the division between realists opposing democracy and democrats who reject realism is absurd and artificial, we must ask: How did it come about?

John H. Herz makes the point that political realism "arises inevitably whenever people become fully aware of the failure of repeated attempts to 'reform' political life, to create a 'better' world, or to oust the 'wicked' . . . History, which is the burial ground of such attempted changes, is also the birthplace of realist disillusionment." [23] Realist disillusionment, exactly. This does not mean, as is often said, that realism spreads pessimism and produces disappointment. Disillusion is a consequence of illusion. It is idealism that produces disillusionment, not realism. Realism would prevent it, if it were effective in time. And this is precisely the point: realism gains strength too late. I mean that the trouble with political realism is that it too often tends to arise when we are already confronted with failure. A first answer to our question is, then, that realism tends to have an anti-democratic sequel because it happens to be a retarded realism: retarded in the sense that it follows the disillusionment brought about by overidealistic policies, instead of preceding disillusion and helping to prevent it. And, of course, a realism that appears when it is too late to act positively is likely to react negatively.

However, this is only a general answer, and in order to get to the core of the matter we must be more specific, thereby distinguishing between democracies of the French type, which I call rationalistic, and those of the Anglo-American type, which I call empirical. For the misinterpretation of realism is characteristic of the first. I mean that the war between realists and democrats is a peculiar feature of the democracies which were inspired by the revolution of 1789.

What is meant by *democrazie di ragione,* by rationalistic democracies, and what distinguishes them from those I call empirical? One obvious difference is that whereas the democracies of the French type were born *ex novo* from a revolutionary rupture, the Anglo-American democracy is the outcome of a gradual process of historical growth. This fact entails further differences that are worth noting. Bryce grasped one aspect when he wrote that the French people adopted democracy "not merely because the rule of the people was deemed the completest remedy for pressing evils . . . but also in deference to general abstract principles which were taken for self-evident truths." [24] And Tocqueville with great subtlety seized on another important difference when he noted: "While in England those who wrote about politics and those who engaged in it shared the same life . . . in France the political world was sharply divided into two non-communicating provinces . . . In one [the politicians] administered; in the other [the writers] formulated abstract principles. Above the real society . . . little by little an imaginary society took shape in which everything seemed simple and coordinated, uniform, just, and rational." [25]

In the final analysis, however, the difference that is at the bottom of all the others is a difference in *forma mentis:* it is the difference between a rationalistic, and an empirical-pragmatic mental pattern. [26] And we must be clear about this point.

For the empirical *forma mentis* it is perfectly natural to conceive problems from a practical point of view. So much so that with pragmatism the criterion of truth itself becomes instrumental and operational. Whenever an argument sounds convincing in theory, but does not seem to work out accordingly when put into practice, the empirical attitude is to rely on the latter test and to disregard the sheer logical force of the argument. This amounts to saying that the empirical mind is open to an "extensional orientation," in that it calls on us to look outwards, to touch things with our hands, to pay attention to the relation between symbol and symbolized, between name and *designatum.*

This emphasis on the connection between word and thing is

especially important in politics, since politicians are inclined to use emotive signs in order to produce "signal" reactions (automatic, unthinking reactions) and not "symbol" reactions (delayed and thoughtful reactions) in their audience. In politics the aim is to use not the word that is most accurate but the one that has the greatest emotional appeal; and we use that word, no matter how incorrect and misleading it may be, again and again. This is inevitable since we stir men to action by arousing their feelings, not by appealing to their minds. But this is why political discourse tends to revolve so much around emotive signs that have very little to do with the referents in question and with the real problems.[27] And this is why it is so important to call attention to the relation between sign and referent, word and thing.

Given the characteristics of the empirical mind it is easy to understand why a realistic attitude is innate to it. An empiricist spontaneously uses a word as a substitute for the thing, and hence as a means of arriving at the thing. That is, he instinctively tends to give linguistic terms a descriptive meaning. And realism consists essentially in this, in a thorough-going *description* of reality. That is why the debate about realism is of only secondary importance in the Anglo-American, but of primary importance in the rationalistic democracies.[28]

For the rationalistic *forma mentis,* the criterion of truth is coherence, not applicability or predictable consequences. Rationalists are concerned with the construction of orderly logical relationships, and do not wish to be asked whether such relationships tell us anything about the real world. In Kantian terms, rationalism leans much more to analytic than to synthetic judgments. So while empiricism develops an "extensional" attitude, rationalism encourages an "intensional" attitude[29] whose concern is the logical consistency of an argument rather than its effect in practical application.

In other words, the logical rigor of rationalism tends to contradict reality rather than adapt to it. Of the two interpretations that can be made of Hegel's equation, "The real is rational" (and vice versa), the one that tends to be chosen by the rationalistic mind—because it is most congenial to it—is the version of the Hegelian revolutionary left: "It is the real that must submit to the rational"

—and not the conservative adaptation: "It is the rational that must adjust itself to the real." So much so that the right wing of Hegelianism has left practically no trace of itself, while the left wing has produced Karl Marx.

From this it follows that, whereas it is perfectly natural for an empiricist to see politics as a practical problem in which a course of action must be judged by its workability and its consequences, the rationalist is poorly equipped to face practical problems. He prefers not to deal with them. Rationalists are interested in constructing prototypes, in seeking models, in looking for *the* definitive solution. They want to reform reality in accordance with reason, which is the same as saying that *an unrealistic attitude is congenial to rationalism.* While empirical democracies are naturally realistic, rationalistic democracies are inclined to be anti-realistic.[30] And this explains, going to the roots of the issue, the hostility between realists and democrats.

In the unrealistic (i.e., rationalistic) democracies, the realists are the refugees of the system. It is only normal that they should react negatively to a system characterized by an anti-realistic bias. And this starts, evidently, a vicious circle, for a democracy deprived of internal realistic correctives becomes more and more an unreal democracy. Thus, so long as our democracies are so conceived that ideals and practice never meet, it is easy to understand why realists cannot find a place for themselves in the system, and why political realism and the approval of antidemocratic policies happen to be so frequently linked. But, clearly, this is not because realism is against democracy as such. It is only the enemy of unrealistic, i.e., rationalistic democracy. Will we succeed in tempering our rationalistic heredity with realism, and, on the other hand, will we succeed in making our realism open to ideals? I should say that *in vitro* this is the problem facing those who are concerned with the democracies that were born under the aegis of the French *raison.*

NOTES

† *Politik als Wissenschaft,* I, 4.

1. Lasswell and Kaplan have attempted to measure the difference between

Aristotle and Machiavelli as follows: "A rough classification of a sample of three hundred sentences . . . yielded these proportions of political philosophy (demand statements and valuations) to political science (statements of fact and empirical hypotheses): Aristotle's *Politics*, twenty-five to seventy-five. . . . Machiavelli's *Prince* . . . consisted entirely (in the sample) of statements of political science in the present sense." *Power and Society* (London, 1952), p. 118, n. 15.

2. One should keep in mind the first words of *The Prince:* "All states and powers which have held and hold rule over men are . . . either republics or principalities." In Chap. III the modern meaning of "state" acquires further clarity by Machiavelli's following remark: "When the Cardinal of Roano said that the Italians did not understand war I replied that the French did not understand the state." However, it should be kept in mind that Machiavelli's use of the word "state" was not consistent. As F. Chiappelli has conclusively demonstrated (*Studi sul linguaggio di Machiavelli*, Firenze, 1952, pp. 59-74), both in the *Discourses* and in the *History of Florence* Machiavelli still uses the term state in the medieval sense, that is, in the same sense that today we say "status" or "situation." Cf. Chap. XII, I, note 3, below.

3. F. Chabod (*Del "Principe" di Nicolò Machiavelli* [1926]) noted that towards the middle of the fifteenth century a secularization of politics had taken place in Italy which differed from what was happening elsewhere in this respect, that the Italian prince of the Renaissance did not cloak his power with any sacred or charismatic attributes. For him it was *potestas*, power, which gave him *auctoritas*, not vice versa.

4. Scholarly interest in Machiavelli is inexhaustible. The most recent work on him is by G. Sasso, *Niccolò Machiavelli, storia del suo pensiero politico* (Napoli, 1958), which contains the latest bibliography.

5. Cf. Carl Schmitt's *Der Begriff des Politischen* (Hamburg, 1933), which gives the most coherent theorization of this approach. To Schmitt, war is not the continuation of politics with other means, as the well-known saying of Clausewitz puts it, but, on the contrary, it is politics which is the prosecution of war with other means. In other words, Schmitt derives his concept of politics from the notion of *hostis*, starting from a state of war in order to explain peace. Cf. *Archiv für Sozialwissenschaft und Sozialpolitik* (Aug. 1927).

6. Cf. Sections 4 and 5, below.

7. For the cultural climate of the period see the instructive and caustic picture presented by Eugenio Garin, *Cronache di filosofia italiana (1900-1943)* (Bari, 1955).

8. It is sufficient to point out, to explain Croce's impact, that it is anticipated that the final edition of his works will require eighty volumes and that

47

his bibliography records four thousand titles. Cf. Fausto Niccolini, *"L' Editio ne varietur* delle opere di B. Croce" in *Bollettino dell' Archivio Storico* XIV-XVI (Napoli, 1960-61), pp. 1-539.

9. Cf. *Materialismo storico ed economia marxistica* (Bari, 1919), Preface to 3rd ed., p. xiv.

10. *Filosofia, poesia e storia* (Napoli, 1951), p. 1172.

11. Cf. *Pagine sparse* (Napoli, 1943), Vol. II, p. 382. Cf. also *Pagine sparse,* Vol. II, p. 373, and *La critica* (1925), p. 347.

12. For an assessment of the political philosophy of Croce, cf. N. Bobbio *Politica e cultura* (Torino, 1955) Chaps. VII and esp. XIII: "B. Croce e il liberalismo." Cf. also G. Sartori, *Croce etico-politico e filosofo della libertà,* lectures (Firenze, 1956), also G. Sartori "La teoria dello stato in B. Croce" in *Studi politici,* II and III (1957), pp. 153-181, 351-382. The essentials of Croce's political philosophy are to be found in the writings collected in *Materialismo storico ed economia marxistica* (1896-1906), in *Etica e politica* (1915-1930), and in the numbers of the review *La critica* of the years 1923-1925.

13. Cf. G. Sartori, *La filosofia pratica di Benedetto Croce,* lectures (Firenze, 1954), esp. Chap. VIII.

14. Cf. in *Etica e politica* (Bari, 1943), the essay of 1926 "La concezione liberale come concezione della vita," and the conclusive article of 1939 "Principio, ideale e teoria; A proposito della teoria filosofica della libertà" in *Il Carattere della filosofia moderna* (Bari, 1940), pp. 104-124. Note that here and throughout this book "liberalism" and "liberal" are used in the accepted meaning by Croce and in Europe in general, a meaning which is quite different from that in American usage, as I explain in Chap. XV, 1-3, below.

15. For additional comments on the Crocean concept of politics, cf. G. Sartori, "L'identificazione di economia e politica nella filosofia crociana" in *Studi politici,* II-III (1954).

16. I am considering the strict methodological question under discussion, abstracting from the situation in which and against which Croce argued. In terms of a historical evaluation one should of course recognize the merits and efficacy of a position through which liberalism is reconstructed as the moral ideal of an everlasting freedom.

17. Cf. *Etica e politica,* p. 284.

18. This is Burnham's interpretation, or better, his labeling. James H. Meisel has rightly pointed out, however, that Mosca was certainly no admirer of Machiavelli (cf. *The Myth of the Ruling Class, Gaetano Mosca and the Elite* [Ann Arbor, 1958], pp. 246-285, esp. 264-265). As a matter of fact, Croce was more of a "Machiavellian" than all the aforementioned authors.

With these reservations in mind, Burnham's labeling may be accepted in a broad sense and for a prima facie orientation.

19. This being the real title of the book known to the English-speaking public with the misleading title *The Ruling Class*.

20. Michels' theory will be examined later (cf. Chap. VI, 6). Mosca's doctrine has been thoroughly analyzed by Mario delle Piane in *Bibliografia di G. Mosca* (Firenze, 1949) and *G. Mosca, classe politica e liberalismo* (Napoli, 1952). James H. Meisel's *The Myth of the Ruling Class—Gaetano Mosca and the Elite* is a really outstanding scholarly study, and despite Meisel's views on the elitist approach, Mosca's thinking is understood sympathetically and in depth. Instead, a comprehensive study on Pareto is yet to be done.

21. On Mosca's liberalism all critics agree in substance. In addition to the works cit. of Delle Piane and Meisel, cf. Pietro Piovani, "Il liberalismo di G. Mosca" in *Momenti della filosofia giuridico-politica italiana* (Milano, 1951), and A. Passerin d'Entrèves, "Gaetano Mosca e la libertà" in *Il politico*, IV (1959). Moreover, as N. Bobbio notes, one must make a distinction even with respect to Mosca's polemics against democracy: "The democracy against which he constantly directed his attacks was the pseudo-scientific theory . . . according to which the better political societies are those where the majority governs. . . . But if 'democracy' was understood in the only sense which, according to Mosca, corresponded with the facts, that is, the tendency which brings on a gradual or total renewal of the political class, he . . . was favorable to the development . . . of such a tendency, even if he wanted it to take place with the utmost circumspection." *Gaetano Mosca e la scienza politica* (Roma, 1960), Quaderno 46, Accademia dei Lincei, p. 11. Actually Mosca's aversion to democracy, shared also by Croce, was above all a condemnation of the parliamentarianism of his epoch. (Cf. Delle Piane, *G. Mosca, classe politica e liberalismo,* Introduction.) On the background of anti-parliamentarian criticism, and for a better understanding of the political position of all the authors in question, see Rodolfo De Mattei, *Il Problema della democrazia dopo l'unità* (Roma, 1934), and "Cultura e letteratura anti-democratiche dopo l'unificazione," in *Dal trasformismo al socialismo* (Firenze, 1940).

22. That Pareto too might have resented, in the long run, Mussolini's dictatorship is suggested by G. La Ferla, *Vilfredo Pareto filosofo volterriano* (Firenze, 1954), esp. pp. 160-171, a work which approaches in a suggestive manner, even if not completely, the complex figure of Pareto. The fact remains that Pareto's latest writings (cf. the collection ed. by Mario Missiroli, *Trasformazioni della democrazia* [Modena, 1946]) reveal a mood of self-complacent appraisal of his own pessimistic predictions.

23. Cf. *Political Realism and Political Idealism* (Chicago, 1951) p. 27.

24. Bryce, *Modern Democracies* (New York, 1924), Vol I, p. 208.

25. *L'Ancien régime et la révolution* (Paris, 1856), Bk. II, Chap. XIII, pp. 222-223.

26. Rationalism, in this context, is opposed not to irrationalism but to empiricism. K. R. Popper in this case suggests the word "intellectualism" (cf. *The Open Society and Its Enemies*, Vol. II, p. 224 and Chap. XXIV *passim*). I prefer "rationalism," because intellectualism is too narrow and furthermore it has a connotation that tends to be negative, whereas my criticism of rationalism covers only its application to empirical problems. When an empiricist handles non-empirical questions he is equally open to criticism. See Chap. XI, 6, below.

27. Cf. Chap. XVII, 4, below.

28. Comparatively speaking, of course. Even Americans have to be reminded of the need of "realism," a task undertaken, for instance, by John H. Herz in *Political Realism and Political Idealism*. The difference is that in the context of Anglo-Saxon empiricism the realistic approach, far from being a *hybris,* spontaneously becomes an integral part and the internal corrective element of the democratic *forma mentis.* I am postponing the development of this argument to Chap. XI, 2-3, where I shall illustrate in detail the difference between empirical and rational democracies.

29. For the intension, or connotation, and the extension, or denotation, of a term, see Cohen and Nagel, *An Introduction to Logic and Scientific Method* (London, 1934), pp. 30-33.

30. To be sure, "rationalism" and "empiricism" are not attitudes that are assigned to peoples by Fate. It is clear, for example, that there is a correlation between realism and nurture, in the sense that realism follows an adequate span of historical experience. European short-lived democracies are unrealistic in internal matters, but much less so in their foreign policy, where continuity has been maintained despite the changes of regime. On the other hand, American democracy is internally realistic, but hightly idealistic in foreign policy, a relatively new field in its experience. This explains why the emphasis of realism is laid, in the United States, mostly on this latter field. Reinhold Niebuhr's books and especially Hans J. Morgenthau's *Scientific Man versus Power Politics* (1944), followed by *Politics among Nations* (1948), are the outstanding examples at hand. Cf. the recent balanced appraisal of Kenneth W. Thompson, *Political Realism and the Crisis of World Politics* (Princeton, 1960).

50

Chapter IV

Perfectionism and Utopia

"If there were a people of gods;
they would govern themselves
democratically. So perfect a gov-
ernment is not suited to men."

—Rousseau†

1. The Misunderstanding of Deontology

IF DEMOCRACY is threatened from without by realists it is even more seriously threatened from within by perfectionists. And we cannot eliminate bad realism unless we rid ourselves at the same time of bad idealism (perfectionism). To speak of "bad idealism" implies that there is a correct idealism and suggests that the problem is to locate the difference between the two—between perfectionism on the one hand, and the proper use and understanding of ideals on the other.

Every discussion of democracy basically revolves around three concepts: popular sovereignty, equality, and self-government. These concepts can be deduced from one another, for popular rule postulates that all are equally sovereign, and therefore postulates equality (or, to be precise, isocracy: equal power); and it can also be inferred from popular sovereignty that self-government has to replace government over the people. Now what is the exact nature and role of these concepts? Merely posing the question should put us on safe ground, because it can easily lead us to realize that we are dealing with the

51

deontology of democracy, that is, with normative ideals. But evidently the question is not posed often, for there are not many people who treat the notions of popular sovereignty, equality, and self-government as the prescriptions they really are. And the fact that the guiding principles of democracy are so often used and discussed without a clear awareness of their nature is at the root of what I call democratic perfectionism.

According to my definition, then, the perfectionist is someone who takes democratic ideals for something they are not because he has never asked himself what they are. As a result he pays little attention to the difference and *décalage* between ideals and practice, and therefore, by the same token, he does not know how to turn, or how to apply, prescriptions to reality. I say "does not know" because it should be clearly understood that not all rosy-hued pictures of democracy are due to a perfectionistic error. Perfectionism is tied to unawareness. When we purposely maximize the democratic ideal we can stop at the right moment—when the advantages of exaggerating democracy still overcome the disadvantages. Whereas stopping at the right moment is precisely what the perfectionist does not know how to do.

Perhaps not enough attention is paid to the circumstance that the ideals which oppose democracy derive their major strength and validity from the fact that the democratic ideal is badly understood and expounded. Carlyle's statement that democracy "is forever impossible" is convincing because too many democrats actually demand the impossible. If the formula *vox populi vox dei* [1] had not been presented as an article of faith, it would not have been so easy to rebut with *vox populi vox diaboli*. Of course, when *demos* is deified it is easy to retort that "It is the everlasting privilege of the foolish to be governed by the wise," [2] and we can even understand how Nietzsche's scourging remarks about "slave morality" (which, according to him, characterized democracy and Christian civilization in general) found so many approving readers. [3] However, the more we read popular anti-democratic writing, the more we realize that its targets are the pretensions of democracy rather than democracy itself; or, to put it differently, the mythology of democracy rather than its actual performance. If it were not for the exaggerations of the perfectionist democrat, there would not be much material left to make up a case against democracy. But otherwise the indictment appears convincing: for democratic mythology, as such, is indefensible in terms of good logic and sound thinking.

The debate on equality, a debate which has gone on from time immemorial, perhaps provides the best illustration of the case in point. Let us take Jefferson's classic formula, "All men are created equal." [4] For Jefferson this was a "self-evident truth." Now, setting aside conjecture about the nature of self-evident truths, it is evident that this proposition is constructed syntactically in such a way as to suggest that it is dealing with a fact. If, however, we submit it to logical analysis, we see that it is a prescription to be correctly formulated as follows: You must consider men as if they were created equal.[5] Personally, I believe that Jefferson was right (candor apart) in presenting his prescription in the form of an outright indicative statement, since a self-evident truth is certainly more effective than an exhortation which depends on our good will. It would be out of place, not to say stupid, for us to require that the democratic creed be revised so that it is logically rigorous and formulated with syntactical precision. However, when we are arguing on logical grounds we must meet objections with logic, not dogmas.

It is not a fact that all men are equal. Rather it is a fact that they are not equal but very different. Except that equality is not concerned so much with matters of fact as with value principles and rules of behavior such as: We must recognize ourselves in the other, or It is our duty to treat others as our equals, not as our inferiors, and so forth. There is no need to emphasize how much our civilization owes to similar maxims. Let us simply point out how easily an elementary correction can cut short an endless argument. By this I do not mean that once the axiological meaning of the term equality is established everything is settled. I only mean that the statement "men are not equal" can be accepted as a fact by any democrat simply because it is an objection that does not concern him. The real point is another one.

It is perfectly possible to attach to the precept of equality a different value from that assigned to it by democratic beliefs. But in this case the argument concerns the point that, to a democrat, equality

53

is just, whereas it is not the justice value that his opponent is prepared to place before all others.[6] The advantage of looking at the question in this way is that it brings the hierarchy of values of the different political positions into the open, which makes it possible to talk about real differences of opinion instead of engaging in a fruitless discussion in which both sides are wrong.

Similar remarks can be made with respect to the concepts of "government of the people," meaning self-government, as well as of the "sovereign people." If these concepts are understood in their proper function there is nothing wrong with them. But if they are mythologized they expose the democratic creed to slashing refutation and, even worse, they undermine from within the proper functioning of a democratic system. The unmerited disrepute of present-day democracies among their beneficiaries is largely because a fatuous mythology has raised the stakes too high. The ingratitude typical of the man of our time and his disillusionment with democracy are the reaction to a promised goal that cannot possibly be reached. This means that the real danger threatening a democracy which officially has no enemies left, is not the competition and opposition of counter-ideals but the impossible demands for a democracy that is too pure and too perfect to exist.

We shall have to handle with care, then, the problem of the perfectionistic perversion of political ideals. And for greater clarity and precision it will be useful to distinguish between two kinds of democratic perfectionism, the contemplative and the active. I call the former myth, and will call the latter utopia.[7] Mythological perfectionism misconstrues the meaning and scope of democratic deontology. Utopian perfectionism attempts to convert literally the mythology into reality. According to this definition the utopian form of perfectionism is its final and actually its destructive form. A myth has the function of combatting other myths, if nothing else. Moreover, a myth can remain a form of escape, or of flight from the world. But while the mythologist confines himself to the *logos,* the twentieth-century utopian poses as a reformer: he has become a man of action, when not a revolutionary.

It will be noted that, despite their present-day technical use, I am using "myth" and "utopia" in their older and more common meaning.[8] And this for reasons that are relevant to our argument.

2. Myth and Utopia Reconsidered

I have stated that we cannot eliminate bad realism unless we rid ourselves at the same time of bad idealism (perfectionism). The statement can be also presented in the converse: namely, that we can hardly sever the bad from the good idealism unless we rid ourselves of bad realism. And the relevance of this remark to the concepts of myth and utopia is that their present acceptance in the technical vocabulary of politics is derived to a great extent from the realistic approach, and from the unwarranted pretensions of realism at that.

In their ordinary sense we have learnt at school what myth and utopia mean. Myth is, for unsophisticated people, something associated with Greek mythology, and utopia a term coined by Thomas More to connote a fiction which has "no place," that is, a nonexistent and impossible world. But if we read authors such as R. M. MacIver or Lasswell and Kaplan (let it be noted that I am citing pro-democratic, not anti-democratic scholars) we discover that their myth has nothing in common with what is commonly understood as being mythological or mythical. Likewise, if we consult Mannheim's works we find that he speaks of utopia in a "relative sense" that carries nothing of the original and etymological meaning of the term.

To MacIver and those who follow his terminology myth is to be understood as a neutral term that covers all "value beliefs and notions that men hold." [9] This amounts to saying, in substance, that everything is myth except exact knowledge[10] and techniques. Thus, when MacIver speaks of the "myth of democracy" [11] the reader is not supposed to understand this to mean that democracy is as real as Zeus and his Olympus-located family. Myth, in MacIver's connotation, "abjures all reference to truth and falsity." [12] Accordingly, in their attempt to provide a framework for political inquiry, Lasswell and Kaplan make a wide use of the category "the political myth," since, they write, "The term myth is not to be interpreted as necessarily imputing a fictional, false, or irrational character of the symbols. . . ." [13]

I will resist the temptation to discuss whether we do have the semantic power, so to speak, to take a word that actually conveys a fictional meaning and decide that it does so no longer.[14] Leaving aside the question of principle as to the fruitfulness of this stipulative approach,[15] two specific questions arise. My first point is: if we cannot say myth in its original and commonly understood meaning, what should we say when we do wish to speak of mental primitivism, fabulation, irrational mind, and clumsy theorizing? The second question is: if myth covers—as MacIver writes—"the most penetrating philosophies of life, the most profound intimations of religion, the most subtle renditions of experience, along with the most grotesque imaginations,"[16] how can we locate, and actually why should we try to locate, the difference between ideas and ideals, and furthermore between proper and erroneous use of ideals? Clearly we cannot.[17]

An example of how misleading the loose and too generous use of "myth" can be, is offered by Burham's conclusion—in his book on the Machiavellians—that since democracy, understood as government of the people, is impossible, it follows that the theory of democracy as self-government should be understood as "a myth, formula, or derivation" (respectively the terminology of Sorel, Mosca and Pareto).[18] Now, I will assert very definitely in the next few pages that if self-government is understood literally, then it is impossible. Nonetheless I am unwilling to underwrite the indiscriminate assertion that self-government is a myth (in Sorel's, or in MacIver's, or in any meaning), because in this way we are lumping together precisely that which we must always divide. Self-government is a myth only when the concept is misconstrued; but if it is understood for what it is, as an ideal that has the function of stimulating active participation of the citizens in the political process, then there is nothing mythological about it, and I do not see why we should concur in discrediting an ideal because it may be overvalued and misinterpreted. Calling self-government a myth is opposing excessive idealism with excessive realism, and thereby forgetting the fact that, apart from the total self-government that is impossible, there is a minimum of self-government that is possible, and that it is precisely this minimum that makes for the difference between the democratic and the non-democratic way of governing.

The allegedly neutral and all-embracing use of "myth" has come about because political scientists wish to appear disenchanted—in the wake of realism. But I do not think that the technique of adopting a disillusioned vocabulary amounts to making a profitable use of what we can learn from the realist school. I am not against semantic innovation. But in the case of "myth" we have changed the established meaning of a term against the fundamental rules of definition: namely, so as to augment ambiguity (between the current and the technical meanings), and so as to widen, instead of lessening, the coverage of the concept. And as we still need to say "myth" in its original sense, I stick to the rule that we should not give a term a new meaning whenever its former meaning is not obsolete and cannot be replaced. To speak of democracy as the "myth of democracy," and to rebaptize and lump together such different things as (i) ideas, (ii) ideals and values, (iii) irrational and elementary beliefs under the label "the political myth" is to the disadvantage of articulate and clear thinking, and—as a consequence—also of democracy. It is a strange thing: we often resist the findings of the realists, and then accept their vocabulary uncritically, instead of accepting their findings (when correct), and refusing their vocabulary (when biased).

The present-day use of "utopia" confronts us with similar problems. A first distortion of its etymological meaning came about with Comte, but its final distortion is to be credited to Karl Mannheim. Utopia, for Mannheim, is simply a state of mind that "transcends" existing reality in a revolutionary direction. To speak of a state of mind that transcends what exists in a given time is, clearly, not to say much, for in some sense the mind always transcends reality and the existent. If we proceed from the *genus* to the *differentiam,* the identification of Mannheim's utopia is therefore to be found solely in its "revolutionary function." So much so that the states of mind which transcend the immediate situation in a conservative sense are called by Mannheim "ideologies." In sum, Mannheim makes utopia into nothing more than the vis-à-vis of ideology, placing the revolutionary ideologies (rechristened utopias) on one side, and the conservative ideologies (ideologies *tout court*) on the other.[19]

Now, if that is what we should understand when saying utopia, utopias are no longer utopias, that is, mental fictions that are located nowhere. And if the word utopia is divested of its specific original

57

connotation, one can well say with Oscar Wilde that "progress is the realization of utopias," or with Mannheim that "it is possible that the utopias of today may become the realities of tomorrow: 'Utopias are often only premature truths.' " [20] By manipulating definitions one can prove anything. However, the net result of Mannheim's arbitrary stipulation is simply the exclusion from our political vocabulary of the term which alludes to the *unrealizable*. I mean that if we define utopia in a non-utopian way, we are left without a name to indicate the politically impossible.[21]

From the angle of the present discussion the pertinent comment is that it would be hard to find a more likely way to encourage and promote perfectionism. That is not to say that this was Mannheim's purpose. Not at all. Mannheim, for his sceptical treatment of ideas and ideals, could well be classified among the political realists.[22] However, the change of meaning of "utopia" which occurs with Mannheim is even more significant from another point of view and in connection with a wider trend.

We live in a time in which scientific humility and scientistic euphoria both concur, paradoxically enough, in shading off the utopian into the merely improbable. Owing to scientific caution we have made a point of never saying "impossible" and of speaking only of degrees of probability or improbability. And owing to scientistic optimism we have come to believe that, in principle, nothing is impossible. Having happily confused technical with moral progress, the perfectibility of science with the perfectibility of man, our age is becoming limitless, in the sense that we are relying more and more on the expectations of a future of *unlimited possibilities*. Of course, if everything is possible, we no longer need a term to indicate the impossible. But if we renounce the term, and if—as I maintain—the impossibilities remain, it may be wise to go back to talking about utopia before we sink into utopia. And this is why, despite Mannheim, I am using "utopia" in its proper etymological sense, to mean a self-contradictory claim to imagine an unreal reality for the purpose of realizing it.

The objection to this will be: How can we establish a priori what is possible and what is not? That is, how can we decide a priori what is utopian? I could get around this objection by retorting that since the present-day utopian has moved into the sphere of action, it is no longer a matter of impossibilities projected into infinite time *a priori* but of impossibilities existing here and now. I.e., I could get around the objection by observing that in discussing an active form of utopianism the issue is not that of the theoretical possibility *in se* of a priori knowledge, but of the pressing practical questions regarding the testing of the utopian undertaking, that is, what we do not accomplish at the moment we are attempting its accomplishment.

However, not even the objection in principle is that formidable. It is true that the theoretical formulation of the criteria of absolute impossibility (that is *the utopian*) presents considerable difficulties.[23] But some elementary examples suffice to show that unconditional impossibilities do exist. For instance, the common saying "You can't have your cake and eat it" obviously indicates an absolute impossibility which does not depend on the circumstances of time or place. Likewise we can say: It is impossible to sleep when awake—or to spend and save the same money—or to take a road that goes to the left and one that goes to the right at the same time, etc. These, too, are unconditional impossibilities that cannot be escaped with the usual phrases that history is a sequence of impossibilities that were made possible, or a cemetery of utopias that were realized.

Passing from the circumstances of everyday life to political situations we still find absolute impossibilities. The difference is that they are more difficult to perceive. There are two reasons for this. The first is that in our personal experience impossibility is revealed immediately and directly to us, as an impossibility to *do,* whereas in politics it is revealed late, indirectly, and as an impossibility to *obtain.* The second reason is that political concepts are so complex, and their meaning so unstable, that it is easy to get around all impossibilities by manipulating words and definitions.

For instance, someone who says that freedom and planning are incompatible, and that therefore it is utopian to want both together, is not necessarily talking nonsense.[24] But if we define the concepts of freedom and planning in a way that makes them compatible then the impossibility disappears. Mind you, the impossibility asserted in the first thesis, if it is well formulated, remains. It is not that the second thesis refutes the first but that we change theses, in that we substitute a realizable program for a utopian program. So it cannot be said that the politically impossible is always overcome. Rather we avoid it by changing our plans. And by doing this, whether we admit it or not, we pay the homage due to those who warned us of an impossibility.

Actually any logician who knows his trade can perfectly well anticipate absolute impossibilities, including political utopias, a priori. Of course we can make mistakes. But since when has the possibility of a mistake ruled out an inquiry? To avoid error, must we give up trying? That is, must we give up thinking?

3. Self-Government and the Politically Impossible

Let us take Marx's utopia, which was to be achieved by the replacement of representative democracies by direct democracy, or more precisely, by a self-government arising from the "withering away of the State." In my opinion, we are justified in considering Marx's self-government an unfounded hypothesis located nowhere, the absolute impossibility of which can be demonstrated *a priori*.

In terms of logical analysis, or at a philosophical level, the notion of self-government raises no problem in that it does not require us to *weigh* the notion according to a scale of intensity and a scale of size. In these terms, when we govern ourselves we have self-government: and that is that. But the same is not true at the empirical level. For if we are faced with the practical problem of realizing a political system based on self-government, then everything depends on the intensity that is attributed to the concept, and correlatively to its extension (both spatial and temporal). In the first place I will put forward the following theorem: *The* intensity *of self-government attainable is in inverse proportion to the* extension *of self-government demanded.*

Let us demonstrate our theorem starting from the hypothesis of a maximum intensity. If we want self-government in the strict and literal sense of the term, we are referring either to inner self-government (self-determination), or to the despot. In this case we have maximum intensity (i.e., the maximum self-government possible), because the extension is zero (self-government *in interiore hominis*). But let us introduce a dimension, a small extension like the *polis,* the ancient Greek city. In this case the term self-government will have less intensity; that is, it will have to be interpreted in a less narrow and less literal sense than before. By saying self-government we now refer to a rapid and comprehensive rotation between power holders and power addressees. As Aristotle put it, in ancient democracies the citizens governed themselves in the sense that all governed and were governed in turn.

Proceeding a step farther, let us assume that self-government is to function over some hundreds of square miles. In this case we shall have still less intensity. Actually, we can now claim very little, since the extension of self-government sought is already such as to permit only a very metaphorical use of the concept. At this point self-government only means being governed from nearby instead of afar; that is, the term still has a meaning antithetic to centralization. The self-government in question denotes, more precisely, autonomous local governments that can be indicated as self-governing because they permit a greater degree of self-government than do political systems which are characterized by centralization and concentration of power. However, for the size that we have envisaged, local government is already a system of indirect government. It is not a self-governing but a representative democracy in which we are governed by intermediaries.

The term self-government becomes, therefore, altogether inappropriate when the extension embraces, for instance, all Italy or France or England. In this case it is hard to see how the citizens could govern themselves in any meaningful sense of the expression. The counterpart of that territorial size can only be some kind of control over government. It follows from this that a phrase like, "A day will come when all humanity will govern itself and will be united in a single self-governing system," would be all the more nonsensical, for we simply have forgotten about the intensity of the concept. That is, we have forgotten that only a zero intensity (approximating zero) can correspond to a dimension n (approximating infinity)—which means that in that imaginary self-government, at zero intensity, there will not be anything remotely resembling the faintest imitation of governing oneself.

Until now I have referred to physical size. But the use of "self-

61

government" involves not only spatial but temporal extension, so that the demonstration must be completed keeping in mind that intensity is also correlative to a temporal dimension. Again, it must be noted that the examination of a logical problem does not proceed in this way, for in logic neither the duration nor the chronological order of referents is taken into consideration. The reason for this is that on a philosophic level our discourse concerns atemporal relations, ideal and not chronological sequences. But when we descend to the empirical level, duration and chronological order count. Operationally speaking, we cannot do first what has to be done afterwards, and there are many things that we can do for a short time but could not do forever.

Let us then reformulate our theorem as follows: *The intensity of self-government possible is in inverse proportion to the duration of self-government demanded.* This means that a maximum intensity of self-government, such as we have, for instance, in moments of revolutionary tension, can correspond only to a minimal duration. In outlining his ideal democracy, Marx took the revolutionary episode of the Paris Commune of 1870-71 as a model.[25] But in doing this he was arbitrarily projecting an instantaneous event into a sort of eternity (the Hegelian end of history), forgetting that the only reason that this experiment in the self-government of the proletariat had a high degree of intensity was that it lasted a very short time. Therefore, as a philosopher speculating about timeless and placeless self-government of the proletariat, Marx is respectable. But as a practical politician—as a man of action—he is an unalloyed utopian. He imagined a stateless society with literal self-government (at maximum intensity), ignoring the inverse relation between the intensity and the spatial-temporal dimension of possible self-government. His ideal of replacing governments by self-governing humanity was impossible then as it is now, and—I am not afraid to predict—will be just as impossible in one or ten centuries.

Formerly our ancestors relied too much on argument and too little on experience, and always said "impossible" and never "improbable." But nowadays we have gone to the opposite extreme of saying "improbable" even when we should say "impossible." No doubt, if everything must be proved by experiment and nothing can be demonstrated by argument, the range of discourse has to be limited to mere "probables," that is to statements and predictions whose truth-value can only be that they are likely or unlikely. But experience cannot replace argument any more than the latter is a substitute for the former. Once more, then, we should take the politically impossible seriously, if we wish to avoid experiences as useless as they are tragic.

4. The Role of Ideals

It is easy to gather from the foregoing that the lines separating a deontology from a mythology, and the political myth from its utopian extension, are indeed thin. In synthesis, utopianism is an extreme case of deontological hypertrophy. And a deontology becomes a myth and a utopia because of a fundamental misconception regarding the nature of deontological discourse and the *raison d'être* for the gap between ideals and reality. Therefore it is especially important to clear up the matter, to master this relation between ideals and the realm of practice.

Benjamin Constant, who was deeply aware of this problem because it had been *the* problem exploded by the French Revolution, sought to solve it by means of "intermediary principles," that is, by interposing a mediant term between "first principles" and reality. He wrote: "When we toss into the midst of a society of men a principle divorced from all the intermediary principles that bring it down to us and adapt it to our situation, we create great disorder; because when this principle is torn from all its links and deprived of all its supports . . . it destroys and overthrows. But it is the fault not of the first principle but of our ignorance of the intermediary principles." [26] The problem undoubtedly is, as Constant saw, to adapt the absoluteness of the principles to the nature of things by submitting the deontology to an intermediary re-elaboration. And Constant was perfectly right when he stressed that "each time a principle . . . seems inapplicable, it is because we do not know the intermediary principle which contains the means of application." [27]

But I should like to take up the argument at an earlier point.

For before dealing with the applicative passage, so to speak, it seems to me that we have to consider what does not pass and should not pass—that is to say, the shock effect of a deontology.

An *ought* is not meant to take the place of *is*. It is meant to be a counterweight, which is a completely different matter. The *ought* is always excessive, it smacks of *hybris*. The reason for this is that ideals are born from our dissatisfaction with reality and have a polemic function, a countervailing role. Therefore the demand is gauged in relation to the resistance that it will meet: it obeys the rule that we must ask for more than we really need. In short, a deontology is not designed to be transmuted into reality. I would go as far as to say that ideals are predestined *not to succeed*. The function of deontological pressure is one of counterbalancing, in that it accompanies the vicissitudes of history ever-present as their non-real, non-acquiescent element.

That ideals are unreal, and are meant to remain such, amounts to saying that if, as an absurd hypothesis, it were possible to convert them, as they stand, into reality, we would not want them any more. Take equality. Is it not one of those ideals that warm our hearts as long as they are kept at a distance? Is it not perhaps true that the closer we come to it, the more aware we become that in abolishing certain injustices we create others, and that literal equality would be as unwelcome as the natural inequality it opposes? Actually, if our ideals were fully realized, we would no longer have many reasons to cherish them. Without deontological pressure and a strong prescriptive charge, democracy would not exist. But a democracy that corresponded exactly to its deontological definition would not be that satisfying. Guns are useful to win battles but we do not fight a war to win guns.

Saying that prescriptive ideals are not designed, as such, to be converted into reality is the same as saying that if we attempt to realize them literally we shall fail, in the sense that the outcome will not correspond to the aim. And this starts a vicious circle. Since the utopian attempt to enforce ideals does not succeed, we are finally brought to believe that it is the ideals which are worthless. I maintain the contrary, which is that if the practical application inevitably fails it is not the fault of the ideals but of the kind of test we choose for them. For we fail to see that while prescriptive stimuli move and guide reality, per se they are not and *cannot be* this reality. They are only an ingredient of the realm of practice destined to counterbalance it with a value tension.

So if what ought to be does not pass over into reality, let us not always blame reality. Because of their absolute and excessive nature, ideals are not made to be converted into facts, but to challenge them. Of course this does not imply that we do not have here, also, a problem of intermediary principles—a problem of finding an operational formulation for ideals. And that is why I should like to conclude with some observations on the logic underlying the application of deontology.

5. The Opposite Danger

The democratic ideal can act on very different situations, either against a non-democratic system or within a democratic form. And so long as democracy remains an ideal that opposes autocracy we can maximize it beyond measure. In fact, the more we exaggerate it the more efficacious it may be. But this is no longer the case once democracy takes the place of its defeated adversary. At this point the deontology no longer has the task of destroying an inimical system but has, instead, the task of enhancing the system it has created. If, therefore, the *ought* remains unchanged, it begins operating in reverse. I mean that when *within* a democracy, we retain the democratic ideal in an extreme form, it begins to work *against* the democracy it has produced. That is to say that if a deontology is not modified in proportion to its growing success, it turns into what J. H. Herz calls the "opposite principle": it produces inverted results. That is why, as Herz writes, "Political idealism has its time of greatness when it is in opposition to decadent political systems. It degenerates as soon as it attains its final goal; and in victory it dies." [28]

We can draw from this the following intermediary rule (in Constant's sense): *To the extent that an ideal is converted into reality, to the same extent it must be adjusted in accordance with its distance from the target.* In the case under discussion, the more a democracy is actually maximized, the more the democratic deontology must be minimized.

The democratic principle in its pure, maximal state, calls for "all power to the people." Taken literally, this principle is unequivocal. But as soon as we consider it in operation, we find that it takes on two opposite meanings. As long as it operates within a nondemocratic system, it functions as a principle that limits power (the opponent's power, of course), whereas when it operates within a democracy it asks for unlimited power. In the first case, therefore, the effect of the democratic deontology is to delimit power, but in the second to recreate a limitless power. This means that, at a certain point, the principle of "all power to the people" is converted from a weapon against absolute power into its opposite, a new absolutist principle.

It could be said that the absolutism of a monarch is not the same thing as the absolutism of the people. And the perfectionist will agree: "Indeed, what I want and what democracy demands is the unlimited power of the people." But I should like to show that he is wrong to cling to the maximal ideal, because the difference between the theses, "all power to the monarch" and "all power to the people," is only nominal. The difference between the two statements is reduced to practically nothing because, as we remember, the attempt to replace autocracy by democracy can succeed easily as far as the titular right to power is concerned but only to a small extent when the actual exercise of power is at stake.[29] And the reason the actual exercise of power does not shift is that beyond a certain point it cannot shift —not that there are shrewd conspirators plotting to rob the people of their sovereignty, as the perfectionist is inclined to imagine.

A democracy, then, is a political system in which the people exercise power to the extent that they are able to change their governors, but not to the extent of governing themselves. It follows from this that the only way the sovereign people can maintain the degree of power they need and are capable of wielding is not to give their governors unlimited power. This means that a system can survive as a democracy only if the principle "All power to the people" is gradually modified, as democracy comes closer to being realized, to "All power to nobody." A democracy can last only if the maximization of the democratic ideal does not lead to rejecting as inadequate the principle of the control of power. If, on the contrary, the perfectionist interpretation of the tenet "all power to the people" is intransigently maintained, it will end by undermining constitutional guarantees and the techniques of representative government. At this point we, the people, lose control. And we get nothing in exchange, because the amount of power that we can actually exercise remains the amount indicated by the formula "control over power." So all we shall get in exchange are governors who are out of our control—whose power is no longer limited. And a situation in which the governors have all the power and the governed have no power, is purely and simply absolutist.

If, then, we do not want our ideal to die in victory we must not lose sight of the threat of the opposite danger,[30] and must therefore transform the battle cry "all power to us" into the peacetime principle "nobody must have all the power." For the first formula is tied to the enemy it was opposing, and therefore, unless it is gradually converted into the second, it will simply bring absolutism back to life.

All this having been said, I am not so naïve as to think that the problem of combating perfectionism is a problem—let us say—of logical rectification. Democracy is to politics what a market system is to economics. The rule of the game is competition and, to pursue the analogy, a multi-party system works in very much the same way as a system of oligopolies. Just as we know no better method of protecting the consumer than forbidding monopolistic concentration of economic power, we do not know a better means for defending freedom than letting parties compete among themselves. The difference, however, is that competition among economic producers is submitted to the control of consumers who do indeed consume and are therefore in a position to appraise goods that are offered to them in tangible form. Competition among political parties, on the contrary, easily escapes the control of the political consumer. Political goods are not tangible and cannot easily be evaluated, for they amount to little more than promises and words, whose terms of reference are too complex and too far removed to be properly appraised.

The difference, then, is that unfair competition in politics has no effective correctives. And when competition becomes a matter of bewitching rather than accomplishment, of promises rather than deeds, the rule of political competition takes on the ill-famed name of demagogy. This means that the fate of democracy is dangerously entrusted to a type of competition which, in the absence of effective methods of control, is chiefly based on *surenchère*—on outbidding—on what is appealing even though it is not credible.

Clearly, between demagogy and perfectionistic outbidding there is a relationship of cause and effect; and it is equally obvious that the demagogic incubation of democratic perfectionism is not due to insufficient intellectual awareness. Even responsible people feel thwarted by the mechanism of the system. This being granted, it remains true that the best way of making a result inevitable is to resign ourselves to its inevitability. We certainly cannot escape something that we do not even attempt to escape. And the best way of paving the way for something we call fated is to repeat at every opportunity that it is fated.

This is why I have dwelt on a logical analysis of democratic perfectionism. Whatever the pattern of the future may be there is no need for us to help demagogy with our mistakes. Granted that democratic mythology and the resultant utopianism give grounds for growing concern, there is no need to accuse Fate in our search for alibis, if it is we who have abdicated from our responsibility of keeping myths within their proper limits. In this case it is not that we are overwhelmed by events but that we ourselves are incapable of directing them and keeping them under control.

NOTES

† *Contrat social,* III, 4.

1. On the origin of this phrase, cf. Francis Lieber, *On Civil Liberty and Self-Government* (Philadelphia, 1880), p. 405 and Chap. XXXV *passim.*

2. Carlyle, *Latter-Day Pamphlets,* I, "The Present Time" (London, 1850), p. 27.

3. Cf. his *Genealogie der Moral* (1887), unquestionably one of the most influential pamphlets of anti-democratic literature. The *Genealogie* (together with the *Anti-Christ*), is the counterpart of Nietzsche's theory of the Superman and the *Herrenklasse.*

4. I refer to the Preamble of the Declaration of Independence of the United States (July 4, 1776), instead of quoting the "men are born and remain free and equal in rights" of the French Declaration of the Rights of Man and Citizens of 1789, because the American text is more characteristic.

Jefferson puts down as a premise the statement that men are created equal, and seems to draw out by way of implication their inalienable right to life and liberty. For the meaning of Jefferson's thesis see, e.g., H. A. Myers, *Are Men Equal?* (New York, 1945), pp. 34-35, 63-64, 136-137.

5. A more sophisticated analysis can divide this prescription into (i) a mere attitude statement or (ii) a value-statement. In the former case we are just saying "Away with hierarchy!" or "Enough of privilege!"—whereas in the latter we are assigning a value. It is often difficult, however, to separate the two kinds of statement, and the distinction is not relevant in this context.

6. These questions will be discussed later in Chap. XIV, esp. sect. 6.

7. I am not following the sense which this distinction had in Sorel, who treated the myth as an expression of the will. For Sorel, "utopia is the last manifestation of faith in reason; myth the first act of rebellion against reason. Utopia is nearly always intellectualistic; myth has always a religious basis." (Giovanni Spadolini, *Sorel* [Firenze, 1947], Introduction, p. xxi.) Whatever the merits of Sorel's approach may be, for the purpose of our analysis it is not important to bring out the voluntarist aspect of the political myth. What concerns us here is to follow the crescendo which attributes to utopia a more marked meaning of "impossibility."

8. Except for an innovation concerning "utopia," which is presented as an active and no more as a contemplative mentality. In this respect, but only in this one, I follow Mannheim's conceptualization.

9. R. M. MacIver, *The Web of Government* (New York, 1947), p. 4.

10. *Ibid.,* pp. 447-448 n.

11. *Ibid.,* pp. 39, 51.

12. *Ibid.,* p. 5.

13. *Power and Society* (London, 1952), p. 117.

14. Lasswell and Kaplan, for example, assert that they use "myth" in a neutral sense and explain it as follows: "The present concept is close to a number of others . . . Marx's 'ideology,' Sorel's 'myth,' Mosca's 'political formula,' Pareto's 'derivations,' Mannheim's 'ideology' and 'utopia'. . . ." (*op. cit.* p. 117). Besides the astonishingly heterogeneous collection of references, it is a fact that for the majority of these authors the labels in question had a derogatory connotation.

15. The question of stipulative definitions, that is, of arbitrariness in defining, will be fully discussed here in Chap. X. Cf. also Chap. XVII, 4, 5.

16. *Op. cit.,* p. 5.

17. Besides MacIver's cosmic definition of myth, I also wonder whether his basic dichotomy between myths and techniques is felicitous. For one thing,

there is too much disproportion between the two terms: if "myth" is too wide, "techniques" is too specific. In the second place, it is questionable whether there is a necessary relationship between them, in the sense that a myth does not necessarily contain the exigency of converting itself into reality, and thereby of making recourse to techniques. Finally, from myth to techniques there is too great a jump, the gap is too wide: an essential intermediary link seems to be missing.

18. *The Machiavellians, Defenders of Freedom* (New York, 1943), p. 236.

19. Cf. Karl Mannheim, *Ideology and Utopia* (London, 1936), esp. pp. 173 f. Lasswell and Kaplan, who formerly followed MacIver, are now accepting Mannheim's conceptualization, which they have synthesized with precision in the following definition: "The *ideology* is the political myth functioning to preserve the social structure: the *utopia* to supplant it." (*Power and Society*, p. 123.) Actually I find their reception of such an artificial and debatable opposition hard to understand, particularly since Lasswell and Kaplan themselves remark in a footnote that "countermyth" would be "a less misleading term than utopia" (*loc. cit.*). This having been recognized, why promote the use of misleading stipulations?

20. Cf. Oscar Wilde, *The Soul of Man under Socialism* (Saugatuck, Conn., 1950), p. 18, and *Ideology and Utopia*, p. 183. The sentence quoted by Mannheim is from Lamartine.

21. Mannheim admits that "among ideas which transcend the situation there are, certainly, some which in principle can never be realized" (*op. cit.,* p. 177), but he does not permit our naming them, unless we resort to a distinction between realizable and unrealizable utopias—a distinction which reveals in itself the difficulties which result from Mannheim's arbitrary definitional manipulation.

22. It is the derivation of Mannheim from Marx that has somewhat obscured the fact that his "ideologies" pertain to the same family of Pareto's "derivations." In effect, even though Pareto never uses the term ideology the concept is basic to his thinking, as N. Bobbio has well pointed out (cf. "Vilfredo Pareto e la critica delle ideologie" in *Rivista di filosofia*, IV [1957]). For a critical analysis of Mannheim's "suspiciousness of ideas" and of the concept of ideology, cf. Chap. XVIII, 2, below.

23. I have tried to go deeper into this problem in my lectures *Questioni di metodo in scienza politica* (Firenze, 1959), pp. 180-186, 228-241.

24. Cf. Chap. XVI, 1, 2, below.

25. The Marxian concept of democracy will be analyzed in Chaps. XVII, 1 and XVIII, 3. I use "Marxian" when referring to Marx himself, and "marxist" to the followers.

26. *Des réactions politiques* (1797), Chap. VIII.

27. *Ibid.*

28. *Political Realism and Political Idealism*, p. 42.

29. Cf. Chap. II, 3, above.

30. Cf. John H. Herz, *Political Realism and Political Idealism*, p. 168 and pp. 168-189 *passim*.

Chapter V

Governed Democracy and Governing Democracy

*"No one denies that there is often a wide
discrepancy between professions of faith
and actual practice, between principles and
actions. The question is how we should
interpret such discrepancies."*

—J. H. Hallowell †

1. Elections, Phantom Public, and Public Opinion

POLITICS IS ULTIMATELY the relationship between the governing and the governed—a relationship which may take the outright form of a direct power *over* the governed or work out smoothly as a power to get things done. It has been argued that the dichotomy between the governed and the governing holds for all systems but democracy, as the peculiar feature of a democratic government is that it makes nobody entirely subject or entirely sovereign. Now it is quite true that democratic decision-making makes it impossible, if we follow its entire course, to locate a dividing line between the positions of the governed and the governing. Nevertheless, to say that it is difficult to indicate the exact boundary between obedience and command is not the same as saying there is no boundary. And even if there were none, our frame of reference would still be useful, for it would lead us to define democracy as the only system which succeeds in escaping the eternal dilemma of politics by making the governed and the governing one and the same.

This, however, is not the case. But we may well ask to what degree is this limiting hypothesis realized. We all agree that in order to have democracy we must have, to some degree, a government of the people; but we also know that if there is a government, it has to be a government over the people. The problem is how these two requirements can be reconciled. And the thorny point is obviously not raised by saying "government over the people" but by the phrase "the governing people."

The question, then, is: When do we find the *demos* in the act or the role of governing? The answer is easy—during elections. The assertion that in a democracy power is exercised by the sovereign people, is warranted because we are measuring the system in electoral terms. And not only are we perfectly justified in doing so but it would be very wrong to overlook the importance of elections. If it were not for elections, if it were not for the fact that we do not trust presumed consensus of opinion, there would be no bridge between governed and governing and hence no democracy. However, we still must consider that elections are a discontinuous and very elementary performance. Between elections the people's power remains quiescent, and there is also a wide margin of discretion between elementary electoral choices and the concrete governmental decisions that follow.

Elections are only the time when single expressions of will are counted. Elections register the voter's decisions; but how are these decisions arrived at? Elections compute opinions; but where do these opinions come from and how are they formed? What, in a word, is the genesis of the will and opinion that elections limit themselves to recording? Voting has a pre-voting background. While, then, we must not forget the importance of elections, we cannot isolate the electoral event from the whole circle of the opinion-making process. If the actual sovereign is not the citizen but the voter, in his turn the voter is none other than the citizen in the critical instant in which he is asked to act as sovereign. And when we shift our attention to this larger picture, we see that popular sovereignty is only a phase of the over-all political process.

73

The actual weight and importance of this obligatory path of the political process through the sieve of popular sovereignty remains to be determined case by case, and depends on a series of conditions, the most important of these being the circumstances in which so-called public opinion is formed. Electoral power per se is the mechanical guarantee of the system, but the substantive guarantee is given by the conditions under which the citizen gets the information and is exposed to the pressure of the opinion-makers. Elections are the means to an end—the end being a "government of opinion" of the kind so masterfully described by Dicey, that is, a government responsive to and responsible towards public opinion.[1]

We say that elections must be free. This is indeed true, but it may not be enough; for opinion too must be, in some basic sense, free. Free elections with unfree opinion—that is, with no public opinion—express nothing. The retort will be, I suppose, that in every society, be it democratic or not, there is always, inevitably, a public opinion. This answer, however, calls our attention to the need of distinguishing between (i) an opinion that is public merely in the sense that it is disseminated *among* the public, and (ii) an opinion which the public to some degree has formed by itself. In the first sense, we have an opinion *made* public but in no way produced *by* the public: therefore public only in the geographical meaning that it is located *in* the public. In the second sense, we have instead an opinion *of* the public, meaning that the public is the subject. In the first sense, any society can be credited with a public opinion. In the second sense, no public opinion exists unless it is based on, or related to, personal and private opinions; and therefore a present-day totalitarian mass society has no public opinion, but only State-made opinions enforced *upon* the public.

Until a few decades ago there was no reason to draw this distinction. Until the advent of mass media and of totalitarian control of the public, to say "popular opinion" meant, and could only mean, "opinion *of* the people," that which the subjects, not the sovereign, had in mind. But nowadays we can find a popular opinion which is is in no meaningful sense the people's opinion. Hen ، the distinction is crucial, and ambiguity as to the meaning of public opinion should be carefully avoided.[2] I shall therefore refer to public opinion only when it is a relatively free and autonomous opinion, that is, to the extent that it expresses a relatively independent will of the people and not when it becomes a mere reflection of the will of the State.

Of course, even a free and autonomous public opinion is, in many senses, neither free nor autonomous. What is actually meant by these requirements is free from State control of the opinion-making process and instrumentalities. As a rule of thumb, the conditions for a relatively self-sufficient public opinion are provided by a system of plural and alternative centers of influence and information—we might say by free competition among mass media and between opinion leaders. This does not imply that the audience usually plays one source of information against another, and that it makes up its mind after having compared and discussed the various arguments. This is seldom the case. Actually, the benefits of mass media decentralization and competition are largely mechanical and unintentional. They are so, mainly because a polycentric system of opinion-making helps to produce a plural, heterogeneous, and—above all—unpredictable and uncontrollable distribution of opinions. In short, a plurality of persuaders reflects itself in a plurality of publics, and a plurality of publics is the minimal but already sufficient condition for a successful operation of the system as a whole—I mean, of a system in which we can truthfully speak of the power of public opinion.

To acknowledge that whenever we meet with an efficient, unrestrained totalitarian monopoly of mass media there is no true public opinion,[3] does not settle the question of just how true public opinion is in the case of a loose, plural system of opinion formation. If the expression "public opinion" is supposed to evoke the image of the common man, we may still ask: to what extent does the public of the common people actually play a role of its own and exert a real influence in all this? Voting studies have, in effect, brought out a very poor picture of the ordinary voter, so poor that one is forced to wonder whether the public in question is anything more than a merely passive audience.[4] The average citizen is neither interested nor active in the political discourse. His information is indeed thin and his perception of the issues is distorted and aprioristic. His choices correspond to patterns of identification connected with a prevailing allegiance or with overlapping affiliations to the family, the peer

75

group, the class, the church, etc.[5] Psephology, the study of electoral behavior, has abundantly shown to what extent the citizen's vote depends on his social, economic, and religious environment, and also —as the French electoral sociology points out—on historically-based collective electoral predispositions.[6] We are thus forced to recognize that the expression "public opinion" stands for an *optimum*. In many respects and instances the public has no opinion, but only a very inarticulate public feeling, made up of moods and drifts of sentiment. In matters of internal policy no less than in foreign affairs, behind the so-called public will what we often find is, as Walter Lippmann says, a "phantom public."[7] But this conclusion needs some qualifications.

When we invest public opinion with the responsibility of making intelligent and rational decisions on definite questions, it is true that we are dealing with a phantom public. Schumpeter exaggerates little, I believe, when he writes that "the typical citizen drops down to a lower level of mental performance as soon as he enters the political field. He argues and analyzes in a way which he would readily recognize as infantile within the sphere of his real interests. He becomes a primitive again. His thinking becomes associative and affective. . . ."[8] He exaggerates little because a similar drop in mental performance can be observed whenever we cross the border from our field of specialization and interest. An astronomer who discusses philosophy, a chemist who speaks about music, or a poet who talks about mathematics will not utter less nonsense than the average citizen interviewed by a pollster. The difference is that the astronomer, the chemist, and the poet will generally avoid making fools of themselves by pleading ignorance, whereas the citizen is forced to concern himself with politics and in the midst of the general incompetence he no longer realizes that he is an ass. So the only difference is that in other zones of ignorance we are warned to mind our own business, while in the political realm we are encouraged to take the opposite attitude, and thus we end by not knowing that we know nothing.

But there is another side to the question. If, instead of asking public opinion to express ad hoc judgments that are articulate, informed, and rational, we think of public opinion as a pattern of attitudes and a cluster of basic demands, then our phantom takes on consistency and stability. In this connection Berelson has suggested an illuminating analogy. "For many voters," Berelson writes, "political preferences may be considered analogous to cultural tastes. . . . Both have their origin in ethnic, sectional, class, and family traditions. Both exhibit stability and resistance to change for individuals, but flexibility and adjustment over generations for the society as a whole. Both seem to be matters of sentiment and disposition rather than 'reasoned preferences.' While both are responsive to changed conditions and unusual stimuli, they are relatively invulnerable to direct argumentation. . . . Both are characterized more by faith than by conviction and by wishful expectation rather than careful prediction of consequences." [9] From this angle, then, public opinion reveals a formidable inertia and a gluey resistance; and therein lies its strength and its limitations, which are correlative.

Therefore, as long as the public is allowed to have an opinion, public opinion is a protagonist which should not be underestimated. It would be entirely mistaken to infer from the poor quality of the ordinary citizen that he amounts to an absentee. He may well be politically illiterate, but he is there. Tenacious in its tastes, identifications, and expectations, impervious to direct argument, public opinion enters the circle of political decision-making demanding a heavy toll. But it is just that—a toll. Policy-making does not spring from a "cultural taste" any more than music from the people who attend a concert, or literature from readers. Public opinion assures the success or failure of a policy. But it does not initiate it. The average voter does not act, he reacts. Political decisions are not arrived at by the sovereign people, they are submitted to them. The processes of forming opinion do not start *from* the people, they pass *through* them.

Thus, it is only by looking at elections and forgetting about electioneering and all the rest that democracy may be viewed as a one-way decision-making process going from bottom to top. Actually, we are confronted with a continuous circular process whose dynamics are activated from the top rather than from the bottom. Even in the most favorable circumstances it almost never happens that popular sovereignty is the real starting point. Before exerting an influence the people are influenced. Before they want something, they are often made to want it. "What we are confronted with in the analysis

77

of political processes is largely not a genuine but a manufactured will. . . . The will of the people is the product and not the motive power of the political process." [10]

Moreover, elections should not be considered only *a parte ante,* but *a parte post* as well. In the latter focus, it is only in a very vague sense that elections can tell those who have been elected how to govern. [11] Primarily the results of voting establish who shall govern. And it is not the fault of the instrument, i.e., the imperfection of the electoral system employed, if elections can reveal only rarely and inadequately the will of the majority in regard to specific policy issues. I mean that the remedy for this cannot be found in creating more refined channels and more sensitive electoral techniques, because if the machine is imperfect it is not cruder than its mechanics, the voters.

Let us be honest. The average voter is called on to make decisions on questions about which he knows nothing. In other words, he is incompetent. And the decisions that each of us make in fields in which we have no skill are, obviously, decisions that have been suggested by someone else, either a competent or a pseudo-competent person. And attention must be paid to the pseudo-competent person, because incompetence consists precisely in not being able to tell the difference between competence and incompetence. How then can we reasonably expect electoral instrumentalities to say more than the voter has to say? We are lucky enough if the voter is not tricked by an erroneous identification into choosing a representative that in no way impersonates his feelings and desires. [12] It would be almost a miracle if he managed to indicate a policy for every issue. Therefore, I see no grounds for complaint if voting does nothing more than indicate, within a general political orientation, the person or the party that we are "coinciding in opinion with." [13]

If this is the actual meaning and performance of elections, then the assertion that voting power is a "governing" power is metaphorical. There is power and power, and in this process the *demos* exercises a power of control and/or of pressure which amounts to a set of vetoes and basic claims in regard to those who govern. But while the people condition a government, they do not themselves govern. This means that when we talk about governing or governed democracy

the verb "govern" is used in two very different senses, or with different intensity and accuracy. When we speak of the people as governing, we exaggerate, or we give the verb a vague, feeble meaning.
When we speak of the people as governed we use the verb "govern" in
its narrow and proper sense. And there is quite a difference. The difference is so great that we may end up with the conclusion that while
the ideal would require a governing democracy, observation of the
real world shows that what we actually have is a governed democracy.

So the unvarnished answer to the question, "To what degree
and in what sense is the *demos* governing?" could be that a realistic
examination of existing democracies shows us the exact reverse of the
ideal: namely, that democracy has functioned only when an aristocracy has governed. The deontology postulates a government of the
people, observation shows that the people are governed by minorities.
Democracy is supposed to be a system of self-government but it
turns out to be a polyarchy.

As we see, the gap between deontology and reality is indeed very
great. And I have purposely presented it in a summary and rather
crude fashion because it seems to me that before taking the nuances
into account it might be well if we accept the challenge in terms of
black and white. Given this gap, then, what conclusions do we draw
from it? This is the point at issue. And unless we know how to
deal with the relationship between ideals and practice it is very likely
that we will fall into three errors of judgment: the perfectionists's,
the realist's, or the sceptic's.

2. Perfectionism, Hyper-Realism, and Scepticism

The perfectionist argument runs as follows: "If a democracy
does not correspond to its prescriptive requisites, it is not a democracy." But, as we have seen, this is an incorrect application of the
normative discourse. Since a prescriptive definition is not an existential
definition, it is true *ex hypothesi* that what is prescribed *does not exist.*
There are two ways of gauging the relationship between *ought* and
is. The right way is to ask, "What is the incidence of deontological
pressure on reality?" thereby ascertaining whether, and to what
extent, it fulfills its counterbalancing function. The wrong way—
the perfectionist way—is to say that whenever the facts do not corre-

79

spond to the prescriptions the ideal is being betrayed. This is wrong for two reasons: the obvious reason that if the ideal coincided with the real it would no longer be an ideal; and the more subtle reason that what *ought* to be is not meant to replace what *is*.[14]

What the perfectionist fails to take into account is that, however much the people that are supposed to be governing are being governed, it remains true that in either case what is in question is a *demos* who matters. So it is not that in the first case we have democracy, and in the second case despotism; it is simply that we are always faced with a fact-value tension. In the second place, it is quite unreasonable to measure the extent of democracy by a standard of "realized perfection" instead of by comparison of the democratic with other ways of governing. For both reasons the perfectionist fails to realize that, despite everything, we have obtained a political system in which those who are governed do choose, influence, and control those who govern.

Just as a misconceived idealism can lead us to the repudiation of existing democracies, so on the other hand a misused realism can lead us to ridicule faith in democracy. In contrast to the perfectionist demand for a literal democracy, there is the realist contention that all deontological fictions should be thrown overboard, the argument being, this time, that since facts contradict precepts, the *ought* is a fraud or a powerless *flatus vocis*.[15]

But here we are making, in reverse, the same mistake as before. For a fact, in itself, cannot contradict a prescription. What ought to be is by definition what *is not,* and therefore its not being is no charge against the deontology. In this case, also, there are two ways of formulating the question. The right way is to ask what would happen if the deontological pressure were really powerless. The wrong way is to use our factual knowledge to undermine the whole set of prescriptions which make possible a democratic *modus vivendi*.

It should be stressed that underlying the arrogance of this misapplied realism, there is a large measure of short-sightedness. It is exactly because we believe in popular sovereignty that democratic leaders understand their role as a service, and it is also because of a democratic *animus* that the promise to govern *for* the people is more than a mere promise. Certainly the objection can be made that in present-day democracies there is more inequality than equality, or rather, more hierarchy than isocracy. But how can we fail to recognize that the ideal of equality does have an impact on the *modus vivendi* of a democracy and realize the extent to which democratic civilization has levelled, in less than a century, intersubjective relationships?

Also, it might be objected that popular sovereignty is a *fictio*. But can it be denied that it is an effective fiction? Thanks to this *fictio,* democratic mechanisms include in the political process those who would otherwise be excluded. And how can we say that a people who are periodically consulted, are the same thing as a mass of subjects who are ignored? In a democratic system the leaders depend on the approval of the electorate; they must obtain the consent of those they govern. How, then, can we infer from this that popular sovereignty is a fraud?

Finally, let the objection be made that in spite of the higher living standard and cultural level of the masses, the electoral expression of popular sovereignty does not live up to the expectations, or better, to the generous illusions of the last century. In 1895 Mosca said, "When we say that the voters *choose* their deputy we use a very inaccurate word. The truth is that the deputy *has himself chosen* by the voters." [16] Universal suffrage has since been achieved, but today no less than in Mosca's time mass parties and their powerful machines succeed just as well in placing their choice (the party nomination) above the people's choice. Nevertheless, if the party actually selects the person, the people still select the party. Therefore big words like party-dictatorship and party-tyranny overstate the case. Whatever the individual selective value of elections may be, we must not forget that elections are important for what they implicitly cause or prevent—simply by virtue of the fact that they happen, of the fact that elections *are* being held.

There is then a middle-of-the-road fallacy—perhaps the most insidious one—expressed by the dictum of the disenchanted: Since all political systems are ultimately based on elites, *there is little difference* between an oligarchy and a democracy. The perfectionist and the hyper-realist types of one-sidedness, once we have been put on guard, are easy to detect. But the detection of a balanced nihilism is not that easy. In the first place, we are inclined to believe that a *via media* is more likely to be a safe road. That a median approach is not, in itself, more credible than any other, and that even a *via media* can be based on wrong averages often escapes recognition. In the second place this middle-way fallacy is often disguised as a form of scientific prudence and of value-free objectivity.

This is all the more reason, however, for showing that arguments of the there-is-not-much-difference type enjoy esteem because our knowledge of political phenomena is very superficial. In the case of economics, for instance, given that perfect competition never exists in the real world, no economist would deduce from this that all cases of imperfect competition are more or less alike, because they are all imperfect. But in the field of politics amateur thinking is still widespread and we often try to hide the gaps in our knowledge by painting them a uniform grey, with disenchanted scepticism that pretends to be profound whereas it is only a cover for emptiness.

3. Party-System and State-System

The classic way of stating the difference between democracy and dictatorship is exemplified by the argument that the first is a multiparty system, whereas the other is a one-party system. But recently the distinction has been challenged by stressing that if competition among leaders does not occur *between* parties, it will always occur *within* the single party. So—the argument runs—we have competition among leaders in any case, and therefore no great difference between democratic and non-democratic patterns of decision-making can be found along these lines. Yet, notwithstanding the foregoing argument, the difference remains, and to my view this is a typical example of how a thesis that appears to be the fruit of a more careful investigation may lead us, instead, to a more superficial understanding.

Of course, the problem is to know how to look for the difference. Thus I shall not argue that whereas the structure of a totalitarian party is undemocratic, in a democracy we are dealing with parties that have a democratic organization. On these grounds I might be answered by Michels' objection that the degree of democracy within a party is in inverse proportion to its size and organization,[17] so that not even the so-called democratic parties remain democratic as they change from being "opinion parties" serving as mere electoral committees, to being permanently organized parties ("organizational parties"). But let us approach the argument from another angle, that is, looking at the role of parties in each system, and correspondingly at the respective role perceptions of the party leaders.

Competition among leaders in a one-party system is a struggle between leaders confronting each other *directly*. The problem for the leader of a faction is to gain possession of the keys to the party and/or the State, thereby controlling them both. Here we only have a "leader-leader relationship": competition is a face-to-face struggle between rulers. In a multi-party system, on the other hand, competition among leaders is not merely inter-factional, but is primarily inter-party. And therefore party leaders confront each other *indirectly;* that is they vie with each other with an eye to the voters. Here the competition between leaders depends on the electorate that they wish to lead.

What are the implications of this? In the first case, State and party duplicate each other, whereas, in the second, they split and come unjoined. In the first instance, he who controls the State and he who rules the party have the same role perception, and both use the power levers at their disposal in the same way and for the same ends, while in the other instance the opposite occurs. That is to say that the single party becomes one with the State, identifies itself with the State; whereas a party that has to operate in a multi-party system identifies itself, willy-nilly, with the point of view of society. No matter how oligarchic and bureaucratized its internal structure may be, a party that has to compete in elections cannot come to identify its platform with the State's point of view. We may put it thus: that in the first case the State's point of view absorbs the party's, while in the second it is the policy as envisaged by the party that ends by becoming State policy.

Now, it is clear that there is a world of difference between planning political action from the party altimetric level, and planning it from the State altimetric level. Parties are placed between the positions of command and obedience, halfway between the governed and the governing. The party operates from a lowered platform, where, if anything, it more easily accedes to the requests of the

83

governed than to the needs of government. Therefore, the very fact that the central motor of the system is placed between the electors and the elected, forces the way of stating the problems of policy-making into a democratic pattern.[18]

This last remark brings us to the second basic difference between a polyarchic democracy and an oligarchic autocracy, which is that in a democratic system the mental pattern of the political class ends by becoming *sui generis*. I am not alluding simply to the fact that a democratic system allows a free and diffuse circulation of elites, but to the related fact that democratic mechanisms leave a mark on the *forma mentis* of leadership. The democratic leader tends increasingly to assume a marketing orientation, the extroversion and flexibility that David Riesman has given the label of "other-direction." [19] This development is not without drawbacks, because an "other-directed" leader may become incapable of leading; but the more this happens, the more it confirms my point regarding the extent to which auto-cratic rulership and democratic leadership fall wide apart.

The difference between a multi-party system and a one-party system can be stated as follows: by virtue of its very mechanics a multi-party system democratizes power, while a one-party system makes it autocratic. For when many parties exist simultaneously, a party governs only insofar as it takes the part of the governed; whereas a single party governs permanently and has only the internal problem of who will govern the party itself. The roles and the corresponding role perceptions are so different in the two contexts that one may well wonder if it is proper to use the term *party* for both systems.

A party is a part, and it therefore implies a counterpart. If there is no counterpart, there is no part, but a whole. In fact, a one-party system is a *no-party* system. The so-called *single party* resembles a real party as much as a man called Mr. Green resembles the color green. The single party does not promote a party system: it prevents it. It is a mobilizing device, not an agent of voluntarization. What we find in totalitarian systems is only a "sub-State system"—a State agency operating as the *longa manus* of the totalitarian arrangement, and performing the role of a subsidiary coercive channel-and-control system of the rulers over the ruled.

And here we are reminded of how important terminology can be. For all we have to do to avoid discovering similarities and affinities among systems that actually have nothing in common, is to speak of "State-system" or "no-party system" as opposed to "party system." The latter postulates a free society and therefore requires parties; the other does not want a free society and therefore it eliminates them. The two worlds are indeed the antithesis of each other. I am ready to agree that all these remarks do not refute the basic argument that democracy is a variant—the open variant—of the elite principle.[20] However, these variants involve such basic differences in the role and nature of the political class, and consequently of the political system as a whole, that any generalization which tends to present as *more-or-less-alike* a polyarchic democracy and a unicentric autocracy falls short of the mark no less than the perfectionist or the hyper-realist approach.

4. Self-Government and Political Apathy

Our democracies, then, are governed democracies. But this does not mean that their performance is in contradiction to, or is the opposite of, what democracy ought to be. What the perfectionist, the bad realist, and the sceptic fail to understand is why the expression "governed democracy" is not a contradiction in terms, that is, why a governed democracy is still a democracy. The point is that although we are governed, we are governed democratically; and this is so because of the value-pressure, because the *is* of a governed democracy is molded by the *ought* of a governing democracy.

It remains to be seen whether the labels used in this chapter can be interpreted differently, as for example Georges Burdeau does in his massive and ambitious *Treatise of Political Science*. According to him, democracies start as governed (*démocratie gouvernée*), but they have now become governing (*démocratie gouvernante*).[21] That is to say that for Burdeau the distinction has a chronological value. Now it is true that the dynamics of democratic systems has been so striking that it should be indicated by ad hoc labels; but whether the transformation under discussion has the meaning given to it by the French scholar seems to me highly questionable. For Burdeau, in present-day democracies an omnipotent popular will increasingly imposes itself on the State. But we must not confuse appearance with substance and *more democracy* with worse, if not fictitious, democracy. Certainly, in almost all democratic countries government is exposed to growing pressure from below, and the reality of mass democracy as well as the goal of populistic democracy press more and more boldly on the structure of the liberal-democratic State. Yet I fail to see how mass democracy can be understood as a genuine incarnation of the will-of-the-people ideal of democracy, and I find it even harder to believe—as Burdeau asserts—that some countries, notably the so-called popular democracies, have actually achieved the stage of a governing democracy. For there is a point in the parabola of mass democracy where the dependence of the leader on his followers increases on the surface but diminishes in fact. And my feeling is, notwithstanding Burdeau's enthusiasm, that the discrepancy between words and deeds has reached a danger point. To be sure, the sound and the fury are there; but what is the substance behind the smoke screen?

Harold Laski once observed that "much of what [has] been achieved by the art of education in the nineteenth century [has] been frustrated by the art of propaganda in the twentieth." [22] Stuffing people's minds—*bourrer les crânes,* as the French say—and persuading our fellow man by dint of deafening noise is one thing, and educating him to understand and judge for himself is another. That is to say that if the opinion of the public is the keystone of the system, then the system is in danger, since increasingly refined weapons have been invented to attack the public mind whereas no armor has been discovered to protect it. Burdeau evidently believes that the role of the public has become increasingly important. In my opinion the opposite, if anything, is happening.[23] And the prospects for the future are even more discouraging. For the more a populistic mass democracy advances, the more important the role of a charismatic ruler in molding public opinion becomes. And the use that mass media can be put to in a situation where the State has the monopoly of propaganda opens up terrifying possibilities of subliminal persuasion, soul engineering, and brainwashing. Orwell's *1984* is a nightmare but not an impossible one. Our technical know-how has reached a point at which man's mind can be easily manipulated. Not much is needed, then, to drain an extreme nominal maximization of popular sovereignty of all real substance.[24]

In other words we had better not take demagogy for a *paideia* and end by believing that by fostering activist modes of intervention and response we are approaching the ideals of democracy. Demagogy only shifts popular sovereignty from the locus where it maintains a capacity for judgment and reasonableness to situations where it loses it. It is well known that a crowd of 10,000 people will approve enthusiastically a proposal that would undoubtedly be rejected if it were presented to the same people divided into groups of fifty. A hundred years ago Carpenter explained the phenomenon of mass events by the law called the "Carpenter effect," and Michels expressed the gist of the argument when he stated that "it is easier to dominate a mass than a small audience." [25] By this path, then, we arrive only at democracy by acclaim, that is, at a massification of popular sovereignty which reduces the actual will of the people to a sham.[26]

In truth, behind Burdeau's diagnosis I can glimpse only the rise of a new political class and the displacement of an elite by a counterelite not in the name of another principle but by the inflation of the original principle. I do not want to go back to a discussion of whether or not a governing democracy will ever be possible. If we define it as literal self-government—i.e., as the identity of the governing and the governed—I have already explained that I consider this utopia to be an absolute impossibility.[27] If, however, in speaking of governing democracy we simply wish to indicate a trend toward more self-government, then I shall state on what conditions I am prepared to believe that a governing democracy may be approached. Progress toward Burdeau's greater democracy could only be proved, in my opinion, if in the over-all process of decision-making majorities (or at any rate larger and larger sections of the minority) took the initiative and minorities alone remained inactive. And let me add that I consider such a development improbable.

The key question is: How do we account for the political apathy of the average citizen? And, part of the same question: How can we explain the high degree of ignorance, irresponsibility, and irrationality implied by this apathy and revealed in his political judgment? In other words, who is responsible for the lack of political interest and the low degree of participation of the common citizen? The old justifications that were profferred when universal suffrage was fought for and when the first disappointment in its results was felt, no longer hold good.

Is apathy due to lack of practice? No, because we have learned that one does not learn how to vote by voting. Is it the fault of illiteracy? No, because one can read and write and still be politically illiterate. Is it the fault of poverty and of a low standard of living? No, because the experience of the welfare State and, we can now almost say, the leisure State, contradict this hypothesis: political participation does not increase as wealth increases, and we find that absenteeism is comparatively greater in bourgeois than in workers' parties.[28] Is insufficient or tendentious information responsible? No, because information is plentiful and easily accessible. Even if we accept the Marxist connotation of "tendentious," the answer is still a negative one because, as Plamenatz puts it, "The workers, when they vote, understand the issues about as much and as little as their employers. That they do not do so, that they are kept in ignorance, that the political vocabulary current among them is one evolved in the interest of the rich—all these statements appear to me to be false. The political vocabulary in current use is much larger than it was two hundred years ago, and most of the words and phrases added to it were invented by radicals and socialists. Indeed, many of them were either coined by Marx or else made popular by him. The language of politics, as it is spoken in Western Europe, is as much 'proletarian' as it is anything else." [29]

In short, the rise in the average living and cultural standard has not changed the inert members of society into active ones. The majority remain passive not because they do not know how to read, but because of what they read; not because they cannot learn about politics, but because they are not interested in it. It is nobody's fault in particular, and it is time we stopped seeking scapegoats. Today, just as in the past, the democratic citizen in most instances does not know what the questions at issue are, what solutions have been proposed, what consequences are likely to follow, and even what the candidates running for office stand for. Now, if all this is so, even when the alleged impediments and obstacles have been removed, it is clearly useless to look for culprits who do not exist. The real explanation is quite different and is obvious enough.

The truth is that the only matters we understand are those with which we have personal experience and that the only ideas we really can master are those that we are capable of formulating by ourselves. Even if we are exposed to an uninterrupted stream of information, "without the initiative that comes from immediate responsibility, ignorance will persist in the face of masses of information, however complete and correct."[30] Moreover, information is not knowledge, and does not provide, per se, a real grasp of the matters under discussion. We are capable of making perfectly contrived speeches in a completely mechanical and mimetic fashion without really knowing what we are saying and without realizing in the least what practical consequences are implied and will inevitably follow. In conclusion, man is not a winged creature. And since the beginning of history whoever ignores this elementary truth has always brought us to the brink of a precipice only to explain, after we have fallen over, that we should have known how to fly. This is the logic used by those who blame the patient and not the therapy, and it is a logic that I am happy to leave to others.

As for Burdeau's "governing democracy," my feeling is that it is not the way democracies grow, but if anything the way they fall. For what is really meant by the label "governing democracy" is not an alternative to representative (or governed) democracy, but the ideal which pervades it; and all that the ideal can accomplish in the real world it is indeed accomplishing. Burdeau has only dressed in new clothes and modern terminology the old distinction between direct and representative democracy. Except that, moving crabwise, he projects a model of the past into the future. And in this way he makes a wrong diagnosis, as well as a wrong prognosis. His diagnosis is erroneous because so-called popular democracies are certainly not governing democracies. And even if we seek to save his diagnosis by transforming it into a prognosis, I still think that Rousseau's remarks about the prospect of a governing democracy remain relevant, for it was he, the modern originator of this notion, who warned us

89

that a literal democracy can never exist since it is contrary to the nature of things for the greater number to govern and for the lesser number to be governed.[31]

5. Democracy Defined: The Power of the Active "Demos"

Politics is, and always will be, the output of the politically active. Thus democracy is, and can only be, the political system in which the power resides in the active *demos*. Of course, looking at the figures, we shall discover that the active demos is only a *minor pars:* but this discovery should not be taken with dismay. Even if the *demos* turns out to be a numerical minority or rather a constellation of minorities, the principle remains intact as long as the rule is respected that opportunities are offered to all without exception. The foregoing definition can be implemented accordingly by saying that democracy is the power of active democratic minorities, the word "democratic" meaning that the recruitment of these minorities must be open, and that they must compete according to the rules of a multi-party system.

We arrive at similar conclusions if, instead of starting from *demo*-cracy, we start with the concept of *iso*-cracy. We can say either that democracy *ought to be* equal power for everybody, or that democracy *is* equal power for each and all. In the first case we establish a norm, with a corresponding right; and it is clear that the right has not been violated just because it is not exercised. In the second case, as the sentence has a descriptive formulation, it can only mean that an isocracy offers the whole *demos* the opportunity to participate actively and equally in policy-making.

I have said that democracy *can* only mean that the power resides in the active people. Let me add that this is right; I mean, this is also what it *should* mean. For if we do not accept this conclusion as valid, there are two possibilities. Either we ask that political apathy be met by coercion, or that those who are politically active be penalized in favor of the politically inert. And these solutions are both absurd. In the first hypothesis it is evident that a democracy cannot impose more than the obligation to vote; otherwise we can no longer speak of free people. Moreover, initiative—i.e., the capacity to intervene actively in the political process—cannot be produced by coercion, for coercion obtains compliance but can hardly make a citizen qualitatively better than he is. In the second hypothesis, which calls for penalizing active minorities because of the apathy of the majority, the result would be general apathy and this would be indeed a queer way to obviate apathy.

Let me sum up. Prescriptively—and therefore potentially—democracy is "equal power for everybody." Actually, democracy is "the power of the active demos," which amounts to saying that power resides in those who avail themselves of it. We may complain that the gap between the prescriptive definition of democracy and its actual performance is very great. This is indeed so. But, again, whose fault is it?

For a long time we have blamed the norm; that is, our complaint has been that the norm "the people must be sovereign" was not fully realized. But we must not confuse the enactment of a prescription with its utilization by those to whom it is addressed. To enact the democratic or isocratic rule means that we have to remove the obstacles which prevent its utilization. It cannot mean more than this, for the actual utilization is a matter for those whom it concerns. It is high time, therefore, that we realized that when we complain about democracy, we are complaining about the *demos*. The defects of our systems are democratic defects, and it does not make sense to maintain that the power belongs to the people and then bewail the fact that they do not use it, or use it badly, or what you will. For this is precisely what observation of the rule that the people are the rulers implies. This point should therefore be stressed: the distance that separates the prescriptive from the descriptive definition of democracy depends on the *demos,* on the quality and intensity of its political output. For it is clear that if the right to the equal exercise of power were made use of by all of the nominal holders of power in the same way, the descriptive definition would merge, in the last analysis, with the prescriptive definition.

One final remark. It has become fashionable nowadays to say that the classical theory of democracy is unrealistic and should therefore be replaced by a more realistic theory. This, however, is not my position. I feel that it is not so much a question of changing theories but rather of understanding what we are dealing with and talking

91

about and, more particularly, of stating correctly in what context the allegedly unrealistic definition belongs. In my opinion, in order to arrive at the "real" definition there is no need to put aside, or reject, the "ideal" definition. All we have to do is to know the rules of the knowledge game (if I may use this metaphor)—and especially the rules for applying a deontology.

NOTES

† *The Moral Foundation of Democracy* (Chicago, 1954), p. 15.

1. Cf. A. V. Dicey, *Lectures on the Relation between Law and Public Opinion in England during the Nineteenth Century,* 3rd ed. (London, 1924), *passim.*

2. For a general orientation, a helpful anthology of material relative to the problem of public opinion is *Reader in Public Opinion and Communication,* eds. B. Berelson and M. Janowitz (Glencoe, 1953).

3. I shall make this point more definite in section 4, below.

4. Until now, political and social scientists have generally been rather cautious in assessing the bearing of their findings on the theory of democracy. Cf., however, B. Berelson's "Democratic Theory and Public Opinion," *Public Opinion Quarterly* (Fall 1952), as well as *Voting* (Chicago, 1954), Chap. XIV. Cf. also the volume edited by E. Burdick and A. J. Brodbeck, *American Voting Behavior* (Glencoe, 1959), in which Burdick and a number of contributors attempt generalizations from the electoral data to political theory.

5. In this connection the most relevant evidence is provided by ecological analysis and survey studies. For the United States, cf. Lazarsfeld *et al., The People's Choice,* 2nd ed. (New York, 1948); Berelson *et al., Voting;* Campbell *et al., The Voter Decides* (Evanston, 1954) and the subsequent Michigan Survey Research Center studies. All this literature has been extensively surveyed by R. E. Lane, *Political Life: Why People Get Involved in Politics* (Glencoe, 1959). A condensed, useful synthesis is Lipset, Lazarsfeld, Barton, and Linz, "The Psychology of Voting," in *Handbook of Social Psychology,* Vol. II, Chap. XXX. British scholars have paid more attention to trend reports. However, three small-scale survey studies are comparable with and relevant to the American findings: Benney *et al., How People Vote* (New York, 1956) for the Greenwich, 1950 survey; R. S. Milne and H. C. Mckenzie, *Straight Fight* (London, 1954); Milne and Mckenzie, *Marginal Seat 1955* (London, 1958). For the French findings, the representative volume is *Les Élections du 2 janvier 1956,* eds. Duverger, Goguel and Touchard (Paris, 1957). With respect to the French ecological analysis cf. note 6.

92

6. French electoral sociology derives from the electoral geography of André Siegfried. Cf. the joint studies *Études de sociologie électorale* (Paris, 1947), and *Nouvelles études de sociologie électorale*, ed. F. Goguel (Paris, 1954).

7. Lippmann's *The Phantom Public* (1920) and his *Public Opinion* (1922) are not only pioneer but still standard works.

8. Cf. *Capitalism, Socialism and Democracy*, 2nd ed. (New York, 1947), p. 262, and all of Chap. XXI, where Schumpeter criticizes the "classical doctrine of democracy," meaning its "will of the people" conception.

9. *Voting*, p. 311.

10. Schumpeter, *op. cit.*, p. 263.

11. Cf. Robert A. Dahl: "I have shown both that elections are a crucial device for controlling leaders and that they are quite ineffective as indicators of majority preference. These statements are really not in contradiction. A good deal of traditional democratic theory leads us to expect more from national elections than they can possibly provide. We expect elections to reveal the 'will' or the preferences of a majority on a set of issues. This is one thing elections rarely do. . . ." *A Preface to Democratic Theory*, p. 131.

12. Let us not forget that *impersonare,* to impersonate, was one of the original basic meanings of *repraesentare.* Cf. H. F. Gosnell, *Democracy, the Threshold of Freedom* (New York, 1948), p. 132.

13. This is how W. Bagehot expressed the idea of representation. Cf. "Parliamentary Reform" in N. St. John-Stevas, *Walter Bagehot* (London, 1959), p. 432.

14. Cf. Chap. IV, 4, above.

15. This is notably the line—and the methodological error—of the whole work of Pareto. Pareto's is a limiting case, but analogous reservations can be made against many of the theses of the realistic school, including the writings of Thurman Arnold, *Symbols of Government* (New Haven, 1935) and *The Folklore of Capitalism* (New Haven, 1937).

16. *Elementi di scienza politica,* 3rd ed. (Bari, 1939), Vol. I, p. 206.

17. See Chap. VI, 6, below.

18. The extent to which the party localization of decision-making "democratizes" power is revealed by the apprehensions of those who assume the governing point of view, and are thereby preoccupied by the enfeeblement of the executive and by the devitalization of the power of government. Cf. among recent works Walter Lippmann, *The Public Philosophy* (Boston, 1955), pp. 55-57; and G. Maranini, *Miti e realtà della democrazia* (Milano, 1958), *passim.*

19. To be exact, Riesman's "other-direction" is not specifically related to the problem of leadership. Cf. in general *The Lonely Crowd* (New Haven,

1950), esp. Chaps. I, XII, and also "The Democratic Character" in *The Political Writings of H. D. Lasswell* (Glencoe, 1951), pp. 465-525, for some penetrating insights on "the open ego."

20. On the contrary, the election studies confirm, if anything, the need of elites and of qualified leadership. The problem will be discussed in the following chapter.

21. Cf. Vols. V, VI, VII of his *Traité de science politique,* and especially the last two, which are dedicated to the *démocratie gouvernante.*

22. *A Grammar of Politics,* 4th ed. (London, 1937), p. 147.

23. Cf. C. Wright Mills, *The Power Elite* (New York, 1957), p. 309: "Surely those who have supposed the masses to be . . . on their way to triumph, are wrong. In our time . . . the influence of autonomous collectivities . . . is in fact diminishing. Furthermore, such influence as they do have is guided; they must now be seen not as publics acting autonomously, but as masses manipulated at focal points into crowds of demonstrators. For as publics become masses, masses sometimes become crowds. . . ." Cf. also Kornhauser's *The Politics of Mass Society, passim.*

24. In this connection I have stressed the need of speaking of propagandas, not of propaganda in the singular—that is, of establishing a typology which would enable us to treat separately the case of soul engineering and the potentials of the unrestrained, extreme hypothesis of the sterilization and distortion of language. Cf. G. Sartori, "Natura umana, verità, propaganda" and "La propaganda e le propagande" in *Studi politici,* II and III (1952), pp. 198-238, 369-411. From this angle I find American literature—impressive as it is—somewhat culture-bound in its attempts to appraise the meaning and the ultimate implications of the Nazi and (especially) the Soviet propaganda.

25. Cf. *La sociologia del partito politico* (Torino, 1912), pp. 24-27.

26. In Freud's vocabulary, a mass regresses to a "primary group" in which the individual disowns his super-ego, falls back to the emotional state of a horde, and gives himself to a hypnotist kind of leader. Cf. his *Massenpsychologie, passim.*

27. Cf. Chap. IV, 3, above.

28. The reason is obvious. The worker who comes out of the factory finds in the cell or section of his party a compensation for the monotony and estrangement inherent in industrial work. Naturally, the higher degree of organizational activity in politics of manual workers reflects a class-distinct "status-polarized" party system, as Campbell and his associates say in *The American Voter* (New York, 1960), Chap. XIII. Where, as in the United

States, "status-polarization" is not felt, no significant difference between low- and middle-class involvement in politics is likely to exist.

29. In *Democracy in a World of Tension*, pp. 318-319.

30. Schumpeter, *op. cit.*, p. 262.

31. Cf. *Contrat social*, III, 4.

Chapter VI

Democracy, Leadership and Elites

*"Government is always government by the few . . .
But this fact does not settle the question of the
degree of democracy. To confuse the percentage of
leaders . . . with the test of democracy is to make an
elementary mistake, since a society may be democratic
and express itself through a small leadership. The key
question turns on accountability."*

—H. D. Lasswell †

1. Majority Principle and Minority Rule

ALL POLITICAL SYSTEMS at a certain point in their development increasingly reveal the defects, or literally the *deficit,* the deficiencies, inherent in their virtues. The democratic principle tends to be a levelling one. Hence, as a democracy grows and takes root, it is faced with the problem of retaining verticality—that is, the vertical structure of authority and leadership—and of succeeding as a system of government.

Let us immediately settle a preliminary point by admitting that democracy is not anarchy. This means that in accepting democracy we agree to solve the question of power and command in a positive fashion. A democracy does not pursue liberty and equality simply by canceling leadership. Whoever considers that the command-obedience relationship is incompatible with democracy is adopting a position that is more consistent with the anarchic than with the democratic

96

approach. If we start from the premise that being free and equal means that we should not be led or governed, it follows that as long as we are governed there is neither liberty nor equality. But that is not the question. "That question—as has been pertinently observed— was answered for us ages ago when civilization began. It was soon learned that a leaderless society is not a society at all, for whenever two or more men form a society and live together there is no such thing as uncontrolled, unrestricted, uninfluenced behavior." [1]

The approach to the problem of leadership in a democracy lies somewhere between the extremes of the anarchistic refusal to pose the problem and the autocratic non-solution of it. While anarchy is simply an attitude of revolt against power, autocracy resigns itself to not solving the problem at all. It submits to it as inevitable and accepts it as being justified, in the last analysis, by *Faustrecht*— the might-is-right principle. Democracy is instead the political form that both poses the problem and feels capable of solving it. It does not aim at destroying vertical structures but at taking advantage of them provided that they are rendered harmless.

This is all very well, but when we tackle the problem at close range unpleasant associations are aroused. In English some of the sharp edges can be blunted because the idea of command can be softened by the use of the verb "to lead." It should be noted, however, that Italian, French, German, and other languages do not have a satisfactory equivalent of leadership. When "leadership" is translated, it turns into something much closer to rulership or to headship. And this may help us to understand how it happened that the leadership principle was more easily accepted in the democracies where one can say "leaders," than in those where one must say, more bluntly, "rulers." [2]

In any case, whether we say rulers or leaders, we are referring to a minority, to an inner circle, to people who belong to the few. Hence even democracy appears to be a minority system in which the few lead and the many are led. Thus arises the disturbing paradox of a majority principle operating through minority rule. It is true that there are many distinctions to be made in this connection. [3] However, when oversensitive defenders of democracy embark on an attack on the so called elite theory—and the attacks are recurrent—

97

they disregard all nuances and distinctions, and reject wholesale, as being anti-democratic, all positions that are tainted by a minority emphasis.

It is not difficult to understand what motivates them. No matter how many *distinguo's* we make, we have to reckon with minorities who count for much and lead, and with majorities who do not count for much and follow. In any case, we are here confronted with inequality, disparity, superiority—all the things that are repugnant to the democratic ideal. Yet we must ask whether this polemic attitude is justified in the light of present-day conditions. Furthermore, it is doubtful whether this is a correct way of approaching the question. To clear the way I will therefore begin from that tangled skein of questions that concern the relation between majority and minority.

2. The Tyranny of the Majority

The terms "majority" and "minority" can be used in diverse contexts, and in different senses. In one meaning, which we might call *constitutional,* majority and minority refer to the protection of the right of opposition, i.e., of the right of the minority or minorities in parliament. The expression "majority rule and minority rights" generally refers to this problem. If the opposition is hampered we may then speak of tyranny of the majority in the constitutional meaning of the expression. Also, what Jefferson and Madison had in mind when they spoke of an "elective despotism," that is, of the possibility of the legislative branch of government becoming despotic, was another form of tyranny of the majority in its constitutional sense: the form known as assembly government. Their hypothesis was that if the elective body (and specifically the lower house) is not checked by the separation of powers, it will concentrate in its own hands an unrestricted, and therefore tyrannical power.[4]

In a second, let us say, *electoral* sense, "majority" applies to the rule of the game, i.e., the principle that whoever votes with the majority, or as the majority votes, is on the winning side. However, this only implies that our vote has not been wasted, for it has helped to elect the candidate we voted for. It does not follow that our representative will be part of a parliamentary majority. Therefore the elector can win on the first level (in his electoral district) and still lose on the second (in the legislature), for there his side may be in the minority. This is why in the electoral sense we speak of majority *principle* and not of majority *rule*. The difference is that when we speak of majority in the context of elections, the expression "minority rights" no longer has any meaning, for in this situation the minority simply means those who must submit to the will of the majority. In this respect, then, *the minority has no rights*. It consists of those whose vote was lost because their candidate did not pass the post.

Then there is a third, a *social* meaning of "majority," which is the meaning attributed to the expression "tyranny of the majority" by Tocqueville and John Stuart Mill. What troubled Tocqueville and, following him, Mill, was the danger of a spiritual tyranny, that is, of an extreme and suffocating social conformity. Here the issue is not the majority-minority relationship, but the relationship of society to the individual. The antithesis is between the majority and freedom of the individual, or between the majority and intellectual independence. "The democratic republics make despotism superfluous," said Tocqueville, "because the majority itself draws a formidable ring around thought." [5] And Mill opened his essay *On Liberty* as follows:

"When society itself is the tyrant—society collectively over the separate individuals who compose it— . . . it practices a social tyranny more formidable than many kinds of political oppression, since . . . it leaves fewer means of escape, penetrating much more deeply into the details of life, and enslaving the soul itself. Protection, therefore, against the tyranny of the magistrate is not enough: there needs protection also against the tyranny of prevailing opinion and feeling, against the tendency of society to impose . . . its own ideas and practices as rules of conduct on those who dissent from them . . . and to compel all characters to fashion themselves on the model of its own." [6]

At first sight it may seem odd that a large part of democratic (not, it should be noted, anti-democratic) literature is so much more concerned with a tyranny of the majority than with a tyranny of the minority. But reflection shows that this is not so strange. Since democracy replaces a tyranny by some minority, and since its rule is that the majority is always right, it is only natural that the far-seeing fathers of democratic theory sought to anticipate the opposite danger —the danger that had not been faced—shifting their attention to the new weak point, to the sector that remains undefended.

Are these concerns justified? Recently the tyranny-of-the-majority formula has been played down.[7] But here we must distinguish between the terminological form and the actual substance of the problems under discussion. There is no doubt that terminologically the expression is often inaccurate since it was invented for the sake of contrast, as the other side of the coin of tyranny-of-the-minority. But we cannot dismiss a problem simply because its wording is not always fitting. Also we must pay attention to the various contexts in which the expression has been used. We should not criticize the formula wholesale, for if we do so, we are confusing the issue. Let us start, then, by being specific.

In the first place there is the constitutional problem, which may be envisaged either as the danger that Jefferson and Madison called "elective despotism" (tyranny of the legislative over the executive branch of government), or as the danger of a tyranny of the majority over the minority (the opposition) in the legislative assembly. And concern about either is justifiable, as experience has shown.

It is well to remind ourselves, in relation to the first concern, that an "elective despotism" became a reality soon enough in the French *gouvernement conventionnel,* and that the subsequent evolution in Europe of parliamentary systems has in a number of cases led to the paralyzing of the executive by assembly government. Now I agree that the so-called dictatorship of the legislative assembly in itself is not despotism: but it may well be conducive to it. That this degeneration has not occurred in the United States is immaterial here, and it leads us, if anything, to suspect that the United States owes much to the constitutional checks created by the Philadelphia constitution-makers, and that the separation of powers is more important than Dahl and other present-day scholars seem to believe.

As for the second concern, I feel that criticism of the tyranny-of-the-majority argument is even less justified. When we put our minds to the problem of the limited exercise of power we soon discover

100

that it is precisely in this instance that juridical checks cannot adequately cope with the problem, and consequently that it is precisely by means of internalized restraints that a majority, be it legislative or executive, is kept from abusing its power. If this is so, then to declare that a governing majority that ignores the rights of the opposition is not a tyrannical majority is clearly a way of helping to make this self-restraint inoperative. And I fail to understand, on the other hand, what is logically wrong with the argument.[8]

Then there is the tyranny of the majority envisaged by Tocqueville and Mill. This is evidently a case by itself. In fact, it is only in this particular context that we can accept the objection that a tyranny of the majority is impossible because only a minority can produce tyranny. However, before dismissing Tocqueville's fears too lightly, let us examine the issue more carefully, distinguishing between two aspects of the question.

In the first place there is the danger of over-conformity which Mill designated (more accurately than Tocqueville) as "social tyranny." This is where Tocqueville's thesis has its weak spots, partly because the cause of the evil does not lie entirely or even largely in the principle of equality—as he argued—and also because in this context the use of the word "tyranny" is undoubtedly metaphorical.[9] But even if we admit that "the majority's influence on thought" is not tyranny in the technical and political sense, but only a possible condition of it, I nevertheless do not believe that Tocqueville's misgivings should be underestimated. For he saw that the key to the system is public opinion. And public opinion is a power behind the power of government only if it is a fusion of private opinions, that is, opinions that are to some extent spontaneous and not merely other-directed. Therefore the present-day man's low resistance to social pressure, his willingness and even eagerness to conform, his availability, constitute the weak point of the system. Tocqueville perceived this fact in 1830 as clearly as was possible at that time. So, despite the imperfections of Tocqueville's account I still think that he was more farsighted than many of his critics.[10]

If, instead, Tocqueville's fear of an "absolute sovereignty of the majority" refers to the danger of the despotism of victorious electoral majorities, I agree that there is little to worry about on that score, for the majorities in question are only fluctuating aggregates, arithmetical entities whose main function is fulfilled once they have designated their leaders. The possibility of a tyranny of the electoral majority is indeed slight, since it is not really the majority (of citizens) who rule, even in a democracy. But here too let us not jump to the conclusion that the danger does not exist at all. It is true that the effective protagonist of a tyranny will never be the multitude, for the good reason that the multitude can paralyze leadership, but cannot lead. However, if the many can easily render a democracy leaderless, inefficient and practically defenseless, it follows that, although the majority cannot be the tyrant, it can open the way for one.

So even if Tocqueville's thesis can be refuted by saying that there are always minorities acting behind the façade of majorities, and that in any case it is always one minority that displaces another, we still must admit that the French writer did foresee the trend that threatens democratic systems. And in order to recognize the importance of Tocqueville's insight, all we have to do is to look beyond his reification—beyond a tyranny of the majority understood as a material numerical majority—and discover its immaterial implication, that is, the *law of numbers.* I do not believe in the danger of a literal tyranny of the majority, but I do fear the *lex majoris partis,* the destructive effect of the law of quantities.

3. Election and Selection

Let us ask an embarrassing question: Why does the greater number count for the most? [11] The answer might be: because it constitutes the larger portion of what is considered a good, i.e., of the popular will. This may be so, but why should the larger portion make for a greater *value?* The retort will be that assuming that one will has the same value as another, the greater the number of wills gathered together, the greater is their collective "weight of value." The trouble with this argument is that, no matter how much we elaborate upon it, the determining factor of its conclusion is always a quantity.[12] And therefore the objection arises again: a value is not a weight, and cannot be identified with larger portions.

"Ten million ignorances do not make up one knowledge," wrote Taine in his famous preface to the *Origines de la France con-*

temporaine in 1875. A French *doctrinaire,* Royer Collard, formulated the objection with great precision: "The will of a single person, the will of many, the will of all, is only a force that can be more or less powerful. Neither obedience nor the slightest respect is due to these wills purely and simply because they are wills." [13] And Jefferson saw what the crux of the problem was when, in 1801, in his first inaugural address, he warned, "Although the will of the majority is in all cases to prevail, that will to be rightful must be reasonable." [14] And here we have touched on the sore point. Assuming that the quantitative rule is to be respected at all costs, the rule expresses and stands for a value only insofar as it is "rightful" and "reasonable."

Our first question seems then to run aground. Except that a shrewder disputant would probably follow another path, and instead of seeking an answer to the question, "Why does the greater number have a greater value?" would object that the question itself is captious. For the point at issue is not a value but a technique, i.e., the criterion adopted in a democratic system for arriving at decisions. The procedural rule best suited to the working of a democracy is that the alternatives which are most wanted, that is, wanted by most people, are those that should be followed. And that is all. So we are talking about an instrument, not about a value. I agree with this completely, and wish to stress that it is precisely the point we must always keep in mind.

To go back in time it is worth recalling that the feudal world of divine right crumbled because people wanted to live in a society whose guiding principle was not privilege, but merit. Democracy is born from the vindication of the principle that the unjust rule of the non-elected (those who exercise power by right of heredity or conquest) be replaced by the rule of the selected. Men wanted to choose the person who was to rule them, and they demanded the right to substitute ability—which is a criterion based on a value—for chance, which is not a value criterion. In respect to the limiting ideal of leadership depending on worth and ability, the democratic principle is that no one can decide by himself that he is better than others; it is the others who must decide this; and the method for ascertaining who is *erkennt,* who is outstanding, is election. "Elect" comes from *eligere,* and expresses the idea of selecting by choice, not by chance.

To go even farther back in time, we might do well to recall that this is the meaning that "election" has always had, and still has, for the religious orders, which have engaged in elections successfully and uninterruptedly for more than a thousand years. Even if few are aware of it, we are not newcomers as far as the use of electoral techniques is concerned. The various electoral methods and precautions (starting with the secret vote), the principle of simple and of qualified majority, were transmitted and taught by the monastic orders which as early as the sixth century were faced with the complicated problem of choosing their superiors. And there is nothing surprising in this fact. Since the monks could not resort to the principle of heredity or to force, they had to find a way of electing their leaders. And as a result of experiments carried on over centuries, the electoral constitutionalism of the various religious orders has achieved a refinement and a complexity that is unsurpassed [15] and that could teach us a great deal. For, in the entire tortuous evolution of their techniques, the principle of the *major pars* has never been separated from that of the *sanior pars,* or the *melior pars.* Notwithstanding the fact that the case of religious orders refers to optimum conditions, these men, knowing that even they were not angels, were concerned with ways to guarantee the choice of the ablest and the fittest with a care and a realism that never lost sight of the danger of a majority of the worst dominating the minority of the best. And they therefore never tired of emphasizing the distinction between *major pars* as means and *melior pars* as end.[16]

To return from their *sapientia* to our *insipientia,* from their wisdom to our own injudiciousness, it has taken us only a few decades to pervert by counting the principle of choosing. Although elections were supposed to be a quantitative instrument designed to make a qualitative choice, the quantitative emphasis has quickly usurped the place of the qualitative. The mechanism has taken control of the mechanic, and if the original intention was to count in order to choose, present-day democracies tend to function through a great deal of counting and very little choosing. The law of numbers valuates quantity. That is to say that, instead of qualitating quantity it *devaluates quality*—an unhappy confusion of arithmetic with values. As we can see, it is easy to conclude that there is little likelihood of a tyranny of the majority. The fact remains, though, that behind that figure of speech there lurks the *lex majoris partis*. And if the law of numbers, which is a means, is taken for an end, then it destroys capable leadership and government becomes anonymous, irresponsible, and amateurish—a situation which is with reason to be feared. Indeed, the grave danger that threatens democratic systems lies in a *selezione alla rovescia,* in the mis-selection of leaders.

It will be argued that this process is inescapable, that the replacement of quality by quantity is inevitable. But let us not overlook the large part played by lack of foresight in bringing about the so-called inevitable. It is not that the mathematical implications of the electoral rule present insoluble problems, but rather, that their solution requires thought. Whereas if we recall the controversy about adopting more democratic electoral systems, it will be apparent that while the instrument fascinates everybody, even today few people worry about what the instrument is for.

What do we mean by saying that an electoral system is more democratic? The most frequent answer seems to be that an electoral system is democratic insofar as it registers the exact proportion between votes and seats, so that a house of representatives is to the voters as a map is to the territory it pictures. Accordingly, the most democratic system would appear to be the most proportional system of proportional representation, and the big problem becomes that of working out a system that eliminates over- or under-representation of certain sections of the electorate. And it is worth noting that not even those who use the single-member district system are impervious to this argument, if one is to judge from the fact that the most exhaustive and the most heartfelt defense of proportional representation comes from English writers.[17] Now, I am not one of those people who deny that proportional representation has virtues, especially when we think of situations in which the single-member district system would function even worse.[18] But I do deny that it can be defended on the grounds that are used to defend it. That is, I do not believe that it makes much sense to discuss which electoral systems are preferable *because* they are more democratic. For the problem is not only that—and furthermore, is no longer that.

It is not *only* that because the election of leaders is a rule-of-the-

105

people kind of problem insofar as we are thinking in horizontal terms—I mean especially as long as we are concerned with the problem of the extension of the suffrage. And that is why the problem is *no longer* that. When everybody votes, the democratic aspect of the question becomes marginal, as little else, or little more, can be done to make an electoral system still more democratic. At this stage to be blocked by this issue while other pressing problems are neglected is like continuing to discuss whether a ten-year-old boy should still wear short pants, forgetting that he is now fifty and has been wearing long pants for some time. It is very easily understandable that the qualitative aspect of the electoral techniques was lost sight of in the heat of the struggle for the quantitative extension of the electoral franchise. But there is no reason today why that aspect should not calmly be given the attention it deserves. Every age has its problems. And after the horizontal aspect of the electoral problem has been settled there remains the vertical.

Actually, the closer we come to solving the electoral question horizontally the more important it becomes to solve it vertically as well. And we shall never treat it successfully by doubling the dose of the same medicine. I mean that it makes no sense to formulate the vertical aspect of the problem in the same terms as the horizontal by repeating that the best system is the one that is "most democratic." It makes no sense, to begin with, because the problem is now one of reduction, not extension. And this is the more difficult task by far. To be exact, we are faced here with not one but two of the most difficult processes in the world: (i) making one person out of two an infinite number of times, and (ii) selecting the better of the two, likewise an infinite number of times.

So, the vertical aspect of the electoral problem is, in the first place, to avail ourselves of the mechanisms of power transmission with a view to integrating multifarious and discordant wills into a single authority. It is worth noting that from this point of view the argument in favor of proportional representation is inverted, since the very virtue of such a system—which is its truer democratic representation—is also its greatest technical defect, since it carries over to parliament, to the vertex of the power pyramid, the problem of reduction and integration that it might be wiser to solve on the way.

Then there is the problem so well synthesized by Bryce when he warned that men desire to be well governed before and more than they desire self-government.[19] And here I fear that even the critics of proportional representation do not pass the test. For those who defend the single-member district system stop at the argument that it is more practical and more efficient, since it assures a stable, responsible government. But they also avoid the problem of quality. In effect, it is symptomatic that the very critics of proportional representation at a certain point accept the ground of discussion selected by their adversaries. It is not true, they retort, that the single-member district system is less democratic; it is really more democratic, since the will of the people is more respected in a system where, in the final analysis, the government is directly designated by the electorate, than in a parliamentary system which interrupts all direct channels of responsibility between electorate and executive by permitting shifting governmental coalitions to hide behind the smoke screen of parliamentary deals. Now it is quite true that in the continental systems based on proportional representation it often happens that parliamentary deals patently alter the will of the electorate, and that it becomes very hard to pin down who is responsible when the electorate is confronted with a number of shifting governmental coalitions. Yet, this *souplesse* may be interpreted, technically speaking, as the fire escape, if not the advantage of the system, whereas we might wonder if the alleged more democratic quality of the English system of direct responsibility would not turn out to be, in less favorable circumstances, its technical defect.

In the summing up, then, not only the defenders of proportional representation but also the uninominalists show how the essential issue is lost sight of by both sides: for they all go on discussing which electoral system best expresses and corresponds to the will of the people. The intriguing side of the story is that they all would agree, upon turning the page, that the will-of-the-voters notion of democracy is unrealistic, and that if the functioning of the system depended on its meeting this requirement, it is hard to imagine how it could work.[20] Perhaps the time has come, then, to be a little more consistent. For there is no sense in discussing electoral techniques without relating them to electoral behavior.[21]

For one thing, the issue as to which system provides the truest kind of representation has to be tested against this question: representation of what? Of the articulate knowledge and will of each voter? No doubt if there were any such thing, "true representation" would be important. But hardly so in the light of the actual voting performance.[22] On the other hand, it can hardly be maintained that one electoral system is more democratic than another because it makes leaders more responsive to the voice of the people: there is no significant difference in this respect between single-member and proportional systems. Actually, if we wish to make the system still more democratic the only real progress in this direction would be—as Rousseau well knew—to lessen the scope and the bearing of elections by having the citizen replace the voter. At the limit, the most democratic method would be not to vote at all. If we vote, then, it is not to make a democracy more democratic, but to make democracy possible: that is, to make it function. In the very moment that we admit the need of having recourse to elections, we minimize democracy, for we realize that the system cannot be operated by the *demos* itself. Clearly, then, the purpose of elections is to select leadership, not to maximize democracy.[23] And if the *raison d'être* of elections is to select leadership, then the best electoral system will be the most selective system, the one which best provides for the qualitative choice of leaders.

The distressing implication of the aforesaid conclusion is that it highlights the fact that for about half a century we have failed to meet the question. For, clearly, to say that the best electoral system is the most democratic system is as good as saying that the best airplane is the one that never flies. How helpful! What is worse, despite the impressive record of failures of democratic leadership, there are still very few people who seem to realize that unless the *major pars* becomes concerned with the choice of the *melior pars*, democracies have little chance of surviving;[24] and even fewer seem to be concerned with finding the devices that could make electoral systems more selective.[25]

It may be that after mature reflection we shall be forced to come to the conclusion that the problem cannot be solved because there is no adequate corrective for the law of numbers. I say "may be" because until the question is raised and everybody becomes aware of its existence, we cannot be sure. However, even if we eventually discover that internalized norms of behavior cannot, in themselves, cope with the problem, we can try to deal with it through constitutional techniques. Once we realize that this is *the* critical issue, we can solve it on one level or another. It is a question of finding the strategic point. But unless we have the courage to raise the question openly it is quite certain that we shall never be able to solve it at all. Let me add in this connection that if the problem were to be approached on the constitutional level, even then we should have to start from zero. Our constitutional theory is hardly more mature—as far as the problems of the future are concerned—than our electoral theory. We speak about "more democratic" constitutions just as *hors de propos* as we speak about more democratic electoral systems;[26] for we forget once again that if citizens do not obtain a good government they cannot be satisfied with the promise of some mythical future self-government.

Curiously enough, it is the same people who bombastically complain about how little the values of democracy are revered, who forget values altogether when the examination of a value problem confronts them with an unpopular issue. It is well to stress, therefore, that we have to be concerned not only with the values that the enemies of democracy deny, but even more with the values that are given so little weight by democrats themselves. In our specific case, a democracy that is unable to produce valuable leadership, or that surrenders to worthless leadership, is a democracy which the *demos* itself ends by feeling is not worth preserving. Let us not delude ourselves. The law of numbers, as such, is no better than the law of chance. The proof can be seen in the fact that the frequency with which mathematical chance has placed in office inept and irresponsible individuals, can be matched by the frequency with which the democracies of the twentieth century have revived the cult of the man sent by Providence.

Let us not be tempted to forget, therefore, that a democracy cannot pass the test, in the long run, unless it succeeds as a system of government. For if a democracy does not succeed in being a system of government, it does not succeed—and that is that.

4. Minorities and Elitism

Let us now turn to the question of minorities—of course, not the minorities that are the section of the population that has been defeated in elections, but the groups that are designated as elites, political class, ruling elite, power elite, top leadership, and so forth. I have purposely recalled a number of current labels because one of the main difficulties here is that there is little agreement on terminology, that our quest for a more articulate vocabulary has until now produced more confusion than clarity, and that some semantic problems have to be faced from the outset.

If one reads the English translation of Michels' *Political Parties,* one finds "leadership" where the German text carries *Führertum* and the Italian text *sistema di capi.* Now, Michels never thought of leadership: what he had in mind was rulership, or headship. And this example can be generalized by pointing out that Italian, German and French have no term for leadership, but a terminology which conveys the idea of headship and rulership. And this semantic background helps us to understand why the European literature on the subject ends up so often by stating the following drastic either-or alternative: either there is no rulership, or there is no democracy. The alternative would be correct if it could be completed by saying: this does not imply that leadership too is incompatible with democracy. But the distinction between headship-rulership on the one hand, and leadership on the other is difficult to perceive when there is no term for rendering the meaning of leadership. As a consequence, much of the European literature on democracy has interpreted the antithesis between rulership and democracy as if it implied that democracy should be leaderless. From this point of view English-speaking authors have been fortunate, since "leadership" conveys a middle-way semantic orientation, so to speak, which crosses the lines of the either-or drastic alternative. Thus, they have not been trapped into a false dilemma, and Anglo-American literature has had no trouble in stating that leadership is perfectly compatible with democ-

110

racy. Nevertheless this semantic advantage has been somewhat dissipated. For just as the Europeans say headship/rulership for all cases, the Anglo-American scholars say leadership for too many cases, thereby putting both rulership (proper) and leadership (proper) out of focus.

Of course, just as Europeans put forward the warning: there is rulership and rulership—one meets in English with the equivalent warning: there is leadership and leadership. Yet, when we seek the term to be used for the other leadership (the non-democratic kind) we find no established use and a great deal of misuse. English does have "headship," but this term is seldom used.[27] It also possesses "rulership," but even this term is not consistently and deliberately used as the opposite of democratic leadership. This is shown by the fact that the anti-democratic approach to the problem is now more and more frequently spelled out as "elitism"—in my view a very unfortunate terminological and conceptual choice.

"Elite" owes its wide currency to Pareto, and this is presumably the reason why elitism is looked upon with suspicion and the label is nowadays currently associated, in the United States, with undemocratic thinking. However, this association is misleading and historically inaccurate. To begin with, few of the critics seem to realize that "elites" was for Pareto a broad sociological and basically neutral concept that he used very much in the sense of the English expression "leading minorities."[28] One might retort that no matter what Pareto had in mind, the fact remains that his theory of elites (like Mosca's theory of the political class) has been put to use by fascism. However, this is simply not true, neither for Pareto nor for Mosca. As Norberto Bobbio rightly points out, "In the two major doctrinaires and creators of the doctrine of fascism, the philosopher Gentile and the jurist Rocco, the theory of elites had no part, not even peripheral. . . . The actual followers of the theory of the political class have not been fascist writers, but anti-fascist and democratic writers. . . . The only serious attempt . . . to apply and to refine Mosca's ideas . . . has been made by the demo-radical pupil of Gobetti, Guido Dorso; and the only re-elaboration of Pareto's ideas . . . has been undertaken by the demo-liberal Paretian Filippo Burzio."[29]

In the first place, then, we cannot speak of elitists *en bloc*. The

111

generalization is arbitrary, because—historically speaking—the concept of elite has been used just as much in liberal and democratic as in aristocratic theories. In the second place, the assumption that elitism has, as such, an anti-democratic implication perpetuates a methodological fallacy and should hence be rejected on logical grounds. If the existence in every society of a leading or ruling elite is a fact, then such a fact can be neither pro- nor anti-democracy. What is against democracy is to seek anti-democratic goals, not to seek factual truth. Therefore, until we see how an author relates the facts to a value choice we cannot and should not pass a value judgment about his value choice (how obvious, if we stop to think about it!).[30]

Third, attention should also be called, in this connection, to the problem of terminological waste. The derogatory meaning of elite that is conveyed by the label "elitism" reverses the original connotation; for, etymologically, elite means "worthy of choice," and it is the only term in the current political vocabulary that conveys the idea of selection, of power based on qualitative superiority. It is, in fact, the modern equivalent of the ancient notion of *melior pars*. Is it really wise, therefore, to reject that concept, or at any rate to discourage the use of the term that permits us to express it? I do not think so. Because we need to distinguish between *de facto* power and rightful power, between those who lead (the actual political class) and those who are capable of leading (the potential political elites). And for this purpose we must be able to speak of elites without guilt complexes.

The foregoing discussion warns us that we are hardly likely to make any progress in dealing with the problem of leadership (i) by using misleading labels such as elitism, and (ii) by using the existing terminology loosely and interchangeably. And my suggestion is that we should try to use one label ad hoc for each type of power structure. Thus, I shall use *leadership* or *leading minorities* in connection with a democratic system, and *rulership* or *ruling minority* for autocratic systems. To say democratic leadership as opposed to autocratic rulership, as Hermens suggests, is indeed a useful terminological device[31] which helps us to eliminate wrong approaches and superfluous debates. For example, the question whether a ruling elite model—as Dahl says[32]—can be applied to a democratic system would be ruled out by definition as an improper question, and this because, *ex hypothesi,* if there is *one* elite of the *ruling* kind, this already means that there is no democracy.

There is, of course, the problem of those labels which can be applied in reference to any system whatever, such as Pareto's elite and Mosca's political class.[33] Yet, even in this case a great deal of confusion can be avoided if we make it clear that "political class" in reference to a democratic system should be taken to mean a specification of functions, or simply an a posteriori classification; whereas in reference to a non-democratic system, it should be understood substantively, as being equivalent to a closed group, if not to a caste. Likewise, it would be very helpful if the term "elite" were consistently expressed in the plural when we refer to democratic *elites* in order to keep before us the fact that they are fluid, open, and scattered; whereas we should use the singular for autocratic regimes to recall that the *elite* in question tends to be a hereditary or co-opted body.[34]

There remains a preliminary and basic problem, which can be boiled down to the question: do leading minorities really exist?— meaning are they as influential and as relevant as they are supposed to be? Robert A. Dahl in his criticism of the ruling elite model seems to imply that there is little sense in speaking of elite, political class, controlling groups and so forth, unless we can spell out and establish the identity of *who is there.* Now, I believe that Dahl makes a very good point insofar as his criticism is directed against the fairy tale of the "sixty families" and its scientifically-cloaked revivals.[35] Actually, if we assume that a given political system is controlled by one power elite, or ruled by a single elite group, then Dahl is right in requesting that this group be properly defined and that we prove that its preferences, when opposed by other groups or the majority, regularly prevail. But I cannot follow Dahl any longer if we neither assume that there is one elite, nor that this one elite exercises a power of the rulership type—that is, if the assumption is that a political class and the leading minorities are made out of numberless controlling groups, and that executive political decisions are the outcome of endless bargaining among these groups. In short, I do not think that

113

Dahl's point can be generalized, i.e., that his specific criticism warrants the general conclusion that the minority approach to the study of politics should be, as such, discarded.

If we wish to investigate the over-all validity of the elite assumption, then I would have three reservations in mind. To begin with, I will admit for the sake of argument—as Dahl suggests—that the elite model is an operational model, and therefore made to be tested empirically. Nonetheless, just because we are not able to trace the thread of political decision-making to a particular group of people, is not a sufficient reason for excluding the possibility of their existence. Leadership may be a fundamental aspect of the political process even if the process is too complex and often too elusive to allow us to designate the wire-pullers and the people who have the last say. In other words, if the limitations of empirical research lead us to state, "We have not found anything," we cannot derive from that statement the conclusion that the problem we wish to investigate does not exist.

In the second place, the validity of the model does not depend entirely on whether or not the power holders happen to be identifiable within a democratic system. I mean that we cannot legitimately conclude that the model is useless unless we can show that it does not apply to *any* system. And this has not been shown. In fact, it is my opinion that Nazism, communism, and fascism, for example, have been characterized precisely by the identifiability of their respective ruling classes. On the other hand, I am well convinced of the thesis that the attempt to pin down physically the power elites and the leading minorities operating within a democratic system is a hopeless and elusive undertaking. However, I would in this respect reverse Dahl's argument, by saying that this very fact provides an excellent test for democracy, and that this difference confirms the usefulness of the approach since it permits us to define democracy *a contrario* as the political system where power is scattered to such an extent that the decision-making process can hardly be personalized.

In the third place, Dahl's argument could not in any case be decisive on methodological grounds. Mental tools are not uniquely or necessarily operational tools. Some are, some are not. Some of them are used for seeking, and some for thinking. The concept of elite is presumably an ideal type of the latter sort. In any case, and in terms of principle, the most that empirical testing can prove is that the model cannot be fruitfully used for empirical testing, at least at the present stage of our technical ability. This does not prove that something is wrong with the concept; it only shows that it should not be used wrongly. And therefore the attack against elitism cannot be supported on Dahl's grounds—by denying the very existence of elites.[36]

5. The Need for Leadership

Having cleared the way, we can now ask: Must we go on being suspicious of elites and leading minorities? The democratic mind, especially the rationalistic type,[37] is instinctively wary of them. It is willing to admit that elites and leading minorities exist, but it feels that they are shortcomings of the system. They can even be accepted, but as necessary evils. My questions are: Is this reaction, or attitude, justified? Why are elites necessarily an evil? Do we still have to beware of them?

There are, generally, two ways of supporting the phobia against minorities. The first argument is that the existence of leading minorities is in patent contradiction to a system which is supposed to hinge on majorities. And the second is that the existence of an "upper minority" which is on a different level from the rest of society is incompatible with the principle of equality. However, these arguments are not formidable.

As far as the interplay between the governed and the governing is concerned, majorities and minorities alternate in various ways and on various levels and are concurrent elements in the decision-making process. Hamilton formulated his fears by saying, "Give all the power to the many, they will oppress the few. Give all the power to the few, they will oppress the many." [38] This is perfectly true, except that the secret of democracy lies precisely in not giving all the power either to the few or the many, but in distributing it in turn and jointly to the former and the latter. Consequently, it is not accurate to say that the existence of a minority system within the context of a majority principle is self-contradictory. For we are here using the term majority in a sense that does not conflict with the meaning we

115

give to minority. The antithesis does not exist—it is terminological not logical.

When we say "majority" we denote a procedure—the rule according to which decisions are made. Among the possible courses of action, the one that is approved by the majority of the voters is adopted. When we speak of "minority" we are referring to the groups that exercise a decisive influence on the process of forming opinions. Minorities try to mold opinions and to obtain the consent of the majority; the majority decides which minority wins. We might describe this interplay in the following way: a minority becomes a majority, or, inversely, the majority is thrown into a minority. In this respect a democratic government can be defined as a system where the majority designates and supports the minority that governs. Where is the contradiction? Of course there are discrepancies, because in the real world things never work out as smoothly as stated by the theory. But worldly imperfection cannot prove that the existence of leading minorities is inconsistent with the principles of democracy.

Actually, the apparent strength of the argument is explained by the fact that we use the same labels to indicate very different things. It is important to stress over and over again, therefore, that there is all the difference between a minority that is an oligarchic body, and minorities which are groups performing certain functions. If a controlling group is a closed unit, and transmits its power by heredity or co-optation, then it is a ruling class incompatible with democracy. But if the leading minority happens to be a polyarchy of "multiple elites" (as Riesman puts it) which is the end product of a process of endogenesis of leaders, and if instead of a caste division there is free vertical movement, then it is a democracy that we have before us. The same remark applies to the generalization that all governments hinge on a political class. When we speak of a political class to which there is low access, the term class denotes a corporate body that is held together by *ésprit de corps*. But when we speak of political class in a democratic society, i.e., in connection with high access, the term class simply designates a category, a professional group. Here the people who perform the role of political leadership are a class much in the same way that doctors and lawyers are.

116

Also the second argument—which holds that since leading minorities are both a sign of, and a result of, inequality, their existence conflicts in principle with the concept of equality—is vitiated by similar confusions. What kind of equality do we refer to? If we mean economic equality and especially equality among classes in the Marxist sense, then only the existence of an upper (economic) class may appear inconsistent with democratic doctrine, but not the existence of a political class, or rather of a political leadership which is decided by election. If by equality we imply—taking a radical view—that there must be no leadership, then we shift from the democratic to the anarchic position, and the question becomes whether or not an anarchic order is conceivable and possible. It is a question as old as it is futile, and Montesquieu said nothing new when he wrote that "the principle of democracy is corrupted not only when the spirit of equality is lost, but also when the spirit of extreme equality is assumed, and everyone wants to be equal to those whom he chooses to govern him." [39] Rousseau, although his antagonist, seemed to echo him when, in his *Discourse on Inequality,* he concluded that "it is against the laws of nature, no matter what way we define them, that an imbecile lead a wise man."

I should like to add that no matter how we define the imbecile and the wise man—indeed not an easy problem to solve—the fact remains that the degree to which any political and social organization meets with acceptance is the degree to which its leaders are considered worthy and capable of leading. Our entire existence is interwoven with remarks of the following kind: "He is not worth much; so and so is first rate." We judge men, and we are only willing to execute the orders of those we respect. And it is exactly for this reason that certain democracies have trouble obtaining obedience,[40] while some autocracies have been supported and accepted willingly.

Let me emphasize again that if equality is a basic value-principle of democracy, we must not forget that it is that—a value principle. A process of levelling can be carried out either by submerging elites or by making people rise to the elite level. Demolatry chooses the first path. But if we want to reinforce democracy we must recognize that equality is a value only insofar as it makes us conscious of quality, thereby using the elites—the qualitative elites—as its point of refer-

117

ence. Thus, our problem cannot be solved simply by the observation that leading minorities exist and that they will probably continue to do so. That able and competent minorities are an integral element of democracies is not a necessary evil but the determining factor in such systems. Pro-democratic elites are not an imperfection but an essential guarantee of the system. The more we study democracy, the more we realize how complicated and precarious it is. And the more we seek ways and means for assuring its survival, the more we become aware that a democratic society asserts itself and gains ground as government *for* the people insofar as responsible and reliable minorities devote themselves to that purpose.

The truth is that democracies depend—as the most thoughtful scholars have observed—on the quality of their leadership. Thucydides reminds us that the greatness of Athens reached its height with Pericles precisely because "by his rank, ability, and known integrity [he] was enabled to exercise an independent control over the multitude." [41] Bryce said: "Perhaps no form of government needs great leaders so much as democracy does." [42] Fifty years later, in 1937, after all the experience of the intervening period, De Madariaga wrote: "Despite appearances, liberal democracies are dependent on leadership even more so perhaps than other, more authoritarian forms of government; for . . . their natural tendency to weaken the springs of political authority must be counterbalanced by a higher level of . . . authority on the part of their leaders." [43] In the same years Karl Mannheim had reached the same conclusion: "The lack of leadership in the late liberal mass society can be . . . diagnosed as the result of the change for the worse in selecting the elite. . . . It is this general lack of direction that gives the opportunity to groups with dictatorial ambitions." [44]

Democracy is the most daring experiment in man's faith that has ever been, or ever can be tried. It moves along the tightrope created by the greatest possible axiological and deontological tension. It is therefore very much exposed to the danger of extremes, and consequently of breaking the delicate balance between *is* and *ought,* between what can and what ought to be done. In short, democracy is terribly difficult. It is so difficult that only expert and accountable elites can save it from the excesses of perfectionism, from the vortex of demagogy, and from the degeneration of the *lex majoris partis*. And this is why adequate leadership is vital to democracy. It has been said that leadership is needed only to the extent that the role of the people remains secondary. But I had rather say that it is when the pressure from below is greatest that eminent leadership is more necessary than ever. For it is at this point that perfectionism on the one hand, and mass manipulation and mobilization on the other, throw the system off balance.

In the light of this, distrust and fear of elites is an anachronism that blinds us to the problems of the future. For we must really be behind the times if we think that democracy is still threatened by the existence of a ruling aristocracy, in the feudal sense of the term. What really threatens us is the opposite danger—that the reaction against rulership might lead us to the extreme of an absence of leadership. I am not saying that democracy should not oppose aristocracy; I am only pointing out that the time is past when democracy has to be on guard against it, and that it is unintelligent to fear a danger that has been largely overcome when the opposite danger—mediocracy—is looming ahead.[45]

Demolatry notwithstanding, quite a number of democracies have been overthrown by popular insurrection, and many dictatorships have been legitimized by plebiscite. Conversely, all existing democracies have been founded and established by *ad hoc* elites and minorities. What we have to fear, then, is that democracy—as in the myth of Saturn—may destroy its own leaders, thereby creating the conditions for their replacement by undemocratic counter-elites.

The point is, therefore, to see clearly what kind of leadership we need, and hence to single out the features of democratic leadership. In respect to the relationship between the leader and the led, decisions are democratic when the leader is responsible to the led and is controllable and controlled by them in many ways, whereas a decision is hierarchical when the power holder exercises strong, untrammeled control over his subordinates. This means that, vertically, democracy can be defined as a process of decision-making in which the leaders are receptive to the preferences of those who are led. In terms of goals, democratic leadership intends to stress the role of the whole group, to encourage shared decisions, to decentralize responsibility,

119

to take advantage of the ability and talents of all—in short, to activate the entire social body.[46]

Our problem is how we are to be ruled, not to avoid being ruled. If, as Filippo Burzio felicitously put it, the non-democratic elites "impose themselves" while the democratic elites "propose themselves," [47] our problem is to reject the former and to encourage the latter. In conclusion, the formula for democracy is, or should be, the following: neither to eliminate nor submit passively to power, but to make it a function; to control the leaders in the exercise of this function; and to put in office responsible, accountable, and capable leaders.

6. The Iron Law of Oligarchy

There still remains a fundamental objection that cannot be ignored. I am referring to Michels' "iron law of oligarchy." Ultimately it is an objection that questions the very possibility of democracy, and that leads us to examine the preliminary problem of how and where we should search to find democracy. Michels, as is known, is not the author of a general theory of democracy. He concentrated his attention on the political party, and the original title of his most important work, which was written in 1910, was *The Sociology of the Political Party in Modern Democracy.*[48] But the conclusions that one can draw from an examination of this field are undoubtedly relevant to the entire problem of democracy, and this for two reasons.

This first is that a democratic system is, in practice, a party system. As Kelsen put it, "Modern democracy is founded entirely on political parties; the greater the application of the democratic principle the more important the parties." [49] Political parties have indeed become such an essential element in the political process that in many instances we might legitimately call democracy not simply a party system but a "party-cracy" (*partitocrazia*), meaning that the locus of power is actually shifted from government and parliament to party directorates. Nor is this all. The study of the phenomenology of parties is symptomatic from another point of view as well. For if the democratic way of life springs from the voluntary creation of small and free communities *inter pares,* parties too are formed as

120

voluntary associations and are, in fact, their typical political expression in a large-scale democratic system. From this angle, then, parties become the type of political organism that most closely resembles, or should resemble, the prototype of every authentic democratic form.

There is no doubt, therefore, that Michels put his finger on a strategic point. Nor can we deny that the problem he singled out is of great significance. For he dealt with the question of organization, and there is no field of human endeavor, nowadays, that does not seek to enlarge and to perfect its organization. "Organization" is indeed a key word of our time. From all points of view, therefore, we must not underestimate the importance of his conclusion, which is that organization destroys democracy and turns it into oligarchy. Michels writes: "He who says organization, says tendency to oligarchy. . . . The machinery of organization . . . completely inverts the position of the leader in respect to the masses. . . . Wherever organization is stronger, we observe a smaller degree of applied democracy." [50]

According to Michels, this is an "iron law," a process which cannot be stopped. It is inevitable that every party seeks the greatest possible number of members, and it is also inevitable therefore that "opinion parties" gradually turn into "organization parties." And since the power of the leader increases as the need for organization grows, all party organization tends to become oligarchical. Michels ends his major study with the following assertion: "The existence of headship is an inherent phenomenon of all forms of social life. It is not incumbent on science to find out if it be a good or an evil. . . . However, there is great scientific as well as practical value in establishing the fact that every system of leadership/rulership is incompatible with the most essential postulates of democracy." [51]

Many criticisms can be made of Michels' diagnosis. In the first place, he speaks of oligarchy and organization without ever clearly defining these concepts. (He confuses, for instance, an iron law of bureaucracy with an iron law of oligarchy.) And as there are many different types of organization, we cannot conclude, without qualification, that all are necessarily oligarchies incompatible with democracy. In the second place, Michels' field of observation is too limited, being chiefly restricted to the German Social-Democratic Party. In the third place, he is not justified in passing from the premise, "Parties

121

are not democratic," to the conclusion that "Democracy is not democratic." The proof he adduces is too narrow for the breadth of his conclusion.

Notwithstanding all this, Michels' diagnosis by and large still holds.[52] For the first objection can be met by observing that the basic argument about organization is a generalization which, vague as it is, does express a law that has not been invalidated. The second objection can be answered by saying that Michels' sample, the pre-1914 German Social-Democratic Party, is always relevant to the large mass parties of Europe, which are certainly not more democratic in origin and form. And the third objection can be met by pointing out that if we extend the investigation to cover all the organized sectors of political activity, including the trade unions, we shall probably not find in other organizations more democracy than Michels found in political parties. And in this case the conclusion that "democracy leads to oligarchy" [53] would find adequate proof.

It can be seen that I do not underestimate Michels' argument. However, I do not accept his conclusion because I do not accept his approach. Actually I consider his argument the most pertinent example of how we may seek democracy without ever finding it. If we agree to measure the degree of democracy by comparing its organizational forms with the prototype of voluntary associations, it will be hard to prove that Michels is mistaken. But he is wrong because his comparison is wrong, for we cannot proceed from a face-to-face democracy to a nation-wide democratic form as if the two things were comparable and belonged to the same continuum. Michels reasons just as the "democratic" critics of our democracies do, and his formulation of the problem is identical with that of the Rousseau school.[54] As far as the approach is concerned, Michels is no different from Proudhon, Marx, or Bakunin. They all refer to the matrix of voluntary associations, and using this yardstick come to the conclusion that the political democracy under which we live has no organized form that corresponds to that model.

At this point, we can make two contrasting forecasts. Either the advent of democracy must be postponed until all of the organized superstructures that repress it—beginning with the State—have been dismantled, or we must admit that these superstructures are indispensable and therefore that democracy is unrealizable. In the first case we consider it possible to enlarge to infinity the prototype of voluntary associations and to convert it into that gigantic self-operating collective entity which Marx and the Anarchists dreamed of. In the second case, we recognize that in the process of enlargement the model is distorted, and so we conclude that large-scale democracy is purely utopian. However, in spite of the divergence of the prophecies, the two conclusions, insofar as they affect the present, are the same: our so-called democracies are apocryphal.

The practical outcome of these contrasting positions is the same, because both Michels and the perfectionist, the pessimist and the optimist, are looking for democracy with the same lantern. And the trouble lies in the lantern, that is, it lies in the measurer and not in what is being measured. This is shown by the fact that although critics have an easy time claiming that present-day democracies are not democracies, they cannot explain how it happens that these so-called "false" democracies are so different from actual "non-democracies." And they cannot explain it because they have never understood how political democracy is produced. Their mistake lies in using a static technique of appraisal, that is, in appraising the degree of democracy within a political system by a correspondence test with a model that has no alter ego, instead of looking at democracy as a chain-reaction to be judged dynamically. They seek democracy in structures and not in interactions. They want to find it immobilized *in,* within something, instead of seeking it *between,* as a dynamic relationship *among* groups and organizations. To put it briefly, their mistake consists in looking for life in a body that is already dead, in searching for democracy where it no longer exists. This does not mean that structures are not important—they are—but they are important and affect our argument insofar as their *effects* are concerned.

Michels sought democracy *inside* political organizations. But how could he find it there? Organizing is the arranging of a vast organism according to rigid structures and definite hierarchical levels. We organize in order to create not a democratic form but a body that is primarily orderly and efficient—which is not the same thing. So, the real problem begins at the point where Michels left off. In-

123

stead of looking inside an organization, let us observe the relations between separate and competing organizations.

Why do they compete? Evidently because they seek allies from the outside, as their strength comes from the majorities that follow them. And how do they compete? Evidently by promising benefits and advantages to their followers. The result is that the unorganized majority of the politically inactive becomes the arbiter in the contest among the organized minorities of the politically active. So, no matter how oligarchic the organization of each minority is when examined from within, the result of the competition between them is democracy. And this is because the power of deciding between the competitors is in the hands of the *demos*—the onlooker who benefits from a quarrel between other people.

In short democracy on a large scale is not the sum of many little democracies. Political democracy is, *in primis,* a method or procedure by which, through a competitive struggle for sanctioned authority, some people are chosen to lead the political community.[55] Democracy, then, is the product, or the sequence of effects (secondary and composite) that result from the adoption of that method.

7. Democracy Defined Vertically: An Elective Polyarchy

The subject matter of this chapter is the stumbling block of most discussions about democracy. This is because it is not easy to grasp how the system really works. The classic theory of democracy is unable to explain it, because it leans too heavily on the role of the individual voter and the majority, i.e., on the assumption that for the system to be democratic it must be the output of a majority will.[56] If this were the case or if this were all, we might well wonder how democracy could ever solve its problems and survive as a going political organization. The point is, however, that the classic approach loses sight of the part, vital for democratic purposes, that is played by the mechanisms of the system, which oblige its operators to compete vis-à-vis the consumer market. Therefore, in order to understand how the system actually works, we have to formulate the question this way: Why does an elective polyarchy produce democratic results?

In defining democracy as an elective polyarchy I follow, on the whole, the definition put forward by Dahl. There is, however, a difference, for in my opinion what characterizes democracy is not so much that it is an *egalitarian* polyarchy—as Dahl says—[57] as that it is an *electoral* polyarchy. By this I do not mean that the egalitarian tension is not a typical element in the system. But as far as the vertical aspect of a democracy is concerned, its importance is secondary, and the element of egalitarianism that goes into the construction of the power pyramid tends, if anything, to obstruct its vertical dimension (equality, as such, does not postulate the need for leaders). On the other hand, the amount of equality that actually goes into the vertical construction can be inferred from the conditions that make elections democratic.

Democracy, then, is an elective polyarchy, and we must say "elective" because some polyarchal systems are not based on popular suffrage. In that case the system will be competitive without being democratic. There will be a leader-leader relationship, but hardly a leader-led relationship other than as a unidirectional all-to-one relation. That is to say that in a non-elective polyarchy we will find a reciprocal control *among* leaders, but no reliable kind of control *of* leaders, or *upon* leaders. In order that the non-leaders may be able to restrain, influence, and control leaders, they must have the power to choose them—that is, regular elections must regularly occur.

It will be noted that the descriptive definition of democracy that we have arrived at is ostensibly distant from the prescriptive ideal and the etymological definition that we started with. Yet, a closer examination will show that the gap is not so wide. For when we call democracy a polyarchy, we are not simply saying that many leaders take the place of one. If that were all the difference, there would not be much to rejoice over. Likewise, when we specify that we are talking of an elective polyarchy, we are not saying that we are simply allowed to choose among various possible leaders. If that were all, one might again conclude, in a disillusioned vein, that the leaders change but the domination remains. However, this is not the case. For we must not forget that the definition in question has to be understood dynamically. It means that democracy consists in the procedure (i) that continuously creates open, competitive minorities, (ii) whose behavior is guided by the "rule of anticipated reactions," [58] that is, by the expectation of how the voters will react at the next elections.

In full, our definition says that democracy is a procedure that produces a polyarchy in which competition on the electoral market results in the attribution of power to the people.

According to the main argument developed in this chapter, our definition can be reformulated as follows: democracy is a political system in which *the influence of the majority is assured by elective and competitive minorities to whom it is entrusted.* This definition not only stresses that "If we cannot expect citizens always to check leaders . . . then we are forced to rely heavily on checks exerted by other leaders,"[59] but also has the virtue of bringing out the vital role of leadership, as it implies that minorities are a *sine qua non* condition of the system.

The above definition, however, is only descriptive, in that it does not bring out the requisite conditions for the good functioning of the system. Electoral competition does not assure the quality of the results but only their democratic character. The rest—the worth of the output, so to speak—depends on the quality of leadership. So if we are considering specifically the qualitative aspect of the problem, our definition will have to be rephrased as follows: democracy should be *a polyarchy of elected elites.* We may also put it this way: democracy ought to be a *selective system of competing elected minorities.*

All of this may seem very complicated. But that is because democracy is indeed a complicated form. And our definitions cannot make it simpler than it is; they can only trick us into making it *seem* simple. It is easy to say that democracy is the "people's power." The question is to understand how this is possible, and in what way the people's will can make itself usefully felt. What is required is thus a reply to the question: On what does the proper functioning of an experiment in democratic government depend? This is the question that I have attempted to answer.

Do my conclusions add up to "another theory" of democracy? At first sight it may seem so. It has been said that there are two theories of democracy, the mandate theory, which is the orthodox one, and the competitive theory, developed by Pendleton Herring in *Politics of Democracy,* and especially by Schumpeter in *Capitalism, Socialism and Democracy.* I have undoubtedly been working along these lines. Yet, I am unwilling to accept the so-called new theory as another theory. For I by no means reject the mandate theory; I have only said that it has a prescriptive validity. And if I have followed the competitive theory, I have done so stating that it is the descriptive theory. Therefore the definition that has been suggested in this chapter does not contradict the classical theory and does not attempt to replace it. It is rather an extension and completion of it. For the fault of the classical doctrine is that it stops midway and does not go to the end of the road.

In other words, the inadequacy of the orthodox theory of democracy does not imply that it should be replaced (for in doing that I would be stating a theory about something else), but that it should be developed to its complete extent. The classical conception is simply an unfinished picture, and my point is that the time has come to finish it. Up to now we have not had enough evidence at our disposal to know what landfall we might make. But now we do. It can be understood why at an early stage all the emphasis had to be placed on the *demos*. But now that we have reached maturity, the theory has to be balanced. And that is why I have laid emphasis on democracy as a system of government, and thus on the importance of admitting—in our over-all outlook—the principle of leadership openly, without the usual guilt complexes. Otherwise our theory will remain unbalanced, only prescriptive and not sufficiently (if at all) operational, continuing the unhappy results that our unrealistic attitude and our head-in-the-sand policies have long been causing.

It is pertinent to wonder in this connection why this completion is so laborious. This is chiefly because we fail to make the distinction between the scientific validity and the ideocratic (and subordinately ideologic) use of a statement,[60] or at any rate we fail to place the distinction between its scientific exactness and its ideocratic value at the proper juncture. Thus, the elite argument is classified *en bloc* as aristocratic. Methodologically speaking, this single-package way of disposing of the problem is definitely wrong, and I fear that little progress will be achieved by political theory unless we realize—speaking in general—that when an argument is based on a finding, this finding can only be true or false, and that it is only its subsequent ideocratic or ideological role that falls under the aristocratic-democratic categorization. It follows that the elite concept (i) cannot be classified either as aristocratic or democratic until the purpose is taken into account, and that (ii) it can be *both* aristocratic and democratic, depending on how it is put to use. To assert from the outset that the elite concept is aristocratic amounts to (i) passing an ideological judgment on a statement of fact, and to (ii) disguising a biased premise as the conclusion that it is not. For the correct conclusion is that the elite findings which are put to use for the purpose of showing that democracy is impossible make for an aristocratic theory of elites; whereas elite findings which serve the purpose of helping to constitute the best possible democracy are precisely a democratic theory of elites.

One might say that this is an aristocratic theory of democracy as against its demolatric version. However, what is the value of the demolatric theory of democracy? The voting studies and the opinion polls have confirmed beyond the point of doubt that we have to reckon with a leader-seeking and leader-needing public. On the other hand, our findings prove that the imagery of a self-governing *demos* is either a deceptive myth or a demagogic device, and that in both cases it can only foster the bankruptcy of the system. All the evidence points out, then, that our goal cannot be a headless society but a political community in which coercion yields to inducement, a *vis coactiva* is replaced by a *vis directiva*. I therefore venture to suggest that the democratic theory of elites is in the light of present-day factual knowledge the core of democratic theory itself. To know the facts and to refuse to acknowledge them by putting two and two together—as many people are still doing—is an unhealthy and, in the long run, suicidal policy.

NOTES

† *The Comparative Study of Elites* (Stanford, 1952), p. 7.

1. F. S. Haiman, *Group Leadership and Democratic Action* (New York, 1951), p. 7.

2. Cf., however, note 37, below.

3. Cf. section 4, below.

4. Cf. *Federalist Paper* No. 48 and Jefferson's *Notes on the State of Virginia.* I am overlooking the other meanings of "majority" in Madison, both that

which we might call federal (which takes into consideration the possible tyranny of the majority of the larger and stronger states over the smaller ones), and that which refers to the problem of "factions": the first because it is an extension of the general principle to the specific case of the United States, and the second because to examine the two problems together is bound to create confusion (as Madison himself shows).

5. *De la démocratie en Amerique* (Paris, 1951), pp. 265, 266. *Cf. passim.* Vol. I, Pt. II, Chap. VII, "De l'omnipotence de la majorité aux États-Unis, et de ses effets."

6. *On Liberty* (Oxford, 1947), p. 4. Cf. also Chap. IV, "Of the Limits to the Authority of Society over the Individual." For his indebtedness to Tocqueville, cf. Mill's *Dissertations and Discussions* (Boston, 1864), Vol. II, pp. 79-161.

7. Cf. F. A. Hermens, *The Representative Republic* (Notre Dame, 1958), p. 192: "The time has come to do what J. P. Quincy advised us to do: 'Put that venerable bugbear, the tyranny of majorities,' to rest." Cf. also the criticism of R. A. Dahl, *A Preface to Democratic Theory,* Chap. I and p. 133; and the reservations of David Spitz, *Democracy and the Challenge of Power* (New York, 1958), Chap. V. While I accept some of Spitz's points, I find Dahl's brilliant logical analysis open to question with regard to the fitness of his methodological approach.

8. Let me comment, in this connection, that it is either inconsistent or merely destructive (i) to assert that constitutional checks are effective only to the extent that they are supported by the social checks inherent in a pluralistic society, and subsequently (ii) to underplay the warning and the attitude which help to make effective these social checks. Clearly, unless a society is alerted and sensitive about the unrestrained use of power on the part of the governmental majority, how can we expect the societal checks to replace the juridical ones? If constitutional scepticism is followed by symbolic scepticism (if I may use this shorthand) all that remains is the crude fact of pluralism. And to believe in the mechanical efficacy of a situation of social pluralism is even more naïve than to believe—with Montesquieu—in the mechanical miracles of the separation of powers.

9. Cf. Spitz, *op. cit.,* p. 52: "all too ready acquiescence, even subservience, of the individual to the will of the majority is not . . . , as Bryce saw, tyranny."

10. Some recent books seem to confirm this judgment, e.g., Christian Bay, *The Structure of Freedom* (Stanford, 1958), which, among other sources, draws, although in a disorderly way, upon the findings of the behavioral sciences. Bay puts forward as the ultimate goal "a maximum freedom of expression for all" (p. 6), on the assumption that our main problem is to increase the ability of men to resist manipulation and that we need not "convergence toward a better and more uniform pattern of citizenship, but development

toward the greatest individuality and divergency compatible with citizenship" (pp. 63-64). Is not this the thesis of Tocqueville and Mill? Cf. also the revival and development of Tocqueville's preoccupation in Barrington Moore, Jr., *Political Power and Social Theory* (Cambridge, 1958), pp. 83-87, 182-183, regarding the hypothesis of a "popular totalitarianism."

11. For the history of the principle of majority, cf. Ruffini Avondo, *Il principio maggioritario, profilo storico* (Torino, 1927).

12. Historically speaking, this concept has found its value legitimation in the natural rights assumption; but I doubt that the majority of those who "value" the popular will have, today, the right to appeal to the natural law foundation. The withering away of the natural law support has been well emphasized by P. Piovani, *Giusnaturalismo ed etica moderna* (Bari, 1961) *passim*.

13. Cit. in B. de Jouvenel, *Du pouvoir*, p. 310.

14. Cf. S. K. Padover, *The Complete Jefferson* (New York, 1943), p. 384.

15. Only the evolution of the constitutionalism of the Republic of Venice presents perhaps an even greater degree of perfection and constitutional wisdom. Cf. the fundamental study of G. Maranini, *La costituzione di Venezia*, Two Vols. (Venezia, 1927 and 1934).

16. The importance of the constitutionalism of religious orders and of the evolution of their electoral techniques has been pointed out by Leo Moulin in "Sanior et major pars," *Revue historique de droit français et étranger*, III and IV (1958), pp. 368-397, 491-529. I am greatly indebted to this study.

17. Cf. for all E. Lakeman and J. D. Lambert, *Voting in Democracies* (London, 1955).

18. The criticism against proportional representation made by F. A. Hermens in *Democracy or Anarchy?* (Notre Dame, 1941) is excessive, and does not pass the test of an accurate historical analysis. For a more balanced view of the merits, shortcomings, and likely consequences of each type of electoral system, see M. Duverger, *L'Influence des systèmes électoraux sur la vie politique* (Paris, 1950).

19. Cf. *Modern Democracies* (New York, 1924), Vol. II, p. 501. Much in the same vein W. Lippmann writes: "Men do not long desire self-government for its own sake. They desire it for the sake of results." *Public Opinion* (New York, 1922), p. 312.

20. Cf. Berelson's comment: "If the democratic system depended solely on the qualifications of the individual voter, then it seems remarkable that democracies have survived. . . . After examining the detailed data on how individuals misperceive political reality or respond to irrelevant social influences, one wonders how a democracy ever solves its political problems" (*Voting*, p. 311).

21. To this end cf. the discussion and the bibliography in Chap. V, 1, above.

22. As previously stated, elections are in no significant way indicators of majority preference. Dahl, among others, has made the point very well by stating that "all an election reveals is the first preference of some citizen among the candidates standing for office" (*A Preface to Democratic Theory*, p. 125, and pp. 125-132 *passim*).

23. The old-fashioned way of making this statement would be that we vote to appoint "executors." However, this is precisely one of those myths that election studies have dispelled: actually we need leaders, not mere executors.

24. Among the few exceptions see Luigi Einaudi's essay, "Major et sanior pars" in *Il buongoverno* (Bari, 1954), esp. pp. 92-93.

25. In this respect, instead of resuming contact with the problems, we have if anything been losing it more and more. For instance, John Stuart Mill, although a follower of Hare's system of proportional representation, was always mindful of the qualitative problem, so much so that he took particular care to insure the influence of "the best" by means of a plural voting based on educational criteria.

26. Cf. Chap. XIII, 7, below.

27. Cecil A. Gibb has, however, aptly differentiated leadership and headship. Cf. "Leadership" in *Handbook of Social Psychology*, p. 882.

28. *Minoranze guidatrici* is actually the best Italian synonym for Pareto's "elites" (cf. Pasquale Jannaccone, "V. Pareto sociologo," in *Discussioni e indagini economiche e finanziarie* [Torino, 1953], Vol. I, pp. 259-276). We are thus faced with the paradox that the term which comes closer to leadership is accused (under the elitism labeling) of embodying par excellence the anti-democratic approach.

29. N. Bobbio, "Fatti e valori nella teoria delle 'elites'" in *Comunità*, No. 80 (1960), p. 4. For Guido Dorso, cf. "Classe politica e classe dirigente," in *Dittatura, classe politica e classe dirigente* (Torino, 1949); and for Filippo Burzio, *Essenza e attualità del liberalismo* (Torino, 1945).

30. Cf. Chap. III, 4, above.

31. Cf. F. A. Hermens, *The Representative Republic*, esp. pp. 31-35. Hermens mentions the criticism he evoked from Michels, who pointed out that "the differentiation between governments by leadership and governments by rulership is a distinction without a difference." My remarks on the un-translatability of the concept of leadership help in explaining Michels' reaction.

32. Cf. "A Critique of the Ruling Elite Model" (*American Political Science Review*, June 1958, pp. 463-469).

33. The two concepts are often coupled (and even fused, as for instance, in the expression "ruling elite," which gives the impression of being a compound

of Mosca and Pareto). Let us therefore remember that for those who conceived them the two concepts had only one point in common: the thesis that every society is divided into those who are governed and those who govern, and that the latter are a minority. The political class of Mosca is a political concept referred to the problem of the organization and exercise of political power; the elites of Pareto are a concept of social dynamics (with a wider scope) focused on the qualities that are necessary to become part of that class (the theory of residues), and on the causes of their origin and decadence (the theory of the circulation of the elites).

34. On the problem of the elites in general see the collective volume *Le Elites politiche* (Bari, 1961).

35. In this connection, i.e., in relation to the query, "Is there a ruling class left in the United States?" I agree with Riesman's answer that "ruling class theories applied to contemporary America seem to be spectral survivals." (Cf. *The Lonely Crowd*, p. 238, and Chap. XI *passim*). The opposite view is held notably by C. Wright Mills. However, I fail to see how Mills can denounce the existence of *one* power elite when he himself remarks that "the power elite today involves the often uneasy coincidence of economic, military, and political power" (*Problems of Power in American Democracy*, ed. A. Kornhauser [Detroit, 1957], p. 166). I wonder if his "uneasy coincidence" is not better focused by Riesman's "veto groups" system.

36. For a more exhaustive discussion on Dahl's thesis see the reports pro and con of Joseph La Palombara and Georges Lavau respectively, as well as my own remarks in *Le Elites politiche*, pp. 153-157.

37. Gunnar Myrdal has aptly noted that "The idea of leadership pervades American thought and collective action. . . . It is a result less of a conscious ideological principle than of a pragmatic approach. . . . For this reason it is also much less part of America's self-knowledge. . . ." (*An American Dilemma* [New York, 1944], Vol. II, p. 709). This then is another case where one grasps the fundamental difference between the rationalistic and empirical mental pattern (cf. Chap. III, 5, above), which will be discussed at greater length in Chap. XI, below.

38. Cf. *Debates . . . on the Adoption of the Federal Constitution*, ed. J. Elliot (Philadelphia, 1941), V, p. 203.

39. Cf. *L'Esprit des lois*, Bk. VIII, Chap. II. Montesquieu added: "Democracy must avoid two excesses: the spirit of inequality, which leads . . . to the government of one person; and the spirit of extreme equality, which leads to the despotism of one person." In the following chapter he clinches the point: "The spirit of true equality is as far from that of extreme equality, as the sky is from the earth. The first does not consist in a system where everyone commands or no one takes orders, but in a system in which one com-

mands and obeys one's own equals. Its aim is not to have no masters at all, but to have only one's equals as masters."

40. One is reminded of Alain's remark: "A contested power quickly becomes tyrannical." *Le Citoyen contre les pouvoirs* (Paris, 1926), p. 150.

41. *History of the Peloponnesian War,* trans. Richard Crawley (New York, 1950), Bk. II, Chap. VII, pp. 142-143.

42. *The American Commonwealth* (New York, 1888), III, p. 337.

43. S. de Madariaga, *Anarchie ou hiérarchie* (Paris, 1936), p. 56.

44. *Man and Society in an Age of Reconstruction* (London, rev. 1940 English ed.), p. 87. One could keep on citing at length. Cf. finally Lester G. Seligman: "The question may thus be seriously raised as to whether the democracies have been defective by impeding the . . . rise of adequate leadership." *American Political Science Review,* Dec. 1950, pp. 904-915.

45. Cf. A. D. Lindsay, *The Modern Democratic State* (London, 1943), p. 261: "If democracy is to survive it will have to employ and use every bit of skill and knowledge and leadership it can get hold of. This complicated inter-dependent world in which we are living cannot be run without knowledge and skill, foresight and leadership. Any cult of incompetence can only lead to disaster."

46. Cf. in general *Studies in Leadership—Leadership and Democratic Action,* ed. Alvin Gouldner (New York, 1950), and for a condensed synthesis, "A General Framework for the Study of Leadership," in *The Language of Social Research,* eds. Lazarsfeld and Rosenberg (Glencoe, 1955), pp. 511-518. One must keep in mind, however, that a large part of American literature on leadership stems—implicitly when not explicitly—from studies conducted on small groups. Now at the level of large-scale political organizations no direct communication between leader and group is likely to be possible, and therefore it must be emphasized that small-group findings can be only in a small degree relevant at the political level.

47. Cf. *Essenza e attualità del liberalismo,* p. 19.

48. The book appeared in German in 1911 and in Italian in 1912; since Michels was bilingual both texts may be considered original. It was translated into English in 1915, and reprinted in 1958, *Political Parties: A Sociological Study of the Oligarchical Tendencies of Modern Democracy* (Glencoe). I have not used this translation, however, because of the terminological difficulties pointed out at the beginning of section 4 of this chapter.

49. *Vom Wesen und Wert der Demokratie,* Chap. II. Democracy as a party system will be examined in Chap. XI, 4, below.

50. *La Sociologia del partito politico,* p. 33. For a concise summary of Michels' theses "on the oligarchic tendencies of political organizations" see his *Studi sulla democrazia e sull' autorità* (Venezia, 1933), pp. 58-59, and the follow-

ing passage written in 1909: "If there is a sociological law which political parties follow . . . this law, if reduced to its most concise formula, must sound like this: the organization is the mother of the rule of the elected over the electors." *Ibid.*, p. 49.

51. *La Sociologia del partito politico*, p. 419. The German text says *Führertum*, and the Italian text *sistema di capi;* therefore, simply to translate "leadership" (as in the English version) fails to convey the meaning of the text. On the other hand I maintain "leadership" to remind that for Michels the concept of headship also covered the former.

52. To cite only two of the most authoritative confirmations, cf. M. Duverger, *Les partis politiques* (Paris, 1951), p. x: in Michels' work "the oligarchic tendencies of mass organizations are still described in terms of the contemporary situation"; and S. M. Lipset: "The obvious conclusions of this analysis are that the functional requirements for democracy cannot be met most of the time in most unions." ("The Political Process in Trade Unions," in *Political Man* [Garden City, 1960], p. 394.) I have cited the most recent bibliography that directly or indirectly tends to support Michels' law in G. Sartori "Democrazia, burocrazia e oligarchia nei partiti," *Rassegna italiana di sociologia,* III (1960), pp. 119-136. Consult also for a more detailed analysis of the problem and of the difference between Michels' and Max Weber's approaches.

53. *La Sociologia del partito politico*, Preface, p. xiii.

54. Cf., e.g., where Michels states that the representative system is impossible, calling attention to the Rousseaunian postulate that the exercise of the will cannot be alienated, in *La Sociologia del partito politico*, p. 37.

55. Cf. J. A. Schumpeter, *Capitalism, Socialism and Democracy*, p. 269.

56. Cf., although in a somewhat different perspective, Walter Lippmann, *Public Opinion*, p. 312: "The democratic fallacy has been its preoccupation with the origin of government rather than with the processes and results. The democrat has always assumed that if political power could be derived in the right way, it would be beneficent. . . . But . . . the crucial interest is how power is exercised. . . . And that use cannot be controlled at the source."

57. Cf. *A Preface to Democratic Theory*, p. 87, for his classification of political systems and equalitarian and non-equalitarian polyarchies.

58. This is Friedrich's felicitous wording. Cf. his 2nd (1941) ed. of *Constitutional Government and Democracy* (Boston), pp. 589-591. The chapter in question, XXV, has been omitted from the 1950 ed.

59. R. A. Dahl in *Research Frontiers in Politics and Government* (Washington, 1955), p. 62.

60. I make a sharp distinction between ideocratic and ideological function. Cf. Chap. XVIII, 2, below.

Chapter VII

What Democracy Is Not

> *"Technological society, by producing mass*
> *phenomena of individualistic loneliness,*
> *calls into being the totalitarian State*
> *and ends the era of democracy."*
>
> —Y. R. Simon†

1. The "Ex Adverso" Definition

To DEFINE means to assign limits, to delimit. A concept is undefined as long as it is unlimited. That is to say that a definition must embrace the whole of what it defines, but no more. Therefore, if we want to complete our definition of democracy, we also have to see what democracy *is not,* that is, what is the opposite of democracy.

Generally, definitions *ex adverso* are the easiest. As it is difficult to say what white is, we usually say that it is the opposite of black. When we try to define politics positively, we are bound to get into trouble, so we solve the problem by saying that it is neither ethics nor economics, and so forth. Likewise, while it is complicated to say what is meant by democracy, it is, or should be, easier to say what is not meant by it. Except that—and this is more than a coincidence —as soon as we have become aware of the importance of locating accurately the boundaries of democracy, and thereby of clearly establishing the difference between it and its counterfeits, our way of indicating the opposite of democracy has become less and less precise.

Formerly, the contrary of democracy was indicated by words like tyranny, despotism, autocracy, absolutism and dictatorship.[1] But we have recently coined two new terms, totalitarianism and authoritarianism. Thus, when the question, "What is the opposite of democracy?" is asked, we tend to reply, nowadays, "Totalitarianism," or "Authoritarianism." Franz Neumann's last book, for instance, has been given the title *The Democratic and the Authoritarian State,* and totalitarianism has been spelled out by Nisbet as the very negation of democracy despite the warning that "we merely delude ourselves if we suppose that there is always necessary conflict between totalitarian governments and the desires and aspirations of the masses." [2]

Now, there is no doubt that our political vocabulary was in need of some enrichment. But I question whether these two innovations are happy ones or are being used correctly. In fact, I do not consider "authoritarianism" a felicitous terminological coinage and, while "totalitarianism" is a very useful addition to our vocabulary, I wonder to what extent it is suitable as a proper antithesis to democracy.

Of course, it would be pedantic to ostracize the word authoritarianism or to reproach everybody who opposes totalitarianism to democracy. But since we are living in the age of confused democracy —so confused that it is even difficult to determine what democracy is not—we should be put on guard against the misunderstandings that stem from the use of these concepts. There is nothing wrong in that we enjoy saying "authoritarianism" or "totalitarianism." But it is somewhat strange that the antonyms that are less satisfying are being used so much more than the apposite ones.

When we oppose democracy to autocracy, for instance, we can easily and surely determine the point where democracy ends, notwithstanding all of its possible variants and transformations. Whereas when we speak of democracy and totalitarianism, we place a vast no-man's-land between democracy and its opposite. And it is my contention that authoritarianism is even less satisfactory as an antithesis. Thus, to begin with, the problem of the definition *a contrario* of democracy confronts us with this puzzling fact: that the label which should be used most is actually the label that is used least.

2. Authoritarianism and Authority

In the word authoritarianism, the suffix *-ism* indicates a particularly, not to say excessively, energetic authority—an authority which crushes liberty. "Authoritarianism" is thus a pejorative term. But authoritarianism comes from "authority," and the word authority tends instead to have a favorable connotation.

The original meaning of "authority" is probably related to the Latin verb *augere,* to augment. Therefore, in its earliest meaning it indicated that those in authority add something, supplement, confirm, or sanction a course of action or thought. However, as Hannah Arendt has pertinently pointed out, this original meaning has been completely lost, because *auctoritas* derived its meaning from a strictly traditionalistic mental pattern. For the Romans the authority of the living depended on and stemmed from the authority of the city's founders. Thus, what is "augmented" by those in authority is the foundation. *Auctor* was not *artifex,* i.e., was not the actual maker or inventor. History was not seen as the adventure of man's breaking with the past and introducing change, but, on the contrary, as an augmentation of the past, as the expansion and confirmation of an *Ursprung.* The opposite is true for us. In our view of the world, *auctor* has become associated with *artifex,* with the author, the inventor, the maker. We take a dynamic view of history, and thus we do not think of growth as directed towards the past, but towards the future.[3] However, notwithstanding our different perspective, and therefore notwithstanding the fact that *auctor* has become *author*— thereby suggesting the idea of creation, innovation, and initiative— "authority" has always been and still is an approbative term. And it is hard to see how it could be otherwise.[4]

It is all very well to say that the political process is a "power process." But once we have said this, we must distinguish between one type of power and another: between *potestas* and *auctoritas,* between power as force (or domination) and power as authority, between power to coerce and power to get things done. Thus, "authority" is the term that we need for the purpose of indicating not the power that is suspended from above over those who have to submit to it, but, on the contrary, the power that comes from spontaneous investiture and draws its force and efficacy from the fact that it is acknowledged.[5] Authority is, we could say, a power that is based on persuasion, prestige, deference. And when we speak of authority, we refer to a leadership that arouses and receives spontaneous support.[6]

In regard to our problem, the distinction between power and authority is serviceable in that it allows us to specify that democracy is the political system which is built on the mode of exercising power that is called authority, in the sense that the typical feature of democracy is that it tends to transform power into authority, a *vis coactiva* into a *vis directiva*. Far from being repugnant to democracy, authority is its power formula par excellence. The ideal cherished by those who look forward to a genuine democracy is not the conquest of power but, on the contrary, its minimization, and therefore the replacement of "power holders" by what we might call "authority holders."

In the light of this conclusion, it is easy to understand how disturbing the label "authoritarianism" is. There are three reasons for this. In the first place it tends to make our attitude toward the idea of authority ambivalent and vacillating, torn as we are between the consciousness of its desirability and the distressing associations it arouses. As a consequence some people have again started to confuse *auctoritas* with *potestas,* authority with power, with the result that all the typology concerning the different forms of power has been muddled once more[7] and that the very notion of authority has been made meaningless.[8] A second incongruity comes from the fact that "authoritarianism" casts over the problems of the present the shadow of an outworn and gratuitous philosophy of history. The term has in this respect a singularly anti-historical flavor, since authority started to be used in a pejorative sense when the idea of liberty without authority, of a happy state of natural anarchy, had already been long extinct. In the third place, thanks to the interference of the term authoritarianism, we are forced to be real virtuosi of language in order to make a proper use of our terminology. This may seem a frivolous reason for disapproving of its use, but I submit that a democracy cannot permit itself the luxury of defending itself as if its audience were made up of philologists and glottologists.

Since authority and democracy are so closely interwoven that we can hardly speak of democracy without speaking of authority, let us suppose that at a certain point in the discussion we have to use the adjectival form instead of the noun. What are we supposed to say? Shall we call democracy an "authoritarian" system? This is clearly inadvisable. Thus if we wish to convey the idea that democracy typically requires power as authority, our only escape is to resort to the subtle distinction between *authoritarian* (non-democratic) authority, and *authoritative* (democratic) authority, with the result that we find ourselves with the not very appealing expression "authoritative system" to connote a democracy.[9] And in order to avoid misunderstandings, we would have to resort to similar refinements quite frequently. For example, "authoritarianism" has suggested the epithet "authoritarian personality" to indicate the type of personality structure that is not adapted to the democratic way of life.[10] The trouble is, again, that this term leaves the impression that the type of personality which can best serve democracy should be authority-less. Of course, this is not so. But in order to correct this erroneous impression, we shall have to make a distinction between the authoritarian personality and the authoritative personality, with the understanding that the successful functioning of a democratic system depends on the latter type of personality structure.[11]

We can see from all this that we do indeed have to be virtuosi. And I wonder whether it is wise to establish the difference between democracy and its opposite by such fine distinctions. Furthermore, I am also brought to wonder why we should honor modern dictatorships with a distinctive mark that they do not deserve. It is true that when we say "authoritarian State" we mean to express censure; but in the censure a certain amount of praise is also implied.[12] "Authoritarianism" does suggest that an excessive use of authority is involved; yet, this excess remains linked to something that is praiseworthy, it is an excess of authority. And authority is a legitimate need, no society is possible without it. Actually, if the use of "authoritarianism" had not clouded the waters so much, and if we could follow the sensible and usual practice of giving it the meaning of its root (authority) we would assert the very opposite of what is commonly accepted, that is, that it is inappropriate to use a word that evokes the idea of authority in speaking of a tyrannical system, for true authority is destroyed by despotisms, whereas the authoritative personality is necessary to a free society.[13]

If, then, we are seeking the correct antithesis of democracy, authoritarianism will not do, for a word that creates confusion and gives rise to so many unnecessary problems cannot be the proper antithesis. And it should be added that, even setting aside all the foregoing reasons, authoritarianism is not, in any case, a *vis-à-vis* of democracy, for the good reason that the concept of authority is correlative to the concept of freedom.[14]

True freedom, it is said, accepts authority, just as true authority recognizes freedom. Freedom that does not acknowledge authority is arbitrary freedom, *licentia* not *libertas*. Vice versa, authority that does not recognize freedom is authoritarianism. This means that authoritarianism is the opposite of liberty and therefore the opposite of what is historically known as liberalism rather than as democracy. And the difference is not in the least irrelevant. For one thing it still has to be proved that democracy cannot be illiberal, or at any rate a-liberal.[15] And in this hypothesis the use of the term authoritarianism would demand the inclusion of "authoritarian democracy" as a possible category—another confirmation of our assertion that if it is the opposite of democracy that we are seeking, we have not found it.

3. "Total State" Democracy and Absolutism

Let us get on to "totalitarianism." Totalitarianism comes from "totality," and simply expresses, as such, the idea of extension, of something that embraces and pervades everything; and, in a derived sense, the idea of all-pervading penetration and intensity. But according to this meaning it could hardly be denied that, in some degree, a tendency towards totality characterizes every modern State. Demographic pressure, the continually increasing interdependence of all aspects of the industrial society, technological progress and the resultant search for more and more rational, functional, and planned societal forms, to mention only the more conspicuous reasons, lead present-day governments, *bon gré mal gré,* to concern themselves increasingly with everybody and everything.

In this respect, then, we could easily argue that the law of inertia of modern States tends to make them more and more totalitarian, in the literal meaning of the term. All modern States are developing in the direction of the "total State." And the democratic State is no exception. As a matter of fact, the hypothesis that a democratic State can become totalitarian, meaning that it can become an all-pervading total State, is perfectly plausible. For, in principle, no political formula can justify a totalitarian expansion of political power as easily as democracy. Democracy is the government *of* all, and as such it is vested with a greater right than any other ethico-political formula to exercise jurisdiction *over* all. The power that originates in everyone is authorized, *ex hypothesi,* to do everything. "The democratic fiction," de Jouvenel remarks, "lends the leaders the authority of the whole. It is the whole that wills, it is the whole that acts." [16]

It will be objected that this is not the sense in which "totalitarianism" was coined and accepted into the political vocabulary, since in this context it has a technical connotation and should thus be considered a synonym of "authoritarianism" or "absolutism." The reason for this is that, in politics, attention is not paid so much to the extent of power—to its amount—as to the way it is *exercised.* This may be true, but once we have decided that totalitarianism does not indicate an extension—a total State—but has to be understood as an equivalent of absolutism, or of authoritarianism, we have not made much progress. On the contrary.

I shall not embark again on a discussion of authoritarianism, because, whatever the worth and appropriateness of the concept itself, any identification of authoritarianism with totalitarianism is patently arbitrary. Even if it is plausible that every totalitarian system is authoritarian, the opposite, i.e., that every authoritarian system is totalitarian, is not plausible. The only necessary consequence of authoritarian exercise of power is that the freedom of the subjects will be trampled on and, more precisely, that coercion will be at a maximum intensity while voluntarization will be feeble and peripheral. That this should take place in a totalitarian manner is a further condition or hypothesis, which certainly cannot be explained if we make totalitarianism synonymous with authoritarianism.

Rather, it is useful to examine the other equation, namely, that totalitarianism is analogous to absolutism. For this purpose it will be worthwhile to investigate the concept of absolutism, and this in two respects—to see if it can help us to clarify the concept of totalitarianism, and to ascertain at the same time whether the term is by any chance satisfactory as an opposite of democracy.

Absolutus is a term used by the Latin commentators of the Aristotelian concept of *pambasileia* (translated as *rex absolutus*) and it did not have, for a long time, a derogatory meaning. *Potestas absoluta,* absolute power, merely indicated a supreme, perfect, complete, and (in this context and reference) intangible power. It is only with Machiavelli, and especially with Guicciardini, that a *potestà assoluta* is linked with virtual tyranny (and this only in a peripheral way), and that the Latin root *absolvere,* which conveys the meaning of "setting free," begins to be associated with the idea of lack and thereby of imperfection.[17] However, it was not until the 18th century that "absolutism" was coined and used in its modern derogatory sense of "released from" something that we praise. In the modern connotation, then, the absolute power of absolutism denotes a power set free from controls, released from restraints: a limitless, discretional exercise of power that allows no opposition. And the concept appears definite because we are reminded, by association of ideas, of the absolute 17th and 18th century monarchies.

But what interests us is not the past. I mean that if we have to use the word "absolutism" for the present, the fact that it recalls an example from the past is confusing, not only because absolute monarchies no longer exist in the West, but especially because this imagery is related to the patrimonial concept of the State, that is, to a political system in which the State is conceived of as the monarch's estate. Therefore it is obvious that a democracy cannot be absolute in the sense that absolute monarchies were; but that does not prove that a democracy cannot become absolute in some other way.

In what we might term its material meaning, a power that is not opposed by adequate *de facto* countervailing powers is an absolute power. In this connotation, absolutism is related to the concentration of power. The more a society loses its pluralistic structure and the more its intermediary forces are levelled and weakened, the more easily the conditions that make absolutism possible are created. Thus, any State that concentrates all the power in itself is potentially a State that can exercise absolute power. And this implies that even an overcentralized democracy[18] that tends to replace the spontaneous interplay of a multi-group society with its own unicentric will is in a position to exercise an absolutist kind of pressure. Let us not forget, in this connection, that "democratic centralization" was Lenin's slogan.

In a second sense, we have absolute power when it is not disciplined and limited by law. In this meaning the absolute State is the non-constitutional State, that is, a State in which the power holders are not restrained by, or have become released from, constitutional checks and restraints. In this connection the query is: Is the democratic State necessarily a liberal-constitutional State, and more precisely a *Rechtsstaat* of the "garantist" type in which the sovereign *demos* (no less than the former *princeps*) is not *legibus solutus?* [19] Genetically, that is historically speaking, this has been the case. But if we say "necessarily," then the answer is: No, democracy and constitutionalism are not inevitably linked. Actually, present-day maximization of democracy seeks, or at any rate entails, a minimization of the "garantist" aspect of liberal constitutionalism. Democratic perfectionism in particular rejects the classic constitutional State in its impatience to obtain more quickly more than the system allows. But then we cannot fail to see that even in the constitutional meaning of the expression a democracy may become absolute. Incidentally, let us be reminded that this has already been the trend with ancient democracies.

There is finally a third, general and generic, sense of "absolutism" that refers to a mental pattern, to a personality type. The so-called constitutional gentleman, with his internalized moral self-restraints, typifies its opposite, the non-absolute kind of leader. But the constitutional gentleman has become a very rare specimen in our time. Therefore, even from this broad angle, I do not see why the assertion that a democratic absolutism is within the range of possibility should be considered disrespectful. If democracy is not absolutist it is not because it cannot, *ex hypothesi,* become so, but rather because we are made aware of this danger and thereby take the necessary precautions.

143

In effect many authoritative scholars have emphasized that the principle of democracy, in itself, can easily imply absolutism, or that in any case it leaves many openings which may lead to what is meant by saying "absolutism." Democratic legitimacy implies the limitation of power only insofar as it opposes autocratic power, so that once the adversary is defeated, popular sovereignty may well come to resemble its former enemy. A limited power while fighting or resisting another power, popular sovereignty becomes, in its own way, a source of unlimited power when the counter-powers disappear.[20]

E.g., if we contend that democracy is achieved by taking all the power from the despot with one hand to give it to the people with the other, all this operation accomplishes is to present us with an absolutism in reverse. And in this case one is perfectly justified in maintaining that it is precisely democratic legitimacy that gives absolute sanction to power. For there is no appeal when sovereignty is exercised in the name of the people: we are already in the final court of appeal.

As anyone can easily see, the antithesis under discussion is neither clear-cut nor axiomatic. By saying this I do not intend to affirm that democracy and absolutism are compatible. I only wish to make clear that I cannot demonstrate what democracy *is not*—or can never be—if I have to argue the problem on the basis of the concept of absolutism.

The answer to my second question, namely, whether totalitarianism and absolutism should be used as synonyms, and whether the latter concept helps in determining the meaning of the former, is implicit in what I have already said. Absolutism is a loose concept that cannot be pinned down easily. Therefore, it is not very helpful in explaining an already obscure term like totalitarianism. Two one-legged men do not make a two-legged man. I should also like to make, in principle, an objection concerning the economy of language. "Totalitarianism" is a modern word which was invented to give the idea of a phenomenon that seems to us without precedent. What sense does it make then to waste this neologism by dressing it in old clothes? If totalitarianism has to be understood as meaning absolutism, why coin this new term, which has the additional defect of

144

being even more obscure than the previous one, since we have to use "absolutism" to explain it?

4. Totalitarianism

Instead of resorting to synonyms that are not even synonyms, let us return to the direct question: What does "totalitarianism" mean? A perusal of the views put forward by a number of authors in the book *Totalitarianism*[21] shows how ambiguous the word is, and how difficult it is to agree on its meaning. The fundamental question seems to be whether the word should be used to indicate a trait that is common to many different State-societies, or whether it should designate a particular type of political system characterized by its own special syndrome of features.[22] Another question, which is related to the former one, is: Should "totalitarianism" be used for all epochs, including ancient times, or should it be reserved for our time, to indicate an experience whose novelty we wish to emphasize?

It is my opinion that if we take the first path we cannot give a sufficiently definite meaning to the term, nor employ it most fruitfully. Certainly, if we wish, we can say that the ancient *polis* was totalitarian, or, as Franz Neumann remarked, that the government of Sparta and the regime of Diocletian are examples of totalitarianism.[23] Except that the analogy is superficial, and, as Karl Loewenstein rightly points out in this connection, "We are not entitled to qualify certain ancient autocracies as totalitarian because the *telos* of the State-society . . . , rarely articulated in secular terms, was accepted without disagreement by the power holders and the power addressees alike, and so deeply ingrained in tradition that it required neither ideological formulation nor enforcement." [24] When we apply "totalitarianism" to a past epoch, we lose sight of the profound qualitative difference that exists between total domination taken as a matter of course because it is based on tradition and religion, and the total domination which emerges in the modern world, superimposing itself on a Christian, liberal, and democratic civilization.[25]

Besides, following this line, we can come to the point of reducing the notion of totalitarianism to a vanishing point, as E. H. Carr has done. He defines totalitarianism as "the belief that some organized group or institution, whether church or government or party, has a special access to truth."[26] Now, the reason that Carr arrives at such a patently arbitrary definition is that he wants to demonstrate that totalitarianism is as old as the world, that it has always existed and always will, except for a brief parenthesis which he calls the "age of individualism."[27] But what he really manages to demonstrate is the futility of employing the term to interpret the entire course of history. The danger of taking this line is that we arrive at wholly arbitrary stipulations that have no basis whatever in the semantic potential of the word, or at any rate that we give "totalitarianism" so broad a meaning that it becomes meaningless.[28]

The second approach, which is the one indicated by Friedrich, is thus more fruitful, even though it presents considerable difficulties. In his contribution to "Totalitarianism" Friedrich lists five requisites for a totalitarian system: (a) an official ideology, (b) a single mass party controlled by an oligarchy, (c) government monopoly of arms, (d) government monopoly of mass media, and (e) a terroristic police system.[29] It is symptomatic that this list is varied even by those contributors who agree with Friedrich that totalitarianism is a specific political system characterized by several traits.[30] Nevertheless the area of disagreement can easily be reduced to a question of detail if an agreement is reached on the following points: (i) the opportunity of using "totalitarianism" to denote only a present-day phenomenon, and (ii) the necessity of adhering to the semantic connotation of the word, which means remaining within the orbit of the idea of totality.

It is my thesis, then, that a new term has a *raison d'être* if it expresses a new idea. Therefore "totalitarianism" can be used fruitfully if by it we mean to indicate the unprecedented intensity, pervasiveness, and penetration—both in breadth and in depth—that political domination can assume. Our world is revealing such a new aspect and dimension of power as not even the prophets of a new age—Marx and Nietzsche, for instance—have glimpsed or suspected. Hobbes's Leviathan is a baby monster when confronted with Orwell's, and the tyrannies of the past seem innocent and innocuous compared to what totalitarian dictatorships are, or can become.[31] A term was needed to indicate this difference, and "totalitarianism" is effective as this term.[32]

What I disapprove of is its use as a noun, for when used as the grammatical and logical subject of discourse, "totalitarianism" does not say enough, since it designates neither a form of government nor a way of governing. Instead, it becomes meaningful when it is in its adjectival form, when used as a predicate. It is correct to say "totalitarian party" because the specification indicates that it is a party that wishes to suppress all other parties. And it is correct, and necessary, to speak of "totalitarian autocracy" because thus we indicate the modern type of despotism and tyranny. Whereas, on the other hand, it is useless as well as misleading to adopt "totalitarianism" as a substantive to replace the pre-existing terminology.

It is a confusing waste because in this case totalitarianism becomes a cosmic notion that is interpreted by everyone as he thinks fit, and thereby distracts our attention from the essential point. The essential point being that totalitarianism denotes the imprisonment of the whole of society *within* the State, an all-pervasive political domination over the extra-political life of man. When in Italy the saying was, "Everything in the State, nothing outside the State, nothing against the State," this was little more than a rhetorical phrase. But if the proposition "everything in the State" is taken seriously and applied to its limit by the instruments of coercion which technological power has at its disposal, we indeed find ourselves confronted with the thing; that is, "the ultimate invasion of human privacy," [33] the destruction of everything that is spontaneous, independent, diversified, and autonomous in the life of human collectivities; in short, a huge political garrison where a mass society has been incapsulated into the State. And this is precisely what distinguishes totalitarianism from absolutism: "The destruction of the line between State and society and the total politicization of society. . . . This is not merely a question of more or less political power. The difference is one of quality, not quantity." [34]

Yet in these terms we have described only a tendency, an objective, or, as it has been so well expressed, a "nightmare." [35] We have not described a definite type of State, or a definite power

147

structure. And since the possibility of pursuing totalitarian ends strictly depends on the form of the State, we must first determine what the non-democratic form of power structure is—and this will be the opposite of democracy which will permit us to conclude that totalitarianism and democracy are incompatible.

5. Democracy versus Autocracy

We may now review with sufficient accuracy the range of the possible opposites of democracy, or at any rate the ways of indicating its boundaries with the greatest possible clarity. I shall proceed to examine the following concepts, arranged in five groups: (i) tyranny, despotism, absolutism; (ii) dictatorship; (iii) authoritarianism and totalitarianism; (iv) the coercion-consensus continuum, or the monocracy-polycracy distinction; (v) autocracy.

Tyranny, despotism, and absolutism are the old-fashioned terms. Actually they survive in our vocabulary mostly as scare words. Tyranny, it is true, has a long and elaborate record in the history of political thought. It is sufficient to recall the distinction of Bartolo da Sassoferrato and of Coluccio Salutati between tyranny *quoad exercitium* (relating to the way of exercising power) and tyranny *ex defectu tituli* (relating to the illegitimate or violent acquisition of power) and all the following literature of the Monarchomachs on the right to kill the tyrant. Nevertheless it is hard to see how these distinctions, and for that matter all the Renaissance literature on the subject, apply to modern conditions and to the present-day terms of the problem. Our plebiscitary dictators can hardly be considered tyrants *ex defectu tituli,* and our criteria for spelling out a tyranny *exercitio* are too different from the Greek and the Renaissance moral and natural law criteria. On the other hand, despotism is a very inarticulate concept in the political literature, and we have seen the difficulties inherent in the use of absolutism. All in all, these terms only render the general idea of a displeasing and oppressive *exercitium* of State power. And if we want to know more about the tyrannical, despotic, and absolute way of exercising power—as well as of the form of State which is related to this *exercitium*—we must refer to the more modern concepts.

Dictatorship is actually the term that has come to replace

tyranny. However, our use of dictatorship in the meaning formerly given to tyranny is very recent.[36] Indeed so recent that our concept is still very rough and inarticulate.[37] One could almost say that whereas tyranny has been reduced out of its old age to being a scare word, dictatorship still has to emerge from the juvenile stage of being little more than a mere "boo word." For up to the present moment there is no satisfactory theory of dictatorship which establishes a typology and relates the concept to a certain kind of allocation of power, distribution of power, elite recruitment, decision-making, and—in sum—to a definite form and *exercitium* of State power.[38] It is true that if we are making little progress in this direction this is because, or partly because, we have been unable, as yet, to build a frame of reference to replace the obsolete traditional classification of political systems.[39] But it is also true, on the other hand, that present-day scholars are making a generous use of the term but have dedicated little attention to the concept, concentrating, as it were, not on dictatorship but on authoritarianism and totalitarianism. We know comparatively less about our dictatorships than previous authors knew about tyranny, and consequently our queries have to be once again passed over to those new terminological coins.

Totalitarianism and authoritarianism, however, cannot solve our problem either. In opposing authoritarianism to democracy we confuse the issues of liberty and of democracy, we reinforce the obsolete notion of an authority-less democratic ideal, and at the same time we provide a very inadequate image of what awaits us in a technological totalitarian autocracy. As for totalitarianism, its ineffectiveness as an *ex adverso* determination of democracy is revealed by the fact that in the expression "totalitarian democracy," which has been put into circulation by J. B. Talmon,[40] the two alleged opposites have been coupled. We need not discuss whether Talmon's label is pertinent, intrinsically contradictory, or paradoxical. It is sufficient to note that its very adoption points out the weakness of the antithesis democracy-versus-totalitarianism. And it is a real weakness, for in this alternative we are unable to spell out and define clearly one horn of the dilemma, i.e., totalitarianism as a noun. Democracy is in itself an extremely difficult and controversial concept. If we try to define it *per differentiam* with even vaguer and more ambiguous notions, we are just furthering the confusion of ideas.

It might be suggested at this point that we should change approach, and search for what democracy *is not* by having recourse to distinctions of the power-authority, or the coercion-consensus kind (and the like). But in this approach we have a continuum; and this means that conceptual overlaps are not only inevitable but considerable. Who could deny, for instance, that every coercion requires a minimum of consent, and vice versa that hardly any consent is exempt from some degree of coercion? This does not mean in the least that the distinctions are not useful. On the contrary, they are essential. But it does mean that if we use them for the purpose of pinning down the difference between democracy and non-democracy they may well lead us to what I have called a balanced nihilism.[41]

We might switch, however, to Karl Loewenstein's suggestion: "The basic dichotomy of political systems and the patterns of government included therein would be terminologically best expressed by the pair of opposites 'polycracy' and 'monocracy,' the former denoting shared and the latter concentrated exercise of political power." [42] I agree with Loewenstein when he remarks that complex classifications defeat their purpose, and I agree very much with his subsequent treatment of the topic.[43] But regarding this specific suggestion it should be pointed out that also the "polycracy-monocracy" contrast can hardly prevent overlaps, for the argument will always be brought up that even a monocracy is based, somehow or other, on a polycracy.[44] I grant that the objection is not insuperable, but let me again pose the question: Why choose overlapping, or (as in the cases examined previously) misleading and ambiguous concepts when we do have, after all, an unequivocal term which expresses the contrary of democracy?[45]

We are left, thus, with autocracy. It is quite true that even autocracy can be criticized on the grounds that it has not been elaborated any better than dictatorship and the other poorly defined and somewhat inarticulate concepts on our list. Nevertheless, autocracy does have an advantage over the other concepts in that it focuses the attention on the strategic juncture of the argument, namely,

150

on the method of creation of the power holders, and on the source of their legitimacy. So, given the fact that we do not possess an articulate agreed-upon general framework for the classification of political systems, it follows that in the present state of our conceptual tools only autocracy is serviceable for the purpose of defining democracy *a contrario*. Despite other possible drawbacks, if the alternative is "democracy or autocracy," the semantic indication conveyed by autocracy is precise, and we are immediately able to elucidate the concepts and to draw the line that clearly separates democracy from what it is not.

Democracy, viewed as non-autocracy, denotes a political system characterized by the absence of personal power, and more particularly a system that hinges on the principle that no one can proclaim himself ruler, that no one can hold power irrevocably in his own name. Precisely because the autocratic principle is repudiated, the democratic axiom is that man's power over man can only be granted by others. Furthermore, if the designation of leaders does not come from consensus, there is no democracy. Nor is there democracy when consensus is counterfeit and extorted, for there is no consensus if those who are to give it are not free to dissent and if it does not result from choice among a number of alternatives. And no terminological falsification, as well as no amount of subtle display of dialectics, can erase boundary-posts that are as clear and easily identifiable as these.

From this correct *ex adverso* approach we also understand more clearly the meaning and *raison d'être* of liberal-democratic institutions, that is, of the constitutional precautions which, by separating the exercise of power from its investiture and by binding public officials to preordained juridical structures, make it possible to replace leaders, to limit their time in office, to hold them responsible to the people, and to avert abuses of power. The *a contrario* definition of democracy is therefore the following: In democracy no one can choose himself, no one can invest himself with the power to rule, and therefore no one can arrogate to himself unconditional and unlimited power. The difference between democracy and its opposite lies in the fact that in a democracy power is scattered, limited, controlled, and exercised in rotation; whereas in an autocracy power is concentrated, uncontrolled, indefinite, and unlimited. What democracy *is not* is, in one word, autocracy.

NOTES

† *Philosophy of Democratic Government* (Chicago, 1951), p. 309.

1. The terms are arranged in chronological order. Tyrant and despot are Greek names. Absolutism and autocracy have been used only since the eighteenth century. One might wonder why I have listed dictatorship, a Latin term, as last. In its Roman meaning, dictatorship was not a political system but an extraordinary magistracy limited in time and functions. We have to wait until we are well into the twentieth century before dictatorship denotes a non-democratic regime. Therefore, the meaning of dictatorship which concerns us is really a very recent one. These concepts are examined below in Sect. V.

2. Cf. R. A. Nisbet, *The Quest for Community* (New York, 1953), p. 194.

3. Cf. Hannah Arendt in *Authority*, ed. C. J. Friedrich (Cambridge, 1958), pp. 99-102; cf. also Friedrich's essay, p. 30.

4. For greater development and depth see in general the volume ed. by Friedrich, *Authority*, which contains excellent contributions. Cf. also the good collection *Freedom and Authority in Our Time*, eds. Bryson, Finkelstein, MacIver and McKeon (New York and London, 1953); as well as Dolf Sternberger, *Autorität, Freiheit und Befehlsgewalt* (Tübingen, 1959).

5. The *Bulletin international des sciences sociales* in the series of terminological studies under the auspices of UNESCO indicates the following common usage of "authority": "Power that is accepted, respected, recognized, legitimate." (IV [1955], p. 718.) With reference to the distinction which Friedrich makes between corporeal or substantive power (power as a *thing had*) and relational power, or power *over* (cf. *Constitutional Government and Democracy*, pp. 22-24 and 584), authority would be the desirable form of the "relational" mode of power.

6. In a somewhat poetic but effective manner, Jacques Maritain writes: "We shall call 'authority' the right to lead and command, to be listened to and obeyed by others: and we shall name 'power' the force by means of which others can be obliged to listen to and obey. . . . To the extent to which it is power, authority reaches down to the physical level; insofar as it is authority, power is raised to the moral level. . . ." "Démocratie et Autorité" in *Le Pouvoir*, eds. R. P. McKeon, C. J. Friedrich, *et al.* (Paris, 1957), II, pp. 26-27.

7. Many contemporary writers, in fact, use "power" and others use "authority"

for all possible cases, without any precise reason, and without explaining why; thereby revealing that they are blind to the problem which Plato had already seen, that is, whether *auctoritas* is to be explained in terms of *potestas* (Thrasymachus' thesis), or whether *potestas* is to be converted into *auctoritas*. Yet it is on the basis of this distinction that one poses the fundamental alternative between "politics as war" (the *auctoritas* which is might) and "legalitarian politics" (the *auctoritas* which is not *potestas*) which we have examined above in Chap. III, 2.

8. Cf. e.g., Robert Bierstedt's essay, "The Problem of Authority," in *Freedom and Control in Modern Society,* eds. Berger, Abel, and Page. (New York, 1954), in which authority is defined as "institutionalized power" (p. 78), legality is confused with legitimacy (following Merriam), and a number of distinctions are either misleading or irrelevant. Lasswell and Kaplan's (and Merriam's) definition, "authority is formal power" (*Power and Society,* p. 133), also seems inadequate.

9. Perhaps it is for this reason, that is, because he had implicitly in mind authority rather than authoritarianism, that David Easton speaks of "authoritative allocation" and "authoritative decisions." If this is the case, it would seem helpful to contemplate also a strict use of the notion, distinguishing between authoritative and coercive allocations. Cf. *The Political System* (New York, 1953), Chap. V.

10. Cf. for instance T. W. Adorno *et al., The Authoritarian Personality* (New York, 1950); M. Janowitz and D. Marvick, "Authoritarianism and Political Behavior" in *Public Opinion Quarterly* (1953), pp. 185-201; and *Studies in the Scope and Method of the Authoritarian Personality,* eds. R. Christie and M. Jahoda (Glencoe, 1954).

11. Aside from the terminological confusion because of which we should on the one hand approve of authority but on the other beware of the authoritarian personality, I am under the impression that many of the extrapolations derived from this questionable ideal-type are either of little significance (because much more important variables should be taken into account) or arbitrary. E.g., is it really true that an authoritarian family structure supports an authoritarian political regime? And if it is true (actually the opposite can be claimed), is this extremely remote antecedent really relevant?

12. One should bear in mind that "authoritarianism" was coined by authoritarian regimes, and this, obviously, in order to exploit the approbatory connotation of the semantics.

13. Cf. Friedrich: "In a very real sense, in a totalitarian society true authority is altogether destroyed," in *Totalitarianism* (New Haven, 1954), p. 274. This thesis is developed by Friedrich in *Confluence,* No. 3 (1954), pp. 307-316, and elaborated further in a very stimulating way in *Authority,* p. 28 f. Cf. also Hannah Arendt, "Authority in the Twentieth Century," in *Review of*

153

Politics, IV (1956). This was also, despite the different wording and approach, Gugliemo Ferrero's thesis when he distinguished between the power that "comes from above" and the legitimate power that "comes from below," and related the crisis of our times to the "disappearance of the sense of legitimacy." Cf. *Il potere* (Milano, 1947), *passim*.

14. Cf. the history of the idea in G. Quadri, *Il Problema dell'autorità* (Firenze, 1940), two vols.

15. I leave the argument in its outline form since the relationship between freedom and democracy will be examined historically in Chap. XV (but cf. also Chap. XIII).

16. *Du pouvoir*, p. 316.

17. Cf. R. De Mattei "Assolutismo" in *Enciclopedia del diritto* (Milano, 1958), Vol. III, pp. 917 f. Cf. also Emilio Bussi, "Réflexions critiques sur la notion d'absolutisme" in *Bulletin de la Societé d'Histoire Moderne*, Nov.-Dec. 1955.

18. Lasswell and Kaplan distinguish between centralization and concentration of power, and rightly point out that the latter, not the former, is a characteristic of despotic rule (*Power and Society*, pp. 224-225). Accordingly I use "over-centralization" for a centralization which acquires the nature of a concentration.

19. The notions of a liberal-constitutional State, and the problems which are connected with it, will be clarified in Chaps. XIII and XV, below.

20. Cf. Chap. II, 3 and Chap. IV, 3, above.

21. Cf. *Totalitarianism: Proceedings of a Conference Held at the American Academy of Arts and Sciences, March 1953*, ed. C. J. Friedrich.

22. Cf. N. S. Timasheff in *Totalitarianism*, p. 39.

23. Cf. *The Democratic and the Authoritarian State* (Glencoe, 1957), pp. 246-247.

24. *Political Power and the Governmental Process* (Chicago, 1957), pp. 59-60.

25. Other examples of totalitarian anticipations are furnished by Barrington Moore, Jr., *Political Power and Social Theory* (Cambridge, 1958), Chap. II, "Totalitarian Elements in Pre-industrial Societies." Still, it seems to me that our terms (such as dictatorship and totalitarianism) cannot, without being arbitrary, be superimposed on preliterate societies and on oriental despotisms.

26. E. H. Carr, *The Soviet Impact on the Western World* (New York, 1949), p. 110.

27. *Op. cit.* This is also the underlying central thesis of Carr's history of the Russian Revolution, *The Bolshevik Revolution* (London, 1950-1958), 5 vols.

28. Cf. R. A. Nisbet's remark: "Totalitarianism has unfortunately become one of those omnibus words used to absorb indiscriminately every element of the

past and present that we regard as detestable." (*The Quest for Community,* p. 192.)

29. Cf. pp. 52-53. In a successive volume, *Totalitarian Dictatorship and Autocracy,* written in collaboration with Z. K. Brzezinski (New Haven, 1956), Friedrich adds to the five above-mentioned characteristics a sixth one, "a centrally directed economy" (cf. pp. 9, 177-236). It is understood that these five or six traits are interwoven, with a totalitarian system as their syndrome; for the monopoly of armed force as well as economic planning pertain, or, in the latter case, can pertain also to democratic systems.

30. Cf. in *Totalitarianism* the communications of Alex Inkeles and Karl W. Deutsch, pp. 87 f., 308 f. It turns out that if we follow, for example, the criteria suggested by Deutsch, Peter the Great would be a totalitarian despot, while to Friedrich he would not (cf. p. 334).

31. The unique and modern character of totalitarian dictatorships is rendered very well by Friedrich and Brzezinski, *Totalitarian Dictatorship and Autocracy,* esp. pp. 10-13 *et passim.* The authors opportunely point out, as a confirmation of the "modernity" of the totalitarian systems, that four of the six traits they enumerate are "technologically conditioned," and that the two remaining ones (the official ideology and the single party) link the totalitarian dictatorship to modern democracy, of which they are a perversion. "In summary," the authors conclude, "these regimes could have arisen only within the context of mass democracy and modern technology" (p. 13). This genealogy is generally recognized. Gabriel A. Almond has well synthesized on his part the novelty of this concept as follows: "Totalitarianism is tyranny with a rational bureaucracy, a monopoly of the modern technology of communication, and a monopoly of the modern technology of violence." "Comparative Political Systems" in *Political Behavior—A Reader,* eds. Eulau, Eldersveld, Janowitz (Glencoe, 1956), p. 39.

32. In this sense, totalitarianism is perhaps the very word that Tocqueville was trying to find when he wrote: "I believe that the kind of oppression which threatens democratic nations will not resemble any other form previously experienced in the world; our contemporaries would not be able to find anything like it in their memories. Try as I may I cannot find an expression that can reproduce the exact idea I have formed of it; the ancient words despotism and tyranny are entirely inadequate. It is something new; I must therefore attempt to define it, for I cannot name it." *De la démocratie en Amérique* (Paris, 1951), Vol. II, Pt. IV, Chap. VI, p. 324.

33. R. A. Nisbet, *The Quest for Community,* p. 202.

34. Franz Neumann, *op. cit.,* p. 245.

35. "When I try to picture totalitarianism to myself as a general phenomenon," writes G. F. Kennan, "what comes into my mind most prominently is neither the Soviet picture nor the Nazi picture as I have known them in

155

the flesh, but rather the fictional and symbolic images created by such people as Orwell or Kafka or Koestler or the early Soviet satirists. The purest expression of the phenomenon, in other words, seems to me to have been rendered not in its physical reality but in its power as a dream, or a nightmare." *Totalitarianism*, pp. 19-20.

36. It is well to remember in this connection that dictatorship was still used in a very innocent meaning in the age of the Italian *Risorgimento*. Farini in Emilia in 1859 and Garibaldi in Sicily in 1860 proclaimed themselves dictators, and Marx used "dictatorship of the proletariat" in a sense that to him seemed quite compatible with that of democracy. This is because "dictatorship" still denoted either a magistracy (according to the Roman origin of the term), or (as in Marx, who was echoing Blanqui) simply the idea of recourse to the use of force.

37. What has happened to the concept of dictatorship is to some extent parallel to what has occurred to the idea of absolutism. Absolutism could not be understood in a defective sense—as the release of the ruler from obligations from which he should not be freed—until the idea of *potestas amplissima* was confronted with that of *princeps legibus obligatus,* and in a special way, ultimately, with the concept of a State bound by law (the constitutional State). This is indeed why the negative meaning of absolutism is not fully affirmed until the eighteenth century (and never without reservations, as is evidenced by the concept of enlightened absolutism). This applies also to dictatorship. It is only after an adequate and successful experience of "government by consent" that we begin to perceive that *dictare* (to dictate) can stand for a distinct type of political system. It is only at this point that dictatorship can take on a negative connotation (as the opposite of government by consent). Outside of this opposition, the need of *dictare* is implicit in any form of government, and by this route we are brought back to the original meaning of *dictator*.

38. Strange as it may seem, the bibliography on the subject is suprisingly poor. The old and very questionable text of Carl Schmitt, *Die Diktatur* (2nd ed., 1928) is still the one most cited, and has not been superseded. The very classification of the concept is still in the embryo stage, as evidenced by the incomplete study left by Franz Neumann, "Notes on the Theory of Dictatorship," in *The Democratic and Authoritarian State*, pp. 233-256. On the other hand, Alfred Cobban's *Dictatorship—Its History and Theory* (London, 1939) remains by far—despite the 1954 volume of G.W.F. Hallgarten *Histoire des dictatures* (French transl., Paris, 1961)—the best historical interpretation.

39. The attempt made by Lasswell and Kaplan with *Power and Society* to provide this framework (see especially Part III, Chaps. VIII, IX) is perhaps the most convincing example at hand. Despite innumerable valuable precisions and insights, I find it difficult to agree with most of the definitions and classifications adopted. Perhaps their effort would have been more re-

warding if a historian of political theories had been part of the team, since a large part of their conceptualization of the key political terms seems to lack historical dimension, that is, the role those terms have played and the purpose for which they were invented and elaborated. Cf. below Chap. X, 4, 5, and in particular note 19.

40. Cf. *The Origins of Totalitarian Democracy* (London, 1952).

41. Cf. Chap. V, 2, above.

42. *Political Power and the Governmental Process*, p. 13.

43. Actually, Loewenstein too starts from autocracy, taking as the basic classification the distinction between (i) constitutionalism as shared and (ii) autocracy as concentrated exercise of power. Cf. *op. cit.*, p. 29 *et passim*.

44. Cf. e.g., how Lasswell and Kaplan use a threefold division, breaking the dichotomic approach into (i) autocracies, (ii) oligarchies, and (iii) republics (cf. *Power and Society*, p. 218 f.). Although this classification is widely open to question, it points out that Loewenstein's conceptualization inevitably raises the problem of an intermediary or mixed pattern.

45. In conclusion, if we start from the terminal democracy (and there are good reasons why we should), then "autocracy" has a more precise symmetry, even though "monocracy" can be effectively used to point out that when the investiture of power is autocratic, a concentrated exercise of power is correlative to it.

Chapter VIII

The Search for Proofs

"Classical political philosophers . . . were trying to describe political institutions which they considered praiseworthy . . . and they were perfectly right to do this. . . . They also wanted to give reasons for preferring one set of institutions to another, and this was correct too. . . . Where they went wrong was in looking for the wrong kind of reasons."

—T. D. Weldon†

1. Do Political Systems have Foundations?

To DEFINE is not the same as to give reasons for. One may acquire a perfect understanding of democracy without being in favor of it. Definition is not proof, and what is of paramount importance to us is the proof—the arguments that demonstrate that our thesis is true. We are thus confronted with the question: Can the truth of democracy be demonstrated?

That demonstration, not definition, is the primary concern, is shown by the fact that the major undertaking of political philosophers and of political theory has always been the search for the proof that a particular political system is true or—more accurately—good, or just. However, since all demonstrations are addressed to the mind, the argument remains a rational argument even when the focus is not, properly speaking, truth, but goodness, or justice. For, in the second case, too, what is attempted is the demonstration of what

158

true good, or true justice is. To avoid further complicating a sufficiently complicated argument I shall thus examine the issue only
in relation to the primary test—the criterion that we call "truth."

In the final analysis, we are faced with the traditional problem of
political foundations. And modern thinking has reached a stage of
sophistication in which the question, "Do political systems have
foundations?" cannot be avoided. The more so as, since the so-called
revolution in philosophy has taken place, the tendency has been to
answer unequivocally: No, there are no political foundations to be
discovered.[1] Now, if by this is meant—as Weldon has written—that
"There is nothing behind or beyond actual political institutions which
those institutions express, copy or realize," [2] I believe that the prima
facie meaning of the statement is perfectly sound. However, with
this assertion we have only rejected the Platonic approach—the hypothesis that there exists a super-world of ideal prototypes which
men attempt to copy in their world. On these grounds the refutation
is easy, but it is not conclusive, since the search for foundations
cannot be associated merely with the Platonic approach. Actually
the problem which confronts us is whether or not there are grounds
for discussing our political choices in rational terms, and for saying
that we may be right or wrong in advocating a particular political
system.

Let us therefore reformulate the question as follows: Is it possible
to give adequate or convincing reasons to demonstrate that our
arguments in favor of democracy (for instance) are correct or true,
whereas the arguments in favor of autocracy are false? And in
answering this question we must guard against saying No for the
wrong reason; namely, that man cannot be convinced by reason.
This is immaterial. We are not concerned here with the effectiveness
of reason, but with the question of whether we are entitled to search
for valid reasons to demonstrate that we have made a correct choice.
To try to prove that we cannot find any proof by using the argument
that people who hold different beliefs will not be convinced by our
demonstration is a good example of bad logic.

It must be clear from the outset that when we discuss the
question of whether democracy or any other political system has
foundations, in the sense that it can be supported by convincing

159

proof, we start with the assumption that man is a rational animal. For if he is not, or to the degree that he is not, the problem we are discussing does not arise. A non-reasoning animal will not wonder what the reasons are that make him prefer one political system to another. And if he does not wonder, it means he is already convinced without proof, for better or for worse. However, a certain number of persons, although a small number, do wonder, and do behave or try to behave like rational animals. And these people have the right to know whether or not questions like "Why is democracy better than dictatorship?" are "improper questions," as Weldon and others contend.

Being concerned with rational animals, I will employ the classic manner of stating a rational argument; that is, can we make true assertions about political systems to prove that we ought to choose (for instance) democracy? In short, "Is democracy true?" This question cannot be answered, however, unless we first distinguish between the various contexts in which the attribute "truth" is used in ordinary language. For the purpose of our discussion it will be sufficient to distinguish between three meanings of truth: its empirical meaning, its logical meaning, and its valuative meaning. There is, of course, a general meaning of "truth" that covers all these instances. In this general sense I take truth to mean—with Dewey—"warranted assertibility." Nonetheless, the kind of evidence, or the criteria of verification,[3] are different according to whether we have to deal with empirical, logical, or axiological warranted assertibility.

In the empirical sense, truth means *factual truth,* for it is determined by the existence or non-existence of the fact indicated by a statement. An empirical statement provides information and states facts about the world of our experience. Accordingly the method of verification—that is, of finding out whether it is true—is, ultimately, a "certification" based on our sense-experience.[4] Empirical truth is thus based on observation (or, more precisely, on the controlled acceptance of observed facts as real facts) and leans heavily on inductive reasoning. And an empirical theory is true to the extent that its application, that is, its working out in practice, corresponds to what the theory predicted and expected. An empirical theory

160

may also be true in point of logic, but it need not be: for it is our experience, not rules of logic, that verifies empirical truths.

In the logical or strictly rational sense, a statement or an argument is true if it is *non-contradictory*. A series of propositions is logically true when all of its assertions are congruent, and are coherently deduced from each other without break of continuity. This means that a logical argument has to be verified by seeing whether it obeys the rules of logic. It cannot be certified by observation but has to be demonstrated by deductive reasoning. (Of course, this only means that deduction prevails over induction.) A logical theory is true, then, to the extent that its arguments are coherent and exactly deduced from premise to consequence. A logical theory may also be factually true, but it need not be, for it is by having recourse to the rules of logic, not to sense-experience, that logical truths are verified. A rational truth (a logically necessary truth) is only—from the empirical point of view—a logical possibility.

Finally, in the evaluative or axiological sense we call true an assertion to which a positive *true value* (not truth-value) is being attached. We need not discuss here what makes value assertions—the act of assigning value—different from empirical and logical statements.[5] Likewise, it is open to question whether there is an adequate way of verifying axiological propositions. Let it just be pointed out that the validation of values cannot be carried on as an empirical certification or as a logical demonstration. Strictly speaking, value judgments are neither factually true nor logical-illogical but preferable.[6] When we say that liberty or equality is the true value, for instance, we actually assert that it is the value which we prefer.

This being stated, in what sense do we wish to prove that democracy is true? Empirically, logically, or axiologically? For in each case we actually ask a different question, and correlatively we have to adopt a different method of verification.

2. The Empirical Test

Let us begin by exploring the question of whether and how democracy can be proved on empirical grounds. In this context, "true democracy" is a theory of democracy whose purposes are realizable, and are indeed realized, and whose structures fulfill the tasks for which they were designed. True democracy, then, is a democracy which can successfully be put into practice and which functions as a going political system. There can be many true democracies, in the empirical sense, just as long as they pass the test that they must function and succeed in the real world. Conversely, all democracies whose practice perverts their professed goals, and whose accomplishments are very different from their declared aims, are empirically false. In definitely pragmatic terms we demonstrate the truth of democracy to the degree that—literally—*we make it true,* and we prove it to the extent that—operationally—we are able to make it work.

Yet, if we think a minute, we see that all this does not really amount to a demonstration. When I say that a true democracy is one that functions, I have not demonstrated that democracy is true. I have only indicated which definition of democracy should be adopted of those that have been proposed and are logically plausible. What I have not demonstrated is the *demonstrandum.* If I say that, empirically speaking, true democracy is the one which operates most successfully in the light of its historical accomplishments, my entire argument assumes that I have already accepted democracy. So that if one does not accept it, one can seek true autocracy in exactly the same way, asserting, for instance, that of all the possible autocratic systems, the one that achieves its aims most efficiently is the true autocracy. And it is understood that this argument too, fails to demonstrate that other political systems are not true.

Therefore, if by demonstrating democracy we mean adducing arguments in its favor and arguments against autocracy, it will not be very useful to formulate the question in empirical or pragmatic terms. Although a well-functioning democracy may provide a very convincing psychological proof, no rational conclusion can be reached on these grounds. If one is requested to demonstrate what reasons support democracy and what non-reasons weaken the other systems our search for proofs will have to be shifted into the realm of logic. For only if democracy can be supported by logical necessity, shall I be able to demonstrate democracy. But in that case the question we have to answer becomes the following: Is democracy reducible to a logical truth? Can it be explained in terms of rational truth?

3. The Rational Test

I shall use "reason" and the expression "rational test" in the strict sense, to connote a typically logical mental pattern. This is not to say that the empirical or axiological discourses are irrational, but only to say that, in these instances, the rational component has less intensity, or at any rate is not exclusive. It is, then, in the intensive and exclusive meaning of "rational test" that we shall now inquire whether democracy can be justified in rational terms, that is, whether it can be ultimately grounded, explained, and defended logically.

There is unquestionably one meaning of the expression "to rationalize democracy" that makes the operation perfectly possible. For instance, one can have a good time projecting democracies *more geometrico demonstratae*. Rousseau, but especially Morelly and Mably, engaged in something like this. One can very well sit at one's desk and imagine a democracy "without contradictions" which is perfectly able to meet the test of rational coherence and congruity. However, what is the point of such constructions? They do not demonstrate that democracy is true. They simply show how a hypothetical well-reasoned democracy could be outlined. But a democracy that might be logically true is by no means a true democracy that exists and functions. It is only a logical possibility. If we submit it to empirical certification, a democracy based on reason is precisely the one that will not meet the test, and is therefore a false democracy. And if the democracy that meets the rational requirements turns out to be a democracy that cannot exist, the net result of constructing such edifices for the sake of their logical beauty and perfection is not to make democracy convincing but just the opposite. I mean that as long as we insist on demonstrating democracy by rationalizing it, we will only have democracies that function worse and worse.[7] On the other hand, by following this line we cannot even demonstrate that democracy is superior, at least hypothetically, to other systems. In this respect we are in the same deadlock as before. Just as I can hypothesize rational democracies, my opponent is in a position to hypothesize rational autocracies that are equally logical, symmetrical and coherent. Once more the argument does not demonstrate what it was supposed to prove.

We can draw two conclusions from this. In the first place, there is no sense in discussing a political system in terms of the principle of contradiction. Asserting that a democracy is true because it is non-contradictory is as absurd as rejecting it for the opposite reason. In the second place, it is useless, if not dangerous, to try to justify democracy by rationalizing it. The very same thing can be done with autocracy, and thus we find ourselves just where we started, except that we have picked up along the way a number of additional impractical ideas.

However, there are two other queries to make in connection with the possibility of providing a rational explanation of a democratic system. We can ask whether it has a rational foundation, i.e., whether it was constructed on logically defensible and convincing premises; and, secondly, whether it pursues rational goals in a sense that will be explained later. Let us examine the first query.

As makers of history, we can copy nothing. We have to invent. The body politic is not given, it is constructed. And the foundation of our political inventions has to be traced back to a working principle, that is, the basic rule which determines their functioning. To put it more precisely, the foundation of all political systems is to be found in the procedure which is followed to settle controversies and discipline inter-personal and inter-group relationships. Society can exist insofar as there is an ultimate preordained criterion, allowing of no appeal, which is called upon to resolve its conflicts.

What is this procedural basis, or ultimate criterion, in a democracy? It is the axiom, "The people are always right." Even in its most sensible and moderate form—as expressed, for example, in William Jennings Bryan's statement, "People have a right to make their own mistakes"—the criterion that we have agreed to accept for the solution of controversies in a democratic society is that the reason of the many is always *the right reason*, by definition.

Evidently this is not a true rule, either empirically or rationally. If we try to verify it empirically observation will show how often the voice of the people is by no means the voice of God. And I willingly leave to others the task of trying to prove that the rule is logically defensible.[8] For myself, I shall merely observe that the proposition, "The people are always right," is simply the rule of the game by which we have agreed to abide because it expresses the *pactum societatis* which allows a democracy.

In fact, whoever wants to prove that democracy has rational foundations finds himself in a blind alley. That is to say that the entire rationalistic tradition seems to indicate that we cannot find a rational justification for democracy. It is no accident that in the realm of rationalistic philosophy we rarely come across theories of democracy. The rationalistic ideal, from Plato on, has been "noocracy," the aristocracy of the wise,[9] and not irrational, unreasonable, and fickle democracy. In the Platonic approach, it is not the philosopher (he who loves knowledge, *sophía*) but the *philódoxos* (he who follows opinions, *dóxai*) who can be *demóphilos,* that is, a supporter of democracy. Speaking in general, the point is that *ratio* submits to Truth and not to will, to Knowledge and not to opinion, and that its ideal is a definitive and coherent *ordo ordinatus* rather than a provisional, odd, and ever unstable *ordo ordinans*.[10] The only exception to this trend seems to have been Rousseau, a rationalist who rebelled against the *raison* of the Enlightenment.[11] But it is an apparent exception that confirms the rule, for even Rousseau's democracy is ordained to be definitive and untouchable, since it is entrusted to the certain and ever just inspiration of the general will, and not to the fallible, ever changing will of all.[12]

In saying this—let there be no misunderstanding—I do not in the least mean to suggest that autocracy meets the requisites of reason better than democracy. On the contrary, the very fact that rationalistic political philosophies have not succeeded in finding the rational foundation they have so often sought for absolutist systems, shows, if anything, that the opposite is true. Besides, we can easily demonstrate that autocracy cannot be given rational justification if we apply to it the same *reductio ad absurdum* we applied to democracy. In this case our basic principle will be: "The ruler is always right." Now we may call the democratic axiom optimistic, but, if so, what shall we call the axiom, "The ruler can never make mistakes"? Given the choice between two varieties of naïveté, it is hard to see in what way the autocratic *pactum subiectionis* is more logical and convincing than the democratic *pactum societatis*. The autocratic paradigm simply substitutes a non-rational pattern of resignation for a non-rational pattern of hopefulness. And in either case we have before us a rule of the game which defies both empirical and rational verification.

We must conclude, then, that democracy lacks rational foundations which would justify, for example, a statement like the following: He who is for reason is for democracy, whereas he who is anti-democratic does not reason. In other words, we cannot reduce democracy and its opposite to the antithesis between rationality and irrationality. We are not entitled to say, displeasing as it may be, that the rational man should believe in democracy as *the* rational political solution. (And the same applies to autocracy, of course.)

The objection will be made that the foundations of political and social systems consist in the values they embody and profess, not in the procedural rules to which they ultimately submit. I am willing to agree with this, but if this is the case we shall have to move on to the third stage, where the search for proofs becomes a discussion of values. And by requesting that democracy be demonstrated in axiological terms, we implicitly confirm that it can neither be demonstrated nor invalidated in purely logical terms, and—in general—that neither democracy nor any other political system can be, as such, reduced to a rational truth.

This is, in fact, my conviction. If we take "demonstration" in its strict, rational sense, I would not know how to demonstrate democracy any more than I would know how to demonstrate autocracy, socialism, liberalism, republicanism, or the like. Nor do I find this conclusion surprising. For, in the final analysis, democracy, autocracy and the rest are blueprints of societies in being, or societies yet to be, grounded on a basic procedural rule and sustained by value goals. By giving the old Platonic term a pragmatic twist, we could say that democracy, liberalism, autocracy, etc., are "paradigms," models that we project and laboriously seek to adapt and apply to reality. And this is why all political systems slip through our fingers when we try to seize them and to pin them down empirically or logically.

4. Cognitive Truth and Rational Advisability

The question "Is democracy preferable because its value goals are true goals?" is awkward. For there is a widespread feeling nowadays that values, or at any rate terminal values, are beyond the reach of any kind of proof.[13] It is held that values are believed rather than proved, desired rather than explained, cherished rather than justified. Although scholars tend to accept less and less the emotive theory of values[14]—the extreme view that evaluations express only emotions and feelings—and although it is maintained more and more (rightly so, I think) that reason plays an important role in value-decisions,[15] nevertheless it is a fact that we are unable to find conclusive evidence for sentences expressed in this form: Equality is the highest good—or Liberty is the supreme value.

If this is so, however, it would seem that we have come to a dead end. At the empirical level all I can do is to ascertain the correct working definition of democracy—what democracy can be in the real world. In the context of logic my argument has been chiefly concerned with showing that we get entangled in pseudo-problems. And apparently the axiological approach forces me to conclude that the argument has no conclusion, or that it cannot be pushed beyond a certain limit. This means that democracy cannot be confirmed on factual grounds, or on rational grounds, or on the grounds that democratic values are the most valid of all, since I cannot demonstrate this either.

Does the foregoing imply that our search for proofs has failed and that we must resign ourselves to silence? Or must we admit *apertis verbis,* that all political systems, as far as their foundations and worth are concerned, are more or less equally valid? No, these are not my conclusions. Quite the contrary, I believe that if we adopt such positions it is because we have missed the essential point and have not found the right approach. In fact, up to now we have observed and judged a political system in itself and not by comparing it with alternative systems; whereas it is clear that if we wish to bring forth evidence to convince others about democracy, or to make them prefer it, our problem is not one of absolute standards but a problem of confrontation. It cannot be a problem of absolute standards for we have long since abandoned them. But this does not justify our jumping to the conclusion that there are no standards at all. The only justifiable inference is that the question has to be approached differently.

167

It is rather obvious—if we come to think about it—that all we shall discover, as long as we simply look inside a single political system, is an imperfect and unsatisfactory human construction. But suppose we look outside, around us, at all state-societies taken together. In itself, democracy may well be a solution that does not satisfy the rational mind, or a system whose values have no objective priority and cannot be shown to be prevalent. But what of it? The problem of securing proofs for a political system arises, after all, because we are asked to make a choice among possible alternatives. It follows that what we really need to know is: Why choose this instead of that? And the only way to provide an answer for this query is to compare the various systems with each other.

This has been known, to be sure, for thousands of years. But the things that have always been known are often those we forget or disregard. And this is illustrated by the number of writers who nowadays more or less explicitly conclude with the "undecided proposition" [16] that they cannot warrant, or make a convincing case for democracy. This undecided conclusion, however, stems from the fact that we fail to distinguish between two very different issues, namely, the cognitive question of objective truth and the practical question of rational advisability. And if we do make the distinction, it follows that although we may not be in a position to assert, "Democracy in itself is true," we can still say very definitely, "The choice of democracy can be rationally warranted." [17]

5. The Comparative Appraisal

Let us suppose that I am asked to prove that democracy is "worth more" than autocracy, or at any rate to show why I choose a *pactum societatis* and not a *pactum subiectionis*. My first argument would be that autocracy is a much more dangerous and frightening prospect. In the axiom "The people are always right," the word people is actually a shorthand term for a long process of adjustment and compromise, that is, a decision-making process that entails innumerable internal checks; whereas the rule of a despot exposes us to a menacing and overweening *sic volo sic iubeo*. In the first case the system provides for a number of safety mechanisms and devices, whereas in the latter it offers no protection whatever. Moreover, once

I accept the principle that the ruler is always right, I agree to take a blind risk, since I do not know, and as a matter of fact it is no longer important that I know, to whom I am entrusting myself; I am giving absolute and unconditional power to an unknown quantity.

The retort to this might be that efficient and effective power is preferable to the paralysis of power that so often hampers parliamentary government; or that the more limited and less legitimate power of a single despot is less to be feared than an absolutist democracy or a "popular totalitarianism," as Barrington Moore, Jr., calls it.[18] But these arguments, I think, lack historical perspective. For in our time the One who rules alone is, and will be, neither less legitimate nor more limited in his power than the ancient tyrants and kings. He is not less legitimate because today dictatorships can easily become plebiscitary. And we cannot even console ourselves by saying of the despot, "He is but one man; there are but twelve hours in a day," because the physical limits and the other natural obstacles that prevented the tyrants of the past from wielding totalitarian power no longer exist.[19]

My second argument would be that while the solution of the problems of leadership offered by democracy may seem precarious and even paradoxical, the solution offered by autocracy is simply no solution at all. The democratic leader says: "I am their head and therefore I have to follow them"[20]—a statement which expresses both the drama and the nobility of the democratic venture. The autocrat says, or would have to say: "I have made myself your ruler and therefore you must obey me." I agree that the democratic solution, which requires that the general should follow rather than lead his army, has serious drawbacks. But what about the autocratic non-solution, that is simply entrusted to a *quia nominor leo*? Why should I submit to someone who arrogantly declares himself, by himself, the best, and the infallible?

And this leads me to suggest a third reason for preferring democracy. Democracy is open to change. In the final analysis it is a system that tests men and that can succeed in solving the problem of leadership. As Mirkine-Guetzévitch said, "Democracy is perfectible; the path from the *cacocracy* of the mediocre to *agathocracy* is always open." [21] Whereas autocracy is hardly perfectible and rapidly becomes a government based on privilege, a static and closed system with no adequate circulation of elites. I know that one can retort that the democratic selection of leaders does not seem to work out any better than the autocratic coöptation from above. I agree, because in our preoccupation with whether democracy is "true"—in the sense that it mirrors a rational prototype—we do not pay enough attention to the true democracy, the one which works and which, to begin with, succeeds in choosing its leaders. Let us face the unpleasant truth that institutions cannot do for men what men cannot do for themselves. As Plato already well knew, it is not the State that makes citizens just, but citizens that make the State just.[22] This having been granted, is it a reason for giving up hope? A life without hope is precisely what autocracy provides. And this is why I suggest, again, that democracy is preferable.

However, the most difficult part of my task has still to come, for I have not yet come to grips with the problem of values, and therefore with the fundamental objection that my arguments are persuasive only insofar as the following undemonstrated assumption is accepted: that individual freedom, personal security, and respect for human life are "good" and rank among the highest values. I shall be asked: How can you prove that?

It is often assumed that a value statement remains unverified unless we are able to demonstrate it in the form "freedom is best," (or the like). However, this is both an incongruous demand and —as I will point out in the following section—an improper test. For it is incongruous to approach the problem of values in the form "Why is freedom best?" when we are concerned not with a metaphysical but with an empirical issue, and in particular when the reason for our questioning of values is that we hold that metaphysical queries cannot be answered. If we assume, as the value relativists[23] tend to assume, that values only reflect the opinions and emotions of the people who profess them, then the question Why is freedom best? is a sort of trap-question, for it cannot be answered *ex hypothesi*. If values are a think-so, it follows that the pertinent question is: What do people think about values? And a value is validated, in the light of this assumption, if we are able to discover in man some common, basic value-attitudes and feelings.

It might seem that in accepting this approach I have only avoided the first trap to fall into a second. For it so happens—I might be told —that different people partake of different value-feelings at different times and places; in short, that history is a cemetery of values as well as a storehouse of the most conflicting values. But this evidence is, I am afraid, obtained improperly, that is, by questioning people with questions that pass above their heads. If we are addressing a congress of philosophers, it is all right to draw up an articulate map of values, to arrange it in a logical and hierarchical order, and to wonder how this order of priorities can be justified. But it is definitely incongruous to use this philosophical map as a questionnaire for the public at large; whereas this is how we have been handling the affair and have discovered that the world of values is not a cosmos but a chaos. But is the chaos there, or have we (the observers) created it? I take the latter view, for we are bound to obtain chaotic answers if—under the assumption that values are the feelings shared by a community—we forget that we have to look precisely for value feelings, that is, something as basic, simple, and inarticulate as our hypothesis requires.

Accordingly, the undemonstrated assumption of my argument cannot, and should not, be tested in the sophisticated form of a (metaphysical) statement like "freedom is best," but in the light of the following elementary (and therefore appropriate) question: Do human beings in general share some common feelings about some basic values which would be best protected and would be best expressed by a democratic political form? We may ask, for instance: Are there people who prefer uncertainty as to whether they will still be alive tomorrow to the assurance that they will, or who prefer prison to home, or the arbitrary deprivation of liberty and torture to due process of law? I grant that many people throughout the world will not even grasp the sense of these questions. However, if someone who has never tasted liberty and the protection of the law and has lived all his life an animal life is not able to answer, or answers at random, it does not mean that he does not want the values in question. Clearly it is not that he prefers death, prison, and torture, but that he has been living beneath the level of values and does not know that his destiny could be any different. In effect, despite the plurality of value systems as perceived at the sophisticated level of intellectual analysis, there is ample evidence from the very beginning of time that once men have begun to enjoy the values of respect for human life and for the dignity of the individual person, their reaction has always been the same, namely, to prize these values.

So, even if we wish to argue from the extreme position of the emotive theory of values, there are grounds for asserting that whenever people realize that democracy is the device which best protects their life and freedom (with all that this implies), they are emotionally affected and swayed in favor of it. It is not my task here to plead the case for democracy. I only wish to show that if we know how to avoid the wrong questions and tests, it is quite possible to justify our preference for democracy on the basis of a comparative value appraisal. That political paradigms have, ultimately, an axiological foundation does not mean that we must shut ourselves in a shell of inexpressible and indefensible value choices, and thereby have nothing to oppose to the conclusion that all ethico-political ideals are of equal worth.[24] As Leo Strauss puts it, "If we cannot decide which of two mountains whose peaks are hidden by clouds is higher than the other, cannot we decide that a mountain is higher than a molehill?"[25]

6. The Microscope Fallacy

Having indicated the kind of evidence I consider adequate to prove or disprove the validity of a political system, and therefore of political choices, I am prepared to meet the criticism that my test cannot be accepted because it is not sufficiently rigorous. And this raises the question: How much precision is required for warranted assertibility, that is, for a warranted use of the word "truth"?

The answer depends, of course, on the subject matter. It is one thing to deal with an object-world, or a thing-world; it is another one to deal with a referent that is the symbolic world of man. The distinction is too obvious to be worth dwelling on. But it is worthwhile to observe that not even the physical world is measured by a

172

single gauge, since different levels and fields of investigation have different yardsticks. Euclidean geometry is perfectly adequate for architects, while curve geometry is required for dealing with cosmic space; and it would be absurd to say that curve geometry must replace Euclidean geometry because of its higher degree of accuracy, when all an architect has to do is design a building. Likewise—to mention other elementary examples—for someone using a microscope a millimeter is so big a unit that it is useless, whereas a kilometer is perfectly adequate for terrestrial measurement, and light years are suitable for measuring cosmic space, even though they may involve mistakes of millions of kilometers. Yet there would be no sense in saying that unless the distance between the sun and the earth is measured in millimeters, the measurement is scientifically invalid.

But if we turn our attention to the social sciences, we sometimes get the impression that in our anxiety to keep up with the physical sciences we have lost a sense of the proper proportion between the measurer and what is being measured. Thus, it would not be hard to find someone who would just love, if it were possible, to examine the surface of the moon with a magnifying glass even though his only purpose were to draw a map of it. In fact, some social scientists want to be so scientific that they give the impression that if they came across an elephant they would call for a microscope before they were willing to declare what animal it was. This is what I call the "microscope fallacy," meaning that it is a fallacy to think that every level of analysis requires the same precision of measurement, and that the absolute unit of measure is the one that is the smallest, as if, for example, the millimeter were in all instances preferable to the kilometer. In my view this is a misconception of how the natural and physical sciences are conducted, as well as a misconception of how our minds work. To put it more precisely, we are pursuing the ideal of an improbable unified science through an erroneous reductivist epistemology.

In the social sciences, and also in political science, reductivism is expressed by the idea that political macro-analysis can and should be, whenever possible, reduced to micro-analysis. The "group theory of politics" can be taken as an illustration of this approach.[26] Of course, there is nothing wrong in the group focus. The mistake of reducing all political reality to an interplay among groups lies only in the belief that micro-analysis can replace macro-analysis; whereas, on the contrary, we need both, and both are of like importance. That is to say that the error lies in thinking that political society as a whole can be regarded as a cluster of face-to-face groups, and that what we mean, e.g., by the expression "American democracy" can be explained simply in terms of face-to-face relationships or of similar micro-frameworks.[27]

The reductivist way of proceeding is tempting, but it does not sufficiently take into account the way the mind works, that is its inability to keep up with the transformations which are involved; for when we have arrived at the (micro) *terminus ad quem* we have entirely lost sight of the (macro) *terminus a quo*. It is not possible to make a whole intelligible by reducing it to its most elementary units, and then by re-combining component parts which have been previously cut back to the very bone. In the re-combined whole the bones will be there all right, but the flesh will be missing. In other words, to think that micro-analysis, if magnified, can arrive at, or can convey, the same idea expressed by macro-analysis, is an assumption that may be valid for a divine super-mind, not for a human mind. We humans have to proceed in a much more rudimentary and fractional fashion if we want to understand the material we are dealing with; that is, we must work in stratographs. At every level of a given subject-matter we grasp a certain aspect of the problem we are examining; and when we change level, we apprehend another aspect, i.e., we envisage another problem. The cluster of problems which is indicated by the term "State," for instance, is different from the cluster of problems indicated by the expression "the governmental process," and we are only deluding ourselves if we think that in speaking of the latter we are also explaining the former.

These observations are intended to call attention to the fact that there is as little sense in employing for general political theory (macro-analysis) the kind of tests that have been devised for micro-analysis as there is in using a magnifying glass to ascertain if a house is a house. It follows from this that I cannot accept the objection that the comparative method of appraisal cannot prove anything—that is, that it cannot warrant political preferences because it is not a precise method. By the same token we could argue that we need a telescope if we really want to see a person standing opposite us on the other side of the road.

In fact, when we say that the defect of macro-analysis is its low standard of evidence, and that the virtue of micro-analysis is its high standard of evidence, we are making an unwarranted statement, for in speaking of "defect" and "low" we are implying a comparison which is unjustified and misleading. In order to speak of high and low standards of evidence we have to assume the existence of an absolute standard for measuring evidence. Now, not only does no such absolute standard exist, but furthermore it is a mistake to think that it ought to exist and that it would be useful to find it. For the adequacy of a standard of evidence depends solely on its pertinence, i.e., on the existence of proper proportions between the method of measurement and what is being measured. What escapes those who bewail the absence of an absolute standard is that the problem of precision is a problem of inner consistency between the test and what is being tested. This is so true that the probability and frequency of error—regarding the predictive aspect of a theory—is not necessarily higher in macro-analysis than in micro-analysis, except in the sense that the micro-analysts who just assemble facts avoid predictive errors by avoiding predictions.

Therefore, my conclusion is that political systems pose a problem of choice; that choice presupposes comparison between better and worse (not between good and true, or bad and false in the absolute sense); and that it is quite possible to achieve a degree of precision that is adequate for the purposes of this comparison. Hence it is perfectly possible to justify, and (in this sense) demonstrate a preference. Political choices do allow a rational argument. If the opposite is maintained, it is because the nature of the problem under discussion has not been made clear. The problem is not to determine whether or not democracy is factually true, or whether or not it has rational foundations, but whether warranted advisability can be attained in evaluating political alternatives. And since the term "truth" applies to any warranted assertibility, I contend that there is one perfectly legitimate sense in which we are entitled to say that democracy is true. Our search for proofs is not doomed to failure just so long as we know what we want to prove and the way to prove it, and as long as we are not the victims of the microscope complex.

NOTES

† *The Vocabulary of Politics* (London, 1953), pp. 43-44.

1. For an orientation on this "new philosophical attitude," cf. the collection ·ed. by Peter Laslett, *Philosophy, Politics and Society* (Oxford, 1956), and esp. Weldon's brilliant contribution, "Political Principles." However, the basic work which is discussed in this chapter with reference to the problem of political foundations is Weldon's *The Vocabulary of Politics*.

2. *The Vocabulary of Politics*, p. 36.

3. Note that I do not use "verification" and "verifiability" in the technical sense employed in analytical philosophy, which is beyond this context. On the technical meaning (and also for critical views), cf. the essays collected in *Revue internationale de philosophie*, III-IV (1951), dealing with the "Notion de Vérification," with notable contributions from Ryle, Feigl, Pap, Warnock, Aron, and others.

4. Verification can be used either in a strict sense (when applied only to experimental science and to empirical statements), or in the broad etymological sense according to which *veri-ficare* means the process of discovering whether what is being asserted is *verum* (true) in reference to any statement whatever. I use "verification" in the latter, general meaning. For the strict empirical meaning I employ "certification" (*certum* in its difference from *verum*).

5. Actually it is not at all clear yet whether the general class of propositions with evaluative words (such as attitude statements, imperatives, and commendations, ethical or other) should be broken down as was done when the distinction between empirical and logical (analytical) statements was discovered. My own feeling is that too many heterogeneous things are being thrown into the category "axiology." For a preliminary assessment and some constructive suggestions on the subject, cf. John Wilson, *Language and the Pursuit of Truth* (Cambridge, 1958), pp. 65-70 and Chap. II.

6. Of course, there are instances when a value statement can be empirically true (when it reports correctly the actual value beliefs of the people to whom they are referred), and in some sense value-preferences can also be contradictory (as when a person holds at the same time two value goals that are mutually exclusive). However, this does not settle the problem of how the criteria for assigning value can be verified. Values can be verified empirically and logically to the extent that we consider them as the "things preferred," but not as "principles of preference."

7. Cf. my criticism of the rationalistic blend of democracy in Chaps. III, 5 and esp. XI, 3.

8. Cf. Thurman Arnold's pungent remark that democracy means that "it is better for a government to do foolish things which can have popular support than wise things which arouse people against it." *The Folklore of Capitalism* (New Haven, 1937), pp. 44-45.

9. Cf. the well-known passage in Plato's *Republic:* "Until philosophers are kings, or the kings and princes of this world have the spirit and power of philosophy, and political greatness and wisdom meet in one . . . cities will never have rest from their evils" (473), *The Dialogues of Plato,* trans. B. Jowett (New York, 1937). See Bks. V and VI of the *Republic, passim.*

10. A. R. M. Murray's *An Introduction to Political Philosophy* (London, 1953) renders the connections between rationalistic philosophy and authoritarian conceptions much closer, and explains it by going as far back as the theory of knowledge which he believes to be presupposed by rationalism. Nevertheless the Kantian criterion used by Murray to separate rationalism from philosophic empiricism seems debatable, historically speaking, and the relations he demonstrates appear far-fetched. To me the coincidence between rationalism and autocratic propensities on the one hand, and between empiricism and democratic inclinations on the other, is actually very loose, and may only be traced back to mental patterns. My views therefore do not coincide with those stated by Murray. In particular, I do not maintain that an empirical philosophy is a determining factor in the choice of a democratic end, but that, if we pursue that end, then an empirical mentality will better succeed in the application. Cf. Chap. XI, below.

11. Cf. R. Derathé, *Le Rationalisme de J. J. Rousseau* (Paris, 1948). An extreme interpretation is given by Cassirer: "This apparent irrationalist ends with a most resolute faith in reason," "Das Problem Jean Jacques Rousseau" (1932), in Italian transl. (Firenze, 1938), p. 66.

12. Cf. Chap. XIII, 4, below.

13. Herbert Simon writes in a current text: "There is no way in which the correctness of ethical propositions can be empirically or rationally tested" (*Administrative Behavior* [New York, 1954], p. 46). In another classic work, *Politics, Economics and Welfare,* Dahl and Lindblom make the premise: "We do not attempt a demonstration of the ultimate 'rightness' of the values we use as criteria" (p. 25), clearly implying that the rightness of values cannot be demonstrated. For the *status quaestionis,* cf. the review by Adrienne Koch, "The Status of Values and Democratic Political Theory," *Ethics,* (April 1958), pp. 166-185; and also Arnold Brecht, *Political Theory* (Princeton, 1959), pp. 9-14 *et passim.*

14. For this extreme position cf. A. J. Ayer, *Language, Truth and Logic,* 2nd ed. (London, 1946), Chap. VI, and the Introduction, pp. 20-22. For a general

treatment of the subject cf. *Readings in Ethical Theory*, eds. W. Sellars and J. Hospers (New York, 1952), Part V, "The Emotive Theory." Cf. also Arthur Pap, *Elements of Analytic Philosophy* (New York, 1949), Chap. II.

15. For the new emphasis on the role of reason in axiology within logical positivism (or logical empiricism) itself, cf. E. Maynard Adams, "Empirical Verifiability Theory of Factual Meaning and Axiological Truth" in *The Language of Value*, ed. Ray Lepley (New York, 1957), p. 94 f.

16. I have in mind Felix Kaufmann's terminology, according to which a proposition that is neither (empirically) valid nor counter-valid is "undecided." Cf. *Methodology of the Social Sciences* (New York, 1958), p. 66.

17. As H. R. G. Greaves sensibly points out, "There is certainly a stage at which it is pointless to ask further questions or demand more reasons, but in the process of reaching that stage we may expect to find common ground with others in making our appraisals, and this common ground is of great importance." *The Foundations of Political Theory* (London, 1958), p. 35.

18. Cf. *Political Power and Social Theory*, pp. 80 f. The label is well chosen; Moore's thesis, however, is less convincing because the hypothesis of a decentralized and diffused system of repression is hardly conceivable without centralized wire-pulling.

19. Naturally the statement has no absolute value. Cf. on this point the reservations of Karl W. Deutsch in *Totalitarianism*, pp. 308-333, where the problem is approached from the angle of the theory of communication and control. Still the development of electronic machines and cybernetics seems to overcome many of Deutsch's objections, and I fear that we cannot count much on the eventuality that the totalitarian dictator will end up by being overpowered by an "overload" of the chain of command.

20. The origin of the phrase is uncertain. Simmel attributed it to a German. In Italy it was used by the socialist leader Turati. As far as I know, the first to pronounce it was the French radical politician Ledru-Rollin, the father of universal suffrage.

21. In *Scritti in onore di L. Sturzo* (Bologna, 1953), Vol. II, p. 563.

22. Cf. *Republic*, IV, esp. 435.

23. The expression "value relativism" is here by necessity used in a vague manner. For an extensive analysis of its various meanings, cf. Arnold Brecht, *Political Theory, passim*.

24. Although only few political scientists and theorists would openly underwrite this extreme form of value relativism, the degree to which a corresponding state of mind exists in practice, has been aptly underscored by David Easton in *The Political System*, Chap. 1, from the angle of what he calls "decline into historicism." "In the past," Easton points out, "theory was a vehicle whereby articulate and intelligent individuals . . . offered for

serious consideration some ideas about the desirable course of events" (p. 234), whereas present-day students of political theory "have been learning what others have said and meant; they have not been approaching this material with the purpose of learning how to express and clarify their own values" (p. 236).

25. *What is Political Philosophy?* (Glencoe, 1959), p. 23.

26. Cf. A. F. Bentley's pioneer work *The Process of Government* (1908) and David B. Truman, *The Governmental Process* (New York, 1951). For a synthetic presentation see Earl Lathan, "The Group Basis of Politics: Notes for a Theory," *American Political Science Review,* II (1952).

27. The remark may be generalized beyond the strict limits of the group theory of politics, since a considerable number of present-day American social scientists do not seem to be sufficiently aware of the fact that microanalysis is not suited for more general employment, and that small group phenomena cannot be magnified to explain the process and operations of large and complex units.

Chapter IX

Inconclusions

*"We are much too obsessed by the
twentieth century to speculate about
the twenty-first."*

—Raymond Aron†

1. Theory and Philosophy, Politics and Ethics

AT THIS STAGE it might be useful to consider some of the issues
that underlie the problems we are examining. I shall start with the
following two questions. First, should my theory, as it has been developed so far, be understood as a philosophical theory? Secondly,
should the normative element of political theory on which I have
laid so much emphasis be regarded as an ethical concern? I shall
begin with the latter query.

If I were asked what the relationship is between politics and
ethics, my reply would be that I have not tried to answer this question. However, it is advisable to explain why, chiefly in order to
eliminate possible misconceptions. Let this be clear: when we talk
about the normative aspect of politics we are not necessarily talking
about moral prescriptions. Since all norms are not ethical norms, using the form *ought* does not automatically place us in the sphere of
ethics. And it is my contention that if the "good *society*" is the value
or end that we are pursuing, then we are dealing with political, not
ethical norms, for what is in question here is above all the best kind
of community life, and not our inner moral integrity.

180

Naturally, the distinction between political and moral prescriptions (like that between juridical and moral laws) depends on how we define morality. Thus the distinction tends to disappear as soon as we talk of "social morality" or "political morality" in the same way that the boundary between law and ethics vanishes as soon as we find it proper to speak of juridical morality. However, I can see no advantage in going back to the monolithic vision of life, in which there is a fusion of the public and private spheres, and at the same time of the realms of religion, ethics, and politics, as has been the tendency ever since Hegel in his notion of *Sittlichkeit* suggested the idea of a supreme, all-embracing morality. By this I do not mean that the social dimension of moral experience is not a constituent element of it. But Kant's ethics and his categorical imperatives are enough to warn us how misleading and superfluous the qualification "social" is. It is superfluous because it is pleonastic, and it is confusing because it implies an antithesis that does not exist, since selfish ethics or ethics that is indifferent to others is inconceivable.

Perhaps I can make my point clear by recalling a distinction made by Max Weber, a writer who is more familiar than Kant to political scientists and theorists. Weber distinguishes between *Gesinnungsethik* and *Verantwortungsethik,* between an ethic based on principles which we pursue regardless of consequences, and an ethic based on consequences, on our responsibility for the results of our actions.[1] In my view this is indeed a valuable distinction, but not as a distinction between two kinds of morality. For there is only one ethics, only the *Gesinnungsethik.* When we are faced with the *Verantwortung,* that is, the problem of consequences, we are entering another sphere in which we have to deal with the problem of how we should behave as political, and not *solely* as moral animals: I mean, as individuals living in a *polis,* and not solely in themselves. The Weberian creation of a second kind of morality only leads to two unfortunate results: draining politics completely of almost all axiological content (as bad realism does), and overloading ethics with spurious ingredients which confuse its distinctive features and suffocate what is peculiar to it.

I therefore take the view, with Kant, that ethics has to do with good will or good conscience, and that it concerns an inner experience

181

which leads us to perform "disinterested actions," [2] and not actions that are calculated with a view to their useful consequences. It is not that calculation of consequences should not occur, but it should occur *afterwards*—after we have perceived what our moral behavior should be—when other questions present themselves. Hence my approach can be summarized as follows: (i) that politics cannot be understood in purely non-axiological and non-normative terms; (ii) that political ideals and values, however, have to be dealt with as being *political,* not ethical, in nature; (iii) that consequently both political moralism and political cynicism are mistaken positions, the former because it stems from a premature merging of the political with the moral realm, and the latter because it is the result of an unjustified schism between them. Politics and ethics are neither identical nor separated from each other in watertight compartments. And the difficult question of their relationship becomes insoluble if we approach it from points that are too remote, as we do when we reduce politics to nothing but hard facts and needs, and place *all values,* by definition, in the moral sphere.[3] I believe that if we want to understand how ethics and politics communicate, we have to compare comparable elements, that is, political values with ethical values. But this is an argument which is outside the scope of my study, and I must therefore leave it as a suggestion for further consideration.

My second question, namely, whether "philosophy" of democracy would not be a more proper label for this study than "theory" of democracy, raises the problem of what I mean by theory, and also, implicitly, of how I understand the relationship between political philosophy and political science.[4]

My answer to the first part of the question is that I use "theory" in its usual sense, to mean, as Brecht writes, "propositions that try to explain something." [5] I would also follow Brecht in emphasizing the fact that today "political philosophy, political theory and political science are no longer interchangeable terms." [6] Of course, even a mere factual description in some sense provides an explanation, inasmuch as it attempts to explain how things happen, or have happened, in a particular situation. However, the fact that we can legitimately use the word "explanation" even in the latter case does not mean that we cannot draw a line between the how and the why of things. Here, then, I am concerned with theory in the precise sense of an explanation which leads to theory construction. But to make my notion of "theory" clearer, I shall try to outline briefly its relation, on the one hand, to the type of theory called philosophy, and on the other, to the type of theory called science.

The relationship between political philosophy and political science is indeed complicated and controversial. For it is not possible to answer conclusively, as Catlin and others do, by saying that political science deals with means, while political philosophy deals with ends;[7] or, correlatively, that the former only reports on values, whereas the latter evaluates values.[8] Once we have granted that science is concerned mainly with how and the means, and philosophy mainly with why and the ends, this more-or-less kind of explanation does not settle conclusively the question of where philosophy ends and science begins. Nor can the borderline be determined on the basis that philosophy is a second order talk, whereas science is a first order discourse. This, again, is a prima facie distinction.[9] And I believe even less in the distinction which holds that philosophy tries to explain everything while science tries to explain only something. This, no doubt, is often true, but it only scratches the surface of the problem.[10]

Finally, I do not believe in the least in all the distinctions which are based on the premise that political philosophy is a branch of moral philosophy designed to evaluate political practices and goals from the ethical standpoint. This is altogether inexact, and illustrates how often we make the mistake of treating every *ought* as if it were a moral prescription. For although it is true that most philosophers are concerned with what the State ought to be, it is not true that they propose to moralize the State. On the contrary, they have frequently tried to show that this is not possible. Thus—going back to the main point—to define philosophy as anything involving a discussion of values, and science as the discourse which avoids the discussion of values, is not a convincing solution. On the contrary, it makes philosophy too broad and science too narrow,[11] and makes the *Wertfreiheit* issue too important at the expense of other equally important issues.[12]

What complicates our task is not so much that political science is not a homogeneous field, as that philosophy is very heterogeneous.

183

For in the latter respect we actually have to deal with radically different species—empirical and non-empirical philosophy.[13] It follows that a line of demarcation which may be valid if we are considering empirical philosophy, will not be valid any more when we are referring to an idealist philosophy, and vice versa. For instance, my theory can be pushed up to the philosophical heaven or dragged down to the scientific earth, depending on the level of abstraction which is deemed to be the philosophical level. Where a highly abstract idealistic philosophy prevails, I could hardly be considered a philosopher at all, while the opposite might be held where empirical philosophy is dominant. That is to say that whereas in my country I tend to be regarded as a political scientist, my guess is that in the United States many political scientists would be inclined to send me back to where my countrymen do not think I belong, i.e., to the jurisdiction of political philosophy.

As one can easily infer from this example, the *status quaestionis* is indeed puzzling, and largely undecided. For the purposes of the present discussion it will suffice to make clear in which situations it is important to distinguish between what is political philosophy and what it is not, and in which cases the distinction is only of secondary importance. To give an instance of the first case, let us assume that our knowledge of politics has come from a study of Hegel or of the left-wing Hegelians, including Marx, or of the political writings of Giovanni Gentile and Benedetto Croce (to mention the philosophers who have been most influential in Italy). In this case, the following warning is not only relevant but necessary: you know political philosophy, but *only* political philosophy. For we have not acquired any practical know-how, any skill that enables us to deal with actual policy-making and policy planning. It is always worthwhile to read Hegel, but not if we want to deal with empirical problems, and certainly not if we have an operational purpose. In other words, this is a case where political philosophy is strictly separated not only from political science, but also from any empirical theory of politics whatsoever.

Let us take instead the case where our knowledge of politics is related to a pragmatic philosophy, which is more concerned with the *mundus sensibilis* than with the *mundus intelligibilis*. And more

184

precisely let us refer to the present Anglo-American trend of reducing philosophy to little more than epistemology of science or a second-order talk. In this case, demanding a closer relationship between philosophy and science is mostly a way of deploring hyperfactualism and research for the sake of research, fact-finding with no problems. I can well understand, therefore, the recommendation that one hears from time to time in the United States to the effect that the gap between philosophy and science should be bridged, and that what is needed is a more philosophical political science. But let me point out that this recommendation takes on a completely different meaning when the referent is no longer an empirical kind of philosophy but the other kind, the philosophy that proclaims itself *scientia scientiarum* and claims that the only true science is philosophy. From this point of view the aforesaid exhortation becomes very confusing, and I wonder whether it would not be better to avoid this very loose and vague use of "philosophy."

Again, in the case of an empirical approach to philosophy, one may well use the labels "political theory" and "political philosophy" interchangeably. Yet, even in this case I believe that it would be useful to be more specific. For when someone says "political philosophy" it would be correct to understand that he is not interested in any operational, or applied, kind of theoretical inquiry. Whereas if someone says "political theory" and purposely avoids saying "philosophy," he probably means that his theory construction is concerned with practical consequences and does have an operational purpose (although not in the narrow sense given to the term in micro-analysis). Clearly, this makes for quite a difference. And it is also for this reason that I prefer to say that I am dealing with democratic "theory" and not with the philosophy of democratic government.[16]

2. Logical Analysis and Historical Appraisal

Although I do not wish to engage further in the general discussion of the theory-or-philosophy argument, it will be pertinent to consider a specific issue, namely to what extent my theory can be equated with what the Oxford School calls philosophy. For this purpose let us ask whether it is, as Weldon holds, "the purpose of philosophy . . . to expose and elucidate linguistic muddles;"[17] or

185

whether the purpose of political theory and/or philosophy is, as Ayer maintains, "to exhibit the logic of the statements which characteristically figure in discourse about politics." [18] My answer tends to be Yes, up to a certain point, but *not only,* from the point where Ayer's statement ends.

So far I have undertaken a task which is in some respects amenable to the approach followed by Ayer or by Weldon. My main purpose has been to enucleate the logical pattern underlying most discussions about democracy, and to seek appropriate ways for finding the correct answers. This is the angle from which I have examined the Scylla of realism and the Charybdis of perfectionism, or the ostensible paradox of a power granted to the majority by a minority leadership, or the error of seeking democracy where it cannot be found, etc. From the same viewpoint and with the same purpose, I have discussed the problem of defining democracy in the sense of tracing its boundaries, as well as the question of whether we should abandon the claim that political preferences are defensible. These are all issues that concern a rational animal. They have been fostered by logical thinking, and therefore must be solved logically. And I am assuming that they cover the most frequent misconceptions about democracy.

This does not mean that there are no gaps in my list. There are no doubt other statements that characteristically figure in political discourse whose underlying logic has not been taken into account in the preceding pages. Omissions are inevitable. But I believe that what I have presented is already an adequate selection of the fundamental themes. So, if I agreed wholesale with Ayer and others about the purpose of political theory (or political philosophy), my task would be accomplished and this chapter would be the conclusion. However, I feel that the task assigned to political theorists by these writers is only preliminary, and consequently that only preliminary conclusions, if any, can be drawn at this stage.

Although logic is necessary, it is not sufficient. A logical analysis of democracy can offer, at most, a clean shell, a framework ready for use but completely empty. This achievement is not to be belittled. But if we wish to fill out our framework and to give a concrete *content* to our idea of democracy, we must go further and look at history. And this is why a historical appraisal will follow the logical or methodological analysis which I am now terminating.

To be sure, the division of the book into a logical and a historical inquiry is not a rigid one. The problems that I have discussed up to this point have had to do chiefly, but not solely, with logical and methodological muddles. The problems which will be raised in the following section are chiefly, but not solely, related to historical experience. Much of what has already been said is based implicitly on historical evidence, just as a great deal of what I am going to say also involves logical elaboration. Therefore the difference between the two parts of the book is one of emphasis. Nevertheless, we are so often confronted, nowadays, with unfinished business, that I have found it useful to devote a separate section to what tends to be more and more neglected, that is, to the historical dimension of our problems. But let there be no misunderstanding about my interest in historical information. I shall be concerned with the presentness of the past, not with its pastness. And as the present is not only, as Leibniz said, *issu du passé* but also *gros de l'avenir,* that is, not only issued from the past but also pregnant with the future, I wish to look first at our own time to see what it forecasts about our future.

3. Old Knowledge and New Future

It may be felt that in the foregoing chapters some of the most typical features of present-day political life have not been duly weighed. For instance, I have only touched on the party system, or rather on democracy as a party system,[19] and furthermore I have not even mentioned the growth of a countervailing pressure-group system (if I may call it so).[20] Also I have paid little attention to developments within the party system itself, such as the transformation of loosely-knit parties based on consensus of opinion into highly organized and bureaucratized mass parties, with all that this implies. However, these developments and new features would be relevant to my outlook only to the extent that they affected the logic of the statements which are basic to political discourse. And this, in my opinion, is not the case. This is not to deny the importance of the question of "party-cracy" (*partitocrazia*) and its bearing on the functioning of parliamentary government, as well as on other aspects of democracy. But these questions are not necessarily pertinent to my approach.

What I have in mind when I speak of looking more closely into the present is therefore something which is, at the same time, less definite and more all-embracing. It is a widespread feeling that we are now at a turning-point of history. Does this mean that the problems we are now faced with are so new that we are unable to cope with them on the basis of our past or even our present-day knowledge? This query is relevant in that it may cause some perplexity as to what will be the future value of the topics that we are discussing. Assuming that they encompass the main facets of democracy as we have known it up to now, will posterity regard them as being important any longer? Let me just reply that, for the time being, no evidence supports that perplexity, at least in its extreme formulation: that our future will be so radically different from our past, that looking backwards to former times—i.e., to previous experience—will be useless.

It could easily be shown that the world we live in has nothing in common with the world of Aristotle, Machiavelli, Locke, Montesquieu, or even of Tocqueville. Yet if we take the time to read these classics, we find that, despite the distance that separates them from us, they provide us with invaluable historical insight, and that good thinking remains profitable and useful thinking, for the very plain reason that it *is* good thinking. Aristotle's comments on the egalitarian reforms of Phales the Calcedonian would have been illuminating for Marx, if he had read Aristotle instead of only Hegel; and they are still relevant to what is going on in Soviet Russia. I could give many similar examples, for in politics there are issues which remain unchanged under the most changing conditions. And it is the task of political theory to deal with precisely such issues. So the perplexity raised by "political futurism," if I may call it that, should not alarm us.

In this connection I should like to go back to the question of whether the classical theory of democracy has become outdated, since we have outgrown the conditions that it presupposed. Although there is some truth in this argument, I myself take a more cautious view. In fact, what I have been trying to show is that what changes in the

188

lifetime of a political system is not the ideals, or the normative theory, but the way of adapting them to reality. A reappraisal of the value-fact relationship shows that we need not reject the original value goals of democratic deontology. What is more, we *cannot*, for a democracy that rejects its own deontology denies itself. I believe, therefore, that the problem is not the creation of a new normative theory, but its intermediary readjustment in accordance with the gradually decreasing distance separating the ideal from its possible realization and with the changing needs of different epochs. It is true that democratic idealism, as expressed in the classical theory, at a certain point claims more than can actually be achieved in reality, thereby jeopardizing the entire system. But if political idealism is so often suicidal, this is chiefly because it is much easier to know how to handle ideals negatively than positively.

In sum, my contention is that what needs restatement is primarily the relationship between norms and facts, for it is this that badly needs to be assessed. Of course, in revising our view of this relationship we also indirectly modify the classical theory. However, modifying it does not mean dismissing it, and my feeling is that it should be readjusted but not rejected. For what we lack is the ability to use and apply the normative theory of democracy—that is, what its classic framework amounts to—in a positive and constructive way.[21]

I hope that these introductory remarks make clear that my reaction against "political futurism" does not mean that I think we can ignore change, or that we should not consider the possibility of the future's being radically different from the present. The issues which are at stake in any given time and place change with changing conditions, and therefore the relative weight and importance of politics itself might have to be assessed differently in the world of tomorrow. And this last hypothesis deserves attention.

4. Politics and Economics

As far as I can see, nothing unforeseen is in the offing as far as the political form of human societies is concerned. Autocracy, or better, totalitarian autocracy, may take over, but that is not new, even though new technological means of oppression give a modern cast and an unprecedented impact to this oldest and most primitive sys-

189

tem of domination. What is new, instead, is the economic form of our societies, in the broadest sense of the expression.

In the last hundred years we have all become more and more economic-minded. And in the last few decades, if not in this last decade, the industrial-technological revolution has indeed reached a turning-point. In the "industrial society" [22] economic output is no longer absorbed by demographic growth; it has leaped, or can leap, far ahead of it. As Galbraith puts it, a civilization of plenty replaces a system of "organized scarcity." [23] And this changes all our perspectives. "In an economy of growth," Raymond Aron writes, "the problem of distribution takes on a meaning that is totally different from the one it has had for centuries. General wealth used to seem an almost fixed quantity . . . if some one had too much, it meant that it had been taken away from someone else. But when the wealth of the collectivity steadily grows each year by a certain per cent, the rhythm and speed of the increase is more important than the problem of redistribution, even for the non-privileged." [24]

The relevance of this argument to politics is easy to see, at least in terms of a logical extrapolation. For the sake of simplicity let us put it this way. On one side we have a cake, and on the other side we have the problem of *who* cuts it *how*. The size of the cake is the concern of economics, the cutting—i.e., the distribution—is the concern of politics. If the ratio between the size of the cake and the number of eaters remains about the same, then the political problem of how it should be divided is the major problem, or at least the only one which may have different solutions. But if we can easily supply more cakes, or a bigger one, then the economic problem of making a larger cake supplants the political problem of who is to have the greater share. Of course the question is not quite as easy as that. But this simplification will suffice to illustrate the prediction that politics will be less important in the world of tomorrow, at least as far as ideological tensions of the Marxist kind (class struggle, etc.) are concerned. In the long run, everybody will have to become aware of the fact that what matters most is, by far, the size of the cake. As Aron points out, it is already true that "the three themes of Socialist doctrine—private property versus public property, anarchic market

190

versus planned market, capitalist exploitation versus equality—have to a large extent lost their appeal." [25]

The question then arises as to whether a new kind of political discourse will follow as a result of the situation described as the "industrial society." If I understand Aron's argument, his answer would tend to be: No, on the contrary there will only be less political discourse. If so, I am quite satisfied by this answer, as it implies that our new future will not be new, that is, not very different from the present, as far as the problems considered by political theory are concerned. And this is what I was interested in finding out.

Nonetheless, it is worthwhile to examine the implication of the main trends of the industrial age, and particularly to explore what is likely to be the impact of technological industrialization, of a *civilisation technicienne,* on the incumbent mood of our era. And in this connection it is useful to state more definitely the limits of the concept of industrial society, to the extent that it is presented in the form of a world-wide prediction.

5. Industrial Society or Industrial Democracy?

Let us first deal with the repercussions of the industrial society on ideological conflicts and strains. According to Aron and others, the present phase of industrialization is destined to bring about a relaxation of ideological tensions. Is this "end of ideology" really probable? [26] In my opinion this is a short-range conjecture which is strictly limited in space and time. It is limited in space because the only reconciled societies are, or will be, those whose productivity greatly anticipates their demographic growth. And it is temporally limited because Marxism is not necessarily the last of the ideologies, and we must not confuse the decline of a certain type of ideology with the disappearance of ideology as such.

There was a time when people all over Europe used to say *felix Austria,* happy Austria. Had the term ideology been in existence, a clever eighteenth-century observer of the period preceding the French Revolution might have predicted that the age of ideology had passed. The prediction would have been correct to some degree, in that the religious wars between Catholics and Protestants had actually come

191

to an end. However, new religious wars were in the making. It was not to be long before the ideology of nationality (not yet nationalism) was to tear to pieces the prosperous, peaceful, well-administered, admirably conceived and constructed Hapsburg Empire. Then, all in one century, came nationalism and Marxism, and today we are also confronted by a combination of the two, by national-Marxism. How can we delude ourselves with the notion that ideologies, as such, have run their course? If we labor under this delusion, I am afraid that a future historian will be able to refer to a *felix America,* or to a "happy Europe," in a highly ironic sense.

We must distinguish between the genus and the species, that is, between ideology as a conceptual category and its historical expressions like, today, Marxism and nationalism. And there is no reason to forecast that even these historically conditioned ideologies are likely to decline outside the restricted circle of the prosperous industrial democracies of the West, since in Russia an increasing nationalism is taking the place of a decreasing Marxism, and since in the underdeveloped countries the high tide of nationalism and political messianism is still to come. Nor, on the other hand, must we be too optimistic about the long-term duration of industrial peace in the priviliged industrial democracies. It is quite true that an industrial society which is looking forward to an era of plenty, and whose major problem is no longer *labor*—in the original meaning of effort, fatigue, pain—but leisure, is not very vulnerable to the onslaughts of extremism. However, we should not assume that the first reaction to the plentiful life will be the reaction of the generations who will have become accustomed to it. Perfectionism and disillusionment may develop at any stage of economic prosperity (actually they only rise in the wake of economic development, not at the lower stages of deprivation), and the "great emptiness" [27] of an age of leisure is bound to create new rebels, new protest attitudes and other still unforeseen difficulties. [28] For leisure permits us to store energy which we do not know where to expend. In the Middle Ages a similar situation occurred when holidays were almost as frequent as working days; except that free time and work were intimately related, and that, at any rate, leisure time was taken up with religious practices. But what about today? And let us not forget in this connection that superstition

192

and ideological *Ersatz* thrive precisely when religious creeds decline.

Finally, we cannot exclude the possibility that the rhythm of growth required by an industrial society will be slowed down by an increasing distributive and consumer appetite, i.e., that the solidarity required by the system on behalf of its own requirements will be disrupted by the unleashing of individual demands, in which case economic expansion would no longer absorb and counterbalance ideological tensions. Therefore, no world-wide or long-range predictions can be made about the withering away of ideologies as such.[29]

There is another and even more important question, namely whether industrial societies will be, or can be, democratic societies. But here again I do not believe that it is possible to make a generalization applicable to the whole world. For it is necessary to differentiate between economic and political forecasts. It seems likely that all countries without exception are destined to become industrial societies. But that does not mean that they will necessarily become industrial democracies.[30]

It is not at all certain that the common factor of industrialization will bring the various political forms closer. On the contrary, it may well be that industrial necessity—I mean the imperative requirements of industrialization—will bring about a definitive cleavage between societies that are already industrialized and can therefore permit themselves the luxury of democracy, and those that are not yet industrialized and cannot permit themselves that luxury. And the latter hypothesis is certainly as likely as the former. We must not forget that, according to the theory in question, in an industrial society a democracy can be consolidated only if the increase in the size of the cake greatly exceeds the increase in the number of eaters. Whereas the prospect before us is an age of overpopulation, in which demographic growth outdistances industrial progress in vast areas of the world.[31]

This means that only industrial democracies that are already industrialized and already democratic can be given a favorable political prognosis. For the rest of the world the advent of industrial society may well imply, instead, forced industrialization to be paid for by a radical reduction of consumption. And this is exactly what cannot be obtained by democratic procedures which require the consent of the popular will. Therefore it is quite likely that throughout the world industrial dictatorships and not democracies will prevail. Let us face it: in terms of the industrial approach, the outlook for industrial democracies is rather dim. What seems to be in store for the Western industrial democracies is complete encirclement by powerful industrial dictatorships of the communist or nationalist type.

However, I myself do not take such a pessimistic view for three reasons. The first is that it is the privilege of intelligence to foresee events that are too logically patterned to actually happen. That is to say that we must be wary of expecting men to respond to their environment according to a rational pattern; the "pictures in our heads"—to use Lippman's image—may not correspond in any sensible way to the "world outside." [32] The second reason is that the time factor must be carefully weighed, for what happens here and now may not happen elsewhere for a hundred years and, because of this time difference, may never happen at all. However, the prospect is still not encouraging. Actually, if I have reason to hope for a less catastrophic future for democracy it is mainly for a third reason: namely, that I do not accept the underlying assumption of the whole argument—that history will have to be viewed increasingly from the economic angle and understood more and more in economic terms. This amounts to saying that if industrial democracy has a chance of surviving, it is because it is a democracy, and not because it is industrial—that is, because of political and ethical reasons, not economic reasons.

6. A Plea for More Theory

I have engaged in a discussion of industrial society with an eye to this question: What is likely to be the impact of a *civilisation technicienne* on political concerns, and thereby on political theory in general and on democratic theory in particular? I am ready to admit that in the context of the industrial society there will be more economic and less political discourse. An era which is increasingly economically conscious will probably tend to neglect the political form in favor of the economic form of society. But the fact that this is very possible does not make it less unfortunate. Indeed, the prospect that decreasing attention will be paid to political problems makes it all the more necessary to call attention to them. Predictions are not made to induce in us a mood of resignation to our fate or to help us in betting for the winning side. Predictions, rather, are made to warn us of the dangers that lie ahead and to show us how to counteract them in time. And this is why I wish to plead the case for more political concern and to argue against the delusive assumption that political problems can be solved by economic means.

Let us again take up the question of ideology. I am perfectly willing to agree that the technological phase of industrial growth can cure the ills, and especially the traumatic tensions, produced by the first stage of industrialization. But economic medicines can cure only economic disorders, and I do not in the least believe that all spiritual ills come from the same virus. The consequence, ideology, is much vaster and proteiform than the cause, economy. In the second place, and in particular, it is rash to explain ideologies merely in terms of "material causes." Actually, ideologies come from subjective no less than from objective sources, from mental deprivations no less than from material deprivations. As Eric Hoffer vividly reminds us, "The effectiveness of a doctrine does not come from its meaning but from its certitude. . . . Crude absurdities, trivial nonsense, and sublime truths are equally potent in readying people for self-sacrifice if they are accepted as the sole, eternal truth." [33] From this angle men cling to some doctrine because they need to believe, because they need some absolute certainty. And the more we approach an overly mundane conception of life, the more our need to pursue some absolute goal may take on a politico-ideological form.

It follows from this that if we want to keep ideologies within their proper limits the primary rule remains that we must fight them on their own ground, that is, confronting myth with reason, credulity with credibility, dogmas with knowledge. I confess that I am always astonished when I hear it said that the only way to combat communism is to introduce reforms and to improve the standard of living. This is like advising one to build a dike in the middle of the sea, forgetting that no dike would hold if there were no land above sea level. Economic reforms and welfare may check the spread of Marxist ideology (i) in terms of intensity, or tension level, and (ii) to the extent that it encompasses what Cantril would call a "politics

195

of despair." [34] However, there are plenty of non-intense communists, and despair can always be replaced by a more moderate protest-attitude without affecting one's party affiliation in the least. And the relative character of social and economic protest should warn us that the economic therapy, in itself, can hardly be effective.[35] I am not saying that reforms are useless, but that they will not meet the challenge of communism unless adequate attention is paid *pari passu* to the political dimension, and especially to the ideocratic background of the problem.

Politically speaking, the spread of the ideology of communism is, nowadays, an organizational phenomenon. A communist party in its mature stage—such as the Italian P.C.[36]—operates as a State within the State, a Church within the Church, and even as a "closed commercial State." This organizational network creates a sort of isolation belt which provides for all the necessary "communication stoppers," if I may call them that. This amounts to saying that the communication problem is just as serious as the economic problem, and that a political class which can only think of economic means of fighting the appeals of communism may only end up doing the right thing (reforms) in the wrong way and for the wrong reasons, thereby combining bad economics and bad politics.

But I am not concerned here with the dikes—whether merely economic or political as well—but with reminding that our dike-building frenzy too often makes us forget about the solid earth. For what actually contains the expansion of the ideology of communism is the fact that historical materialism and the Marxist-Leninist doctrine do not meet the test of rational and empirical verification. I grant that this may not be sufficient. Nonetheless, if it were not for the fundamental fact that communism cannot be accepted by sound thinking and knowledge, we would not be here in a position to say so. If we were only economic animals, then democracy would soon give way under the pressure of the have-nots. It is because we are also capable of being mental and thinking animals that we may wish to preserve democracy. But then, if a have-not ideology is not to prevail, it is the responsibility of knowledge, as it always has been, to limit its proliferation. Intellectual inadequacy can only be cured by mental means, and the first remedy for poor reasoning is correct reasoning. If we overlook this fact and believe that this is no longer a primary concern, we are lost. And this is my first reason for making a plea for more political theory.

My last remark raises the very general question, What is politics? Admittedly, politics is not ethics. Granted this, we cannot deny that there is an inextricable deontological element in it, an *ought*. And the political imperative, as I have tried to show all along, is not only a technical imperative concerned with the proper means for reaching a desired end, but is in itself an end aimed at the political good life. That is to say that politics is not only a question of "Who cuts the cake in what way"; and that politics cannot be reduced to the mere problem of "Who gets what, when, how."

To reduce politics to a problem of "getting" is indeed strangely primitive for a sophisticated civilization like ours. What do we get, tangibly, from freedom? Nothing, or, in crude economic terms, only the freedom to starve. Yet freedom has been what people have most cherished and sought throughout the whole history of the West. It may well be that we could "get more," economically speaking, from a well-regimented industrial dictatorship. But are goods all that we want from life? However naïve this answer may seem, I do not think so. Of course, if we keep repeating over and over again that in the final analysis the problem of politics is simply how to make "mine" what is "his," we shall end by convincing our audience that it is so. Since man does not have a nature in the naturalistic sense, but, as Ortega y Gasset's felicitous phrase runs, "is what he thinks he is," it is perfectly possible to make him into nothing but an economic animal.[37] In this case, however, neither democracy nor a free society is possible. For if men ask society—or the State—for more than they are willing to give, only a despotic system can hold together a collectivity in which each member is seeking only profit for himself.

In this perspective the advent of industrial society on a world scale should serve as a last alarm signal. For it tells us that the time when the history of the West was also the history of the world has gone, and, further, that the time when Western supremacy could be guaranteed by its technological knowledge and its economic-industrial potential is also past. Let us be frank. As far as economic and technological skill go, we have little left to export. If anything, we

197

have taught others so well that we may have to go to our ex-pupils for instruction. If the West still has a good deal to say and to teach it is in the realm of its politico-ethical civility. For we have been toiling over the creation of the good life, and have been experimenting with the techniques of liberty for twenty-five hundred years. In this respect the rest of the world is in its infancy, having hardly emerged, if at all, from resigned acceptance of the inevitability of despotism.

Our democracy is the outcome of a long process of trial and error aimed at creating a political form which can assure a tolerably secure life for every human being. And this heritage of ours is unique. Let us not lightly destroy it by reducing politics to economics, ideals to instincts and ethics to nothing.[38] This road leads to suicide, and I, personally, have no intention of taking it. My suggestion instead is: why not start, or at least try, to sell less goods and more sound ideals and ideas?

Consequently I shall not concern myself further with either industrial society, or industrial democracy. Granted that the industrial society is, or will be, the stimulus, the response may or may not be a democratic political form. And the outcome will depend more on our ability to steer history in one direction or another than on the allegedly fatal consequences of the physical environment. It is the aim of political theory to remind us of this, and therefore democratic theory can best be served if we speak of democracy per se. For if we concern ourselves with the industrial society at the expense of the democratic society, democracy will succumb. An "industrial man" who is nothing but a consumer-animal will exchange the good life for the comfortable life, and in the long run will lose both.

The notion of industrial society and of industrial democracy is questionable from another point of view as well. For it limits our horizon to the most advanced democracies which are in the most favorable economic situation, whereas we must not forget that the democratic world is larger than the industrial world and that the non-democratic world is larger still. Now, one of our chief concerns is precisely who is going to win the "third world" over. So if we do not want the democratic slice to become smaller and smaller, we must not focus the argument, somewhat parochially, on the optimum case. In principle, theory should try to embrace the retarded as well as the advanced societies, the embryonic as well as the mature democracies.

It may be that in attempting to encompass too much my generalizing will displease both ends of the democratic arc, the most advanced as well as the most primitive. But it is important for the stable democracies with no problems to know about those that have problems. On the other hand, the unstable or potential democracies need a theory which, even though somewhat advanced, is nevertheless within reach of their needs. The clock of history does not move and is not timed everywhere at the same pace. In some places an industrial society is well under way, but in most of the world it is only a distant prospect, at present beyond reach. So, for the purpose of a "general theory," the clock will have to be somewhat slowed down. We have tried to anticipate the future. Let us try now to move with the present at a pace suited to all.

NOTES

† *La Societé industrielle et la guerre* (Paris, 1959), p. 3.

1. Cf. *Politik als Beruf,* 2nd ed. (München, 1926), pp. 55 f.

2. Naturally, disinterested is meant in the Kantian sense of actions which have no economic or utilitarian motivation. Bentley's use of the term "interest" (which is followed by David Truman, Blaisdell, and a number of behavioral political scientists) is entirely different, as interest is understood as a synonym of motivation. In this meaning Kant's "disinterested actions" become meaningless, for they would be "actions without motivation," i.e., inaction. The latter stipulation makes it impossible, in fact, to characterize moral behavior.

3. In this way, and if we divest political behavior as such of any value content we are led to Reinhold Niebuhr's drastic alternative between "moral man and immoral society." Evidently there is a point at which we must choose, and it is quite certain that the alternative between ethics and politics may indeed present itself in an acute, dramatic way. However, in my approach the alternative is not so drastic. The moral man is not only moral, and the political society is not necessarily immoral.

4. I assume thereby that political *philosophy* on the one hand, and political *science* on the other are the extreme points of the continuum "the study of politics," and that political *theory* proper lies somewhere in between. It is understood that both philosophy and science are "theories": but when the

identification of a theory as definitely philosophic or as definitely empirico-scientific is precise, it seems expedient to use theory in an uncommitted sense. This framework has the advantage of the utmost simplicity coupled with historiographic fitness. As for the term *doctrine* I only use it when the overriding purpose and outlook of a political philosophy or theory is to advocate a policy (either conservative or revolutionary). The thesis which unfailingly reduces political philosophy to political doctrine is vitiated by a scientistic bias, and obscures the basic fact that political philosophy and theory do comprehend a cognitive finality (even if sought by methods which may be regarded as unscientific). The cognitive purpose may be defeated by some other hidden purpose. This does not alter the fact that philosophy (or theory) is not, qua philosophy (or qua theory), a doctrine: at most, it can *also* be a doctrine.

5. *Political Theory, The Foundations of Twentieth Century Political Thought,* p. 501; cf. also pp. 501-503, 14-17, *et passim.*

6. *Political Theory,* p. 17. I would disagree, instead, with two other points made by Brecht. First, "that philosophy, insofar as it tries to explain phenomena, is theory, and insofar as it applies scientific methods is science" (p. 16). This is only confusing. Second, if it is true—as Brecht asserts—that "political 'theory,' when opposed to political 'philosophy' now is usually meant to refer to *scientific* theory only" (p. 17), then I find this statement in contradiction with the previous one that political theory and political science "are no longer interchangeable terms." I would say, instead, that political theory as opposed to political philosophy, indicates that the former is empirical whereas the latter is speculative (or at a higher level of abstraction).

7. Cf., e.g., George G. Catlin, *The Science and Method of Politics* (New York, 1927), pp. 347-348, and his article "The Function of Political Science," *Western Political Quarterly,* IV (Dec. 1956). This is, in the final analysis, the approach of Max Weber. My remark is in no way intended to imply that the distinction is not useful: in fact it is indispensable. It does not constitute, however, an adequate, final criterion of demarcation.

8. The two arguments are linked because the Weberian distinction between science of means as opposed to assessment of ends is motivated by the preoccupation of constructing a value-free science.

9. Cf. T. D. Weldon: "It is not the job of philosophy to provide new information. . . . Philosophical problems are entirely second-order problems. They are problems, that is, which are generated by the language in which facts are described and explained." (*Philosophy, Politics and Society,* p. 22.) In my lectures *Questioni di metodo in scienza politica* (Firenze, 1959), pp. 5-68, I take the related but different view that the distinction between "empirical use" (*perceptum*) and "ultra-empirical use" (*conceptum*) of language permits a satisfying determination of the borderline between the

200

empirico-scientific and the philosophical discourse. To return to Weldon's point of departure, perhaps it would be well to clarify that natural science is a first-order talk, that all social and historical sciences are already a second-order talk, so that philosophy is (when empirical) a third-order, or otherwise a fourth-order talk. What matters, of course, is not whether the steps to be considered are four, or more, or less (which will depend on the degree of precision required) but that we perceive clearly that we must distinguish between various levels of abstraction of language, and correlatively the different purposes which require and justify them.

10. Leo Strauss, among others, states: "Philosophy . . . is quest for universal knowledge, for the knowledge of the whole. . . . It is . . . the attempt to replace opinions about the whole by knowledge of the whole. Instead of 'the whole' the philosophers also say 'all things.' " (*What Is Political Philosophy?* p. 11.) I agree, but if we put it in this fashion we have not spelled out a criterion. Besides, we must not forget that science too pursues the goal of arriving at the knowledge of all things, even if the striving towards a "unified science" may (and I believe is bound to) fail.

11. Making philosophy too wide and science too narrow (and sterilized) because, if we take a strict view of the *Wertfreiheit* requirement, then also a very great slice of political science would have to be classified a posteriori as philosophy. Dwight Waldo, among others, has aptly pointed out (i) that language embodies, qua language, preferences; (ii) that the process of acculturation includes the inculcation of basic value attitudes; (iii) that life experience itself prepares us to perceive or not perceive according to a value-alertness. (Cf. "Values in Political Science" in *Approaches to the Study of Politics,* pp. 96-111). On the basis of these antecedents, one is brought to wonder up to what point the social sciences themselves may avoid the accusation of being inevitably value-biased. Naturally, as Jean Meynaud judiciously affirms, "To ascertain the inevitable limits of scientific objectivity and to claim the right to express value judgments are two different positions." *Introduction à la science politique* (Paris, 1959), p. 15.

12. In my essay "Der Begriff der 'Wertfreiheit' in der politischen Wissenschaft" (*Politische Vierteljahresschrift,* I [1960], pp. 12-22), I stress that a science is not a science simply because it is value-free, but primarily because of (i) an adequate vocabulary, and (ii) a consistent application of logical and methodological rules. For a more radical criticism (with which I do not concur) see Gunnar Myrdal, *Value in Social Theory—A Selection,* ed. P. Streeten (London, 1958), *passim.*

13. Not to mention the difference between the classical and the post-classical philosophy that has been well spelled out by Leo Strauss. Cf. *What is Political Philosophy?* esp. pp. 27-29, 74-77, 78 f. My remarks apply only to modern philosophy, that is to say, from when the classical foundations were covered up.

14. In my own vocabulary Hegel's *Philosophie des Rechts* is a fourth-order talk, whereas an empirical political philosophy (Dewey's for instance) would be a third-order talk.

15. Cf. in *American Political Science Review*, II (1950), Francis G. Wilson (p. 384) and Thomas J. Cook (p. 388); *ibid.*, IV (1951), J. Roland Pennok, "Political Science and Political Philosophy," pp. 1081-1085; *ibid.*, II (1956), H. Eckstein, "Political Theory and the Study of Politics: A Report," pp. 475-487; and W. H. Harbold and D. G. Hitchner, "Some Reflections on Method in the Study of Politics," *Western Political Quarterly*, IV (1958). On the same line, cf. finally Peter Winch, *The Idea of a Social Science and Its Relation to Philosophy* (London, 1958).

16. Whatever may be the worth of the framework outlined above, the point is that in the present fluid and controversial situation the heading "theory" permits an escape from the paralysis (or at least the complexes of timidity) inherent in quantitativism, hyper-factualism and value-phobia, without requiring that we have recourse to a fourth-order talk.

17. In *Philosophy to Politics and Society*, p. 23.

18. Foreword to Weldon's *Vocabulary of Politics*.

19. But on this point cf. Chap. XI, 4, below.

20. See G. Sartori, "Gruppi di pressione o gruppi di interesse?" in the symposium *Contributi italiani al IV congresso mondiale di scienze politiche* (Milano, 1959), pp. 94-129.

21. Cf. Chaps. IV, V, and esp. Chap. VI, 7, above.

22. We may also speak of "post-industrial" society (cf. David Riesman, "Leisure and Work in Post-Industrial Society," in *Mass Leisure,* eds. E. Larrabee and R. Meyersohn [Glencoe, 1958], pp. 363-385), and (why not?) also of "automation society." These labels, however, anticipate on the average, in the sense that they put into focus an advanced case such as the case of the United States.

23. Cf. J. Kenneth Galbraith, *The Affluent Society* (Boston, 1958), *passim*.

24. Cf. R. Aron, G. Kennan, R. Oppenheimer, *et al., Colloques de Rheinfelden* (Paris, 1960), p. 12.

25. *Ibid.*, p. 13.

26. In addition to the aforementioned *Colloques de Rheinfelden,* cf. also: Edward Shils, "The End of Ideology?" *Encounter,* Nov. 1955; Daniel Bell, *The End of Ideology: On the Exhaustion of Political Ideas in the Fifties* (Glencoe, 1960); and S. M. Lipset, *The Political Man,* Chap. XIII.

27. Cf. Robert M. MacIver, *The Pursuit of Happiness* (New York, 1955), Chap. VI.

28. Cf. *Mass Leisure, passim*. Many contributors emphasize the seriousness of the problem of what to do when we have nothing to do. For a rapid synthesis see also Georges Friedmann, "Le Loisir et la civilisation technicienne," *Revue internationale des sciences sociales*, IV (1960), and the articles which follow on the sociology of leisure (pp. 551-630). Friedmann distinguishes according to analogous preoccupations between *temps liberée* and *temps libre*, meaning by the latter the positive exploitation of the "freed time."

29. That the phrase "the end of ideology" applies strictly to the West, whereas in the East and the third world the process is taking place in the opposite sense, is stressed opportunely by Daniel Bell, *The End of Ideology*.

30. Let it be understood that I do not use "industrial democracy" in the same sense as the Webbs do—to say that workers should run their own industrial plants—but refer the political form 'democracy" to the industrial age. On the theories of the Fabian movement and on the achievements of the workers' management of industry, cf. H. A. Clegg, *A New Approach to Industrial Democracy* (Oxford, 1960).

31. Per capita food consumption in many parts of Asia and Latin America is lower today than it was twenty years ago; in some places, even lower than in 1914. And this precisely because the rise in production does not keep pace with the rise in population.

32. Cf. W. Lippmann, *Public Opinion*, Chap. I.

33. Eric Hoffer, *The True Believer, Thoughts on the Nature of Mass Movements* (New York, 1951) Part Three, Chap. XIII, Sect. 57.

34. Cf. Hadley Cantril, *The Politics of Despair* (New York, 1958). The implication of what I am saying above is, however, that Cantril overstates the angle of despair and overlooks, for instance, the fact that a communist party is a perfect instance of the political "organizational man."

35. Even assuming, in so saying, that there is a necessary correlation between communism and poverty, which is not the case. Gabriel Almond, among others, has well shown that poverty is only one of the causes of communist allegiance. Cf. *The Appeals of Communism* (Princeton, 1954), esp. p. 83 f. One need only glance at the electoral maps on the distribution of the communist votes in Italy in G. Braga, *Il Comunismo fra gli italiani* (Milano, 1956) to see that the communists are very strong in aeras with a high standard of living and relatively weak in many depressed zones.

36. The case of the PCI (*Partito Comunista Italiano*) deserves to be cited and is the one to be studied with most attention because it is the strongest and best organized communist party in the West, not only with respect to the number of members (about 2,000,000) but also regarding the quality of its bureaucracy and leadership. Cf. Aldo Garosci, "The Italian Communist

Party," in Mario Einaudi, J. M. Domenach, and A. Garosci, *Communism in Western Europe* (Ithaca, 1951), and Braga's *Il Comunismo fra gli italiani.* For the more recent figures see Cantril's *The Politics of Despair,* pp. 4-10. Despite the impressive rise in prosperity, the communist vote from 1948 to 1960 (the last administrative general election) tends, if anything, to grow. Prosperity has lowered the tension ratio, but not the allegiance. It should be added that it is very likely that the left-wing Italian Socialist party would lose a considerable number of votes in favor of the communist party if it disavowed the "class unity" slogan. Thus the potential pro-communist vote in Italy is comparatively much higher than in France and could easily rise, one may guess, to 30 per cent of the total vote.

37. Ortega y Gasset has written some fascinating pages on the "non-substantiality" of the so-called nature of man. Cf. esp. *Historia como sistema* (Madrid, 1941), VII.

38. See in this connection Eric Voegelin's denunciation of the "Gnostic cliché." His words on this subject are harsh, but not unjustifiable. Cf. *The New Science of Politics* (Chicago, 1952), pp. 129-131 *et passim.*

Part Two

The Evidence
A Historical Appraisal

"What is past is prologue."
—Shakespeare, *The Tempest,* II, 1

"The actual facts are what I wish to describe, and it seems as if nothing could be simpler, for they are all around us. But the facts are obscured to most people by the half-assimilated ideas and sonorous or seductive phrases that fill the air; and few realize exactly what are the realities beneath the phrases."
—James Bryce, *Modern Democracies,* New York, 1924, I, Preface, viii

Chapter X

What Is Democracy?
The Truth-Value of Definitions

*"Our search for enlightenment has met
with more emptiness than content, and
in sum we know that an infinity of things
our parents believed true are false, and
we know very few truths which they did
not know."*

—Galiani†

1. Are Definitions Arbitrary?

ANSWERING the question, What is democracy? amounts to giving a definition of the word democracy.[1] The next question is: What is a definition? According to John Stuart Mill, "The simplest and most correct notion of a definition is a proposition declaratory of the meaning of a word, namely, either the meaning which it bears in common acceptation, or that which the speaker or writer . . . intends to annex to it."[2] Mill did not attach much importance to the difference between the meaning specifically given to a word by the speaker or writer, and its common meaning. But today some philosophers do. They make a clear-cut distinction between a stipulative definition and a lexical or lexicographical definition.[3] In the former case the speaker announces: I propose to use this word in this sense, and this is *my* definition of it. This, being my own "deliberate,

207

arbitrary, self-conscious choice of a name for a certain thing," [4] is a stipulation. In the latter case the speaker reports how a word is generally used, that is, what people usually mean when they use it. This, being the kind of definition that dictionaries are supposed to give, is called lexicographical (i.e., written in lexicons).

Nobody will deny that there is a difference between these two cases. Even Mill was aware of this. And thus it is relevant to ask why the difference did not seem as important in his time as it does now. The answer is that, on the one hand, it pleases us to stress the conventional nature, and also the arbitrary character, of language; whereas, on the other hand, we are trying to escape from the ultimate implications of this approach.

The distinction between lexical and stipulative definitions leads to this further distinction: lexical definitions may be true or false, depending on whether the report on how a word is commonly used is accurate or inaccurate, while stipulative definitions—as Maurice Cranston writes—"cannot be divided into the true and the false. *They are arbitrary.* You can stipulate that 'black' shall mean white, for example, by pointing to a patch of snow and saying, 'Whenever I say "black" I mean this colour.'" [5] If in saying "can," one is using the verb in the sense of "anything can happen," or as in the sentence, "I can commit suicide," the example would be merely trite. But the conventionalists do not mean only that. They maintain that this procedure is perfectly legitimate so long as two conditions are observed: (i) that the stipulation be explicitly stated; and (ii) that the stipulator always use, e.g., the word "black" in the same way.

This does not explain, however, how listeners are to respond when they see white and someone says "black." The Oxford philosophers meet the question by suggesting that we are entitled to approve or disapprove of a stipulation on the basis of its utility. In other words, although stipulations cannot be divided into true and false, they can be divided into useful and muddling. At first sight this criterion seems to work. Thus if we take again the example given by Cranston the problem is immediately solved, since everyone will probably agree that to say black when everyone else says white is merely confusing. But the only reason this example does not raise difficulties is because nothing is really at stake when we talk about colors. When we discuss politics, however, it is a very different matter; and I am afraid that in this context very few issues, if any, will be solved by saying that a certain stipulation is muddling.

In his pungent essay, *Politics and the English Language,* George Orwell pointed out that "the great enemy of clear language is insincerity" and that there is therefore a "special connection between politics and the debasement of language." Ordinary political language is insincere language, for it is less an instrument for expressing thought than a means "for concealing or preventing thought." [6] Actually, except in the case of some intellectuals, political discourse is more often than not either a device for achieving and maintaining power, or a device for stimulating action. And I fear that political double talk, or even double think, is not only inevitable but even acceptable within certain limits, since one cannot rouse an audience to action simply by cold reasoning. I do not wish to sound cynical. I am only trying to point out the special difficulties that a student of politics is bound to encounter. For he has to work in a field where it may be considered useful to becloud problems, and definitely not useful to clarify them. Indeed, an important part of politics may be described as the art of confusing political issues (and this is not necessarily the wicked part). So, in connection with the "utility test" suggested by the Oxford philosophers, a scholar will have to ask: What is the definition of "useful" in this context? Useful for whom? Useful from what angle?

Of course these questions can be answered, and most scholars do act as if they knew what the answer is. But the answer cannot be arrived at if the question is formulated in the conventionalistic manner; namely, What is a useful definition of "useful"? For a merely practical criterion—that is, a non-cognitive criterion—opens the way to an endless regression. For instance, if someone were to say that political science is useful for political practice, and that in practical politics it is useful to muddle political problems, I do not see how Cranston and the others could object. That is, I do not see how they can prevent their criterion from working in reverse, from inviting confusion because it is useful. Thus if definitions could not be divided into true and false and if they were only arbitrary stipulations, the problem of defining democracy would have to be formulated as follows: Anyone is entitled to stipulate that democracy means whatever seems to be useful from the stipulator's viewpoint. And it would become an insoluble problem.[7]

It is apparent, then, that if we adopt the approach that has grown out of the so-called revolution in philosophy, we shall have to confirm Treitschke's prediction that logic would become democracy's worst enemy. Someone may retort at this point that I have forgotten that only stipulative definitions are arbitrary, and that there are still the lexical ones. But I will answer that falling back on dictionary definitions is of no help.

Following the procedure indicated by Cranston, let us begin by taking a group of dictionaries. If I consult enough of them I shall discover that democracy means so many different things to different people that I shall have to conclude that it has contradictory meanings. What is the next step? If I wish to be safe and remain on the solid ground of the true-false criterion there is no next step. My inquiry will end with a report like the following: Democracy means to the Russians what autocracy means to the West and vice versa. Is this conclusion acceptable? If it is, then there can be no democratic theory. In fact, it is useless to think. All we have to do is to take a census of what people are taught to believe, and produce statistics and percentages which will enable us to determine the winning majority.

So we shall probably decide to adopt a stipulative definition. In this case, however, we shall be offering a definition having no truth-value, i.e., whose value is "arbitrary,"[8] and we shall be able to defend it only on the grounds of its utility. But to someone whose goals are different from mine it may be useful to say: By democracy I mean a system in which everybody obeys a single ruler, without question. And thus we are back where we started. For if this stipulation is opposed to mine, both definitions can only be viewed, according to this approach, as private conventions. And, again, accepting such a conclusion is tantamount to saying that the question of who is wrong and who is right can only be decided by statistics and, ultimately, by force of arms. Whoever is on the side of those who conquer the world will have told the truth. For at this moment all the dictionaries will define democracy according to the victor's definition, and in this way one of the stipulations will become true! *Quia nominor leo* because I am named Lion.

Clearly, we are in trouble. And in order to get out of it we will have to reconsider the whole question from the beginning by asking: what is the truth-value of definitions? And, in particular, how valuable can our definition of democracy be? No theory of democracy can be formulated, I believe, unless this question is settled. I will therefore have to deal with the conventionalist's approach in detail.

2. A Distinction with no Difference

To clear the way, it will be useful to show that the distinction between lexical and stipulative definitions is only confusing—first, because it does not hold good; secondly, because it creates superfluous complications; thirdly, because it distorts our understanding of the actual process of thinking and defining.

To show how fragile the distinction is, all we have to ask is: whence do dictionaries derive the meaning of words? That is, what kind of definition is the lexicographical? Obviously dictionaries are only inventories of stipulations that have been generally adopted. What we find in lexicons are still stipulations. The only difference is that whereas a lexical definition refers to old conventions, a stipulative definition may suggest a new one proposed for future observance. However, in both cases we are dealing with conventions. Thus, if stipulative definitions are arbitrary, then so are lexicographical definitions. It follows that to grant that dictionary definitions can be true or false is begging the question, for only our report as to how certain people actually use a certain word may be true or false, not the definition itself, which remains a stipulation and is therefore to be adopted or rejected only on the basis of utility.

It may be argued that there are other differences between lexical and stipulative definitions. First of all this difference: while the lexical definition is not normative (it does not say that the term democracy, for instance, ought to be used in a certain way), the stipulative definition is legislative or normative since it tells us how the term should or should not be understood. But this is not true. I can easily pro-

211

vide myself with an "ought definition" by following the lexicographical path of using standard authors as authorities. And I can equally
well propose a stipulative definition that is purely descriptive. The
fact that I am profferring it for future observance does not mean that
it is prescriptive. Therefore, if we want to discuss whether a definition
of democracy is supposed to state the rules according to which the
term *is* used, or *ought* to be used, we are dealing with a separate
problem which is usually solved by saying *is* when we agree with
general usage, and *ought* when we do not. Be this as it may, the
is-ought criterion does not correspond to the lexical-stipulative criterion.

It may be suggested, however, that a difference between the two
kinds of definitions can be found in the fact that the lexical one is
impersonal—a we-answer—whereas the stipulative one is subjective—
an I-answer. Yet, this difference is only apparent. Taken at its face
value, what I say is always and only what *I* say, that is, all definitions
are "I-definitions." But if what I say has any value at all, it must
be more than an I-definition, no matter what its verbal formulation is.
So, for the purpose of deciding whether a definition is valid or not,
there is no point in determining whether I am speaking in impersonal
terms, i.e., relying on the authority of others, or whether "I" openly
takes the place of "we," i.e., I am speaking on my own authority. In
any case, it would be perfectly easy to conceal the "I" under the
mantle of a *pluralis majestatis,* but it would not change things in the
least.

The difference, then, between lexical and stipulative definitions is
so irrelevant that it is not worthwhile making a point of it. There
is only one kind of definition, the stipulative; and this kind of definition can only be divided into old and new linguistic conventions.
If we take the conventionalistic position, we must be consistent; we
cannot stop halfway. We cannot maintain that only stipulative definitions are arbitrary. Dictionaries will not help us escape the conclusion
that all definitions are arbitrary.

And this conclusion cannot be mitigated by maintaining that a
lexicographical definition is less arbitrary than a stipulative one. This
last line of defense hinges on the argument that the area of arbitrariness is limited for the former by the need for some common under-

standing and by the requirements of public discourse, while there is no such limit for stipulations since they refer only to our private area of *liberum arbitrium*. However, if this thesis appears convincing it is only because the term stipulation grossly overstates the case. Of course, if people are encouraged to be eccentric[9] by being told that it is perfectly all right to call a dog "cat," or vice versa, just so long as the stipulation is made clear, then I grant that stipulations will differ widely from lexical definitions. So much so that we shall be able to communicate only with the help of old, and none other than old, dictionaries. However, this has not been the case up to now. And in order to understand how we actually behave in these matters, it will be useful to make clear what really happens when we declare: I propose to attach this meaning to this word.

The label "stipulation," is meant to stress the element of innovation—as well as of arbitrary freedom[10]—in definition. According to R. Robinson, "In stipulation we freely make any word mean anything we choose."[11] But this is a distorted report of the actual proceedings. Actually innovation is very rare and is certainly not our main concern. What we usually do is to make a choice among the existing meanings of a word. That is to say, our chief purpose is to reduce ambiguity. If we happen to end up with a new meaning, it is only because we have to say something for which there seems to be no word already in existence. In any case, our so-called stipulations are based on thoughtful and careful reasoning. Furthermore, it is not at all true that in the rare cases where we are impelled to redefine a term we fail to take into account the need for common understanding. How, then, is a stipulative meaning any more arbitrary than a dictionary meaning?

The truth is that the distinction between the two types of definition cannot be defended even on these grounds. Our thinking takes the form of a continuum in which we begin by consulting dictionaries or by reading the definitions of others, and end by making a choice. And if we have to decide what point in this process is the most arbitrary, I am inclined to say that it is more likely to be at the beginning than at the end. So not even in this moderate form does the distinction seem valuable. Once again, if we wish to take the conventionalistic approach, we have to carry it through to the end.

3. Criticism of Conventionalism

Having cleared the way, we can now state the issue in a simple query: Is it true that, within an established language, the meaning of words is *only* a matter of convention so that we must conclude that definitions are neither true nor false but arbitrary stipulations? The issue is, ultimately, what test we are to adopt for accepting a definition. Let it be clear from the outset that we are not concerned with the origins of speech. How the first meaningful utterance appeared—that is, how a certain meaning became associated with a certain articulate sound—is both obscure and immaterial. Even assuming that language originates from random and arbitrary emission of vocalizations and that therefore convention was the basis of language for *Homo Neanderthalensis*, the point is that it is no longer the *sole* basis of language. But if this is so, on what grounds should we attribute a validity to arbitrary stipulations? While I am unable to answer this query positively, I can instead see a number of reasons for answering negatively that the so-called new approach is a wrong approach. And I shall try to warrant this conclusion by examining the following four questions:

1. Are definitions rules of the language game?
2. Is the useful-confusing criterion adequate?
3. Are definitions like axioms?
4. Has conventionalism an alternative?

In regard to the first question, I maintain that the conventionalists are *inconsistent;* in regard to the second, that the criterion of utility, understood as a practical way to solve cognitive problems, is totally *inadequate;* in regard to the third, that the whole position is based on a *false analogy;* and in regard to the fourth, that we have been trapped by a *false dilemma.*

First, inconsistency. If we ask why it is that our definitions can be neither true nor false, a frequent answer is likely to be: because they are like rules. That is, modern conventionalism tends to understand definitions as rules, and more exactly as linguistic rules of equivalence. I shall assume that this is correct.[12] Even though I consider the expression "rules of the language game" to be nothing more than a clever metaphor, I shall begin by taking it seriously. But then I find that the game theorists of language contradict themselves. For there is no sense in speaking of rules and then asserting that it is perfectly legitimate to break them. If we maintain that everybody has the right to make whatever stipulations he wants, there are no rules; and if there are rules, then we cannot maintain that their infringement is legitimate. The right of a player who wishes to change the rules is not to interfere with the game, but to withdraw from the game. Thus there is no sense in saying that we are perfectly entitled to call "black" what others call white. If definitions are "like rules," where does our right to transgress them come from? To grant this right amounts to saying that no game is possible.

Let us suppose that a chess player finds himself in a game where his opponent uses the queen's moves for the king's. According to the philosophers who refer to the game model, it is perfectly correct for the second player to do this so long as he announces it and does it consistently. But the first player will decide instead that his opponent does not know how to play chess, and therefore cannot be permitted to play. And in my opinion the player who does know how to play is right, and the philosopher is wrong. For he who moves the king as if it were the queen is not creating another game; he is destroying that game, and in truth would destroy any game. My first point, then, is that inasmuch as definitions are rules we must ask that they be observed. To encourage their violation is flagrant inconsistency.

Secondly, inadequacy. To get closer to the heart of the problem let us ask: When we say that we adopt a definition because we find it useful, what do we mean? The question is: *Useful for what?* My guess is that most scholars would reply: Useful for science, useful for the progress of knowledge. Maybe, but then, clearly, we are speaking in this case of cognitive utility. And once we admit this, I wonder how much difference there is between the true-false and useful-useless criteria.

There certainly is one difference, namely, the difference between a realistic and a nominalistic theory of knowledge—between the "correspondence theory" of truth and what we might call the logical, methodological, or "coherence theory" of truth. Now there is no

215

doubt that this is an important question, on which philosophers are very bitterly divided. But it is a question that is relevant only in the context of what may be called the large logic (which embraces gnoseology, epistemology, and methodology), and not in the context of "small logic," that is, in the context which concerns those who are not professional logicians. For us—no matter whether we are political philosophers or political scientists—the problem is reduced to a question of warranted assertibility, and the query whether truth is an *adequatio intellectus et rei* [14] (as the correspondence theory holds), or whether it is only the truth of the statement made (as the nominalists contend), may remain undecided. We do not need to solve this question, and the reason for this is that we proceed in the same way, no matter what the metaphysical background and foundation of our investigation is deemed to be. I mean that the dispute about the nature of truth affects the form rather than the substance of the matters dealt with in our field. Scholars who believe in the correspondence theory of truth are surer of themselves, and speak of their conclusions as expressing truth with a capital *T*. The others are more modest, think of truth with a small *t,* prefer to talk of truths in the plural, and in some cases shy away from the word completely. But to eliminate the word does not amount to eliminating the concept.

Even if we take a relativistic view of truth, when we say that a definition is useful, we mean that it is useful for cognitive purposes. That is to say that the sentence, "This is a useful definition," is a shorthand implying that we are leaving the metaphysical problem of Truth undecided. If we expanded the sentence, it would stand for the following: Although I am trying to find out something which I consider true, I do not wish to get entangled in the problem of what Truth is. Neither do I. Nevertheless the fact remains that a definition which is useful for cognitive purposes is "true" in the sense that it is useful in the search for truth. And if we refuse to recognize that the criterion of utility is simply a modest and cautious way of dealing with truth, the criterion ceases to work. For we would then be checked by the dilemma: Useful for political understanding, or for political practice? Useful for science, or for the power holders? To put it bluntly, a position that is justified on the basis of sheer utility may only promote conformity to the will of the sovereign. And since political authors have to earn a living like everybody else, it is important that we unequivocally acknowledge that unless the concept of utility is understood as a subclass of the category "search for truth," it has nothing to do with science or knowledge in general.

My second point, then, is that the difference between "true" definitions and "useful" definitions amounts to the difference between an arrogant attitude toward Truth and a humble attitude toward truth (or probable truths). In other words, when we are concerned with knowledge, truth and utility are not two different criteria, but formulations at a different level of modesty of the same criterion. It is not possible to escape the problem of truth, as the Oxford philosophers and other scholars believe, by adopting a merely utilitarian or practical test. If we wish to solve a cognitive problem we have to rely on a cognitive criterion. Whether we call it truth or usefulness is immaterial, as long as it is clear that the latter term is only an understatement of the former. To advocate utility per se is simply to smuggle into the discussion a test that is wholly inadequate. For unless the concept of usefulness signifies *cognitive usefulness,* it cannot help us to determine that a certain definition is useful, while its opposite is not.

Third, false analogy. The question at this point is: What is the place of definitions? Is a definition the starting point of an investigation, or the conclusion of it?

There is no general answer to this question, for in some cases we start from definitions and in others we arrive at them. But this does not depend on our pleasure; it depends on whether or not we are referring to axiomatic or postulational language (like geometry). In the case of geometry, for instance, we start from a set of definitions, which we call axioms and postulates, precisely because everything follows from them. But in existential discourse the procedure is very different. This may not be apparent at first sight, for even in the latter case we often introduce our discussions with a definition. However, this is either a didactic device, or else we place a definition at the beginning of our discourse because it is the conclusion of a process of investigation that others have already carried out. In any case, no matter what the physical location of a definition is, its logical place is at the end. And this is so, even if in our exposition the

217

definition-finding process is omitted. For we know what is meant by a certain term only because we have previously discussed it and tested it.

The bearing of the foregoing analysis on the issue under discussion is to show that the conventionalists' argument rests on a misleading analogy. For we are often confronted with the statement that a definition is neither true nor false, on the grounds that definitions are "arbitrary" starting points. Now this clearly implies that the conventionalists think that a definition is like an axiom. But this is correct only if the philosopher is to become a mathematician. It is false if the mathematician is to become a philosopher, and, in general, whenever natural language is in question. It is indeed true that in non-existential language a definition—i.e., an axiom and a series of postulates—cannot be true or false because it is just an arbitrary beginning. But this is no longer so in existential language. In this context to say that a definition is arbitrary is the same as to say that it is false or wrong: for in this case we are in a position to pass judgment, since definitions are here the outcome of an inquiry. Likewise, it is perfectly correct to speak of a set of axioms as "useful," since they only serve as the starting point of a postulational system: in fact, we mean that we need them just for this purpose. But when, in existential discourse, we say, "This definition is useful," we mean something else, i.e., that we have found out by means of experiment, observation and reasoning that it leads us to conclusions that can be warranted (as true). From this angle as well, we are once again led to the conclusion that there is no qualitative difference in natural language between the true-false and the useful-confusing criterion.

In sum, my third point is that those who maintain that in the last analysis a definition is only an arbitrary statement of what we decide a term shall mean, are applying the rules of axiomatic discourse to non-axiomatic discourse. And this is a fallacy. In effect, within existential discourse an arbitrary statement of what a word will mean for the speaker is not a definition, not even a preliminary stage of the process of defining. It is just nonsense. For here the place of definitions is *at the end* of an investigation.

Fourth, false dilemma. If my purpose were only negative it

would not be necessary to press another charge. But I am interested in raising the question, "How do conventionalists prove their contentions?" because it will lead us to the constructive part of the argument. The winning argument of the new look in philosophy seems to be that conventionalism has no alternative. Words can have only conventional meanings, and thus definitions must be arbitrary, because it cannot be otherwise. Apparently we are confronted with the following dilemma: either one takes the conventionalistic stand, or one is bound to fall back into the old delusion of "real essences" and of "absolute standards." [15]

It is sometimes surprising to see skilled and clever logicians themselves become victims of well-known logical fallacies. For it is obvious enough that from the premise, "This is not white," we cannot infer: Then it must be black. Likewise, from the statement, "There are no absolute standards," it does not follow that there are no standards at all. Why should the only alternative be arbitrariness and linguistic chaos? And the question is rhetorical, for there is no doubt that from the premise, "There are no real essences," we cannot correctly conclude: Therefore there is *nothing*. This being—let us face it—the unavoidable implication of the stipulative theory of language.

Now, to begin with, I have already shown that at the bottom of our so-called linguistic conventions there is *something*. For they are the outcome of a long, thoughtful, and purposeful process of choice among the known and accepted meanings of a word, plus an occasional element of rational—not arbitrary—innovation. This amounts to saying that to the extent that definitions can be traced back to stipulations, such stipulations are not arbitrary. If they are, or when they are, they are discarded. Arbitrariness is so far from being the typical feature of the defining process, that it is in fact the criterion by which we decide that a definition is wrong or useless. Moreover, the use of a word, i.e., its accepted meaning in actual use, is not only established by reason, but, even more, through experience. The latter being—as we shall see—my basic contention.

But let us recapitulate. My final criticism is that the either-or dilemma—conventionalism-or-metaphysics—which has been presented by certain schools of present-day logic is unwarranted. It can be applied to non-existential language, and in fact it has been suggested by misleading analogies drawn from mathematics. But as far as existential language is concerned, the alternative in question does not apply. Our freedom to stipulate freely is not restricted by a metaphysics of real essences, but by the fact that the meaning of descriptive terms is based (i) on thoughtful, rational decisions, as well as (ii) on past and present experience.

4. Words, Meanings, and Experience

We can now turn from the general issue to our specific concern, which is to give positive reasons why the question, "What is democracy?" cannot be answered by statistics (i.e., by saying that democracy is what a large number of people agree to call democracy), or by private stipulation, i.e., by putting forward a convention of one's own which cannot be challenged *ex definitione* because it is a stipulation.

If definitions of the non-axiomatic kind belong at the end of an argument, then the range of possible definitions of democracy is already severely curtailed. The first part of the book has, I hope, offered ample evidence of this. Yet rational examination may lead to various possible interpretations of democracy. But our freedom to select among the logically possible or conceivable kinds of democracy is further restricted by historical evidence. And this means that the definition of democracy is, to a great degree, a matter-of-fact definition which is arrived at by examining what happened to possible democracies.

This helps to explain why the term democracy no longer means that which is indicated by the Greek root. From the point of view of "utility" it would undoubtedly be expedient to stick to the etymological definition, for everything would then be clear, simple, and coherent. Nevertheless, if we look at the way "democracy" is actually understood in current political dealings, we discover that the present-day meaning has very little to do with the idea of a self-governing people. Despite the literal meaning, we think of a majority rule which respects minority rights, and I have previously defined democracy as an electoral polyarchy, or an elective system of competitive minorities.[16] Now, there would be no *logical* reason, strictly speaking, for departing from the literal meaning. That is to say that, going to the bottom of the matter, the reason is not logical but *historical*. The actual use of "democracy" has been shaped by experience and reflects what we have learned as practitioners.

My argument can be summarized as follows: the meaning of the word democracy is not conventional because it is historical. The statement should not be understood in the trivial sense that we accept the definition of democracy which has the authority of repetition, but in the sense that we accept a certain definition because it has been tested by historical experience. Obsequiousness to tradition is often a mere equivalent of mental inertia, whereas the kind of investigation required for rediscovering the historical dimensions of "democracy" requires hard work and application. It is in no way an easy task to follow the itinerary by means of which words acquire, with the passing of time, a semantic rigidity which results precisely from the fact that they are filled with historical content and substantiality.

It has been pertinently said that man is assimilated history—history incorporated in his being.[17] But this is so because of language, because language is a storehouse which reminds us of past experience, a "keeper-alive" or a "conservator"—as Mill said—of former practice.[18] More precisely, words such as democracy are shorthand reports intended to convey ideas about how we are to behave *as experienced people* in matters regarding which each generation starts by having no experience. And if this is so, if the term democracy is a carrier of historical experience whose meaning is stabilized by an endless trial-and-error historical process, it follows from this not only that the demand for freedom of definition is hard to distinguish from the right to be ignorant, but also that the stipulative theory of language fails to grasp the very essence of language.

Even assuming that at the origins of speech we may find conventions, we ourselves are not beginners, and we do not start with a *tabula rasa*. We are not architects trying to find out how to build a skyscraper, but inhabitants dwelling on the thirtieth floor, that is, with at least thirty centuries of records behind us. We tend to be ironical about "the noble savage" and "the man of nature" that so fascinated the Illuminists. But the conventionalists' approach to language is founded on a similar metaphysics; for it hypothesizes a language of the year zero while we are living in the twentieth century A.D., at a

221

moment in which the term democracy has become a designator, or indicator, of a pattern of behavior which has been molded by a long and painstaking process of trial and failure concerned with the question: How can we be governed without being oppressed?

5. Historia Magistra Vitae

In a less sophisticated time, I could have introduced my thesis by simply saying *historia magistra vitae,* history is the teacher of life. But now that modern logicians make life so hard for us, I have had to make a detour and add to Cicero's dictum by saying *historia magistra definitionis.* And in this connection I should like to suggest that we pay more attention to history than many contemporary scholars are inclined to do. It is often said that political scientists do not have to bother with history. However, if we examine this statement carefully we shall see that it does not contradict my recommendation. It means either that (i) as political scientists we should not be concerned with the history of political ideas, or that (ii) our interest in history is not the same as the professional historian's. *Cum grano salis,* I agree with both these statements.

That does not mean that I advocate ignorance of the history of political ideas.[19] It only means that we should distinguish between the history of philosophy and political doctrines on the one hand, and history as a record of experience on the other. The implication of the distinction is that, *qua* political scientists, we have to reckon with the history of political ideas only to the degree that they reflect and contain some kind of historical learning and testing. As for the second point, I agree that there is an unquestionable difference between the aspect of the past which interests us, and the aspect studied today by pure historians.

Modern historians have developed a keen feeling for the diversity of events. Every event is seen as being unique (*einzigartig* and *einmalig*). It follows from this that the attitude of present-day historians could be better expressed by the formula, "History never repeats itself," than by Cicero's dictum. This amounts to saying that whereas the earlier historian resembled the political theorist in the sense that he thought of history as an art of precepts learned from the past, this is no longer the case. And there are two reasons for this. For one thing, all modern learning has become more and more specialized, so that the historian has to fulfill only his particular task of recounting *wie es eigentlich gewesen,* how it really happened, as Ranke said. However, if historians today reject generalizations and stress the uniqueness and unrepeatability of historical events, this is also done in opposition to the natural sciences, for the purpose of severing the *Geisteswissenschaften,* from the *Naturwissenschaften.*[20] For these reasons, both of which are certainly valid, the present-day historian is very different from his predecessors and has shifted his focus of interest away from the political scientist's and the political theorist's. But this does not justify our disregarding history: it simply means that we have to do for ourselves what the professional historians no longer do for us. Historical information remains very important to us, provided that we know how to exploit it for our own purposes.[21]

The foregoing permits us to appraise the objection that history does not teach us anything because there is no repetition in history. Although many political scientists officially take this view, it is my impression that for many of us it is more a slogan to which we pay an initial lip-service rather than a principle which really affects our subsequent proceedings. And if we take seriously the assertion, "History never repeats itself," then this is another example of what I have called the microscope fallacy.

To be sure, historical events are unique: but if they are seen from the perspective of the professional historians. If we use lenses that are as strong as theirs, every pear will also seem unique. However, this does not mean that in botany we cannot speak of "the pear" in general. Also every individual human being is unique, but sociologists and other social scientists would have to look for another job if we did not recognize the fact that for certain purposes we may treat individuals as if they were alike. *Mutatis mutandis,* there is enough repetition in history to allow us, if we know how, to learn a good deal from the past, because the past is not only pastness. So all that I am willing to concede is that, unfortunately, it is quite true—as Bernard Shaw pungently remarked—that we learn from experience that men never learn from experience. However, this is no reason for extolling ignorance, and we shall certainly not be better off without historical insight and knowledge.

In fact, we have no choice. Explicitly or implicitly, a very large number of our assertions are based on examples and evidence drawn from the past. And it is hard to see how it could be otherwise, and how the theory and science of politics could do without the testing ground of history. In empirical investigation, logic is an instrument of rectification, i.e., logical method is solely a method, which cannot prove *per se* that an empirical statement *must* be true. On the other hand, history is the only large-scale experimental laboratory that we have. Thus, political theory and political science arrive at empirically valid conclusions to the degree that they elaborate a systematic set of predictions which are based on historical testimony.

I say "predictions" because political science is different from historiography in that it examines the past in order to foresee the future, that is, to extrapolate what can be done and what, vice versa, is not feasible. And I say "testimony" instead of "experience" because experience in the narrow, strict sense of the term is something too limited and autobiographic to be sufficient for dealing with large-scale problems of historical construction. It is true that our personal experiences are a decisive element in the focusing of problems. Nonetheless, the basic test is provided by the fact that our so-called experiences come to us in the form of testimony.

It must be clear, however, that when I suggest that we look at history, I do not mean that we should proceed in the manner of the professional historian. On the contrary. For instance I will be more interested in looking for unity in diversity, than for the diversity which splits unity. Whereas historians are apt to consider that all democracies are different from one another, I will speak of democracy in the singular, notwithstanding its varieties. As I have already pointed out, for some purposes it is correct to say that *the* pear (the generalized pear) does not exist, as there are only different kinds of pears; and for other purposes we can also say that not even the kinds exist, as each pear of the supposedly same kind is different. In other contexts, however, these disquisitions are irrelevant, because what concerns us is to prevent the general class, "pear," from being confused with the class, "orange." Likewise, my concern here is to see to it that the general class, "democracy," is not mixed up with counterfeits.

For the purposes of political theory what is relevant is not to show, as the historian may do, that variety proliferates in history, but on the contrary to show that history reduces variety. These two statements are only apparently contradictory, because the historian is fighting against misleading generalizations, whereas I am fighting against the logical abstractness implied in the game theory of definitions.

Therefore, from this point on, my primary concern will be to review the problem of democracy in historical terms. A word like democracy acquires a definite, helpful, and usable meaning only if we remember that it is an abbreviation summarizing the acquisitions and values of a civilization. Since all this is only *implied,* it is easily forgotten. That is exactly why we have to call attention over and over again to the need for constant awareness of the historical background of our shorthand. I grant that we live looking ahead, and that we have to be interested in what democracy can and should be rather than in what it has been. However, if we want our projects to succeed, our predictions must be based on historical testimony. Otherwise we are building *in vacuo,* on nothing and for the sake of nothing.

NOTES

† Letter, Nov. 7th, 1778.

1. Admittedly, there is a difference between defining a term and explaining the meaning of a term, just as there is a difference between indefinability and incomprehensibility. However, in this context, I am not using "definition" in the technical sense which would require the aforesaid distinctions.

2. J. S. Mill, *System of Logic* (London, 1898), Book I, Chap. VIII, p. 86.

3. As a general source see Richard Robinson, *Definition* (Oxford, 1954), esp. Chaps. III and IV.

4. *Ibid.,* p. 60.

5. M. Cranston, *Freedom,* pp. 35-36. (The italics are mine.)

6. In *Selected Essays* (London, 1957), pp. 152, 154, 157.

7. Of course, conventionalists assert that this is no problem at all. Weldon, for instance, writes: "What is futile is to puzzle ourselves as to whether the

American or the Russian use of 'democracy' is the true or correct one"
(*The Vocabulary of Politics,* p. 23). I will raise this issue in Chap. XVII, 5.

8. Cf. R. Robinson: "Lexical definitions have a truth-value but stipulative
definitions have not. . . . *It is an arbitrary choice.* . . ." (*op. cit.,* pp. 62,
63). (The italics are mine.)

9. It is not that the authors in question recommend eccentricity; quite the
contrary. Thus Robinson lists no less than fifteen "rules of stipulation that we
may usefully lay upon ourselves" (*op. cit.,* pp. 80-92), beginning by asserting
that "the supreme rule of stipulation is surely to *stipulate as little as possible"*
(p. 80), and concluding by admonishing that we should "remind ourselves to
be *responsible in stipulation"* (p. 91). However, what is the justification of
these rules? Robinson replies that "if they are justified [their justification]
can only be . . . to lessen the disadvantages of stipulation" (p. 92). But
the admission "if they are justified" shows the contradiction of the whole
position. For what is the sense of advocating a stipulative approach that
eventually ends up by recommending to stipulate as little as possible? The
truth is that this approach does encourage people to be eccentric, and I hardly
see how we can discourage stipulations by advocating a stipulative theory of
language.

10. On the "freedom of definition," cf. also L. S. Stebbing, *A Modern Introduction to Logic,* 7th ed. (London, 1950), p. 426 f.; C. G. Hempel, "Fundamentals of Concept Formation in Empirical Science," in *International
Encyclopedia of Unified Science* (Chicago, 1952), II, 7, p. 14 f.; and Uberto
Scarpelli, *Il Problema della definizione e il concetto del diritto* (Milano,
1955), esp. pp. 65-66.

11. R. Robinson, *op. cit.,* p. 65.

12. Although it can convincingly be argued that it is not. See Michael Scriven,
"Definitions, Explanations and Theories," in *Minnesota Studies in the
Philosophy of Science* (Minneapolis, 1958), Vol. II, pp. 139-150.

13. For a more thorough examination, cf. Arthur Pap, *Elements of Analytic
Philosophy,* Chap. XIV: "Theories of Truth."

14. Correspondence between mind and thing: this is the Thomistic formula.

15. Cf. Weldon's *The Vocabulary of Politics,* Chap. II, pars. 2 and 3.

16. Cf. Chap. VI, 7, above.

17. Cf. G. Burdeau, *Méthode de la science politique* (Paris, 1960), pp. 121-123.

18. *System of Logic,* Book IV, Chap. IV, 6, p. 455. In another passage, on p.
448, Mill writes: "Language is the depository of the accumulated body of
experience to which all former ages have contributed their part."

19. Of course not. In some sense the stipulative theory of language both encourages and follows our growing inability to master the ideas received from

the past. Cf. with reference to this question the subtle observations of Leo Strauss on the need "to transform inherited knowledge into genuine knowledge by revitalizing its original discovery" (*What is Political Philosophy?* pp. 73-77). Strauss writes: " 'Our ideas' are only partly our ideas. Most of our ideas are . . . abbreviations and residues of the thought of the past. . . . Therefore if we want to clarify the political ideas we have inherited we must actualize their implications . . . and this can be done only by means of the history of political ideas" (p. 73).

20. This distinction between "sciences of the spirit" and "natural sciences," as has been discussed and formulated by Windelband in *Geschichte und Naturwissenschaft* (1894), but above all in *Einleitung in die Geisteswissenschaften* by Dilthey (1883) and in *Die Grenzen der naturwissenschaftlichen Begriffsbildung* by Rickert (1896-1902), is at the origin of contemporary historiography. Their thesis was that whereas physical sciences are "nomothetic" in that they search for abstract universal laws, historical sciences are "idiographic" because they deal with the unique.

21. The relationship between the older historical methods and the newest approaches has been perspicuously pointed out by Frederick M. Watkins: "The respective strengths and weaknesses of the historical and the behavioral approaches are, indeed, curiously complementary. The strength of the historical approach is that its results are synthetic and dynamic. . . . The weakness is that the results are by no means rigorous. . . . The behavioral approach, on the other hand, is inspired by the highest standards of objectivity and rigor. . . . The corresponding limitation is that its conclusions tend to be merely analytical and static." *Approaches to the Study of Politics*, ed. R. Young, p. 152.

Chapter XI

Empirical Democracies and Rational Democracies

"While most lasting empires and constitutions have been built without preconceived ideas and over-all plans, structures which have been too consciously designed have lasted just long enough to fall heavily on builders and spectators alike."

—R. Ruyer†

1. Democracy Is a "Historical Product"

SINCE THE discovery of history by the Romantics the sentence, "This is a historical product," has become commonplace. If we take this statement at its face value it is nothing more than a banality, since it is obvious that everything that has existed or does exist in history is a historical product. But the statement can be interpreted so that its meaning is not banal.

In the first place, when we say, for example, that democracy is a historical product, what we actually mean is that a democratic system is possible insofar as history has created the conditions and the prerequisites for its working. This is why we also speak of historical maturity, alluding to the fact that we must take account of the temporal factor, and that an experiment in democracy has little

228

chance of survival if it is attempted prematurely. It would be more precise to say, in this sense, that democracy is the product of a *certain history*—I mean, of a given historical background. And in this qualification there is already a hint as to why democracy can only be exported with difficulty.

If the sentence, "This is a historical product," is analyzed further, it also takes on another meaning, or rather calls our attention to the *sui generis* nature of our problems. In this sense, when we speak of a historical product we are speaking of something that in the final analysis defies both rational dissection and deliberate, artificial reproduction. Historical products hold secrets that scientific reason cannot penetrate. And this is because, in historical—as opposed to natural—events, imponderable factors which we cannot measure or isolate come into play. When we wish to plan and steer history deliberately, we are confronted with "invisible entries," with factors which we can only glimpse, and to which we can therefore give only vague names, like *ethos, Volksgeist* (spirit of the people), custom, cultural pattern, vitality, and so on. We know that these are very important entries in our bookkeeping system and in our calculations, but we do not know how to identify, weigh, and count them, either in regard to their interplay or in regard to their respective coefficients of dynamism.[1]

In this sense the sentence, "This is a historical product," warns us of the limits that prevent us from lording over history in the same way as we do over nature. Historical products always contain hidden entries that cannot be expressed in clear and distinct ideas, and therefore confront us with unknowns that a rational animal cannot properly master or create anew. For instance, the *animus* is an imponderable which can hardly be directed and nurtured deliberately. Yet, the bearing of this "symbolic imponderable" on the outcome of our attempts to plan history is decisive. And from this viewpoint we can better understand why, when a democratic form is transplanted to a different historical humus, something unforeseen and uncontrollable always happens.

Rousseau, who looked at the English constitution through the eyes of Montesquieu, sent word to the Anglo-Saxons that even though they thought they were free, they were actually slaves.[2] But he based his judgment on those elements of the particular historical product, the evolution of the English constitution, which Montesquieu's rational transcription succeeded in tracing out. And I understand very well why Rousseau did not find this soulless skeleton reassuring. I mean that in a historical vacuum Rousseau's thesis that a people who are limited to electing their representatives are free only at the moment that they vote (for they become slaves again immediately after) is a perfectly plausible thesis. Except that the British were really free enough, for their liberty was based on custom, on common law, and on an unwritten constitutional *praxis*. Thus, what Rousseau should have said, strictly speaking, was that the written constitution that Montesquieu had deduced from English practice was not sufficient to guarantee freedom to people who imported it.[3]

The sentence "Democracy is a historical product," can have a third meaning. It may also call attention to two different methods of historical fabrication, one of which is spontaneous and the other preconceived and intentional (relatively speaking, of course). In this sense it emphasizes the difference between unplanned and planned history-making, between the man who considers himself the obstetrician rather than the father of history, and the man who regards himself as its *dominus,* if not its creating God. Thus the proposition, "American democracy is a historical product," does not have the same meaning as "Soviet economic planning is a historical product" (even though, in the banal sense of the statement, the Soviet experiment equally belongs in the category of historical facts). Nor does it even have the same meaning as the sentence, "French democracy is a historical product," because the revolution of 1789 was a deliberate break with the past while the Declaration of Independence of 1776 was a claim for the right to advance along the path of the liberties already existing in England.

The difference is that when the statement in question refers to American democracy, we mean that American democracy is an authentic historical product, that is, a historical product in the specific and fullest sense of the expression.[4] For American democracy grew out of a gradual, uninterrupted process of spontaneous historical endogenesis. "Historical product" in this sense, then, indicates the genuine mode of historical development i.e., a pattern of behavior which *goes along* with history instead of going against it.

If American democracy is a genuine historical product, this is because it was patiently constructed by a *forma mentis* that seems to be tuned in perfect harmony with the fabric of time. That is to say that American democracy is the fruit of an empirical mental pattern that proceeds cautiously by historical addition, a pattern that is so different from the rationalistic radicalism which characterized the French Revolution that it started a revolution in order to lend strength to historical continuity rather than to break it.[5] Whereas the rationalist tends to re-build everything *ab imis* and to start with a *tabula rasa,* the empiricist prefers mending what he finds at hand to re-making it anew. What matters for him are not so much principles as precedents. *Stare decisis* is the formula that expresses his legal approach; and to stand by what has already been done, and in this sense to stick close to the facts, is his criterion of historical planning. And this is the secret of the Anglo-American type of democracy.

In this sense, then, calling American democracy an authentic historical product is the same as saying that it is an empirical type of democracy. Whereas saying that a democracy of the French type is not a historical product in the same sense, amounts to asserting that it is a rationalistic democracy built on abstract theory rather than on practice.[6]

2. Rational Mind and Empirical Mind

I am, of course, speaking of empiricism not in the technical sense, but as a mental pattern that has characterized the whole course of English history, and that, in its pragmatic form, now characterizes the American way of life and thought. I assume that it is equally clear that I am not speaking of pragmatism in a technical sense either. When I say that Americans are typically pragmatic, and that their genius consists of a *forma mentis* that is basically practical and instrumentalistic, I am using the terminology of Peirce, James, and Dewey to indicate a *Gestalt* that existed long before these terms were coined. For English empiricism turned into pragmatism at the very moment that it was faced with, and challenged by, a limitless virgin continent to be conquered.[7]

231

Clearly there is a difference, a considerable difference, between the progenitor and the progeny, between an empirical and a pragmatic mental pattern. Empiricism is well expressed in the cautious, patient Wait-and-see motto, while pragmatism can be better expressed in the adventurous, dynamic Try-and-see formula. However, if we compare these two patterns to the rationalist mentality, the difference between them becomes less significant. So, for brevity, I shall say "empiricism" to indicate both English empiricism and American pragmatism, or, in any case, to indicate their common base.

While the empirical (empirico-pragmatic) mentality stays *in medias res,* close to what can be seen and touched, the rationalist mentality soars to a higher level of abstraction and hence tends to be far removed from facts. While the former is inclined to accept reality, the *raison* tends to reject reality in order to re-make it in its own image; while empiricism tends to be anti-dogmatic and tentative, rationalism tends to be dogmatic and definitive; while the former is eager to learn from experience and to proceed by testing and re-testing, the latter goes ahead even without tests; while the empiricist is not deeply concerned with rigorous coherence and distrusts long chains of demonstration, the rationalist is intransigent about the necessity for deductive consistency—and therefore, in the summing up, while the former prefers to be reasonable rather than rational, the latter puts logical rigor above everything and thus is rational even if it means being unreasonable. While the empirical approach takes the attitude that if a program does not work in practice there must be something wrong about the theory, the rationalist will retort that what is true in theory must also be true in practice—that it is the practice, not the theory, that must be wrong.

Of course, the borderline between the empirical and the rational approach is not clear-cut. They do not express two kinds of logic but different degrees of alertness and sensitivity within the context of a common logic, of the same formal logic. Also, I am not implying that everybody who speaks English is an empiricist, and that everybody who speaks French or German or Italian is a rationalist. Obviously, we are dealing with prevalences, or prevailing tendencies, and it is clear that every culture has its rebellious minorities. There is a rationalistic current in Anglo-American thought, just as we find an anti-rationalistic line (which is sometimes empirical but, it is interesting to note, more often plainly irrationalistic) in the history of European culture. However, these exceptions and nuances do not alter the basic fact that the difference between empirical and rationalistic cultural patterns is an essential key to understanding the dissimilarity and mutual incomprehensions (in politics as well as in other fields) of the Western world. And that is why it is important to look at the underlying cultural patterns if we want to understand the difference between democracies of the Anglo-American type and, let us say, of the French type.

I shall start with some impressionistic evidence; then I shall examine in detail how the empirico-pragmatic attitude characterizes the Anglo-American definition of democracy, and, subsequently, in what way this definition is inadequate for those who do not receive democracy from history but have to create it out of their own heads.

3. Political Rationalism

It is certainly no accident that democratic regimes in a large part of Continental Europe evolved in the direction of parliamentary, if not assembly, systems, whereas a similar development did not take place either in England (where parliamentary government is an inaccurate name for a cabinet system) or in the United States. And if we take 1830-1831 and 1848 as our reference points for the past, and the post-World War I and II situations for the present, it is striking to see how the difference between French-type and Anglo-American-type democracies has, if anything, increased with regard not only to the written but also to the living constitutions. Why is this? And further how can we explain the fact that the difference has increased in spite of the unwavering admiration for the English model professed by European constitutional theory from Montesquieu on?

The explanation is that neither the good intentions of the constitution-makers nor the unhappy experiences that often accompanied the various "more democratic" rewritings of our constitutions were able to forestall the logical implications springing from the original sin, so to speak, of the European systems. For the democracies of the French type are cerebral: they are created by *la raison* and embraced with rational consistency and out of faith in reason. This means that

233

they were constructed deductively, with logical rigor, from premise to consequence. Hence, since the major premise—to which everything must lead and from which everything must follow—is that "the *demos* is sovereign," these systems have really never freed themselves from the chains of Rousseau and remain shackled to the will-of-the-people concept of democracy.[8]

Of course, it is not that the Anglo-American democracies deny that popular sovereignty is the system's point of departure and of reference. However, to see how differently the empirical mind and the rationalist mind work, all we have to do is observe their respective notions of "the people." For the Italian, the Frenchman, or the German, *il popolo, le peuple*, or *das Volk* is—semantically and conceptually speaking—a singular entity, and it conveys the idea of a *One* precisely because the concept is carried to the level of abstraction that is congenial to the rational mind. From this it follows that it has always been the tendency of European political theory to speak of the People as an entity spelled with a capital *P*, and that, while the Anglo-Saxons have never trusted Rousseau's *volonté générale* or the Germans' *Volksseele* and *Volksgeist*, these concepts have enjoyed high esteem on the continent, as shown by the lasting influence of Rousseau, Hegel, and Marx. The difference, then, is that from the very beginning the rationalistic democracies have leaned heavily on a concept of the People which the Anglo-Saxons have instinctively considered to be perilously close to a mythological oversoul, to what they call the organismic fallacy. While the British constitution does not recognize any such entity as "the people" as having a constitutional status, Continental democracies have developed what Herbert Spencer once called a superstitious belief in a kind of divine right of popular sovereignty.

The same difference that we find at the point of departure exists at the point of arrival. Let me just observe that in English-speaking countries it is customary to speak of "government," while Europeans almost always say "State." Now, there is the same distance between government and State as between the people (plural) and one People (singular). Once again, it is a difference in the level of abstraction. The rationalist is concerned with the State and not with the government, or governments, because (unlike the empiricist) he is ill at ease if he has to deal with things that are too fluid and changing. He wants the essence, something solid, basic, and permanent.[9] The empiricist, even when he uses the word State, will not forget that behind the entity there are persons—individuals. So let us not delude ourselves. "State" does not mean, in the English and American vocabulary, the same thing that it means to a European, because for the latter the problem of the State is completely separate from the problem of government; it is a problem of juridical form, not of persons.[10]

But to grasp the difference between empirical and rationalistic democracies it will be rewarding to follow their respective methods of logical construction step by step. For even if it is true that every democracy is based on the same premise, viz., that "the power belongs to the people," our conclusions may still differ widely, depending on how they are drawn from the initial premise. The links of the chain of argument can be narrow or wide, tight or loose, rigid or flexible. And rationalism proceeds from premise to conclusion with no flexibility, joining one link of the chain to the next one as tightly and securely as possible.

Assuming, as we read in the first Article (mind you, the first) of the constitution of the Weimar Republic (which, from a rational point of view, was undoubtedly an excellent constitution), that *die Staatsgewalt geht vom Volke aus,* that the power of the State emanates from the People, in a tightly knit system of argument the first consequence of this premise is that the democratic significance of the various possible electoral techniques takes on a preponderant and vital importance,[11] so preponderant that it totally obscures the other side of the problem, that is, leadership and efficient government.[12] This is shown by the fact that all the Continental democracies have adopted proportional representation[13]—the implication of this being that the Anglo-Saxons' arguments in defense of the single-member district system have not seemed as convincing on the Continent as they have in England and the United States. And we can see why. When one has to start from the very first step, beginning anew from the literal definition, it follows that the burden of linking an ideal of direct, self-governing democracy to a nation-wide indirect democratic system of government comes to rest heavily, and entirely, upon electoral foundations and legitimacy so that the problem of "true" and "equal" representation becomes all-important.

The second consequence of the premise, "All the power belongs to the people," is—if we are to be logical—that the principle of a balance of power among equal organs of the State cannot be considered democratic, for a constitution is democratic (the argument runs) to the degree that the body which represents the voice of the people prevails. And the force of this argument is revealed by the fact that democracies of the French type have become, even though in varying degrees, assembly systems.

The implications of this development are far-reaching. To begin with, while the Anglo-Saxons say "the executive" chiefly because it is the traditional and ceremonial term, democrats of the French type often take the expression very seriously and use it literally: if the government is called the executive this means—they claim—that it must be an executor, and only an executor. Thus governmental paralysis has ultimately become a typical and, on the whole, predominant feature of the "well-reasoned" democracies. And the executive is not the only victim of this "demo-cratic consistency." The bicameral system, too, has suffered from it, with the upper house becoming more often than not a pure and simple duplicate of the lower house. While the English, for example, are willing to consider the House of Lords a representative body, albeit *sui generis,* this is incomprehensible to a Continental democrat. Similarly, while Americans regard judicial review as a fundamental characteristic of their system, attempts to introduce something like it in democracies of the French type encounter the objection that a judicial power which is permitted to oppose the executive and (worse still) the legislative body contradicts the logic of a system that is based on the people's power. And so judicial control is looked upon with suspicion, as an anti-democratic device aimed at jeopardizing the principle of popular sovereignty.

The final consequence, again very logically, is that the notion of democracy takes on a much more demanding, intransigent meaning within the rationalist framework than it does in the Anglo-Saxon possibilist version. And how could it be otherwise? The further we take a rigorous rational-deductive line of argument, the less we depart from merely analytic statements. Thus the problem of democracy tends to be expounded touching always the same chord, in a mono-chord key, as if democracy were a monocracy in which the People is the One. So the final consequence is that a rational democracy is bound to be a very strenuous undertaking—an advanced and extreme type in which "true democracy" is regarded as being a political system in which the *demos* is entrusted with power not to avoid being misgoverned, but in order that people themselves should govern.

I am not suggesting—let it be noted—that the rationalist kind of democrat is necessarily a political extremist. My point is, rather, that he is likely to be an intellectual extremist. It is quite true, of course, that the distance between theoretical and active extremism may be slight, as is shown by the fact that political extremism is widespread in democracies of the French type, while it is less frequent in countries where an empirical mental pattern prevails. However, my point is that the rationalist mentality is extreme even when its logical rigor is not carried over into the field of practical politics. Burdeau is a case in point.[14] For when he speaks of a "governing democracy" as if it were a reality, he is supposedly speaking as a detached observer. But in truth his diagnosis springs from a rationalistic tradition in which logical consistency, that always requires the drawing of the ultimate conclusion, overcomes and distorts the facts.

4. Candide in America

In the empirical approach the peculiar and essential features of a democratic system appear to be (i) the existence of more than one party, and (ii) the safeguarding of minorities. That is to say that the standard Anglo-American definition of democracy is: A multiparty system in which the majority which governs respects the rights of minorities. Of course, this definition raises no problems as long as it is addressed to an audience familiar with it. But let us put ourselves in the shoes of one of the many twentieth-century Candides who land in the United States. His reaction will be very different. Let us suppose, for example, that our Candide comes across the passage from James Burnham which says, "The fundamental characteristic of democracy in the sense in which we use the word (regardless of what it meant to the Greeks who invented it) is the concession of the right of political expression to minorities." [15] He will certainly be astonished: nor should his astonishment surprise us. After all, until that moment he had usually heard "democracy" used in connection with "majority." It is as if a somewhat naïve European asked an African native what crocodiles were, and the native answered: What matters is that you be careful where you place your feet when you go near a river, and, if you value your life, that you never bathe in it. The similarity of the two cases is that neither Burnham nor the African native answer by saying what *the thing is*. We are told instead what *we must do* if a certain thing, or event, is to be sought or avoided.

In other words, Burnham's is a typically pragmatic and instrumental definition. Likewise when we define democracy as a party system in which the majority respects the minorities, we are answering not so much the question, "What is democracy?" as the question: How does democracy work? The point is, then, that the Anglo-American doctrine goes directly to the question of practice. It is not concerned with explaining the concept but rather with indicating the instrument. And therefore it puts forward a *procedural definition* which establishes the rules for the proper functioning of the system.

Naturally, after spending some time in the United States, Candide will understand more. For example, he may see without much difficulty the reason why American authors pass quickly over the *demos* and rapidly arrive at parties. For it is the parties, not the people, that have to be created and that pose practical problems which can be solved in different ways. And parties are necessary because without them—or at any rate without some equivalent of parties—how can the people express their will in any effective way? So democracy is defined as a party system because if there were not two or more parties the people would have no electoral alternatives from which to choose, and therefore would not be able to express effectively their agreement or disagreement. Thus Candide can easily be made to understand that the absence of parties or the existence of a single party indicates a lack of liberty.

So far so good. But Candide will begin to have trouble when he is confronted with the subsequent thesis that minority rights are a fundamental characteristic of democracy. This is indeed a most delicate and difficult point, and it is well to dwell on it, not only for the sake of alien visitors, but for the sake of the supposedly learned native democrats as well.

If a democratic system is to shun paralysis, it is clear that the party that controls the majority of parliamentary seats must have the right to govern and to impose its will and its laws on the minority parties. On the other hand, it is also clear that this right has, at least in principle, far-reaching implications, for a democracy ends up by giving a very discretionary legislative power to the elective assemblies. Therefore, from the latter point of view, we are warned that if the majority makes excessive use of its right, the system will no longer function as a democracy. The argument goes as follows: If a majority exercises its power without limits, it will not be difficult for it to maintain itself as a permanent majority; and if we have a majority that cannot be turned into a minority, then we are no longer dealing with a democratic majority—that is, with a system whose rule of the game is the majority principle. For a majority principle requires changeable majorities, with the various parts of the body politic being able to alternate in wielding power.

The argument is sound, but I doubt that our Candide has yet been convinced by it. For the crucial point remains to be clarified. In effect, we still have to explain why this rule of the game is so important, and why it is that everything depends on the opposition's being permitted to have its turn in exercising power. Guglielmo Ferrero said concisely: "In democracies the opposition is an organ of popular sovereignty just as vital as the government. To suppress the opposition is to suppress the sovereignty of the people." [16] Why?— one might ask. And the question is justified, because clearly there is nothing in the majority principle itself that obliges us to conclude that the majority must respect the opposition, or the minority.

If we do conclude this, it is for a reason that we have not yet given, i.e., that we are concerned about protecting individual liberty. Now, "Liberty for the individual means nothing if it does not imply the right to pursue a course of conduct and to hold and advocate views which do not have the approval of the majority." [17] This, then, is the real reason for our taking the part, at a certain point of the

239

argument, of minorities against the majority. But if this is so, then we still have to explain why individual liberty is so important; important, be it noted, not just because we happen to like it (it may be that Candide does not share this taste) but important precisely because it is essential to the very survival of a system based on popular sovereignty.

Kelsen observed acutely: "Even he who votes with the majority is no longer entirely subject to his own will. He is aware of this when he changes his opinion"; for "in order to be free again, he, the individual, would have to find a majority in favor of his new opinion." [18] Let me comment on this. Clearly, if minorities are not protected the possibility of finding a majority in favor of the new opinion is unlikely, since he whose opinion changes from that of the majority to that of the minority immediately falls into the ranks of those who have no right to make their opinions heard. Therefore, unless the liberty of minorities is respected, not only would the first electoral test determine, once and for all, those who are free and those who are not; but also the liberty of those who voted for the majority on that occasion would be lost forever, because, in practice, they would not be permitted to change their opinion. Thus the first election will be, in effect, the only true election. And this amounts to saying that such a democracy dies at the very moment of its inception.

This may seem to be a *reductio ad absurdum*, but it is only such because our democracies do permit dissent, and because in entrusting the government to the majority we do safeguard the right to oppose it. If we can reply to Rousseau that the citizen of a representative democracy is free not only at the instant he votes[19] but always, it is precisely because he can decide at any moment to transfer his allegiance from a majority opinion to a minority opinion. It is in this *being able to change his opinion* that his enduring liberty is rooted. So it was with good reason that Lord Acton could write: "The most certain test by which we judge whether a country is really free is the amount of security enjoyed by minorities." [20] Liberty for each and all acquires its authentic meaning when we are in the minority, and the safeguarding of minority rights is therefore the most vital requisite of an open society.

I wished to present the foregoing arguments in a somewhat

pedestrian fashion because I am under the impression that many of those who are not satisfied with the American model of democracy—and there are many such people in the world—are rejecting something that they have never understood. Nonetheless, it cannot be denied that the argument as developed so far has a limitation. And it is the limitation of any "practicalism," to use the term that James was fond of. The empirical approach to the problem of democracy is characterized by focusing attention on the practical devices by means of which democracy is realized (parties), and on the most delicate procedural aspect of the democratic way of governing (respect for the opposition). This is undoubtedly the most useful focus but, clearly, the resultant concept of democracy presupposes that democracy is taken for granted. In other words, English-speaking people define democracy under the assumption that it is an accepted belief, and that there is no need to demonstrate what is generally acknowledged.

The Anglo-American doctrine does not have to deal with questions of principle, with fundamentals, or, as we say in my country, with the conceptual issue. It suffices for it to define democracy with respect to its technical articulation and procedure. But that is the very reason why this definition, which is perfectly adequate in its own context, appears inadequate and marginal in other contexts. For people in other countries are by no means agreed as to what constitutes democracy, what kind of democracy is possible, or even what they want from democracy. This means that all the steps of the argument which the Anglo-Americans can leave out, others have to follow, one by one. Thus, when we limit ourselves to saying that democracy is a party system, or that it is the government of a majority which respects minorities, we are not giving an answer capable of satisfying someone who asks us: What is democracy?—meaning by this: Which democracy is a true democracy?

5. The Underlying Premises

If we think it over, it is rather obvious that the Anglo-American theory of democracy cannot satisfy outsiders. It is not that there are lacunae in it but simply that Anglo-American doctrine is concerned with its own democracy, not the democracy of others. We Europeans have to be won over to democracy, and therefore we want it fully explained, we seek its "essence." The Anglo-Americans do not need to worry about essence; it is sufficient that they concentrate on procedures.

To start with, let us take again the notion of democracy as a party system. It is a "marginal definition" in that it defines democracy by one of its mechanisms. Granted the importance of that mechanism, the fact remains that this is not a primary definition for it presupposes a whole series of basic clarifications.

In the first place it presupposes that an answer has been given to the preliminary question whether democracy is, or can be, a government *of* the people (in the literal sense). If we do not clarify this *antea*, this antecedent point, the whole party conception of democracy can be undermined by the claim that a direct democracy with no party diaphragms is far more authentic than representative democracy. The multi-party system characterizes democracy insofar as it has been previously demonstrated that direct democracy is impossible, or is possible only in conditions that cannot be met.[21] In short, for the party (that is, representative) conception of democracy to be accepted, we must first settle the question whether a system without intermediaries, in which the will of the people is directly expressed, might not provide "more democracy."

This is not all. For democracy defined as a multi-party system presupposes the answer to another preliminary question, namely, "What is consensus?" Otherwise the advocates of a one-party system could say that their single party is democratic on the grounds that it is also supported by general agreement. On this account we have to focus attention back to the modes of consensus, and start by carefully distinguishing between the procedures for achieving democratic consensus and the plebiscitary sanction given to modern dictators—the latter often being, as Max Weber has observed, "in its most genuine meaning, a kind of charismatic dominion which cloaks itself in a legitimacy derived from the will of the subjects." [22] There is no need to emphasize that we are confronted here with very troublesome issues, also because the problem of consensus is intermingled with the problem of public opinion, and consequently with questions such as the one raised by Lowell, namely, that "in order that it [public opinion] may be public, a majority is not enough, but the opinion must be such that while the minority may not share it, they feel bound by conviction, not by fear, to accept it." [23] These and other similar underlying questions do not have, in Europe, a merely scholarly bearing; they have also a direct bearing on the actual political debate.

The same reservations can be raised about the definition of democracy as a system of government regulated by a limited majority rule. The implicit assumption here is that democracy already exists, and that everybody agrees that it should be maintained exactly as it is. George Santayana well recognized this when he wrote that "to put things to vote, and to accept unreservedly the decision of the majority, are points essential to the English system; but they would be absurd if fundamental agreement were not presupposed. Every decision that the majority could conceivably arrive at must leave it still possible for the minority to live and prosper, even if not exactly in the way they wished. . . . In a hearty and sound democracy all questions at issue must be minor matters; fundamentals must have been silently agreed upon and taken for granted when the democracy arose." [24]

It follows that the thesis that democracy is to be understood as the limited exercise of power by those who ultimately have the right to wield it as they wish, will not appeal to the people who fear that their democracy will be destroyed, or who want to replace its existing form with a new one. And there is no use in hiding the fact that under these circumstances the rational (not reasonable) mind can find various ways of justifying the unrestricted rights of the majority. A typical feature of the rationalistic approach is, in effect, that it tends to argue problems in terms of limiting cases. And if we reason in this way, we easily arrive at the following drastic either-or position: In order to have majority rule, the rights of the majority must be absolute, for once we accept the principle of minority rights we shall have minority rule; and since we cannot permit the few to exercise power over the many, we must agree that the many have no obligation to respect the few.[25]

This is, in fact, one of those problems which can be solved empirically, not rationally. When we come to the moderate application of the majority rule, we have reached the point where constitutional precautions are no longer sufficient. A majority that controls the government and the passage of legislation does not abuse its power, ultimately, so long as it limits itself by itself; and this implies a developed sense of fair play, deep-rooted democratic habits, and internalized self-restraints. All of this remains outside the orbit of solutions which can be discovered and enacted by rational thinking. Thus it is not surprising that the rationalistic democracies are not inclined to consider the limited majority principle to be a requisite condition of the system.[26] It is not surprising also because problems that we are unable to solve, we prefer to ignore.

Of course, the *de facto* difference between a situation in which democracy is generally accepted and situations of controversial democracy has to be accounted for, in the sense that an attitude of tolerance is more likely in the former than in the latter environment. On the other hand, consensus and cleavage do not come from nature but from nurture, and we should not, therefore, fail to perceive that a "consented democracy" is more likely to be attained where—as in the English-speaking countries—the principle of a majority rule respecting minority rights is addressed to an empirical mentality that rejects rigid positions of principle, refuses all theological intransigence and tends to conceive of democracy as the institutionalization of the art of compromise. It is such an interpretation of the system that makes it possible for majority and opposition to live together profitably, an enterprise which is much more difficult when the absolute quality of rational convictions and of Cartesian rigor comes into play. All in all, then, outside of the Anglo-Saxon world even the limited majority principle becomes a controversal issue: for it is not a first principle but a derived principle, not a *definiens,* one might say, but a *definiendum.*

And we still have not penetrated fully behind the scene. For both the definition of democracy as a party system and its definition as a self-restrained excercise of majority power, are based on the implicit major premise that what we are discussing is *liberal* democracy. Whereas democracies born under the aegis of Rousseau and the classical writers of antiquity are not necessarily, or spontaneously, liberal democracies.

6. An Appraisal

How should we appraise the two types of democracy in question? Given the fact that they are two subspecies of the same genus, at first sight the difference between the Anglo-American and the French type might seem to be merely the difference between a small-scale and a large-scale approach to the same conception: that is, between a theory concerned with the ways and means of democratic government, and a theory which has to start from ultimate principles. But, as we have seen, this difference also implies a dissimilarity of mental approach. And in this respect the empirical and the rational way of conceiving democracy never coincide. It is important for us all to be aware of this fundamental diversity because, otherwise, Europeans are unable to appreciate the American model, and on the other hand Americans cannot really figure out what is going on in Continental Europe.

There is no doubt (or at least so it seems to me) that the empirical mind is best suited for the requirements of a democratic modus vivendi. Its tendency to proceed by trial and error; its flexibility and its adherence to facts; its instinctive concern with the way things work out—all this seems expressly designed for succeeding in spontaneous historical construction, as well as for dealing with the concrete problems of a free society. We can therefore easily understand how it happens that democracy develops successfully in English-speaking countries, while in countries where a rationalistic mental pattern prevails its fragility is only equaled by its ambitiousness. For, as Goethe said, there is nothing more inconsistent than supreme consistency.[27] And the fruit of extreme consistency, at least in politics, is that the rationalistic democracies are always in danger of becoming imaginary democracies, far too removed from reality to be able, in the long run, to master the problems arising in the real world.

It would indeed be very useful, then, if European rationalism would develop a keener attitude and ability to face practical problems with a practical logic, remembering that "in social dynamics . . . nothing is easier than being deluded by a rationalistic logic, which abandons itself to foolhardy extrapolations and pays no attention to secondary and composite effects." [28] Yet, my criticism of rationalism should not be interpreted as an unconditional approval of empiricism and pragmatism. For these mental patterns, too, have their limitations and their excesses.

It is difficult to deny that Anglo-American democracy deserves first place as far as accomplishment and historical achievement are concerned. Yet its appeal is not very strong, and is certainly not in proportion to its merits. Rousseau, Hegel, and Marx travel throughout the world, and the last is read (and perhaps understood) even in China; whereas no English or American author has been able to gain any comparable influence outside the borders of his own culture. In short, rationalism travels, and empiricism does not. Why? It is not difficult to answer. In order to be able to circulate, a political doctrine must acquire a universality, a level of abstraction and a theoretical backbone to which the empirical mentality—wrongly, in my opinion—pays too little heed. And this precisely in the cases in which the rational approach is well justified and serves the purpose it is meant to serve.

We have thus arrived at a situation which seems to me paradoxical. While the diffusion and penetration of ideas—at least in their ideological form—increases all over the world, pragmatism makes a point of being able to do without them. And while we are forced to envisage political problems on an ever expanding scale, American thinking narrows its focus, concentrating on smaller and smaller detail, on analyses that are valid only here and now, or there and now—*as if this were all.*

If the rationalist is not trained to solve practical problems, on the other hand "practicalism" lacks an adequate intellectual grip in terms of rational construction. (These are, of course, very broad generalizations.) American culture, especially if we consider its indigenous roots, is perfectly equipped to train a formidable *homo faber,* but there is the danger of its not being able to live up to its responsibility to educate the *homo sapiens* (in the humanistic sense) who is needed to nourish and complement him. It is my conviction, therefore, that it would be to the advantage of both sides if the rationalistic and empirical approaches could meet halfway. And this is the path I shall attempt to pursue in examining the historical achievements which have produced and sustain modern democracy.

246

NOTES

† *L'Utopie et les utopies* (Paris, 1950), p. 85.

1. Cf. G. Sartori, *Questioni di metodo in scienza politica* (Firenze, 1959), pp. 187-195.

2. *Contrat social,* III, 15.

3. In effect, the advice given by Montesquieu to his readers was somewhat naïve. He wrote: "To discover political liberty in a constitution no great labor is requisite. If we are capable of seeing it where it exists, it is soon found, and we need not go far in search of it." (*L'Esprit des lois,* Bk. XI, Chap. 5.)

4. I point to the United States because it covers an experience that is more characteristically democratic with respect to the English model. It is symptomatic that as late as 1952 a study sponsored by the Hoover Institute revealed that only 50 per cent of the English people regarded the term democracy as a correct name for their political system, whereas 88 per cent of the Americans considered the label democracy as appropriate. Cf. I. De Sola Pool, H. D. Lasswell, and D. Lerner, *Symbols of Democracy* (Stanford 1952).

5. Cf. the sense of "givenness" of which Daniel J. Boorstin speaks with a felicitous expression, *The Genius of American Politics* (Chicago, 1953). Cf. also, for the suspicion about French rationalism, Norman Jacobson, "Political Realism and the Age of Reason: The Anti-Rationalist Heritage in America," *Review of Politics,* IV (1953).

6. Cf. Chap. III, 4, above.

7. For further elaboration, cf. G. Sartori, "La democrazia americana di ieri e di oggi," in *Il pensiero americano contemporaneo,* ed. F. Rossi-Landi (Milano, 1957), pp. 299-357, esp. pp. 303-329.

8. Two recent books published in Italy are a good instance of this. Cf. Lelio Basso, *Il Principe senza scettro: Democrazia e sovranità popolare nella costituzione e nella realtà italiana* (Milano, 1958): and Giorgio Fenoaltea, *Il popolo sovrano: Realtà e illusione della sovranità popolare in Italia* (Firenze, 1958).

9. It should be noted in this connection that the universities of Continental Europe teach *Staatslehre,* the theory of the State, and that "government" as an academic denomination is actually untranslatable. This is because it appears inconceivable to look for a theoretic systemization at that low level of abstraction in which the empirical approach proceeds.

10. In fact, as Maitland observed, the reluctance of the English to use the word "State" is correlative to their reluctance to accept the doctrine of the

juridical personality of the State. Cf. "The Crown as Corporation," in *Collected Papers*, Vol. III (Cambridge, 1911).

11. Cf. G. Sartori, "Electoral Studies and Democratic Theory," *Political Studies*, I (1958), esp. pp. 11-13.

12. Cf. Chap. VI, 3, above.

13. To be sure (as has been noted in Chap. VI, note 18 above), proportional representation cannot be charged with all the evils attributed to it by F. Hermens in *Democracy or Anarchy?* However, I would say that Hermens' thesis becomes meaningful if it is placed in the over-all context of a rationalistic approach.

14. Cf. Chap. V, 4, above.

15. *The Managerial Revolution* (New York, 1941), p. 162.

16. *Potere*, p. 217.

17. Cf. J. Allen Smith, *The Growth and Decadence of Constitutional Government* (New York, 1930), Chap. XIV.

18. H. Kelsen, *Vom Wesen und Wert der Demokratie*, Chap. I.

19. One should keep in mind that Rousseau's thesis was not only currently accepted in the years of the Revolution (Robespierre himself distinguished between "representatives of the people," whom he considered inadmissible, and "agents of the people") but also remember that it has profoundly influenced up to the middle of the nineteenth century a large part of the French doctrine, and not only the extreme positions of a Considerant or a Proudhon, but of Ledru-Rollin and a Catholic like Veuillot as well.

20. *The History of Freedom in Antiquity*. I am quoting from the collection *Essays on Freedom and Power* (New York, 1955), p. 56. Lord Acton was alluding in particular to the problem of religious freedom. His statement nevertheless can be validly generalized.

21. Cf. Chap. XII, 2, below.

22. In *Wirtschaft und Gesellschaft, Grundniss der Sozialökonomik* (Tübingen, 1925), Vol. I, Part I, Chap. III, par. 14.

23. A. L. Lowell, *Public Opinion and Popular Government* (New York, 1930), p. 15.

24. *Character and Opinion in the United States* (New York, 1955), p. 115.

25. This rationalistic position has found support in the United States esp. in Willmore Kendall. See his *John Locke and the Doctrine of Majority Rule* (Urbana, 1941), and "Prolegomena to Any Future Work on Majority Rule," *Journal of Politics*, IV (1950), pp. 694-713. Cf. also W. Kendall and J. A. Ranney, "Democracy: Confusion and Agreement," in *Western Political*

Quarterly, Sept. 1951, pp. 430-439. On the other extreme we find Calhoun's doctrine of "concurrent majority," which in substance theorizes the minorities' right to veto. Cf. *A Disquisition on Government* (New York, 1953).

26. Cf. Bruno Leoni, who marks the boundary which divides the Anglo-Saxon democracies from the Continental ones precisely on the basis of the tendency to use the majority principle in a temperate or absolute way. "Il pensiero politico e sociale dell' 800-900," *Questioni di storia contemporanea* (Milano, 1952), Vol. II, pp. 1133-1136.

27. *Maximen und Reflexionen,* 899.

28. R. Ruyer, *op. cit.,* p. 80.

Chapter XII

Greek Democracy and Modern Democracy

"It is clear that all the conditions of liberty have changed; the very word 'liberty' does not have the same meaning in modern times as it had in ancient times. . . . It is always useful to study antiquity, but it is puerile and dangerous to imitate it."

—E. Laboulaye†

1. Homonymy, Not Homology

THE TERM democracy was coined almost twenty-five hundred years ago. It first appeared in Herodotus' *History* in connection with the notion of *isonomía,* equality before the law.[1] From then on, even though it was eclipsed for a very long interval, it has remained part of the political vocabulary. But in so long a lifetime it has naturally acquired diverse meanings, referring, as it has, to very different historical situations as well as to very different ideals. So with the passing of time both its denotative and connotative uses have changed. It would be strange if this were not so; and it is therefore surprising to observe how little attention is paid to the fact that today's concept of democracy has only a very slight resemblance, if any, to the concept that was revered in the fifth century B.C. When we use the same word we instinctively tend to believe that we are referring to the same thing. However, if this ingenuousness is excusable when we are dealing with contemporary events, it is not when it makes us pass over more than two thousand years of historical achievements, as is the case with Rousseau and with Marx's and Lenin's democratic primitivism.[2]

Ancient democracy is conceived in relation with the *polis*. And the Greek *polis* was by no means the city-State that we are accustomed to call it—that is, a city organized in terms of what came to be named from the sixteenth century onwards "the State"[3]—but rather a city-community. When we speak of the Greek system as a democratic State we are being grossly inaccurate, both terminologically and conceptually. For what characterized that democracy was that it was stateless, in the precise sense that it dispensed with the State and was a democracy to the extent that the *demos* replaced the State. The idea of a democratic *State* was inconceivable for the Greeks; and if they had been able to conceive of it, it would have seemed to them to be a contradiction in terms.

First of all, then, ancient democracies cannot teach us anything about building a "democratic State," and about conducting a democratic system that covers not merely a city but a large expanse of territory inhabited by a vast collectivity. For the *polis* is as different from a territorial State as a river from an ocean. I mean that the problems of political organization in the first context are as much like those in the second, as the building of a raft is like the construction of a steamship. And this is not all. The difference between ancient and modern democracies is not simply one of geographic and demographic dimensions requiring completely different solutions, but also one of ends and values.

Modern men want another democracy, in the sense that their ideal of democracy is not at all the same as that of the Greeks. And it would be strange, indeed, if this were not so. In more than two thousand intervening years Western civilization has enriched, modified and articulated its value goals. It has experienced Christianity, humanism, the Reformation, the modern conceptions of natural law, and liberalism. How can we possibly think that when we advocate democracy today we are pursuing the same aims and ideals as the Greeks? How can we fail to realize that democracy embodies for us

251

values of which the Greeks were not even aware? Yet a considerable part of political literature still speaks of the Greek experiment nostalgically as if it were a lost paradise. All the more reason, then, for looking into the matter with attention.

2. Direct, or "Polis" Democracy

Saying that ancient democracy was the counterpart of the *polis* is another way of saying that it was a "direct democracy" (as well as explaining why). And even though many people apparently fail to realize this, we actually have no current experience with the type of democracy known as "direct."[4] All our democracies are indirect; that is, they are representative democracies in which we are governed by delegates, not by ourselves. Instead, in a direct democracy the citizens themselves exercise political power. In the *polis,* as in its medieval imitations, the system of government was based on the personal, actual participation of all the citizens of the city. There, then, we had a really self-governing democracy.

Of course, we must not take the notion of direct democracy (and of self-government) too literally, thereby assuming that in the ancient city the rulers and the ruled were identical. Not even Cleon, who was an advanced demagog for his time, ever went so far as to maintain that the system was perfectly expressed and only amounted to the whole body of the *demos* in the assembly. Leadership existed even then, and officials were chosen by lot or elected to fulfill certain functions. However, given the limits and imperfections of human affairs, the democracy of antiquity was undoubtedly the closest possible approximation to a literal democracy in which governors and governed worked side by side and dealt with each other face to face. Even though we may question the degree of intensity of self-government in the *polis,* nonetheless the fact remains that the difference between direct and indirect democracy is radical. In this juxtaposition the boundaries between the two are clear. In direct democracy there is continuous participation of the people in the direct *exercise* of power, whereas indirect democracy amounts to a system of *limitation* and *control* of power. In our democracies, there are those who govern and those who are governed; there is the State, on one side, and the citizens, on the other; there are those who deal with politics professionally and those who forget about it, except at rare intervals—whereas all of these distinctions have very little meaning in ancient democracies.

Two questions arise: Is direct democracy preferable?—and secondly: Is it still possible? From a logical point of view we should start with the question of its possibility, for if we discovered that, today, direct democracy is impossible, it would be pointless to discuss its desirability. But men are not that logical. Very often desire precedes knowledge, and while all of us have preferences, few of us stop to inquire whether they are attainable. Desires are given gratis, knowledge costs time and effort. Besides, there is also nostalgia for the impossible. And I am interested in finding out whether the recurrent longing for the classical world is justified.

The preferability of direct democracy is one of those questions that reason would answer in one way, and that historical experience leads us to answer in another. In terms of principle nobody is likely to deny that he who exercises power himself should be better off than he who delegates it to someone else, and that a system based on participation is safer than one based on representation. And how can we logically deny that direct democracy is a more genuine democracy? But history shows that the *polis* and the medieval communes had a turbulent as well as ephemeral existence. And this historical evidence is all the more significant, since in many respects the *polis* was an ideal laboratory for an experiment in the application of pure and simple democratic principles. Not only were the ancient cities very small,[5] but the citizens lived symbiotically with their city, being tied to it by a common destiny of life and death. Despite these optimum conditions democracy based on direct participation turned out to be very fragile even in its unreproducible testing ground, that compact community unified by a converging religious, moral, and political *ethos* which was the *polis*.

Let us not forget that Aristotle, who was a keen observer and witness of the events that led to the downfall of the liberties of antiquity, placed democracy in the class of the corrupted forms of *politéia*.[6] While Pericles in his famous funeral oration called democracy a "government [in favor] of the many,"[7] Aristotle called it "a government of the poor:"[8] and this change of connotation is not simply the outcome of the obvious logical implication that the many can hardly be the wealthy.[9] Aristotle's redefinition, which today we would call sociological or economic, reflects the parabola of Greek democracy. In the fourth century B.C. political cleavage in the *polis* had become extreme. Either the rich governed in their own interest (this was the political form which Aristotle called oligarchy), or the poor governed in theirs (and this was the democracy that Aristotle had before him). The fact that he defined democracy as a government of the poor for their own advantage still impresses us by its topical flavor. Actually Aristotle arrived at that crudely realistic definition for the simple reason that it summarized the breaking up of Greek democracy by the class struggle. And there is nothing surprising in that outcome.

Real self-government, as the Greeks practiced it, required the citizen's devoting himself completely to the public service. Governing oneself meant spending one's life governing. "The citizen . . . gave himself to the State totally; he gave his blood in war; his time in peace; he was not free to put aside public affairs to take care of his own . . . on the contrary, he had to neglect them to work for the good of the city." [10] And there is the crux of the problem. The degree of politicalization required by the formula was so absorbing that a profound imbalance was created among the various requirements and functions of society: for political hypertrophy inevitably brings about economic atrophy. The more perfect their democracy became, the poorer the citizens became. And the Greek *polis* could not escape from the vicious circle of seeking a political solution to economic distress by confiscating wealth in order to make up for insufficient production of wealth. The democracy of antiquity was fated to be destroyed in the class struggle between rich and poor, because it had produced only a political animal and not a *homo oeconomicus* as well.

If we look at the Greek system in this light it helps us to understand, by contrast, that indirect systems of government have advantages which we are too inclined to underrate. For one thing, indirect types of democracy more easily escape being carried to extremes. A government that passes through numerous intermediaries, and is constructed so as to have the process of political decision-making go through numerous stages, is in itself an important stabilizing factor. It is true that today we again speak of class struggle, and that in certain countries it actually exists. But there is a difference. For in ancient times the war between rich and poor was inevitable, growing, as it did, out of a functional imbalance of the system; whereas today it is not inevitable and we can—if we know how—escape it.

This, however, is not all, nor even the essential. For the basic advantage of a system based on the control of power is that it permits the enormous amount of time and energy which a system based on direct personal participation demands for the *res publica,* to be devoted to the necessary non-political activities of society. From this angle whoever continues to look forward to a society in which every citizen is actively and endlessly engaged in the management of public affairs, is clearly blind to the fact that actual participation in government—if it is real and not just talked about—demands that hypertrophic development of political activity which made Aristotle say that a man who has to work in order to live cannot be a citizen; a development that might well re-open the vicious circle of a growing penury in which the solution of the (economic) problem of prosperity is sought in the (political) redistribution of poverty.

So it is by no means certain that direct democracy, if feasible, is preferable to indirect democracy. On the contrary, the frantic politicalization required by such a system would force the economic-minded twentieth-century citizen to devote himself body and soul to politics, which is precisely the development which the indifferent *polites* of our time wishes to avoid at all costs. And this political overload would still leave the problem unsolved. For the advocates of a direct maximization of representative democracy fail to tell us how they would solve the very problems that the Greeks found insoluble.[11]

There remains the question of feasibility. And in this connection it must be stressed that even if direct democracy were preferable, it is nonetheless impossible.[12] For it can exist only within a city-community, only *intra moenia.* Real self-government cannot be presumed: it requires the actual presence and participation of the people concerned. It is impossible to have direct democracy at a distance, to have a face-to-face system of self-government among absentees. At the same time, the greater the number of people involved, the less effective is their participation. From this quantitative angle as well, the notion of self-government easily becomes diluted to the vanishing point. In sum, when vast territories and entire nations are involved, direct democracy becomes an unusable formula. And that is why the ancient republics waned with the cities which gave birth to them; and why despotism and caesarism took the place of direct democracy as soon as the political organisms were extended, as was inevitable, beyond the city.

It is a fact, then, that democracy based on personal participation is possible only under certain conditions; and correspondingly that when these conditions no longer exist representative democracy is the only type possible. The two systems are not, therefore, alternatives to be chosen between on the basis of personal likings. It is true that an approximation of direct democracy exists even today in the form of local self-government. The principle of democratic decentralization, which is the ideal of political pluralism,[13] is an expression of this approximation. Moreover, it is quite true that democracy in the social sense is built upon a network of small communities and is based on the vitality of participating groups. However, in the modern world the group basis of society and local self-government are subordinated to, and conditioned by, political democracy—that is, by a "sovereign democracy" that is very definitely *not* a direct democracy. For we are only deluding ourselves if we consider the referendum and the popular initiative of legislation as modern equivalents and substitutes of direct democracy.[14]

Even if the so-called forms of direct integration of representative democracy functioned as their advocates would like (and this is not the case) they would still be unable to transform a representative into a semi-direct system. If I put a drop of ink in the bathtub, I might say that I had produced inky water, or watered ink. The fact would remain, however, that while I could comfortably take a bath in that water, I would not be able to write with it. And the actual effect of introducing the referendum and the popular legislative initiative as forms of "direct integration" of indirect democracy is about the same; it just makes a representative system more cumbersome.[15] The main reason for this, obviously enough, is that under

256

the present circumstances the techniques of direct government reveal themselves to be what they actually are—very rudimentary techniques that can function only in very simple situations for solving elementary problems.[16]

Clearly, then, when we say that there are two types of democracy, one based on the direct exercise of political power and the other on the control and limitation of power, we are not discussing interchangeable systems but rather the modern solution of a problem left unsolved by the ancients. This amounts to saying that whoever advocates for the modern State the formula of a direct democracy is making a choice in a historical vacuum in favor of a completely imaginary alternative.[17]

One might comment that, in order to realize democracy at all, modern man has had to be satisfied with less democracy. But I do not think that this is so. Although modern man expects less of "literal democracy," i.e., of popular sovereignty, he actually asks infinitely more of "liberal democracy," which is the other thing that he calls democracy. For the difference between the two systems is chiefly one of ideals, not just of referents.

Participation in the exercise of power does not necessarily imply individual liberty. My liberty *vis-à-vis* political power cannot be derived from the infinitesimal portion of that power by means of which I concur with others in the creation of the rules to which I shall be subject.[18] Therefore our principle of the limitation and control of power does not mean that we are achieving more by asking for less, but rather that we are trying to solve a problem that did not exist for the Greeks: the problem of providing a secure freedom for every individual. All of this exceeds by far the democracy of antiquity, which remains for us an incomplete, embryonic democracy exactly for this reason: it was merely a literal democracy concerned only with the people as a whole.

3. Freedom, Old and New

There is as much difference between the ancient and the modern conceptions of democracy as between the ancient and modern conceptions of freedom. The latter is, however, a very controversial issue,[19] since it is not easy to detect the respective characteristics of the

257

modern and the classical notions of liberty. But the fact that the difference is questioned is an additional reason for returning to it.

The extreme position, in the line which we might say of Constant, Tocqueville, and Laboulaye, is perhaps the one expressed by Fustel de Coulanges when he declared: "The belief that in the ancient cities man enjoyed liberty is one of the strangest errors one can commit. He did not have the remotest idea of it. . . . Having political rights, voting, nominating magistrates, being able to be appointed archon—that is what was called liberty; but men were not less slaves of the State for all that." [20] The logic of this judgment might be paraphrased as follows: measured by modern standards, men of antiquity were not free according to our notion of individual freedom.

Unfortunately, "individual freedom" is indeed vague. And if we do not make this concept more specific, the question, "On what basis can it be maintained that individual liberty was unknown to the Greeks?" will be raised over and over again.[21] And rightly so, since there is no doubt that Greek, and more particularly Athenian civilization, was a multiform, vital explosion of individualistic spirit. Nonetheless, between this individualistic spirit and what Constant and the others had in mind, which was "respect for the individual as-a-person," there is an abyss. And perhaps the best way of understanding the distance that separates these notions is to go back to the vocabulary of the ancients.

To the *polites* the distinction between public and private spheres was unknown. As Werner Jaeger put it: "A purely private moral code without reference to the State was inconceivable to the Greeks. We must forget our idea that each individual's acts are ruled by his conscience." [22] For the Greeks "man" and "citizen" meant exactly the same, just as for them *politéuesthai* did not only mean participating in the life of the *polis,* of their city, but definitely meant "to live." [23] By this I am not suggesting that they did not enjoy individual liberty in the sense of a private space existing *de facto.* This would be absurd. But the meaning and value that this notion had is well indicated by the meaning of the Latin *privatus* and its Greek equivalent *idion.* The Latin *privatus,* i.e., private, means "deprived" (from the verb *privare,* to deprive), and the term was used to connote an existence

258

that was incomplete and defective in relation to the community. The Greek *idion* (private) in contrast to *koinón* (the common element) conveys the sense of privation and lack even more intensively. Correspondingly *idiótes* was a pejorative term, meaning he who was not *polítes*—a non-citizen, and therefore a vulgar, unworthy, ignorant man who was concerned only with himself. (Incidentally, it is significant that while the derogatory connotation of *idiótes* has remained in our word "idiot," its original meaning has been completely lost.)

The difference, then, is that the Greeks were not acquainted with the notion of the individual in a positive sense, that is, with the individual *as a person*.[24] And this for the obvious reason that the concept came with Christianity and was subsequently developed by the Renaissance, by Protestantism[25] and by the modern school of natural law.[26] What the Greek individualistic spirit lacked, then, was the notion of a *legitimate* private space conceived as the moral as well as the juridical projection of the single human person. Therefore the Greek experience of political freedom did not and could not signify an individual liberty based on *personal rights*. And this is what Constant and the others meant. When they denied that the Greeks were familiar with the idea of individual liberty, they were saying that the ancients were not acquainted with the *value* expressed by respect for the individual as a person, a notion which has since gained concrete safeguards from the rule of law, "juridical defense" [27] and the declarations of rights.

The fact that an impassioned individualistic instinct flourished throughout all Athenian democracy does not therefore contradict the assertion that the individual was actually undefended and remained at the mercy of the collective body.[28] For that democracy did not respect the individual; rather it tended to suspect him. Distrustful and jealous of outstanding individuals, fickle in its praise, pitiless in its persecution, it was a city in which ostracism was a precautionary, not a punitive measure—a punishment for no crime! It was a democracy from which Ermodore of Ephesus (to cite only one example) was banished because one citizen was not permitted to be better than the others. And in such a system the individual's position was precarious because, as Laboulaye observed, "the only guarantee for the citizen was his part of sovereignty," and this explains, he added,

259

"how it happens that in Greece and Rome it was possible to pass overnight from the greatest liberty to the severest slavery." [29]

Why, then, is the question concerning the distance between modern liberty and ancient freedom so controversial? The unfortunate fact is that authors seldom make clear which Greeks and which period of time they are talking about, whereas, clearly, this makes a great difference. In the first place, Athens is not Sparta—it is its antithesis. As Plutarch told us, "In Athens each person could live as he pleased, in Sparta no one could." [30] In the second place, if in talking about the Greek vicissitudes we consider only Athens, and, what is more, only Periclean Athens, we can obviously prove anything we wish.[31] For the Age of Pericles was one of those extraordinary and felicitous moments of history, in which a perfect harmony springs from a fortuitous combination of elements and events. But when we assert that the individual citizen of the *polis* did not enjoy the independence and security that we consider freedom, we are basing our judgment, as is only proper, on the entire parable of all the Greek democracies. I have said "democracies," but here a further caution is needed: for we must remember that the picture which was considered by the modern revivers of the classical ideal of democracy was broader—so broad as to include Sparta. Paradoxically enough Rousseau and his school idealized and cherished the Spartans and the Romans far more than the Athenians.[32]

All in all, then, what was the classical idea of democracy? We can now answer easily enough. For the Greeks, democracy was only that system of government in which the decisions were made collectively. Hence, in the classical formula of democracy the community allows no margin of independence and no sphere of protection to the single individual, whom it absorbs completely. The *polis* is sovereign in the sense that the individuals that compose it are completely subject to it. As Hobbes well understood, "The Athenians and Romans were free; that is, free commonwealths: not that any particular men had the liberty to resist their own representative but that their representative had the liberty to resist or invade other people." [33] The fact that the city is free does not mean, or imply, that the citizens are.

When Aristotle defined man as a political animal, he intended

260

to define his essence, not merely to indicate an attribute. For the ancients, man was the *polítes,* that is, when they said "man" they meant the citizen of his *civitas.* In other words, the *polis,* not the *polítes,* was primary, and consequently the individual was a part of his city just as an organ is part of its organism. And the basic difference between the ancient and modern conceptions lies precisely in this: that we believe that a man is *more* than a citizen of a State. In our conception the quality and the value of a human being is not monopolized by his political and social self: he cannot be reduced to his "citizen-ness." For us, a man is not merely a member of a collective *plenum.* It follows from this that a number of questions that did not concern antiquity are instead very important to us. Our problems cannot be adequately solved by a system which only provides that the exercise of power be collective. Modern democracy is meant to protect a freedom of the individual *as a person*—a freedom which cannot be entrusted to the "subjection of the individual to the power of the whole." [34]

These considerations lead us to the simple and obvious conclusion that if we want to understand the Greek idea of democracy, we must erase from our mental picture of it everything that was added later. And once we have made the necessary subtractions, all that remains is an ethico-political idea of liberty which can mean very little, if anything at all, to us. Let us not get lost in minor and dubious distinctions, as when we discuss whether the ancients had political and not civil liberties, or vice versa. The truth is, very simply, that their ideas of civil, political, juridical, individual, and any other liberty were not the same as ours. Nor could it be otherwise, since we are separated from the ancients by value acquisitions of which they were not aware.

4. The Modern Idea and Ideal

One of the reasons that we so often lose the sense of historical distance springs from the bad habit of carelessly modernizing the vocabulary, that is, of applying modern terms to epochs of the past in which these terms either did not exist or were deliberately set aside. Thus when the German *Staatslehre* came into fashion, everybody began to consider the *polis* a State;[35] and we still do find, as a

261

rule, *polis* translated as "city-State."[36] Today "democracy" is the fashion, and we immediately forget, or at least bypass, the fact that for more than two thousand years the term democracy had practically disappeared from current usage and had entirely lost its laudatory connotation.[37] During this long period we spoke of "Republic," not democracy. And to say *respublica* is not the same thing as to say democracy.

Semantically speaking, *res publica* expresses the idea of a thing belonging to everybody, or of the affairs of everybody, and is therefore different from the idea of a power belonging to the people. I mean that *demokratía* lends itself to the interpretation of having to do with the "power of a part," whereas *respublica* does not; and while the former term refers to a definite subject (the people), the latter suggests rather the notion of the general interest and the common good.[38] Historically speaking, moreover, the two concepts had parted company from each other to such a degree that the meaning of "republic" had become the antithesis of that of democracy.

In 1795 Kant severely criticized those who had begun to confuse the republican constitution with the democratic, observing that as far as the exercise of power (*forma regiminis*) is concerned, every government is "republican or despotic," and that democracy, in the proper sense of the word, "is necessarily a despotism."[39] We should not assume that in linking democracy with despotism he was reacting against the excesses of the French Revolution. Kant had welcomed the events of 1789, and besides, the identification of democracy with despotism was an accepted notion of the time. Actually Kant was in no way original in his blunt rejection of democracy as a form of tyrannical rule. Madison and Hamilton, thousands of miles from Koenigsberg and in a far different context, did not think very differently from Kant on the subject. Madison always said "representative republic" and never "democracy," because for him the latter meant the direct democracy of antiquity, that is "a society consisting of a small number of citizens who assemble and administer the government in person." And he too was expressing a common judgment when he wrote that ". . . democracies have ever been spectacles of turbulence and contention; have ever been found incompatible with personal security or the rights of property; and have in general been as short in their lives as they have been violent in their deaths." [40]

The Philadelphia Assembly was not thinking in terms of a democracy either, and what was to become the constitution of the first modern democracy was considered by its framers to be a republican, not a democratic constitution.[41] Even the French Revolution had a republic as its ideal, and although in those turbulent years it also pressed for a democracy—the democracy that became known as Jacobin democracy—this was a secondary aim that was cloaked under the name of *république*.[42] Only Robespierre used the word democracy, and then only at the end, in his speech to the Convention on February 5, 1794, thereby insuring its bad reputation (at least in Europe) for another half-century.[43]

The fact is, then, that when we superimpose "democracy" on "republic" we are creating a false historical continuity which keeps us from realizing that in adopting "republic" Western civilization had settled for an ideal more moderate and prudent, less monolithic and radical than democracy: all in all, a mixed ideal of the political optimum that discards—we might say—the "thing of somebody" (no matter whether the One or the *demos*) in favor of the "thing of nobody." So an arbitrary uniformity of terminology hides the very point we ought to see, that is, the completeness of the break between antiquity's attempt at democracy and its modern reincarnation. Consequently it keeps us from raising this rather interesting question: How was it possible for an ideal which (as we well know) can be so deeply inspiring, to be in eclipse for so long a period of history?

If, as I believe, the history of language reflects history *tout court,* the oblivion into which the term democracy fell is indeed significant. For it testifies eloquently, in itself, that the collapse of the ancient democracies was as final as it was memorable. And this very fact suggests that the word has again come into use chiefly because something new has come into existence.

Although the word is Greek, the thing that we are now indicating by it originated outside of Greece, and much later than the age of the *polis*. Actually, the meaning of modern democracies is related to, and conditioned by, the discovery that dissent, diversity of opinion, and contrast are not incompatible with social order and authority. The ideal genesis of our democracies is in the principle that difference and not uniformity is the leaven and the nourishment of States: a point of view that gained ground in the wake of the Reformation after the seventeenth century. We have to be vague here, because it is extremely difficult, if not impossible, to link this new conception of life to a particular thinker, event, or movement.[44] The maturation of this approach was slow and tortuous; and it seems to me that it was one of those cases where men become aware of what they have been discovering and doing only *ex post*.

Certainly this horizon would never have come into view without the Reformation. For it was not possible to understand that plurality and "parts" were not necessarily inimical to unity until the *Res Publica Christiana* of the Middle Ages had broken up. And I do not deny that the experience of the Puritan sects marked an important step in this trend. Not so much for the reasons that are usually given,[45] as that they encouraged the de-politicalizing of society by breaking the tie between the spheres of God and Caesar, thereby shifting the *ubi consistam* of human life to voluntary associations independent of the State, in the sense that the internal bond among the associates became stronger than that which linked them with the body politic as a whole. Having granted this, it does not follow that Puritanism was the decisive and primary agent in the process of creating the liberal-democratic *Weltanschauung*. In this regard the contribution of the Puritans has been, I feel, overemphasized: for their role was just that, a contributory role.[46]

However that may be, what is important is not to discover who was the originator (assuming there was one) but to understand the importance and the novelty of the event. By and large, until the seventeenth century, diversity was considered a source of discord and disorder causing the downfall of States, and unanimity was regarded as the necessary foundation of any government. From then on, the opposite attitude gradually took hold, and unanimity—not dissent and diversity—came to be viewed with suspicion. It is through this revolutionary reversal of perspective that the civilization we call "liberal" has been built piecemeal, and it is by this route that we reach present-day democracy.[47] Autocracies, despotisms, old and new tyrannies are all monochromatic worlds, while democracy is multi-colored.[48] But it is liberal democracy, not ancient democracy, that is based on diversity. It is we, not the Greeks, who have discovered how to build a political system on multiplicity and differences.

If we pass from the germination of the ideal to its realization, it is only about the middle of the nineteenth century that popular sovereignty appears on the stage of history as an influential, lasting, and stabilizing element of the political process, instead of a disorderly, fickle, and disruptive aspect of it. This, too, we should note, is an innovation. With all due respect to nostalgia for the classics, what really happened in Athens, as well as in Megara, Samos, Messene, Miletus, Syracuse—to name just a few other eloquent cases—has been accurately reported by those who were there, and is indeed different from what *ex post facto* idealizers of a Golden Age contend. With the passing of time, "popular power" in Greek society functioned increasingly as a steam-roller, since whatever the crowd approved became law, with no limits on their exercise of a limitless power.[49] Bryce could thus legitimately comment: "Impatient of restraints, even such restraints as they had by law imposed upon themselves, they [the people] ruled as a despot ruler exemplifying the maxim that no one is good enough to be trusted with absolute power." [50]

Our notion of popular power is completely different, and precisely by virtue of this our democracies can endure. If popular sovereignty has risen once again and this time plays a constructive role, it is because it no longer absorbs all the other elements of the political process: rather, it has been absorbed by them. In the decision-making processes of the liberal-democratic systems, the purely democratic element is the most noticeable but it is by no means *the* determining factor. It is not popular sovereignty by itself, no matter how it is interpreted, that is responsible for the proper functioning of our political systems. Other decisive factors must come into play if the principle of democracy is to produce a democratic result, i.e., a free society in which the people, being free, are in a position to really wield a power of their own.

Although the deontology gives an exclusive place to popular sovereignty, we all know that democracy cannot be reduced to this alone. Whenever the people have used their sovereignty to sanction the advent of a dictator—and, unfortunately, this is no longer a rare event—even the most fervent demolater maintains that such a regime is not democratic. By what right? Because we evidently do not believe that democracy amounts *only* to popular power. Otherwise we should have to consider democratic any system to which the people seem to consent.

5. A Reversal of Perspectives

I have stressed the discontinuity between ancient democracy and ours—which is not made up simply of the Greek ideal plus some subsequent additions—because, as a result of saying, for purposes of brevity, *only* "democracy," we forget, or subordinate, what we have left unsaid. The result is that democracy (the expressed word) becomes dominant, and liberalism (the implied concept) subordinate. This is the exact opposite of the truth. For no matter how much a short-range historical perspective can magnify what is merely close to us, the present-day progress of democracy over liberalism is indeed slight compared to the progress made by modern liberalism over ancient democracy. However little we are aware of it, the democracy that we believe in and practice is *liberal* democracy.

We may put it this way: if, according to the Greek criterion of freedom, the Greeks were free, by the same token we certainly would be slaves. The reason for this is that if the Greek concept of democracy were applied to the modern world it would correspond exactly to a totalitarian despotism. Therefore, whoever calls for the "freedom of antiquity" is actually not asking for liberty, but (even though he does not realize it) for its opposite.

As we have seen, the *polites* were subordinate to the *polis*, the *civis* lived for the *civitas*—for his city—not the other way around. And if we think it over it was logical enough, in that epoch, to look at the problem in this way. For, materially speaking, the city and the citizens were so closely tied together that they could be envisaged as one and the same thing. But suppose we make the necessary substitutions. Instead of the square where the *demos* gathered together, let us imagine the territory of an entire nation, and instead of the governing being carried on by the people themselves, let us imagine that governing is delegated to an *ad hoc* organ, the State. Now,

266

clearly, in these conditions, what remains of the Greek system of democracy is nothing but the precept, "The citizen is made for the State, and not the State for the citizen." And this is the very formula of the States in which there is neither democracy nor freedom, the formula which is used today to justify absolute governments. Nor is this reversal in meaning strange. If a principle that was once valid for a democracy is now used by tyrannies, this happens because the factual terms of the political problem are reversed.[51]

In the city-communities of antiquity, liberty was not expressed through opposition to State power—for there was no State—but through participation in the collective exercise of power. But once we have a State that is distinct from, and superior to society, the problem is reversed, and consequently the demand of a power *for* the people can only mean *opposition to* the State, i.e., comes to mean that the State must not have all the power. Whatever respect we have for the individual-as-a-person (and even if we attach very little value to it) the fact is that the micro-democracy of antiquity was not faced with the problem of the relation between citizens and State, whereas modern macro-democracy is. The Greeks were able to be free, in their own way, by starting from the *polis* to reach the *polites*. But this is not the case for us. When the *polis* is supplanted by a megalopolis, we can remain free only if we move in the opposite direction, i.e., starting from the citizen, from the rights of man, and arriving at the State.

As we can see, it would really be absurd for us to give our concept of democracy the meaning it had for the Greeks in the fifth century B.C. If this happens, it is out of unawareness, it is simply because we have adopted their term. I say "unawareness" advisedly. Actually if we were in a position to weigh impure liberal democracies against pure ante-liberal democracy, it is hard to see how we could decide that the former are worth less than the latter. Unfortunately many of our contemporaries are not capable of making this comparison. So what actually happens is that they choose simply on the basis of the word, and of the *short word*. That is to say that if "liberal democracy" appeals to us less than "democracy" the primary reason for this is that we tend to follow the path of least resistance, to rely on the simplicity of a name at the expense of the complexity of the thing.

It is of paramount importance, therefore, for us to realize that when we indicate a free political system by the word democracy we are using this one term for the sake of brevity, and that this use of "democracy" *brevitatis causa* gives rise to dangerous simplifications and omissions. For, more often than not, all there is behind the shorthand is a void, that is, our failure to take into account twenty-five hundred years of trial and error, innovation and correction. It is but a small step from abbreviation as a useful expedient, to abbreviation as an instrument of mental inertia. If then we do not wish to sell our birth-right for a dish of lentils, we must have the patience to go back and fill in the blanks, that is, to make again *explicit* everything that—in saying "democracy"—remains *implicit*.

NOTES

† "La Liberté antique et la liberté moderne," in *L'État et ses limites* (Paris, 1871), p. 105.

1. Herodotus, *History*, Vol. III, p. 80. Cf. on this page Sinclair, *A History of Greek Political Thought* (London, 1952), Chap. III. It is worth noting that even afterwards this association remains preponderant with respect to that between *demokratía* and *eleuthería* (freedom).

2. For Marx and Lenin cf. Chaps. XVII, 1, and XVIII, 3 below. I have also in mind the post-war formulae of "labor self-management," which are typically exemplified in J. Djordjevic, *La Jugoslavie, démocratie socialiste* (Paris, 1959).

3. Obviously this remark opens the question of what is meant by "State." The abstract form of this word as a substantive from the Latin participle *status* (which as such means only any situation or state of being) began to be used in the modern sense only with Machiavelli. However, as Francesco Ercole (*La Politica di Machiavelli* [Rome, 1926], Chap. II), among others, has demonstrated, tne Florentine secretary used the word *Stato* even with the former meaning of "rank" and "condition," as in the French *état* and in the German *Stand* (cf. Chap. III, note 2, above). Actually the modern use was consolidated by Hobbes, who equated the term "Commonwealth" with "State," and above all by Pufendorf's French translation, in which *civitas* was consistently translated by Barbeyrac as *état*. As for the concept, I do not employ "State" in the juridic meaning of the term, but in its empirical and political one, and therefore not in the sense of "politically organized society" which makes State and society coextensive, but to refer to those who are institutionally vested with the power to govern or to

administer a society. A good recapitulation on the history of the problem is found in Felice Battaglia, *Scritti di teoria dello stato* (Milano, 1939). For the relationship between law and State see finally G. Balladore Pallieri, *Dottrina dello stato* (Padova, 1958), and Vincenzo Gueli, *Elementi di una dottrina dello stato e del diritto* (Roma, 1959).

4. Also called "immediate" democracy (by Max Weber), "pure" (e.g., by Madison), "simple" (e.g., by Paine). As for the relationship between direct democracy and the so-called popular democracy of the Soviet type, cf. Chap. XVII, 2, below.

5. The estimates are controversial, but it is certain that the male population of the city of Athens at the time of Pericles did not number more than 45,000 free adult citizens, probably around 35,000. Cf. W. Warde Fowler, *The City-State of the Greeks and Romans* (London, 1952), p. 167. Cf. also the more elaborate counts by Alfred E. Zimmern, *The Greek Commonwealth* (Oxford, 1911), pp. 169-174.

6. Cf. *Politics,* 1279a. For references see William Ellis' trans. (New York, 1923).

7. Thucydides, *The History of the Peloponnesian War*, trans. R. Crawley (New York, 1950), p. 123, and in general pp. 121-130.

8. Cf. *Politics,* 1279, 1280. Plato too had remarked in passing that "democracy comes into being after the poor have conquered their opponents." (*Republic,* VIII, 557). Cf. also Callicles' remark in *Gorgias,* 483: "The makers of laws are the majority who are weak; and they make laws and distribute praises and censures with a view to themselves and to their own interests." (Jowett's trans.)

9. That this is a purely accidental concomitance is the express warning of Aristotle. Cf. *Politics,* 1290a-1290b.

10. Fustel de Coulanges, *La Cité antique* (Paris, [1864] ed. 1878), p. 396. For a vivid description of the "amount of work that this democracy exacted from its people" (p. 395) read all of Chap. XI of Bk. IV.

11. One suspects that this perplexity may have struck even Rousseau. After having called to mind that among the Greeks "the slaves did the work," for "the chief occupation [of the people] was their own freedom," Rousseau exclaims: "What! Freedom cannot stand without leaning on servitude? Perhaps. The two extremes touch each other." Evidently Rousseau had stepped into the mechanism of direct democracy quite well, and for his part he avoided the embarrassment by remarking that the city must be "quite small." He gave us to understand that, perhaps, on this condition the citizen could have looked after his own freedom and also have time for the rest, without falling into the "unhappy position where one cannot preserve his own freedom except at the expense of that of others, and where the citizen can be perfectly free only when the slave is extremely slave." (*Contrat social,* III, 15).

269

12. For a logical demonstration of this impossibility, cf. Chap. IV, 3, above.

13. By "pluralism" is generally meant that trend of thought which opposes the theory of the sovereignty of the State in order to vindicate the equal right of all associations and organizations of the body politic. I am referring evidently to the "old pluralism," typically represented by the English doctrine with Figgis, Maitland, G. D. H. Cole, S. G. Hobson, the early Laski, and also, in part. by A. D. Lindsay and E. Baker (Cf. for all Ernest Baker, *Principles of Social and Political Theory* [Oxford, 1952]), and not to the new American "pluralism" as expressed by the "group approach" of Bentley, E. Lathan and David Truman. As for juridical pluralism, it has found its main exponents in Duguit and Gurvitch.

14. Such was, e.g., the illusion of Giuseppe Rensi, *Gli 'anciens régimes' e la democrazia diretta* (Bellinzona, 1902, pub. also with a different title in Rome, 1926 and in Milan, 1946). Rensi spoke of "modern forms of direct democracy" (p. 35) with reference to the referendum and the right of popular initiative and revision, whereas he used the term "pure democracy" for the genuine direct democracy, that is, for "those systems in which the people have no assemblies to represent them, but manage their affairs . . . as in the Swiss Cantons by means of *Landsgemeinde*" (p. 11). However the distinction between "pure" and "direct" democracy seems to me unacceptable, at least for the purpose of demonstrating that the introduction of the referendum and popular initiative have the virtue of transforming a representative system into something like a direct system. To refer to a direct democracy because of those devices, as is often still done, is simply to project into the future a naïveté of Bryce, and the illusions of the Rousseaunian school and Considerant. Even the early constitutional work of Giuseppe Capograssi, *La nuova democrazia diretta* (Lanciano, 1921), republished in *Opere* (Milano, 1959) Vol. I, pp. 403-573, reflects the same kind of naïveté.

15. Therefore I find that it is somewhat deceptive to distinguish, as, e.g., in M. Duverger, *Droit constitutionnel et institutions politiques* (Paris, 1955), between direct, representative, and semi-direct democracy (cf. p. 226). To speak of a "semi-direct democracy" is clearly to overstate the case and to suggest a "synthetic solution" which does not exist.

16. Cf. Herman Finer's brief but effective recapitulation on the disappointing results of popular legislation and the referendum in different countries, *The Theory and Practice of Modern Government* (London, 1954), pp. 560-568. The manipulation of popular initiative on the part of pressure groups is clearly shown by specific researches such as Key and Crouch, *The Initiative and Referendum in California* (Berkeley, 1936), esp. pp. 565-568; and J. K. Pollock, *The Initiative and Referendum in Michigan* (Ann Arbor, 1940), esp. p. 69.

17. The vestiges of truly direct democracy survive only in the smallest, patriarchal and, I would say, pastoral *Landsgemeinden* of Glaris, Appenzell, and Unter-

270

wald (five cantons, because Appenzell is divided into Rhodes-Intérieures and Rhodes-Extérieures, and Unterwald is divided into Nidwald and Obwald). The cantons of Zoug and Schwyz abandoned the *Landsgemeinde* in 1848; Uri did likewise in 1928. Moreover, in 1922 Obwald deprived itself of all but its elective functions. It is also worth noting that the five cantons represent little more than 3 per cent of the total population of Switzerland. See W. E. Rappard, *The Government of Switzerland* (New York, 1936), Chap. III, IV; and esp. *Da Démocratie directe dans les communes Suisses,* ed. Marcel Bridel (Zurich, 1952).

18. Cf. Chap. XIII, 5, 6, below.

19. The debate was opened by Benjamin Constant with the speech delivered in 1819 at the Atheneum of Paris: *De la liberté des anciens comparée à celle des modernes.* The influence of Hegelian learning has operated in such a manner that the opposition indicated by Constant was not well understood in Italy. In his *Storia del liberalismo europeo* (Bari, 1925), De Ruggiero accedes too easily to Jellinek's criticism of Constant (cf. p. 177). In 1931, Croce, in reevaluating Constant's ideas, remarked that the problem "is singularly minimized or rendered altogether insignificant by the treatment of the difference between ancient and modern freedom which is made by Jellinek in his *Allgemeine Staatslehre"* (cf. *Etica e politica,* p. 296). But even Croce, as Bobbio points out, failed to grasp the essence of Constant's thought. Cf. Norberto Bobbio, *Politica e cultura,* pp. 248-249. Cf. also Guido Calogero in *Saggi di etica e di teoria del diritto* (Bari, 1947), pp. 56-73.

20. *La Cité Antique,* p. 269 *et passim,* Bk. III, Chap. XVIII. Fustel's straight denial was directed at Grote's *History of Greece* (1856), which had described the Greek city as a bulwark of individual liberty. In the German doctrine Fustel's position was followed by Stahl, Von Mohl, and Bluntschli. Cf. for all Chap. VI of Bluntschli's *Allgemeine Staatslehre.*

21. Cf. finally Eric A. Havelock, *Liberal Temper in Greek Politics* (New Haven, 1957).

22. *Paideia: The Ideals of Greek Culture,* trans. Gilbert Highet (New York, 1945), Vol. I, p. 326.

23. As Burckhardt put it, "The citizen realizes all his power and virtue in the state and for the state; all the spirit and culture of Greece are firmly bound with the *polis." Kulturgeschichte Griechenlands* (Berlin, 1934), p. 55.

24. Even Jellinek, who also criticizes Fustel's thesis (cf. *Dottrina generale dello stato* [Italian trans. Milano, 1921], Vol. I, p. 542 f.), reaches the same conclusion: "In ancient times man was never definitely recognized as a person. . . . Only the nineteenth century has scored a general victory with the principle: 'man is a person' " (pp. 573-574).

25. Cf. Niebuhr's discussion on this point: "If Protestantism represents the final heightening of the idea of individuality within terms of the Christian religion, the Renaissance is the real cradle of . . . the autonomous individual. . . . Ostensibly Renaissance thought is a revival of classicism. . . . Yet classic thought has no such passion for the individual as the Renaissance betrays. The fact is that the Renaissance uses an idea which could have grown only upon the soil of Christianity. It transplants this idea to the soil of classic rationalism to produce a new concept of individual autonomy, which is known in neither classicism nor Christianity." Reinhold Niebuhr, *The Nature and Destiny of Man* (New York, 1941), Vol. I, p. 61.

26. The modern, let it be emphasized, not the former ones. As Alessandro Passerin d'Entrèves, *Natural Law* (London, 1951), notes sharply: "Except for the name, the medieval and the modern notions of natural law have little in common" (p. 9). This is all the more reason why—as Bryce remarked—between the ancient and stoic notion of natural law and its modern version there is the same difference as that between a "harmless maxim" and a "mass of dynamite" (*loc. cit.* p. 10). Cf. also Chap. XIV, note 16, below.

27. I am using Mosca's terminology, *difesa giuridica.* C. J. Friedrich finds it a "quaint" expression for "rule of law." (Cf. the 1946 ed. of *Constitutional Government and Democracy,* p. 592. Chap. XXV was omitted from later eds.). However, as I will say later (Chap. XIII, 7, below), the reason for using different labels is that Mosca did not have in mind the Anglo-Saxon rule of law.

28. For this reason, as Burckhardt remarked (quoting Böckh), "The *polis* must have made its people unhappy." For it encouraged the individual "to bring out to the utmost the potential of his personality in order to demand later its most complete renouncement. In the entire history of the world," Burckhardt concluded, "it is difficult to find another nation which paid so dearly for its actions as the Greek *polis.* In fact along with their high cultural development the Greeks must have also developed the sensitivity to realize the sufferings that they inflicted upon each other." (*La Civiltà Greca,* Italian transl., Firenze, 1955, Vol. I, pp. 339-340).

29. Edouard Laboulaye in *L'État et ses limites,* p. 108.

30. Cf. Pohlenz, *Griechische Freiheit,* p. 28. Referring to Pericles' epitaph, Pohlenz brings out that "in every respect the description of Pericles marks the reverse of the Spartan kosmos. The latter is dominated by coercion, and the individual is completely claimed by the state. In Athens there reigns a freedom where the individual is shut in as little as possible."

31. Cf., for instance, G. Glotz, *The Greek City and Its Institutions* (New York, 1930), p. 128: "In the age of Pericles, Athenian political life showed a perfect equilibrium between the rights of the individual and the power of the state.

Individual liberty was complete. . . ." Glotz, however, exaggerates. See *contra* the over-all judgment of W. Jaeger which applies also to Athens: "The *polis* is the sum of all its citizens and of all the aspects of their lives. It gives each citizen much but it can demand all in return. Relentless and powerful it imposes its way of life on each individual and marks him for its own. From it are derived all the norms which govern the life of its citizens. Conduct that injures it is bad, conduct that helps it is good." (*Paideia*, [New York 1939], trans. Gilbert Highet), Vol. I, p. 106. On the other hand, Glotz modifies his evaluation when he begins to discuss the 4th century B.C., as one can gather from this statement: "In the fourth century the principle 'the people has the right to do what pleases it' was pushed to its furthest limits; it was even sovereign over the laws." Glotz, *op. cit.*, p. 133.

32. The quarrel on the freedom of the ancient and modern people is also tied up with the different type of interest one has in the classic world. Those who are mostly moved by an esthetic appeal towards Hellenic culture will always tend to look upon it as a "model." Moreover, many authors follow the policy of stressing the "permanence" of political fundamentals and are therefore induced precisely for this reason to make that past appear close to our present. If we take care of reckoning with these variables many prima facie contradictory assertions are easy to explain.

33. *Leviathan*, Chap. XXI. Of course, the term "representative" is, in this context, used loosely.

34. Benjamin Constant, "De la Liberté des anciens comparée à celle des modernes." Cf. Italian trans. in *Biblioteca di scienze politiche*, A. Brunialti ed., Vol. V, p. 455.

35. This is less the case with writings in English, however. Even though the English writers received from Hobbes the identity Commonwealth = State, the latter term has never become popular (cf. Chap. XI, 3, above), even when, after Cromwell and the revolution of 1649, "Commonwealth" became for a long time a discredited label.

36. And yet Jellinek himself warned—precisely when speaking of "The name 'State' "—that "the history of the terminology of a science is strictly bound up with the history of the science itself. Between the term and the concept takes place an uninterrupted repercussion. Often the word has shown the way to all the science of a people and of an epoch." (*Dottrina generale dello stato* [Italian trans. Milano, 1921], Vol. I, p. 291.) But, then, how can we superimpose the name to a time that ignored it?

37. Even when, in consulting Greek sources, the Latin authors came across *demokratia*, they avoided in every way transcribing that term. Schmalz has noted that in the Latin writers of the classical period up to the 4th century A.D. the term *demokratia* appears only three times, and in passages and authors strictly of secondary order. It is not until the early Middle Ages that

the term is used sometimes by those who referred to Aristotle's *Politics,* but rarely and by writers of little importance, with the exception of Marsilius of Padua and Thomas Aquinas (cf. Schmalz, *Antibarbarus,* I, 415, s. v. *democratia).* The common practice is to follow Ciceronian paraphrases, like *civitas,* or *potestas popularis,* or *imperium populi.* Machiavelli will say "principato popolare" (popular principality), Guicciardini will write "vivere popolare" (popular living), and in Giambattista Vico one finds no trace of the word "democrazia" (democracy). Cf. also for an analysis of the history of the term, R. Wollheim, "Democracy," *The Journal of the History of Ideas,* Vol. XIX (1958), pp. 225-242.

38. Thus classic writers in the English language have nearly always rendered *Respublica* by "commonwealth."

39. *Perpetual Peace,* Sect. II, "The primary requisite of a perpetual peace: 'The form of government of every state must be republican.' "

40. Cf. *The Federalist* No. 10. Cf. also Nos. 1, 9, 37, 70. Hamilton follows the same line of thinking as Madison, even if exceptionally, in a letter of 1777, he wrote "representative democracy" to mean "representative republic."

41. In those years the only one who used "democracy" in a favorable sense was Paine (but with a certain insistence only in *The Rights of Man,* Pt. II, Chap. III) taking care, however, to distinguish "representation ingrafted upon democracy" from the bad "simple democracy." Jefferson too, later, rarely used the phrase "representative democracy" and always warning that a "republican government" has nothing in common with "pure democracy."

42. It is worth noting that Rousseau also placed "Republic" above "Democracy." Cf. *Contrat social,* II, 6: "Therefore I call Republic any state which is governed by law . . . for then only the public interest governs. . . . Every legitimate government is republican." With respect to the forms of government (democratic, aristocratic, monarchic) Rousseau maintained that each form fits a particular type of country, but that democracy is best suited "to states which are small and poor" (III, 8; cf. also III, 4). For the concept of democracy in the Encyclopedists, cf. R. Hubert, *Les Sciences sociales dans l'Encyclopédie* (Paris, 1923), pp. 254-255.

43. However, Robespierre himself treats "democracy" as a synonym of "republic." Ferdinand Brunot in his monumental *Histoire de la langue française* (Paris, 1905-1948), Vol. IX, lists 206 words or expressions which characterize the political spectrum during the years of the Revolution. Although "democratic" is mentioned, it appears as one of the terms less frequently used, and mainly to rival "aristocratic" (another revolutionary neologism recorded in a dictionary of 1791 as follows: *"Aristocratic:* combination of syllables . . . which produce a strange effect on an animal called *democratic").* (Cit. in Brunot, p. 652). R. R. Palmer, *The Age of the Democratic Revolution—The Challenge* (Princeton, 1959), points out that "there are only three texts of the

period . . . where the author uses 'democracy' in a favorable sense, as often as eleven times within a few hundred words; and these three texts are those of Paine, Robespierre, and the man who became Pius VII" (p. 19). In addition, cf. R. R. Palmer, "Notes on the Use of the Word 'Democracy' 1789-1799" in *Political Science Quarterly*, II (1953), pp. 203-226, where Palmer notes that "it was in Italy . . . that the word 'democracy' in a favorable sense, was most commonly used in the years from 1796-1799. This . . . is due also, one suspects, to the fact that since republics were an old story in Italy the new ideas could not be symbolized by the word 'Republic' as in France" (p. 220). On the Italian use of the term, cf. Calogero, De Mauro and Sasso, "Intorno alla storia del significato di 'democrazia' in Italia," *Il Ponte*, I (1958), pp. 39-66.

44. This paternity is often attributed to the Puritans. But in the first place the Puritan mold of our world has not left an outstanding, definitive written testimony of itself and this fact renders all traces evanescent and of controversial interpretation. As William Haller has well shown (cf. note 46 below), the seed that was cast by the Puritans was transmitted to history especially by Milton's *Areopagitica* and *The Tenure of Kings and Magistrates*. But in Milton we have the fusion of the Puritan cause with the highest culture of the Renaissance, Humanism, and the Reformation. In the second place the close derivation of our democracy from the Puritan experience, as maintained esp. by A. S. P. Woodhouse (*Puritanism and Liberty* [London, 1938, repr. 1953]), and by Vittorio Gabrieli in Italy (*Puritanismo e libertà—dibattiti e libelli* [Torino, 1956]), is based mainly on the writings of the "levellers," which more recent writers have justly opposed with the theocentric, theocratic, and even chiliastic character of the Puritan sermon (cf. Richard Schlatter, *Richard Baxter and Puritan Politics* [New Brunswick, 1957]); and F. F. Solt, *Saints in Arms: Puritanism and Democracy in Cromwell's Army* [Stanford, 1959]). Schlatter fittingly reminds us that "to the majority of seventeenth-century Puritans, both English and American, 'democracy' and 'liberty' were despicable."

45. Such as the one which credits the Puritans with affirming the freedom of conscience and opinion. As a matter of fact the Puritans were not less intolerant than their enemies, and if they invoked those liberties it was for contingent reasons. John Plamenatz makes the point very well: "The first champions of liberty of conscience were neither ardent reformers nor ardent Catholics. They were mostly quiet men. . . . Both Catholics and Protestants asserted it against the state and against all churches except their own. Where they were a minority they often found it expedient (whatever their mental reservations) to claim it for everyone. . . . There is nothing inherently liberal or equalitarian about Protestantism as such, about the mere claim to defy authority for conscience sake. For what we claim for ourselves we may deny to others. . . ." In *Aspects of Human Equality* (New York, 1956), pp. 92-93.

46. On Puritanism the two volumes of W. Haller remain outstanding, *The Rise of Puritanism,* and *Liberty and Reformation in the Puritan Revolution* (New York, 1938, 1955 resp.). For the New World, cf. R. B. Perry, *Puritanism and Democracy* (New York, 1944). Against the tendency to overstate the contribution of the Puritans is the undue stress in the opposite direction by Benedetto Croce and by a considerable sector of Italian culture which forgets the Reformation to such a degree as to defer the "theoretic" foundation of liberalism to Romanticism and German idealism (although they admit that "in practice" its mother country was England). Cf. B. Croce, "Principio, ideale, teoria" in *Il carattere della filosofia moderna,* pp. 114-117, publ. in English with the title "The Roots of Liberty" in *Freedom, Its Meaning,* ed. R. N. Anshen (New York, 1940), which constitutes a final synthesis of Croce's liberal philosophy. The fact that our culture has concentrated its attention more on the romantic discovery of the "individual" in his ineffable uniqueness and diversity, than on the Calvinistic sects and the Anglo-Saxon matrix, is partly a consequence of the Counter-Reformation; that is, of the fact that Italy received in one blow from Romanticism what elsewhere had started with the Reformation. Hence the confusion between esthetic and political Romanticism, and in its wake the attribution of the liberal "theory" to the philosophy of Romanticism.

47. This gradual change of attitude can be followed better, even though indirectly, in such studies as C. Robbins, " 'Discordant Parties': A Study of the Acceptance of Party by Englishmen" (*Political Science Quarterly,* Dec. 1948, pp. 505-529), or Yves Lévy, "Les Partis et la démocratie" (*Le Contrat social,* II and IV, 1959) rather than in the speculations on Puritanism. *See also* Sergio Cotta, "La náscita dell' idea di partito nel secolo XVIII," in *Annali Università di Perugia,* Vol. LXI, 1959 (Padova, 1960), pp. 43-90.

48. R. M. MacIver renders this idea effectively in his discussion of "the multi-group society." He observes: "There are other forms of order than the simple uni-centered order. . . . The conception of the all-inclusive, all-regulating state is, as it were, a pre-Copernican conception of the social system. It appeals to the primitive sense of symmetry." Cf. *The Web of Government* (New York, 1947), p. 421. Cf. also R. M. MacIver, *Civilization and Group Relationships* (New York, 1945), Chap. XIII.

49. Cf. Plato, *Republic,* 563: "At length . . . they cease to care even for the laws, written or unwritten; they will have no one over them." (trans. B. Jowett). Cf. also Aristotle, *Politics,* 1292a, 1293a; and also Isocrates and Demosthenes. No sooner had the laws lost the chrism of sacredness which came to them from tradition than they were overthrown by a popular government which as early as 406 b.c., according to Xenophon, could proclaim that it was absurd to believe that the *demos* did not have the right to do as it pleased.

50. *Modern Democracies,* Vol. I, p. 183.

51. Constant perceived, at least partly, this difference when he wrote: "We can no longer enjoy the freedom of the ancients, which consisted in taking an active and constant part in the collective government. . . . This is why our individual independence must be much more dear to us than it was to the ancients; because when the latter sacrificed this independence for political rights they sacrificed the least to leave the most, whereas we in making the same sacrifice would leave the most to have the least." (In *Biblioteca di scienze politiche,* Vol. V, p. 460.)

Chapter XIII

Liberty and Law

"The more corrupt the Republic, the more the laws."

—Facitut†

1. Freedom and Freedoms

WHEN WE TALK of liberalism people find it difficult to understand exactly what is being discussed; when we speak of democracy they think they do. The notion of popular power is almost tangible, while the idea of liberty is hard to grasp—at least so long as we are free. And whereas "democracy" has a descriptive meaning (although, owing to historical change, a misleading one), liberty or freedom has not. For the word freedom and the sentence "I am free to," can be used whenever we refer to the realm of action and will, and consequently stand for the infinite scope and variety of human life itself.

However, and fortunately, it will be sufficient for us to consider this chameleon-like, all-embracing word from one specific angle: that of political freedom. And for this purpose our main problem is to introduce some order, since the major complications arise because we seldom separate the specific issue of political freedom from general speculations about the nature of true freedom. For instance, Lord Acton introduced his *History of Freedom in Antiquity* with the following remark: "No obstacle has been so constant, or so difficult to overcome, as uncertainty and confusion touching the nature of true liberty. If hostile interests have wrought much injury, false ideas have wrought still more." [1] While I agree very much with

278

Lord Acton's diagnosis—the harm brought about by uncertain, confused, and false ideas—I wonder whether his therapy is sound. For the problem before us is not to discover "the nature of true liberty" but, on the contrary, to remove all the extraneous incrustations that prevent us from examining the question of political freedom by itself, and as one empirical question among others.[2]

We must put some order, to begin with, in the contexts out of which we speak of psychological freedom, intellectual freedom, moral freedom, social freedom, economic freedom, legal freedom, political freedom, and other freedoms as well.[3] These are related to one another, of course, for they all pertain to a same man. However, we have to distinguish between them because each one is concerned with examining and solving a particular aspect of the over-all question of freedom. Hence the first clarification to be made is that political freedom *is not* of the psychological, intellectual, moral, social, economic, or legal type. It presupposes these freedoms—and it also promotes them—but it is not the same as these.

The second clarification has to do with the level of discourse. In this connection the error is to confuse the political with the philosophical problem of freedom. Philosophers have very often speculated about political freedom, but only rarely have they dealt with it as a practical problem to be approached as such. Aristotle, Hobbes, Locke, and Kant are among the few exceptions, that is, among the small number of philosophers who have not made the mistake of offering a philosophical answer to a practical question. Locke, particularly, had this virtue, and this explains why he has played such an important part in the history of political thought. His treatment of the problem of freedom in the *Essay Concerning Human Understanding* is different from, and unconnected with, the one we find in the second of the *Two Treatises on Government*. In the former he defines liberty as acting under the determination of the self, whereas in the latter he defines it as not being "subject to the inconstant, uncertain, unknown, arbitrary will of another man." [4]

However, most philosophers have not been concerned with the problem this way. As philosophers, they are concerned with True Liberty, or with the Essence of Liberty, meaning by this either the problem of the freedom of the will, or the question of the supreme

279

form of liberty (conceived variously as self-expression, self-determination, or self-perfection). This is exactly what philosophers are supposed to do, and nobody is reproaching them for having done it. But they should be reproached when they project their metaphysics of liberty into the political sphere and, unlike Locke, do not notice that in this context we are no longer discussing the same problem. And this point is still far from being accepted. In reviewing the relationship between political philosophy and the science of politics, Carl J. Friedrich—after having rightly criticized the mixing of philosophical questions and "the empirical realm of government and politics"—concludes by accepting a relation that I still consider much too close. He asserts: "Any discussion of freedom and of liberalism must, if it takes its argument seriously, confront the issue of 'freedom of the will.' " [5] Frankly, I do not see why. Of course any discussion about the freedom cherished by the West is based on a *Weltan-schauung*—on a conception of life and values. To be more exact, it presupposes that we somehow believe in the value of individual liberty. But I am reluctant to consider the connection any closer than that.

In the first place, I do not see what difference it would make in practice if we were to ascertain that man is not a free agent, and that he is not really responsible for his actions. Should we suppress penal legislation? Should we further give up a social order that is regulated by norms accompanied by sanctions? I do not see how we could. The only thing that would change, I am afraid, is the meaning of penalty, which would lose its value as a deterrent and its justification as punishment. The convict would become a martyr of society, paying for offenses that he was not responsible for. But he would still be condemned, since all societies have to remove from circulation murderers, thieves, lunatics, and all others who, being incapable of submitting to rules, constitute a danger to their neighbors.

The second reason for keeping the philosophical problem separate from the others is that, unless we do, we cannot even understand what the philosophers themselves have been saying. Whoever has had philosophical training knows in what sense Spinoza maintained that liberty was perfect rationality, or Leibniz that it was the spontaneity of the intelligence, or Kant that it was autonomy, or Hegel that it was the acceptance of necessity, or Croce that it was the perennial expansion of life. All these definitions are valid if they are understood in their context. But their validity has to do with a "nuclear meaning," with the search for a freedom that is essential, final, or as Kant said, transcendental. On the other hand, let it be noted, none of these conceptualizations refer to a "relational" problem of freedom. It follows from this, that if we try to use the aforesaid concepts to deal with the problem of political bondage—which is a relational problem—we distort their meaning without solving our problem. As soon as the ideas on freedom of Spinoza, Leibniz, Kant (as a moral philosopher), Hegel, or Croce are lowered to an empirical level for the purpose of dealing with problems that these conceptualizations did not consider, they become false and dangerous. Even dangerous, because if the question of political freedom has been submerged over and over again in a sea of confusion, it is by virtue of the false witnessing that these philosophers have arbitrarily been called upon to bear. So, the second point I wish to make is that political liberty *is not* a philosophical kind of liberty. It is not the practical solution to a philosophical problem, and even less the philosophical solution to a practical problem.

Finally, we must deal with the question of the stages of the process of freedom. The phrase, "I am free to," can have three different meanings, or can be broken up into three phases. It can mean I *may*, or I *can*, or I *have the power to*. In the first sense freedom is permission; in the second sense it is ability; and in the third sense it is a substantive condition. The third meaning is the newest, the last of the series, and for the purpose of the present discussion it can be put aside. I shall therefore confine myself to the two primary meanings of freedom: I may, and I can.

Clearly, freedom as permission and freedom as ability are very closely connected, since permission without ability and ability without permission are equally sterile. Yet they should not be confused, because no one type of liberty can by itself fulfill both these functions. Certain kinds of liberty are designed primarily to create the *permissive conditions* of freedom. Political freedom is of this kind, and very often so are juridical freedom and economic freedom (as understood in a market system). In other contexts the emphasis is instead

281

placed primarily, if not exclusively, on the roots and sources of freedom—on freedom as *ability*. This is notably the case of the philosophical approach to the problem of freedom; and it is also true of the notions of psychological, intellectual, and moral freedom.

The distinction between I may, and I can, corresponds to the difference between the external sphere and the internal sphere of freedom. When we are interested in the externalization of liberty, that is, in free action, it takes the form of permission. When on the other hand there is no problem of external freedom—as in the case of psychological, intellectual and moral freedom—then we are concerned with freedom as ability. Thus terms like "independence," "protection," and "action" are generally used to indicate *external liberty,* i.e., permission. Whereas the notions of "autonomy," "self-realization," and "will" usually refer to the freedom that exists *in interiore hominis.* And this leads us to a third and final clarification: political liberty is not an internal freedom, for it is a permissive, instrumental and relational freedom. In sum, it is a liberty whose purpose is to create a situation of freedom—the conditions for freedom.

2. Political Freedom

Cranston has remarked that "the word liberty has its least ambiguity in political use in times of centralized oppression." [6] This is so true that I suggest we should always approach the problem as if we were being oppressed, that is, assuming that we find ourselves subject to tyrannical rule. And my contention is that the concept of political freedom is not at all ambiguous, provided that (i) we eliminate the confusions of the *alienum genere* kind, (ii) we make clear that it raises a practical, not a speculative issue, and (iii) we specify that it aims at the creation of an external situation of liberty.

Actually, what I find striking in the history of the idea of political freedom is not variety of meaning, but rather continuity of meaning. For whenever the aforesaid provisos are complied with, we always meet with this basic connotation of the concept: that political freedom is "absence of opposition," [7] absence of external restraint, or exemption from coercion. Whenever man asks, or has asked for political liberty (outside of a small community like the *polis*) he means that he does not like constraint, and specifically the forms of constraint associated with the exercise of political power.[8] In other words, political freedom is characteristically freedom *from,* not freedom *to.* People are accustomed to say that it is a "negative" freedom, but since this adjective is often used in a derogatory sense, or at least to present political freedom as an inferior kind of liberty, I prefer to say, more accurately, that it is a defensive or protective freedom.

Critics have repeated to the point of saturation that this idea of freedom comes from an erroneous individualistic philosophy based on the false assumption that the individual is an atom, or a monad. In the first place, I would question the charge that this notion has a philosophical origin, if we mean by this that only a small number of intellectuals are really interested in the individual. If we consider, for instance, the French Revolution (an event that, admittedly, escaped from the control of the *philosophes*), its entire parabola took on the meaning of a vindication of liberty *against* power. During the years 1789-1794, the Third and the Fourth Estate were asking for individual and political liberty in opposition to the State, and not for a social and economic liberty to be achieved by means of the State. The idea that it is a purpose and a concern of the State to promote liberty would have appeared extravagant, to say the least, to the French people of the time. And this not because of their philosophical individualistic beliefs, but for the much simpler reason that they had been crushed for centuries by monarchs, lords, and the meticulous and paralyzing interference of the corporate economic system.

In truth, I think that we need not always call upon monads and the atomistic philosophy of man in order to explain why political freedom tends to be understood at all times—at least when oppression occurs—as freedom *from,* i.e., as a defensive freedom. It is much more important to realize, I believe, that the question of political freedom arises only when we approach the relation between citizen and State *from the point of view of the citizen.* If we consider this relation from the point of view of the State, we are no longer concerned with the problem of political freedom. To say that the State is "free to" is meaningless, unless we wish to introduce the question of arbitrary power. The tyrannical State is free *to* rule at its pleasure, and this means that it deprives its subjects of freedom.[9]

Let this point be very clear: (i) to speak of political freedom is to be concerned with the power of subordinate powers, with the power of the power-addressees, and that (ii) the proper focus to the problem of political freedom is indicated by the question: How can the power of these minor and potentially losing powers be safeguarded? We have political liberty, i.e., a free citizen, so long as conditions are created that make it possible for his lesser power to withstand the greater power which otherwise would—or at any rate could—easily overwhelm him. And this is why the concept of political freedom assumes an adversative meaning. It is freedom *from*, because it is the freedom *of* and *for* the weaker.

Of course, the formula, "absence of external impediments" [10] should not be taken literally, lest it bring to mind an anarchic ideal. The absence of restriction is not the absence of all restriction. What we ask of political freedom is protection against arbitrary and absolute power. By a situation of liberty we mean a situation of protection which permits the governed effectively to oppose abuse of power by the governors. It might be objected that this clarification still does not clarify much. For what is meant by "abuse" of power? Where does the legitimate exercise of power end, and the illegitimate begin? If we review the literature on freedom we shall find considerable disagreement on this point. But we should not fail to perceive that much of the disagreement can be accounted for by the difference in historical situations. The answers to the questions, "Protected from what?" and "Unrestricted to what extent?" depend on what is at stake at any given time and place, and on what is most valued (and how intensely it is valued) in a specific culture. "Coercion" does not apply to every kind and degree of restraint. Nor does "protection" imply defense against everything. In the first place, people must feel that what is involved is worth protecting (the threat of constraint has to be directed against something that they value); and secondly, nobody worries about protecting what is not in danger. Therefore we can be specific only if we examine a specific situation, and know what is being threatened, which threat is feared the most, and which is considered most imminent.

A more difficult issue is raised by the question: Is freedom *from* an adequate concept of freedom? To answer this query we must

284

refer to a broader picture. Clinton Rossiter has summed up the general idea we have of liberty today as consisting of four notions: independence, privacy, power and opportunity. "*Independence* is a situation in which a man feels himself subject to a minimum of external restraints . . . *Privacy* is a special kind of independence which can be understood as an attempt to secure autonomy . . . if necessary in defiance of all the pressures of modern society." However, says Rossiter, at this point we have only mentioned "one-half of liberty, and the negative half at that. . . . Liberty is also a positive thing . . . and we must therefore think of it in terms of *power* . . . and also in terms of *opportunity*." [11] Perhaps there is one slight imperfection in Rossiter's analysis, in that when he says "power" he seems to mean "ability to," in the sense of capacity. To avoid ambiguity, I will include the concept of capacity in our list, and place the concept of power at the end. Thus complete freedom, as we understand it, implies the following five traits: independence, privacy, capacity, opportunity, and power.

Now we can frame our question more accurately: What is the relation between the first half of liberty (independence and privacy) and the second half (ability, opportunity and power)? The answer seems to me to be clear: it is a relation between condition and conditioned, between means and ends. It is, therefore, also a *procedural relation*. It is no accident that these concepts are generally presented in an order in which the notion of independence (and not that of opportunity, or of power) comes first. Unfortunately, this point is seldom made sufficiently clear. Rossiter is by no means an exception to this rule when, in putting his "pieces back together into a unity," not only does he pass over the fact that it is an ordered unity, or rather, an irreversible succession, but, if anything, he tends to stress the opposite. He concludes: "The emphasis of classical liberalism, to be sure, is on the negative aspects of liberty. Liberty is thought of almost exclusively as a state of independence and privacy. But this is precisely one of those points at which classical liberalism no longer serves, if ever it did serve, as a wholly adequate instrument for describing the place of the free man in the free society." [12] This statement is not incorrect. It only omits what is essential.

Political freedom is by no means the only kind of freedom. It is not even the most important kind, if by important we mean the one which ranks highest in the scale of values. It is, however, the primary liberty, as far as procedure goes; that is, it is a preliminary condition, the *sine qua non* of all other liberties. So to speak of "independence from" as an inadequate notion of liberty—as people often tend to do—is very misleading. The other liberties as well, if they are considered singly, are just as inadequate. For adequacy is provided by the whole series, and by the whole series *arranged in a particular order*. It is not sufficient that our minds be free, for instance, if our tongues are not. The ability to direct our own lives is of very little use if we are prevented from doing so. How, then, are the so-called positive liberties adequate if they cannot materialize? It seems to me, therefore, that when we assert that negative liberty is not sufficient we are stating an obvious platitude, while we are not stating what is most important of all; that we need freedom *from* in order to be able to achieve freedom *to*.

It can be argued that political freedom has also a positive aspect (and this might seem to be a reply to those who consider it insufficient and incomplete). Now, there is no doubt that political freedom cannot be inert, that it postulates some activity; in other words that it is not only freedom *from,* but also *participation in*. No one denies this. But we must not overstress this latter aspect, for we must remember that participation is made possible by a state of independence, and not vice versa. Even our subjective rights, as Jhering wrote in his famous pamphlet *Der Kampf um's Recht,* are reduced to nothing if we do not exercise them, if we do not avail ourselves of them. However, it is clearly useless to speak of exercising rights if they do not already exist. And the same holds good for political freedom. It is pointless to speak of "exercise" if there is not already independence. Totalitarian dictatorships require and promote a great deal of activity and of participation. But so what?

My feeling is, therefore, that we ought to resist the temptation to treat political freedom as if it were, in itself, a complete liberty. Those who inflate it by speaking of it as "participation" are disfiguring its basic feature.[14] If we have so often failed in our search for more liberty, the main reason is that we have expected from participation more than it can give. Of course, liberty as non-restraint is not an end in itself, and political freedom requires action, active resistance,[15] and positive demands. Where there is lifelessness and apathy there cannot be liberty. But we must not forget that the relation of forces between citizens and State is unequal; that in comparison with the State their power is destructible; and therefore that their freedom is typified not by its positive aspects but by the presupposition of defense mechanisms. In relation to the State the citizens are the weaker party, and therefore the political concept of freedom is to be pinpointed as follows: Only if I am not prevented from doing what I wish, can I be said to have the power to do it. [16]

There is no reason to be oversensitive when we are told that this conception is incomplete. So it is. Or, rather, it is incomplete in the obvious sense that each specific form of freedom can only amount to a partial freedom, because it concerns only the specific problem which it attempts to solve. Therefore, what really matters is to realize that, despite its incompleteness, political liberty is *preliminary* to the other brands: and this means that it cannot be bypassed. We cannot pass over freedom in the negative sense, if we want to achieve freedom in the positive sense. If we forget for one instant the requirement of not being restrained, our entire edifice of liberties is worthless.

Once we have assessed the question of the procedural importance of political freedom, we may well raise the question of its historical importance to us today. The assertion that political freedom is not enough, meaning that "real freedom" is something else, is totally beside the mark. But the question as to the relation, here and now, between political and other kinds of freedom is, of course, pertinent. Every epoch has its urgencies and particular needs. So we may well maintain, in this context, that since today political freedom is assured, it requires less attention than other liberties—such as economic freedom, or freedom from want, for instance.[17] However, this is a question that can be dealt with only after having reviewed historically the nature of the problems that confront us.[18]

3. Liberal Freedom

It will be noted that so far I have spoken of political freedom and not of the liberal conception of freedom. It is true that the two

287

concepts have become closely linked. However, since the liberal idea of freedom is often considered antiquated nowadays, it is wise to keep the problem of political freedom separate from the liberal solution of it. For it is easy to demonstrate that the freedom of liberalism, being a historical acquisition, is bound to come to an end. But are we prepared to make the same assertion about political freedom? Can we say that even this is a transitory need? If so, let us say so openly, and, what is more difficult, let us try to demonstrate it. Political freedom and liberal freedom cannot be killed with one stone. Rather, it is ·at the very moment that we reject the liberal solution of the problem of freedom that this problem again demands, more pressingly than ever, a solution.

What we ask of political freedom is protection. How can we obtain it? In the final analysis, from the time of Solon to the present day, the solution has always been sought in obeying laws and not masters. As Cicero so well phrased it, *legum servi sumus ut liberi esse possimus*,[19] we are servants of the law in order that we might be free. And the problem of political freedom has always been interwoven with the question of legality, for it goes back to the problem of curbing power by making it impersonal.[20]

There is, then, a very special connection between political freedom and juridical freedom. But the formula "liberty under law," or by means of law, can be applied in different ways. The idea of protection of the laws has been understood, by and large, in three ways: the Greek way, which is already a legislative interpretation; the Roman way, which approaches the English rule of law;[21] and the way of liberalism, which is constitutionalism.

The Greeks were the first to perceive the solution, for they well understood that if they did not want to be ruled tyrannically they had to be governed by laws.[22] But their idea of law oscillated between the extremes of sacred laws which were too rigid and immutable, and conventional laws which were too uncertain and shifting. In the course of their democratic experience the *nomos* soon ceased to mirror the nature of things (*physis*), and they were unable to stop at the golden mean between immobility and change. As soon as law lost its sacred character, popular sovereignty was placed above the law, and by that very act government by laws was once again confused with government by men. The reason for this is that the legal conception of liberty presupposes the rejection of the Greek *eleuthería* —of a freedom that is turned into the principle, *quod populo placuit legis habet vigorem,* what pleases the people is law. Looking at the Greek system from the vantage point of our knowledge, we see that what their conception of law lacked was precisely the notion of "limitation"—a notion which, as was discovered later, is inseparable from it.

That is the reason why our juridical tradition is Roman, not Greek. The experience of the Greeks is important precisely because it shows us how *not* to proceed if we want liberty under law. The Romans, it is true, posed for themselves a more limited problem. As Wirszubski remarks, "The Roman Republic never was . . . a democracy of the Athenian type; and the *eleuthería, isonomía* and *parrhesía* that were its chief expressions, appeared to the Romans as being nearer *licentia* than *libertas.*" [23] Actually Roman jurisprudence did not make a direct contribution to the specific problem of political freedom. But it did make an essential indirect contribution by developing the idea of legality whose modern version is the Anglo-Saxon rule of law.

The third juridical solution to the problem of political freedom is that of liberalism—which was developed in English constitutional practice, found its most successful written formulation in the Constitution of the United States, and is expounded in the theory of "constitutional *garantisme"* and, in this sense, of the *Rechtsstaat,* the State based on law.[24] What did liberalism specifically contribute to the solution of the problem of political freedom? It was not the originator of the modern idea of individual freedom, although it added something important to it.[25] Nor, as we have seen, was it the inventor of the notion of liberty in the law. But it did invent the way to guarantee and institutionalize the dynamic aspect of political freedom.

The originality and value of the approach of classical liberalism can be seen if we compare it with previous attempts to solve the problem. Basically, the legal solution to the problem of freedom can be sought in two very different directions: either in rule by legislators or in the rule of law.[26] In the first approach law consists of written rules which are enacted by legislative bodies; that is, law is legislated law. In the second, law is something to be discovered by judges: it is judicial law. For the former approach, law consists of statutory, systematic law-making; for the latter, it is the result of piecemeal law-finding (*Rechtsfindung*) by means of judicial decisions. From the first viewpoint, law may be conceived as the product of sheer will; from the second it is the product of theoretical inquiry and debate. The danger of the legislative solution is that a point may be reached in which men are tyrannically ruled by other men in spite of laws (as happened in Greece), i.e., in which laws are no longer a protection. On the other hand, the second solution may be inadequate because the rule of law does not, per se, necessarily safeguard the political aspect of freedom (e.g., the Roman rule of law concerned the elaboration of the *jus civile,* not of public law). And while the Greek approach was too dynamic and thereby destroyed the certainty of law, the other is, or may be, too static.

Liberal constitutionalism is, we may say, the technique of retaining the advantages of the earlier solutions while eliminating their respective shortcomings. On the one hand the constitutional solution adopts rule by legislators, but with two limitations: one concerning the method of law-making, which is checked by a severe *iter legis;* and one concerning the range of law-making, which is restricted by a higher law and thereby prevented from interfering with the rights of man, that is, with the fundamental rights affecting the liberty of the citizen. On the other hand, the constitutional solution also sees to it that the rule of law is retained in the system. Even though this latter component part of the constitutional rule has been gradually set aside by the former, it is well to remind ourselves that the framers of the liberal constitutions did not conceive of the State as being a *machine à faire lois,* a law-making machine, but conceived of the role of legislators as being a complementary role according to which parliament was supposed to integrate, not to replace, judicial law-finding. However, an essential feature of the rule-of-law principle is retained: that aspect of the principle of the separation of powers which provides for the independence of the judiciary. (Incidentally, this is actually what the ill-famed principle of the separation of powers demands. *Pace* Montesquieu, who confused the legislative-executive relationship with the one between the State and the courts, English constitutionalism never separated the exercise of power between parliament and government for in this case what is required is a shared, not a divided exercise of power.)

There are, to be sure, many significant differences among our constitutional systems. If we refer to the origins, the unwritten English constitution was directly implied by, and derived from the rule of law; the American written constitution formalized and rationalized British constitutional practice, thereby still leaning heavily on the rule of law; whereas written constitutions in Europe, for want of common law, were based from the outset on the legislative conception of law. But these initial differences have been gradually reduced, since there is at present a general trend—even in the English-speaking countries—in favor of statutory law. Despite this trend, however, we cannot say as yet that present-day constitutions have lost their *raison d'être* as the solution that combines the pros and obviates the cons of both the rule-of-law and the rule-of-legislators techniques. Even though our constitutions are becoming more and more unbalanced on the side of statutory law-making, so long as they are considered a higher law, so long as we have judicial review, independent judges, and, possibly, the due process of law;[27] and so long as a binding procedure establishing the method of law-making remains an effective brake on the bare will-conception of law—so long as these conditions prevail, we are still depending on the liberal-constitutional solution of the problem of political power.

Constitutional systems, both past and present, are therefore, historically speaking, liberal systems. One might say that liberal politics is constitutionalism.[28] And constitutionalism is the solution to the problem of *political* freedom in terms of a *dynamic* approach to the juridical conception of freedom. This explains why we cannot speak of political freedom without referring to liberalism—liberalism, I repeat, not democracy. The political freedom which we enjoy today is the freedom of liberalism, the liberal kind of liberty; not the precarious, and, on the whole, vainly sought liberty of the ancient democracies. And this is the reason why, in recalling the typical

291

guiding principles of the democratic deontology, I have mentioned equality, isocracy, and self-government, but—and perhaps this was noted—never the idea of liberty.

Of course, it is also possible to derive the idea of liberty from the concept of democracy. But not directly. It must be derived indirectly, in the sense that it does not follow from the notion of popular power, but from the concept of isocracy. It is the assertion "We are equal," that can be interpreted as: "Nobody has the right to command me." Thus, it is from the postulate of equality that we can deduce the demand for a "freedom from." However, we should note that this inference is made by modern rather than by ancient thinkers. In the Greek tradition, democracy is much more closely associated with *isonomía* (equal law) than with *eleuthería* (liberty), and the idea of popular power is by far preponderant in the inner logic of development of the Greek system. Moreover, as we have already seen, when the Greeks did speak about liberty it meant something different from what it means today, and they were confronted with a problem of liberty which was the reverse of the modern one.[29]

Therefore, to avoid a historical falsification which also has a vital practical bearing, we must stress that neither our ideal nor our techniques of liberty pertain, strictly speaking, to the line of development of the democratic idea. It is true that modern liberal democracies have incorporated the ideal of a liberty of Man which includes the liberty of each man. But originally this concept was not democratic; it is an acquisition of democracy, not a product of it—which is very different. And we must keep this fact in mind in order to avoid the mistake of believing that our liberty can be secured by the method that the Greeks tried. For our liberties are assured by a notion of legality that constitutes a *limit* and a *restriction* on pure and simple democratic principles. Kelsen, among others, sees this very clearly when he writes that a democracy "without the self-limitation represented by the principle of legality destroys itself." [30] Although modern democracy has incorporated the notions of liberty and legality, these notions, as Bertrand de Jouvenel rightly points out, "are, in terms of good logic, extraneous to it" [31]—and I should like to add, in terms of good historiography as well.

4. The Supremacy of Law in Rousseau

I have mentioned three ways of seeking legal protection for political freedom: the legislative way, the rule-of-law way, and the liberal or constitutional way. But it is held that there is another relationship (which would be the fourth in my list) between liberty and law: "autonomy," i.e., giving ourselves our own laws. And since liberty as autonomy is supposed to have Rousseau's *placet,* many people take for granted that this is the democratic definition of liberty, and contrast, on this basis, a *libertas minor* with a *libertas major*—that is to say, the minor liberty of liberalism (as freedom *from*) to the greater democratic liberty, autonomy. Personally, I question whether those who equate liberty with autonomy are justified in associating this notion with Rousseau. In the second place, which is the supposedly minor liberty: political freedom, or the liberal solution of it? The two are evidently, albeit erroneously, being treated as if they were the same thing. In the third place I wonder whether it is correct to contrast freedom *from* with autonomy, for it is hard to see in what sense autonomy can be conceived of as a political kind of freedom. However these questions deserve attention, and we shall start by ascertaining exactly what Rousseau thought and said.

We can have doubts about Rousseau's solutions, but not about his intentions. The problem of politics, Rousseau affirmed, "which I compare to the squaring of the circle in geometry [is] to place law above man." [32] This was for him *the* problem, because—he said— only on this condition may man be free: when he obeys laws, not men.[33] And Rousseau was more sure of this certainty than of any other. "Liberty," he confirmed in *Letters from the Mountain,* "shares the fate of laws; it reigns or perishes with them. There is nothing of which I am surer than this." [34] And, as he said in the *Confessions,* the question he constantly asked was: "Which is the form of government which, by its nature, gets closer and remains closer to law?" [35]

This was a problem that Rousseau had every reason to liken to the squaring of the circle.[36] While in *Letters from the Mountain* he observed that when "the administrators of laws become their sole arbiters . . . I do not see what slavery could be worse," [37] in the *Social Contract* his question was: "How can a blind multitude, which

293

often does not know what it wills, because only rarely does it know what is good for it, carry out for itself so great and difficult an enterprise as a system of legislation?" [38] For Rousseau this question had only one answer: to legislate as little as possible.[39] He had been coming to this conclusion with more and more conviction for some time, for already in the dedication of his *Discourse on Inequality* he had stressed the fact that the Athenians lost their democracy because everybody proposed laws to satisfy a whim, whereas what gives laws their sacred and venerable character is their age.[40] And this is precisely the point: that the laws that Rousseau referred to were Laws with a capital L—that is, few, very general, fundamental, ancient, and almost immutable supreme Laws.[41]

Rousseau held that the people are the judges and custodians of the Law, not the makers and manipulators of laws. He by no means had in mind the idea of a legislating popular will.[42] On the contrary, he proposed to liberate man by means of an impersonal government of Laws placed high above the will from which they may emanate: that is, related to a will that acknowledges them rather than creates them; that sustains them rather than disposes of them; that safeguards them rather than modifies them. Whoever appeals to the authority of Rousseau must not forget that his Laws were not at all the laws with a small *l* which, by virtue of our formal definition of law, are fabricated with ever increasing speed and magnitude by legislative assemblies in the name of popular sovereignty. His Laws were substantive, i.e., laws by reason of their content. As far as their model is concerned, they were very similar to the notion of law expressed in the theory of natural law.[43] And to appreciate Rousseau's difficulties we must realize that they sprang from the fact that he tried to make immanent the same concept of law that the school of natural law considered transcendent.

He tried to do this by invoking the *volonté générale,*[44] a concept that turns out to be less mysterious than it seems—notwithstanding all the fluctuations to which it is subject—if we remember that it is an expression of the crisis of natural law and, at the same time, of the search for an *Ersatz,* for something to take its place. In the shift from Grotius' *ius naturale* to the Law sanctioned and accepted by the general will, the foundations are different, but the new protagonist (the general will) has the same functions and attributes as the old (nature). Rousseau's general will is not the will of all, that is, it is not "the sum of individual wills";[45] nor is it a *sui generis* individual will freed of all selfishness and egotism. It is somewhere between the two.[46] And to better appreciate its mysterious nature, it is worthwhile recalling Diderot's definition in the *Encyclopédie:* "The general will is in each individual a pure act of understanding, reasoning in the silence of the passions." [47] Rousseau did not accept that definition. Why?

I do not think that what disturbed Rousseau was the rationalistic flavor of Diderot's definition,[48] i.e., his reducing the general will to "a pure act of understanding, reasoning in the silence of the passions." For, although Rousseau's general will is nourished and strengthened by love and by feelings, it is guided by reason.[48] That is, it is still a rational will—"will" as it could be conceived before the romantic outburst, certainly not that voluntaristic will of our time which precedes and dominates reason.[49]

No, what he could not accept was Diderot's answer to the question *Où est le dépôt de cette volonté générale?*—where is the general will located? He could not accept the location of the general will "in each individual." And Rousseau could not settle for this approach because he had to rebuild somehow, within society itself, an equivalent of the transcendence that was formerly placed above and outside the realm of human affairs. In other words, the general will had to be the anthropomorphic substitute for the order of nature and for the natural reason that mirrored that order. So much so that in Rousseau the laws were derived from the general will just as they were previously derived from natural law. He wrote: "Whenever it becomes necessary to promulgate new ones [laws], this necessity is perceived universally. He who proposes them only says what all have already felt." [50] This is like saying that laws are not produced *ex homine,* but are recognized and proclaimed *ex natura:* the general will does not, strictly speaking, make them and want them, but bears them within itself. If it were really a will, when inert it would not exist, and when mute it would not will; while for Rousseau the general will is "always constant, unchangeable, and pure" and cannot be annihilated or corrupted.[51] Which comes back to saying that it is an entity of reason which does not suffer the vicissitudes of human will, or of particular wills.[52]

The general will can be compared, as far as the function Rousseau assigned to it is concerned, to the "spirit of the people," to what the historical school of law later called the *Volksgeist:* not because the two concepts are similar, but because they both attempt to fill the void left by natural law. Both these notions were motivated by the need to discover objectivity in subjectivity, something absolute and stable in what is relative and changeable—in short, a fixed point of reference. The romantics sought transcendence within immanence by locating the former in History (with a capital *H*), in the collective, anonymous, and fatal flux of events; Rousseau tried to find transcendence in Man by placing it in a common ego that unites all men. And just as the romantics of the historical school of law contradicted themselves when, in order to insert their transcendent *Volksgeist* in the orbit of immanence, they had to rely on a privileged interpreter,[53] in the same way and for the same reason Rousseau contradicted himself (thereby revealing the weak point of his system) when, in his search for a link between the general will and what the citizens want, he allowed the majority to be the interpreter of the *volonté générale*.

The contradiction lies in the fact that the will of the majority is subjective and merely stems from the will of all, whereas Rousseau's general will is an objective moral will made up of qualitative elements, for it must be "general" in essence, at its origin, and for its objective.[54] Although Rousseau kept his general will in the orbit of calculable qualities—he even indicated that it is derived from a sum of the differences, i.e., after the pluses and minuses of individual wills are cancelled out[55]—counting can only reveal the general will, it cannot produce its essence.[56] The popular will is additive, the general will is one and indivisible. Even if we grant that in the process of popular consultations an interplay of compensations eliminates individual passions, in order to achieve the quality of general will we need much more: *bonne volonté* (good will), patriotism, and enlightened popular judgment.[57] These are demanding conditions, which amount to a very severe limitation on popular sovereignty.[58]

If the general will "is always good and always tends to the

296

public interest," it does not follow—Rousseau added—"that the deliberations of the people are always right." [59] He later explains: "The people always desire the good, but do not always see it. The general will is always in the right, but the judgement which guides it is not always enlightened." [60] The people would like the good, but that does not mean that they recognize it: therefore it is not the general will that resolves itself into popular sovereignty, but, vice versa, the popular will that must resolve itself into the general will. Rousseau did not ask whether the people rejected or accepted a bill, but whether it did or did not express the general will.[61] In substance, his system hangs on a general will that supplants popular power.

Ironically enough, Rousseau was the proponent of a most unadventurous type of immobile democracy which was supposed to legislate as little as possible, and could survive only on condition that it kept its actions to a minimum. He devoted all his ingenuity and the most meticulous attention to controlling the forces that his ideal would have let loose. His democracy was intended to be defensive rather than aggressive, cautious and wary, not Jacobin and omnivorous.[62] It is no paradox to assert that his democracy was a watchdog democracy, to the same extent that the liberal State of the nineteenth century was nicknamed the watchdog State. He rejected representatives, wanted a direct and, as far as possible, a unanimous democracy, and required that the magistrates should have no will of their own but only the power to impose the general will. The result was, clearly, a static body, a democracy that was supposed to restrict, rather than encourage innovation. It is true that Rousseau spoke of "will," but he did not mean by it a *willing will;* he thought of it as a brake, rather than an accelerator. The general will was not a *dynamis,* but the infallible instinct that permits us to evaluate the laws, and to accept as Law only the Just, the True Law. Rousseau's aim was to free man from his bonds by inventing a system that would obstruct and curb legislation. And this was because he felt that the solution of the problem of securing freedom lay exclusively in the supremacy of law, and, furthermore, in a supremacy of law concerned with avoiding the legislative outcome of the Athenian democracy, that is, the primacy of popular sovereignty over the law.

Rousseau, then, did not present a new conception of freedom. He enjoyed going against the current and contradicting his contemporaries on many scores, but not on this one point: the legalitarian concept of liberty that had found fresh nourishment and support in the natural rights of the natural law revival of the seventeenth and eighteenth centuries.[63] Rousseau never for a minute had the idea of freeing man by means of popular sovereignty, as is maintained by those who have evidently read little of him. The assertion that liberty is founded by law and in law, found in Rousseau, if anything, its most intransigent supporter. Rousseau was so uncompromising about it that he could not even accept the legislative conception of law within a constitutional framework proposed by Montesquieu: for this solution, after all, allowed for changing laws, while Rousseau wanted a basically unchanging Law.

5. Autonomy: A Criticism

It may be asked: did not Rousseau speak of liberty as autonomy at all? Actually we do find in the *Social Contract* this sentence: "Obedience to laws that we have imposed on ourselves is liberty." [64] But when he declared that everybody is free because in obeying the laws that he himself has made he is submitting to his own will, Rousseau was by no means speaking of the autonomy of which we speak today as if it were his discovery.

In the first place, Rousseau related his idea of autonomy to the Contract, that is, to the hypothesis of an original pact in which ideally each party to the contract submits to norms that he has freely accepted. The fact that Rousseau had in mind a democracy that was not in the least inclined to change its Laws shows how important it was for him to keep this liberty tied to its original legitimacy, and indicates that he did not mean this idea to be used as a basis for mass legislation, which is the way we are using it. There is an essential condition that qualifies Rousseau's formula, namely that the people are free so long as they do not delegate the exercise of their sovereignty to legislative assemblies.[65] So his conception has very little to do with obedience to laws that are made for us by others.

In the second place, Rousseau's thesis is closely related to the notion of a small democracy in which everybody participates. His State was the city, and he never thought that his democracy could be applied to large republics.[66] He had in mind Spartans and Romans, and his projects concerned Geneva. Now it is plausible to maintain that the citizens of a small city who govern themselves directly submit only to the rules that they have accepted, and therefore obey nothing but their own wills; but when self-government is no longer possible, when the citizens are dispersed over a vast territory, when they do not participate in the legislative output, does the assertion still make sense? Certainly not for Rousseau.

In the third place, by tracing to Rousseau the concept of liberty as autonomy, we take the premise from which he started and forget the conclusion which he reached. When Rousseau went back to a liberty which is submission to laws which we have prescribed ourselves, his problem was to legitimize Law. If man renounces his natural liberty in order to achieve a superior civil liberty, he does this because the society which he enters subjects him to norms that he has accepted, that is, to just Laws, which liberate, not oppress him. But once Law is legitimized and true Law is established, Rousseau's liberty is liberty under Law. Man is free because, when Laws and not men govern, he gives himself to no one. In other words, he is free because he is not exposed to arbitrary power. This was Rousseau's concept of liberty. And so it was understood by his contemporaries. Even in the Declaration of Rights of 1793, Article Nine stated: "The law must protect public and individual liberty against the oppression of those who govern." This article has a strange ring if we recall that the Terror was under way. Yet, what we have read is Rousseau's definition of liberty.

The truth is that "autonomy" originated from Kant, and that it was Kant who called attention to the concept. Except that for the author of the *Critique of Practical Reason* the notion of autonomy had nothing to do with democratic liberty or any other kind of political or even juridical liberty. Kant distinguished very clearly between "external" and "internal" freedom. And the prescription by ourselves of our own laws is in Kant the definition of moral liberty, that is, of our internal freedom—a completely different matter from the question of external coercion. In the moral sphere we are concerned with the question of whether man is free in the interior forum of his conscience, while in politics we are concerned with ways of preventing man's exterior subjugation. Thus, if we are interested in the problem of man's political freedom, Kant's ethic is of no use to us. And this explains why the word autonomy rebounded from Kant to Rousseau as soon as it took on a political meaning. But the question is: to which Rousseau? To the real Rousseau, or to the one remodeled by the romantics and subsequently by the idealistic philosophers?

With the assurance that is characteristic of him, Kelsen flatly asserts that "political freedom is autonomy." [67] But it seems to me that Kelsen, as well as many other scholars, have adopted this thesis too lightly. For the autonomy about which especially German and Italian theory talk so much is a concept of a speculative-dialectical nature which stems from a philosophy that has indeed little to do with liberalism and democracy.[68] I can understand that many democrats have been fascinated by the idea of autonomy, implying, as it does, a high valuation of the *demos.* But it is a concept that political theory has endowed with the very different function of justifying and legitimizing obedience. This is a perfectly respectable usage, except when we want autonomy for the solution of a problem not its own, namely the problem of safeguarding, maintaining, and defending our liberties.

The truth is that if we may speak of autonomy as a concrete expression of political freedom, this autonomy ended with ancient democracies. The formula of the Greek liberty was—we read in Aristotle—"to govern and to be governed alternately, . . . to be under no command whatsoever to anyone, upon any account, any otherwise than by rotation, and that just as far only as that person is, in turn, under his also." [69] Now, this self-government can be interpreted as a situation of autonomy—even though somewhat arbitrarily, since in Aristotle's description the problem of a *nomos,* and therefore of a liberty related to law, is not raised. However, if it pleases us to speak of autonomy in this connection, then we come to the conclusion that the supposedly new and most advanced conception of liberty advocated by present-day progressive democrats is none other than the oldest and most obsolete formula of liberty. For clearly only a *micropolis,* and indeed a very small one, can solve the problem of political freedom by having—I am again citing Aristotle—"all to command each, and each in its turn all." Certainly our ever growing megalopolis cannot.

Coming back from this very distant past to the present time, we meet with the expression "local autonomy." But let us not delude ourselves: local autonomies result from the distrust of concentrated power and are, therefore, an expression of freedom *from* the centralized State. The liberty connected with administrative decentralization, with the Germans' *Selbstverwaltung,* or with self-government of the Anglo-Saxon type, does not mean what Rousseau or Kelsen had in mind. Situations of local autonomy are in effect "autarchies" [70] and serve as safeguards of liberty chiefly because they allow a polycentric distribution of political power.

It may be said that the notion of autonomy in its political application must be interpreted in a looser and more flexible way, and that it is in this sense that it helps to connote the democratic brand of liberty. Norberto Bobbio observes that ". . . the concept of autonomy in philosophy is embarrassing, but . . . in the context of politics the term indicates something easier to understand: it indicates that the norms which regulate the actions of the citizens must conform as far as possible to the desires of the citizens." [71] This is true—but why use the word autonomy? Orders that "conform as far as possible to the desires of the citizens" are assented orders, which means that the problem in question is one of consensus. And it is important to be precise on this matter, since the intrusion of "autonomy" is causing a great deal of confusion nowadays.

Bobbio rightly points out that while a state of liberty in the sense of non-restriction has to do with action, a state of autonomy has to do with will. [72] This is indeed the point. For the sphere of politics concerns volitions *insofar as they are actions,* and not pure and simple will. In politics what matters is whether I am empowered to do what my will wants. The internal problem of freedom of will is not the political problem of freedom, for the political problem is the external problem of freedom of action. Politics concerns, as Hegel would say, the "objective sphere" in which the will has to externalize itself. Therefore, as long as we interpret liberty as autonomy, we do not cross the threshold of politics; not because autonomy is not essential, but because it is a subjective presupposition of political freedom.

The concept of autonomy is of so little use in the objective sphere, that here an antithesis of it does not exist. We can be coerced and still remain autonomous, that is, inwardly free. And this is the reason why it is said that force can never extinguish in man the spark of liberty. Likewise, we can be safe from any coercion and yet remain sleep-walkers because we are not capable of internal self-determination. Autonomy and coercion are by no means mutually exclusive concepts. My will can remain free (autonomous), even if I am physically imprisoned (coerced) just as it can be inactive and passive (heteronomous) even when I am permitted to do anything I wish (non-coerced). The antithesis of autonomy is heteronomy. And heteronomy stands for passivity, anomie, characterlessness, and the like—all of which are notions that concern not the subject-sovereign relationship but the problem of a responsible self. In short, they are all concepts that have to do with internal, not external liberty, with the power to will, not the power to do; and this goes back to saying that our vocabulary makes it impossible for us to employ the word autonomy in connection with the question of political freedom.

But why should we find it necessary? After all, in politics we are concerned with the practical problem of achieving a state of liberty in which State compulsion be curbed and based on consent. And this is just as much the democratic problem of liberty as it is the liberal problem of liberty. In either case we do not make the laws, but we help to choose the legislators. And that is a very different matter. Furthermore, we are free not because we actually wanted the laws that those legislators enacted, but because we limit and control their power to enact them. If the liberty that we enjoy lay in our personal share in law-making, I fear that we would be left with very few liberties, if any. For, as John Stuart Mill very nicely put it, "The self-government spoken of is not the government of each by himself, but of each by all the rest." [73]

The reply may be that the formula liberty-autonomy is only an ideal. So we are not actually maintaining that somewhere there are people who are free by virtue of their own law-making, or that some place exists where liberty actually consists in the rule of oneself

302

by oneself. What we are expressing is only a prescription. It is only in this sense, therefore, that we put forth an ideal of political freedom that is specifically a democratic ideal. Be this as it may, on substantial grounds I am already satisfied with making the point that "liberty from" and "liberty as autonomy" are not alternatives which can be substituted for each other *in actual practice,* even though, in terms of principle, I must confess that I am still not convinced, for I doubt whether the ideal of self-obedience is really adaptable to the democratic creed, and whether it really reinforces it.

The democratic deontology is authentically expressed in the ideal of self-government, not of autonomy. To the extent that the notion of autonomy takes the place of the notion of self-government, it obscures and weakens it. It obscures it because after having been manipulated between Kant, Rousseau, and Hegel, the idea of autonomy can easily be used to demonstrate (in words, of course) that we are free when we are not. Whoever has lived under a dictatorship knows only too well how easily autonomy can be turned into a practice of submission that is justified by high-level explanations about true freedom. And not only does autonomy easily become a self-complacent exercise in obedience: there is more. For in helping people to mistake a nominal self-government for real self-government it ends up by keeping them from actually seeking the latter. I mean that when we speak of self-government, we can ascertain whether it exists and we know what we have to do in order to approach it; whereas when we speak of autonomy empirical verification is by-passed, and we can stay peacefully in bed and think of ourselves as free.

The rationalistic democracies have, then, been ill-advised in adopting an ambiguous philosophical concept that distracts our attention from concrete, what-to-do problems, and that comes dangerously near to being a sham construction behind which lurks the figure of liberty understood as passive conformity and subservience. In the realm of politics, autonomy is an untrustworthy interpretation of liberty, and its revival indicates how seriously the democratic *forma mentis* as such lacks political sensitivity. Having reappeared on the stage of history after liberalism, that is, in a situation of established political freedom, this *forma mentis* reveals, by the very adoption of the notion of autonomy, that it has not actually suffered the trials and lessons that political oppression imposes.

There is, of course, a type of autonomy that could be considered a *libertas major* even in the sphere of politics; but it would be found in a society that functions by spontaneous self-discipline wherein internalized self-imposed rules would take the place of compulsory laws emanating from the State. We can keep this concept in reserve for a time when the State will have withered away; but as long as the State is growing, let us not be duped into believing in a superior democratic liberty conceived of as autonomy. So long as the State grows let us bear in mind that even though I may succeed in governing myself perfectly, this autonomy does not protect me from the possibility of being sent to a concentration camp—and the problem is just that. This amounts to saying that I believe in the notion of autonomy as moral freedom, in the sense indicated by Kant, but certainly not in autonomy as a fourth type of political freedom.

6. The Principle of Diminishing Consequences

I have wanted to discuss the concept of autonomy fully because this notion is a typical example of that verbal overstraining which tends to jeopardize—among other things—the difficult and precarious conquest of political freedom. Many scholars treat the question of liberty as if it were a logical, rather than an empirical problem. That is, they ignore the principle that I call the law of diminishing consequences, or, as we may also say, of the dispersion of effects.

Thus, from the premise that we all participate (as infinitesimal fraction) in the creation of the legislative body, we boldly evince that it is *as if* we ourselves made the laws. Likewise, and in a more elaborate way, we make the inference that when a person who allegedly represents some tens of thousands contributes (he himself acting as a very small fraction) to the law-making process, then he is making the thousands of people whom he is representing free, because the represented thereby obey norms which they have freely chosen (even though it might well be that even their representative was opposed to those norms). How absurd! Clearly this is nothing more than mental gymnastics in a frictionless interplanetary space. Coming back to earth, these chains of acrobatic inferences are worthless, and this for the good reason that the driving force of the causes (premises) is exhausted long before it reaches its targets. In empirical terms, from the premise that I know how to swim it may follow that I can cross a river, but not that I can cross the ocean. The "cause," ability to swim, cannot produce everlasting effects. And the same applies in the empirical realm of politics to the "cause," participation and elections.

There are at times no limits to the services that we ask of political participation. Yet from the premise that effective, continuous participation of the citizens in the self-government of a small community can produce the "result" liberty (precisely a liberty as autonomy), we cannot draw the conclusion that the same amount of participation will produce the same result in a large community; for in the latter an equally intense participation will entail diminishing consequences.[74] And a similar warning applies to our way of linking elections with representation. Elections do produce representative results, so to speak; but it is absurd to ask of the "cause," elections, infinite effects. Bruno Leoni makes the point lucidly when he writes: "The more numerous the people are whom one tries to 'represent' through the legislative process and the more numerous the matters in which one tries to represent them, the less the word 'representation' has a meaning referable to the actual will of actual people, other than the persons named as their 'representatives'. . . . The inescapable conclusion is that in order to restore to the word 'representation' its original, reasonable meaning, there should be a drastic reduction either in the number of those 'represented' or in the number of matters in which they are allegedly represented, or both." [75]

I do not know whether we can go back to the "drastic reduction" suggested by Leoni. But there is no doubt that if we keep on stretching the elastic (but not infinitely so) cord of political representation beyond a certain limit—in defiance of the law of the dispersion of effects—it will snap. For the more we demand of representation, the less closely are the representatives tied to those they represent. Let us therefore beware of treating representation as another version of the formulae that make us believe (by logical demonstration) that we are free when we actually are not. The fable that autonomy makes for *the* true political liberty is, per se, sufficiently stupefying.

7. From Rule of Law to Rule of Legislators

There are two reasons for my having made a particular point of the connection between liberty and law. The first one is that I am under the impression that we have gone a little too far in the so-called informal approach. Nowadays, both political scientists and philosophers are very contemptuous of law. The former, because they believe that laws can do very little, or in any case much less than had previously been deemed possible; and the latter because they are usually concerned with a higher liberty that will not be hampered by humble, worldly obstacles.[76] Benedetto Croce unquestionably shared this attitude. Yet, philosophers also have a store of common sense, and it is highly significant that an anti-juridical thinker such as Croce himself said: "Those who build theories attacking law, can do so with a light heart because they are surrounded by, protected by, and kept alive by laws; but the instant that all laws begin to break down they would instantly lose their taste for theorizing and chattering." [77] This is indeed a sound warning that should always be kept in mind. After all, if Western man for two and a half millenniums has sought liberty in the law, there must have been a good reason for this. Our forefathers were not more ingenuous than we are. On the contrary.

We must nevertheless admit that the widespread scepticism about the value of the juridical protection of liberty is not unjustified. The reason for this is that our conception of law has changed, and that, as a consequence, law can no longer give us the guarantees that it did in the past. This is no reason for leaving, or creating, a void where law used to be, but it is certainly a reason for staying alert, and not letting ourselves be lulled by the idea that the laws stand guard over us while we sleep twenty-four hours a day. And this is my second motive for paying a great deal of attention to the relationship between law and political liberty.

Montesquieu, who was still relying on the protection of natural law, could very simply assert that we are free because we are subject to "civil laws." [78] But our problem begins exactly where this statement terminates. For we are obliged to ask the question that Montesquieu (as well as Rousseau) could ignore: namely, which laws are "civil laws"?

To begin with, what is law? In the Roman tradition, *ius* (the Latin term for law) has become inextricably connected with *iustum* (what is just);[79] and in the course of time the ancient word for law has become the English (and the Italian and French) word for justice. In short, *ius* is both "law" and "right." That is to say that law has not been conceived as any general rule which is enforced by a sovereign (*iussum*), but as that rule which embodies and expresses the community's sense of justice (*iustum*). In other words, law has been thought of not only as any norm that has the "form" of law, but also as a "content," i.e., as that norm which also has the value and the quality of being just.

This has been the general feeling about the nature of law until recently.[80] Yet, on practical grounds we are confronted with a very serious problem, for law is not given, it has to be made. Only primitive or traditionalistic societies can do without deliberate and overt law-making. Thus we have to answer the questions: Who makes the law? How? And, furthermore, Who interprets the laws? In order for us to be governed by laws, or rather by means of laws, the law-makers themselves must be subject to law. But this is obviously a formidable, strenuous enterprise. The problem has been solved within the constitutional State by arranging the legislative procedure in such a way that the "form of law" also constitutes a guarantee and implies a control of its content.[81] A large number of constitutional devices are, in effect, intended to create the conditions of a law-making process in which the *ius* will remain tied to *iustum,* in which law will remain the right law. For this reason legislation is entrusted to elected bodies that must periodically answer to the electorate. And for the same reason we do not give those who are elected to office *carte blanche,* but we consider them power-holders curbed by and bound to a representative role.

But this solution, or let us say situation, has reacted upon our conception of law. As I have said, we now have a different feeling about the nature of law. For the analytical jurisprudence (that calls up the name of John Austin) on the one hand, and the juridical positivism (of the Kelsen type) on the other, have ended by giving law a purely formal definition, that is, identifying law with the form of law. This shift is actually a rather obvious consequence of the fact that the existence of the *Rechtsstaat* [82] appears to eliminate the very possibility of the unjust law, and thereby allows that the problem of law be reduced to a problem of form rather than of content. Unfortunately, however, the formalists completely overlook (but Kelsen more than Austin) this dependence, that is, the fact that the formal definition of law presupposes the constitutional State. Therefore the high level of systematic and technical refinement achieved by this approach cannot save it from the charge of having drawn conclusions without paying attention to the premises, and of having thus erected a structure whose logical perfection is undermined by its lack of foundations.[83]

The implication of this development, with regard to the political problem that constitutional legality tries to solve, is that Austin, Kelsen, and their numerous following have created, albeit unwittingly, a very unhappy state of affairs. Today we have taken to applying "constitution" to any type of State organization,[84] and "law" to any State command expressed in the form established by the sovereign himself. Now, if law is no longer a fact that is qualified by a value (a *ius* that is *iustum*), and if the idea of law is on the one hand restricted to the commands that bear the mark of the will of the sovereign, and on the other extended to any order that the sovereign is willing to enforce, then it is clear that a law so defined can no longer solve our problems. According to the purely formal definition, a law without righteousness is nonetheless law. Therefore, legislation can be crudely tyrannical and yet not only be called legal but also be respected as lawful. It follows from this that such a conception of law leaves no room for the idea of law as the safeguard of liberty. In this connection even "law" becomes, or may be used as, a trap word.

If the analytic-positivistic approaches of modern jurisprudence are not reassuring—at least for those who are concerned about political freedom—it must be added that the *de facto* development of our constitutional systems is even less so. What the founding fathers of liberal constitutionalism[85] had in mind—in relation to the legislative process—was to bring the rule of law into the State itself, that is,

308

to use Charles H. McIlwain's terms, to extend the sphere of *iurisdictio* to the very realm of *gubernaculum* (government).[86] English constitutionalism actually originated in this way, since the principles of the English constitution are inductions or generalizations derived from particular decisions pronounced by the courts in relation to the rights of specific individuals. And since English constitutional practice—even if it has always been misunderstood—has constantly inspired the Continental constitutionalists, the theory of *garantisme* as well as of the *Rechtsstaat* (in its first stage) had precisely this in mind: to clothe the *gubernaculum* with a mantle of *iurisdictio*. No matter how much the Anglo-Saxon notion of the rule of law has been misinterpreted,[87] there is no doubt that liberal constitutionalism looked forward to a government of politicians that would somehow have the same flavor and give the same security as a government of judges. But after a relatively short time had elapsed, constitutionalism changed—although less rapidly and thoroughly in the English-speaking countries—from a system based on the rule of law to a system centered on the rule of legislators. And there is no point in denying the fact that this transformation per se modifies to a considerable extent the nature and concept of law.

Bruno Leoni summarizes this development very clearly:

The fact that in the original codes and constitutions of the nineteenth century the legislature confined itself chiefly to epitomizing non-enacted law was gradually forgotten, or considered as of little significance compared with the fact that both codes and constitutions had been enacted by legislatures, the members of which were the "representatives" of the people. . . . The most important consequence of the new trend was that people on the Continent and to a certain extent also in the English-speaking countries, accustomed themselves more and more to conceiving of the whole of law as *written law,* that is, as a single series of enactments on the part of legislative bodies according to majority rule. . . . Another consequence of this . . . was that the law-making process was no longer regarded as chiefly connected with a theoretical activity on the part of the experts, like judges or lawyers, but rather with the mere will of winning majorities inside the legislative bodies.[88]

It seems to us perfectly normal to identify law with legislation. But at the time when Savigny published his monumental *System of Actual Roman Law* (1840-1849), this identification still was inacceptable to the chief exponent of the historical school of law. And we can appreciate its far-reaching implications today very much more than was possible a century ago. For when law is reduced to State law-making, a "will conception" or a "command theory" of law gradually replaces the common law idea of law, i.e., the idea of a free law-making process derived from custom and defined by judicial decisions.

There are many practical disadvantages, not to mention dangers, in our legislative conception of law. In the first place, the rule of legislators is resulting in a real mania for law-making, a fearful inflation of laws. Leaving aside the question as to how posterity will be able to cope with hundreds of thousands of laws that increase, at times, at the rate of a couple of thousand per legislature, the fact is that the inflation of laws in itself discredits the law. Nor is it only the excessive quantity of laws that lessens the value of law, it is also their bad quality. Our legislators are poor law-makers, and this is because the system was not designed to permit legislators to replace jurists and jurisprudence. In this connection it is well to remember that when the classical theory of constitutionalism entrusted the institutional guarantee of liberty to an assembly of representatives, this assembly was not being assigned so much the task of changing the laws, but rather that of preventing the monarch from changing them unilaterally and arbitrarily. As far as the legislative function is concerned, parliaments were not intended as technical, specialized bodies; and even less as instruments devised for the purpose of speeding up the output of laws.

Furthermore, laws excessive in number and poor in quality not only discredit the law; they also undermine what our ancestors constructed, a relatively stable and spontaneous law of the land, common to all, and based on rules of general application. For, inevitably, "legislative bodies are generally indifferent to, or even ignorant of, the basic forms and consistencies of the legal pattern. They impose their will through muddled rules that cannot be applied in general terms; they seek sectional advantage in special rules that destroy the nature of law itself." [89] And it is not only a matter of the generality of the law. Mass fabrication of laws ends by also jeopardizing the other fundamental requisite of law—certainty. Certainty does not consist only in a precise wording of laws, or in their being written down: it is also the long-range certainty that the laws will be lasting. And in this connection the present rhythm of statutory law-making calls to mind what happened in Athens, where "laws were certain (that is, precisely worded in a written formula) but nobody was certain that any law, valid today, could last until tomorrow." [90]

Nor is this all. In practice, the legislative conception of law accustoms those to whom the norms are addressed to accept any and all commands of the State, that is, to accept any *iussum* as *ius*. Legitimacy resolves itself in legality, and in a merely formal legality at that, since the problem of the unjust law is dismissed as meta-juridical.[91] It follows from this that the passage from liberty to slavery can occur quietly, with no break in continuity—almost unnoticed. Once the people are used to the rule of legislators, the *gubernaculum* no longer has to fear the opposition of the *iurisdictio*. The road is cleared for the legal suppression of constitutional legality. Whoever has had the experience of observing, for example, how fascism established itself in power knows how easily the existing juridical order can be manipulated to serve the ends of a dictatorship without the country's being really aware of the break.

I shall not go so far as to say that decay of constitutional government—understood as the habit of considering laws in terms of the State, and not the State in terms of laws—has already deprived us of the substance of juridical protection. But I do wish to stress that we have arrived at a point where such protection depends exclusively on the survival of a system of constitutional guarantees. For our rights are no longer safeguarded by our conception of law. We are no longer protected by the rule of law but (in Mosca's terminology) only by the devices of "juridical defense." And since very few people seem to be fully aware of this fact,[92] it is important that we call attention to it. Everywhere, but especially in the rational democracies, there is a call for the democratization of constitutions. Now, this demand indicates nothing other than the steady erosion of the techniques of *garantisme*. The ideal of these reformers is to transform law into outright legislation, and legislation into a rule

311

of legislators freed from the fetters of a system of checks and balances. In short, their ideal is constitutions that are so democratic that they are no longer, properly speaking, constitutions. This means that they, and unfortunately most other people, fail to realize that the more the achievements of liberal constitutionalism are undermined by so-called democratic constitutionalism, the closer we are to the solution at which the Greeks arrived and which proved their downfall: namely, that man was subject to laws so easily changed that they became laws unable to assure the protection of the law.

There are then, as we can see, innumerable reasons for alarm. Whereas law, as it was formerly understood, effectively served as a solid dam against arbitrary power, legislation, as it is now understood, may be, or may become, no guarantee at all. For centuries the firm distinction between *iurisdictio* and *gubernaculum,* between matters of law and matters of State, has made it possible for legal liberty to make up for the absence of political freedom in many respects (even if not all). But nowadays the opposite is true: it is only political freedom that supports the legal protection of individual rights. For we can no longer count on a law that has been reduced to statutory law, to a *ius iussum* that is no longer required to be (according to the formal conception) a *ius iustum*. Or, rather, we can rely on it only insofar as it remains tied to the constitutional State in the liberal and *garantiste* meaning of the term.

Today, as yesterday, liberty and legality are bound together, because the only way that we know to construct a political system that is not oppressive is to depersonalize power by placing the law above men. But this bond has never been as precarious and tenuous as it is at present. When the rule of law resolves itself into the rule of legislators, the way is open, at least in principle, to an oppression "in the name of the law" that has no precedent in the history of mankind. It is open, I repeat, unless we return to the constitutional State with renewed vigor and awareness.

And there is nothing legalistic in this thesis. I believe in law as an essential instrument of political freedom, but only to the extent that political freedom is the foundation and condition of everything else. In other words, what protects our liberties today are "rights," and not the law-as-form on which so many jurists seem to rely. And our rights are the institutionalization of a freedom *from*, the juridical garb of a liberty conceived of as absence of restraint.[83] It is in this sense, and strictly under these conditions, that I have stressed that only liberty under law (not liberty as autonomy), only a constitutional system as an impersonal regulating instrument (not popular power as such), have been, and still are, the guardians of free societies.

We asked at the beginning what place in the scale of historical priorities the principle of political freedom has for us today. If my diagnosis is correct, the answer is: to the extent that *iurisdictio* becomes *gubernaculum* and legality supplants legitimacy, to the same extent political liberty becomes paramount and the need for freedom *from* again becomes a primary concern. Only a few decades ago it might have seemed that the political and liberal notions of liberty had become obsolete. But now it is important to realize that the new freedoms about which we were so keen not long ago are becoming old freedoms, in the sense that the political freedom which we have been taking for granted is the very liberty for which we must again take thought. The pendulum of history goes back and forth. Accordingly, those who are still advocating a greater democratic liberty at the expense of the despised liberal liberty, are no longer in the forefront of progress. They resemble much more a rear-guard which is still fighting the previous war than a vanguard which is facing the new enemy and present-day threats.

By this I do not mean in the least that the question of freedom is exhausted by the liberal solution of the political problem of liberty, or that it is not important to supplement a liberty envisaged as non-restriction by adding a freedom *to* and a substantive power *to*. But it is equally important to call attention again to the proper focus of the problem of political freedom: for it is freedom *from* and not freedom *to* that marks the boundary between political freedom and political oppression. When we define liberty as "power *to*," then the power *to* be free (of the citizens) and the power *to* coerce (of the State) are easily intermingled. And this is because so-called positive liberty can be used in all directions and for any goal whatsoever.

Therefore the so-called democratic, social, and economic freedoms presuppose the liberal technique of handling the problem of power.

313

And I wish to stress *liberal* because it has become important not to confuse the liberal notion of liberty—which is perfectly clear—with the manifold and obscure notions that can be drawn from the much-abused formula "democratic freedoms." It is true that democratic ideals put pressure on the liberty of liberalism, in that they expand a "possibility to" into a "power to," adding to the right of being equal the conditions of equality. But no matter how much democracy permeates liberalism and molds it to its goals, I do not see how we can distinguish and enucleate from the need of liberty as non-restriction a second form of *sui generis* political freedom. To the question as to whether we can oppose to the freedom *from* other and more tangible forms of liberty, I would answer: other freedoms, Yes, of course—but another kind of *political* freedom, No, since it does not exist.

NOTES

† *Annals,* III, 27.

1. *Essays on Freedom and Power,* p. 53.

2. On the problem of freedom in general, Mortimer J. Adler's work, *The Idea of Freedom* (Garden City, 1958), is a precious mine of information (cf. also the bibliography, pp. 623-663). I disagree, however, both with the classification and the method, which he calls "dialectical." The concepts of each author are treated in a historical vacuum, independently of the circumstances and motives which prompted them. Thus in Adler's presentation one misses both the fact that different theses were held for the same reason, and that many differences are due to the fact that the same thing is being said under different circumstances. For further reference to the general problem consult esp. the following collections containing excellent contributions: *Freedom, Its Meaning,* ed., R. N. Anshen; and *Freedom and Authority in Our Time,* eds. Bryson, Finkelstein, MacIver, and McKeon (New York, 1953).

3. I do not use the current labels of freedom from fear, from want, from need, or the formula "freedom as self-expression," since it is seldom clear in what context they belong. With the exception of freedom from need (which is clearly economic), freedom from fear and from insecurity can be understood as instances of psychological freedom, but also as related to political freedom. Still worse, freedom as self-expression can be just as much a psychological freedom as a moral and/or intellectual one.

4. Cf. *Essay Concerning Human Understanding,* esp. Vol. I, Bk. II, Chap. 21 *passim;* and *Two Treatises of Government,* Bk. II, Chap. 4, Sect. 22.

314

5. Cf. *Approaches to the Study of Politics,* ed. R. Young, pp. 174 and 184.

6. Cf. *Freedom,* p. 11.

7. This is Hobbes' well-known definition in Chap. XXI of *Leviathan,* which reads in full: "Liberty, or freedom, signifieth, properly, the absence of opposition; by opposition I mean external impediments of motion." This definition was—according to Hobbes himself—the "proper, and generally received meaning of the word" in England. (For the sake of exactness the definition is placed by Hobbes in the context of "natural liberty": but it overlaps also into the context of civil liberty, of the "liberty of subjects.") I assume that even Adler would agree with my statement about the basic continuity of the concept of political freedom, since he writes in his Conclusion: "In the course of identifying political liberty . . . we found that *exemption from* the arbitrary will of another was commonly present in the understanding of all freedoms" (*The Idea of Freedom,* pp. 611-612).

8. Of course, economic and religious as well as social constraints (as the Tocquevillian type of tyranny of the majority) may also be a concern of public authorities, but they are not necessarily an aspect of political liberty.

9. It does not seem to me, therefore, as H. J. Morgenthau maintains, that political freedom is confronted with a dilemma: freedom for the holder, or for the subject of political power? The concept of political freedom is associated with the latter problem, not with freedom of domination. I agree very much with Morgenthau's conclusions, but I would not say, as he suggests, that there is a case of unfreedom when a power holder is not allowed unrestricted power. Cf. "The Dilemmas of Freedom," in *American Political Science Review,* III (1957), p. 714 ff.

10. This is Hobbes's shorthand. Cf. *Leviathan,* Chap. XIV.

11. Cf. "The Pattern of Liberty," in *Liberty,* eds. M. R. Konvitz and C. Rossiter (Ithaca, 1958), pp. 16-18.

12. *Ibid.*

13. Thus Jhering reminds us that "law is not a logical concept but an energetic and active one." (*Der Kampf um's Recht,* 1st ed. 1873, Chap. I.) Compare with note 15 below.

14. Or otherwise they are following the formula of ancient liberty discussed in Chap. XII, 3, 5, and 6, above; and again in this chap., sections 5, 6.

15. "Les libertés sont des résistances" (liberties are resistances), Royer-Collard, the doctrinaire of the French Restoration, used to say. It is symptomatic how in an author so far removed as Laski one should find a connotation so closely related. Cf. Harold J. Laski, *Liberty in the Modern State* (New York, 1949), p. 172: "Liberty cannot help being a courage to resist the demands of power at some point that is deemed decisive."

16. It should be clear that in the expression "political liberty" I include also the the so-called "civil liberties" (freedom of speech, of press, of assembly, etc.). Civil liberties too are liberties that come under the category of freedom *from,* since they delimit the sphere of action of the State and mark the boundary between the use and abuse of political power. Our political rights stem from civil liberties both as their prosecution and above all as their concrete guaranty. That is to say that political rights are civil liberties which have been extended and protected, and civil liberties are the *raison d'être* (even if not the only one) for the existence of political rights.

17. This issue will be examined in Chaps. XIV, 6, and XVI, 4, 6, below.

18. See below section 7.

19. *Oratio pro Cluentio,* 53.

20. The exceptions are not probatory, for, as M. J. Adler has aptly noted, although there are "(i) authors who maintain that freedom consists in exemption from legal regulations or restrictions and (ii) authors who maintain that freedom consists in obedience to law . . . they are not talking about the same freedom. Though they may appear to be giving opposite answers to the question 'How is law related to liberty?' they are really not taking that question in the same sense." (p. 619). Cf. below, note 76.

21. The similarity of development between Roman and English constitutionalism was perceived by Rudolf von Jhering in his *Geist des römischen Rechts,* and also by Bryce in his *Studies in History and Jurisprudence.*

22. Cf. e.g. Aristotle: "Men should not think it slavery to live according to the rule of the constitution; for it is their salvation" (*Politics* 1310a).

23. Ch. Wirszubski, *Libertas,* etc. (Cambridge, 1950), p. 13.

24. However, I prefer to say "constitutional *garantisme"* instead of state based on law (*Rechtsstaat*) because the latter can also be understood in a restrictive sense as a mere system of administrative justice. In fact the administrative notion of *Rechtsstaat* has prevailed upon the constitutional notion (at least in the Italian and German juridic doctrine). Cf. the pertinent remarks of Giuseppino Treves, "Considerazioni sullo stato di diritto," in *Studi in onore di E. Crosa* (Milano, 1960), Vol. II, pp. 1591-1594.

25. Notably the externalization and generalization of the principle that every man has the right to live according to his own conscience and principles.

26. Dicey's *The Law of the Constitution* (1885), Part II, still remains the classic exposition of the rule of law theory. For the precedents which escaped Dicey, and in particular the contribution of the Italian communes to the elaboration of the principle of the rule of law, cf. the detailed study of Ugo Niccolini, *Il principio di legalità nelle democrazie italiane* (Padova, 2nd ed. 1955).

27. I say possibly because the "due process of law" as understood in the United States has no equivalent in Europe, and in substance considerably surpasses not only the *lex terrae* of the old English law, but the English interpretation of the rule of law as well.

28. Duverger reminds us that "when Laboulaye gave the title *Cours de politique constitutionelle* to a collection of Benjamin Constant's works, he meant to say in substance *Course in liberal politics*. 'Constitutional' regimes are liberal regimes." Cf. M. Duverger, *Droit constitutionnel et institutions politiques* (Paris, 1955), p. 3. To be precise Constant himself had collected those writings in 1818-19, saying that "they constitute a sort of course in constitutional politics. . . ."

29. Cf. Chap. XII, 5 above.

30. *Vom Wesen und Wert der Demokratie*, Chap. VII.

31. B. de Jouvenel, *Du pouvoir*, p. 290.

32. He added: "[Otherwise] you can be sure that it will not be the law that will rule, but men." (*Considérations sur le gouvernement de la Pologne*, Chap. 1).

33. It is the constant thesis in all of Rousseau's writings. In the *Discours sur l'économie politique* compiled probably in 1754 for the *Encyclopédie*, he wrote: "Law is the only thing to which man owes his freedom and the justice he receives." In the dedicatory letter to the *Discours* on *Quelle est l'origine de l'inégalité parmi les hommes* he wrote: "No one of you is so little enlightened as not to realize that where the vigor of the law and the authority of its defenders end, there can be no safety or freedom for anyone." In the first draft of the *Contrat social* (1756), law was described as "the most sublime of all human institutions." In the "brief and faithful" condensation of his *Contrat social* in the *Lettres écrites de la montagne* Rousseau repeated: "When men are placed above the law . . . you have left only slaves and masters." (Pt. I, No. 5.)

34. Pt. II, No. 8. Rousseau had said before: "There is . . . no freedom without laws, nor where there is anyone who is above the law. . . . A free nation obeys the law, and the law only; and it is through the power of the law that it does not obey men. . . . People are free . . . when they see in whoever governs them not a man, but an organ of the law" (*ibid.*). And in Pt. II, No. 9 he writes: "All that the citizen wants is the law and the obedience thereof. Every individual . . . knows very well that any exceptions will not be to his favor. This is why everyone fears exceptions; and those who fear exceptions love the law."

35. *Les Confessions*, Bk. IX. It is a rephrasing of this question: "What is the nature of a government under which its people can become the most virtuous, most enlightened, most wise, in short the best that can be expected?"

36. Rousseau enjoys this comparison, which is also found in a letter to Mirabeau dated 26 July 1767.

37. Pt. II, No. 9.

38. *Contrat social,* II, 6.

39. Cf. B. de Jouvenel in the *Essai sur la politique de Rousseau* which introduces his ed. of the *Contrat social* (Genève, 1947), pp. 123-126. Cf. also *Du pouvoir,* pp. 295-304.

40. The criticism against the legislative fickleness of the Athenians is resumed in the *Contrat social,* II, 4. Cf. also III, 11, *ibid.*

41. The state, says Rousseau, "needs but a few laws" (*Contrat social,* IV, 1). And let us remember that his model was Sparta, that is, the static constitution by antonomasia. Addressing the citizens of his favored Geneva he wrote: "You have good and wise laws, both for themselves, and for the simple reason that they are laws. . . . Since the constitution of your government has reached a definite and stable form, your function as legislators has terminated: to assure the safety of this building it is necessary that you now find as many obstacles to keep it standing as you found aids in building it. . . . The building is finished, now the task is to keep it as it is." (*Lettres écrites de la montagne,* Pt. II, No. 9). The exhortation to "maintain and reestablish the ancient ways" is found also throughout the *Considérations sur le gouvernement de la Pologne* (cf. Chap. III). One must also keep in mind that Rousseau's concept of law is based on custom, which he judges as the most important aspect of law (cf. *Contrat social,* II, 12).

42. In the dedicatory letter to the *Discours* on *L'inégalité parmi les hommes* Rousseau states that the republic he would have chosen is the one in which "individuals are happy to accept the laws." In the *Considérations sur le gouvernement de la Pologne* (Chap. II) Rousseau distinguishes between the common "law makers" and the "Legislator," laments the absence of the latter, and recalls as examples Moses, Lycurgus and Numa Pompilius. Cf. also *Contrat social,* II, 7, where he invokes the Legislator, "an extraordinary man in the state" who must perform "a particular and superior function which has nothing in common with the human race," for "it would take gods to make laws for human beings."

43. The relationship between Rousseau and natural law is studied in detail by R. Derathé, *Jean-Jacques Rousseau et la science politique de son temps* (Paris, 1950).

44. The wording is not Rousseau's, in fact the expression was common enough. Cf. the careful and intelligent reconstruction of the concept in Jouvenel's *Essai sur la politique de Rousseau,* pp. 105-120, 127-132.

45. *Contrat social,* II, 3.

46. We should not look at Rousseau's general will through romantic glasses, and for how it has reached us after the idealistic mediation. Also because, as Derathé points out, "the general will is essentially a juridic notion which can be understood only through the theory of the moral personality which had been formulated by Hobbes and Pufendorf" (*J. J. Rousseau,* etc., pp. 407-410).

47. *Encyclopédie,* "Droit naturel," Sect. 9.

48. Rousseau is just as much a rationalist when, e.g., he declares that in the civil society man must "consult his reason before listening to his inclinations" (*Contrat social,* I, 8), and that to submit to the civil society means to be subject to a "law dictated by reason" (*ibid.,* II, 4). Consider also the following passage in the *Contrat,* II, 6: "Private citizens see the good which they repudiate; the public wants the good which it does not see. . . . It is necessary to compel the first to make *their will conform with their reason;* one must teach the other to *know what it wants*" (my italics).

49. See in this connection A. Cobban's *Rousseau and the Modern State* (London, 1934) and Derathé's *Le Rationalisme de Rousseau* and *Jean-Jacques Rousseau et la science politique de son temps.* Cassirer goes as far as maintaining that "Rousseau's ethics is not an ethics of sentiment, but it is the purest and most definite ethics of the law ever formulated before Kant." ("Das Problem Jean Jacques Rousseau," Italian transl., p. 84). Which is going too far. My deviation from Masson's thesis does not imply that I disregard his fundamental work, i.e., his classic book on *La Religion de J. J. Rousseau* (Paris, 1916, 3 vols.); nor do I wish to deny that Rousseau's political thought is a continuation of his ethics. But I do not see how one can pile together *Émile* (and along with it the *Discours,* the *Confessions,* the *Rêveries,* or even the *Nouvelle Héloïse*) with Rousseau's political writings. Whether Rousseau's sentiment has a romantic character or not, the point is that the "ethics of the sentiment" and the "ethics of politics" belong to radically different contexts: in *Émile* Rousseau educates man "according to nature," in the *Contrat* he "denatures" him into a citizen. As Rousseau himself points out in *Émile* (I), "Whoever wants to preserve in a society the priority of the natural sentiments does not know what he wants."

This is to say that Rousseau considers two hypotheses. When society is too large and corrupt only the individual can be saved. Therefore in *Émile* Rousseau proposes to abolish even the words "country" and "citizen," and exalts love for one's self. In this hypothesis man must devote his attention entirely to himself. But when the city and society are small and still patriarchal—this is the second hypothesis—then one must save the community: this is the problem of the *Contrat.* In the latter case the citizen must cancel the man, the patriot must collectivize his love for himself, and the individual must give his self to the whole; he dies as a "particular" and is reborn as a moral member of the collective body. Rousseau is coherent, but

319

his hypotheses are discontinuous, or better alternative. In the "nature man" the sentiment dominates, but in the "denatured" one (the citizen) passion and love become a catalyst which helps in the production of a society which acts according to reason; and the general will is the very *deus ex machina* of a purely logical construction.

50. *Contrat social*, IV, 1.

51. *Ibid.*

52. It is true that in Rousseau there is also a "subjective" position through which the will can decide about the laws (cf. *Contrat*, II, 12); but that admission is always accompanied by the position that reason discovers their "objective" necessity (cf. *Contrat*, II, 11).

53. The analogy holds true even in this respect: because for Rousseau too the legislator is a "revealer," as Groethuysen has pointed out in his work *Jean-Jacques Rousseau* (Paris, 1949), p. 103.

54. Cf. esp. *Contrat*, II, 4 and 6.

55. *Contrat*, II, 3. Here one can perceive the distance between Rousseau and Hegel, between the philosopher of the eighteenth century and the romantics. In Rousseau's conceptualization we do not find, for there could not be, any of those ingredients used by the romantics for building their organismic, collective entities, we do not find the "soul" or the "spirit" of the people. For this reason Rousseau had to keep his general will proximate to something numerical and computable.

56. In fact Rousseau hastens to specify: "Often there is quite a difference between the will of all (*la volonté de tous*) and the general will" (*Contrat*, II, 3). That "often" reveals Rousseau's difficulties and oscillations. On the one hand he was concerned to find a passage between Law and Sovereign, but on the other hand Rousseau was not at all resigned to accept this consequence: that "a people is always free to change its laws, even the best ones: for if it wants to harm itself, who has the right to stop it?" (*ibid.*, II, 12).

57. B. de Jouvenel has rendered the distinction very well. He states: "The will of all can bind everyone juridically. That is one thing. But it is quite another thing to say that it is good. . . . Therefore, to this will of all which has only a juridic value he counterposes the general will which is always correct and always tends toward public welfare" (*Essai sur la politique de Rousseau*, p. 109).

58. Note in passing that Rousseau's "people" is completely different from the *populace*. The people consists of the "citizens" and the "patriots" only. Both in the project of the Constitution of Poland as in the one of Corsica, Rousseau foresees a meticulous *cursus honorum* which amounts to a qualification for sovereignty. And from the *Lettres écrites de la montagne* one can see very

320

clearly that equality for Rousseau is an intermediate condition between the beggar and the millionaire represented by the bourgeoisie. Between the rich and the poor, between the rulers and the *populace*, Rousseau's "people" is not far removed from Hegel's "general class."

59. *Contrat*, II, 3.

60. *Ibid.*, II, 6.

61. *Ibid.*, IV, 2.

62. Rousseau not only did not have a revolutionary temperament, he was not even a political reformer. Cf. Groethuysen's concise statement: "Rousseau's ideas were revolutionary; he himself was not" (*J. J. Rousseau*, p. 206). In his second *Discours* Rousseau declares: "I would have liked to have been born under a democratic government, wisely tempered" (Dedicatory letter). In the third *Dialogue* he stresses that he "had always insisted on the preservation of existing institutions." In 1765 he wrote to Buttafoco: "I have always held and shall always follow as an inviolable maxim the principle of having the highest respect for the government under which I live, and to make no attempts . . . to reform it in any way whatever." The project on the reform of Poland is throughout a reminder of the use of prudence in carrying out reforms, and one of the most sarcastic refutations of revolutionary medicines is found in this text: "I laugh at those people . . . who imagine that in order to be free all they have to do is to be rebels" (*Considérations sur le gouvernement de la Pologne*, Chap. VI). Only Corsica, Rousseau believed, could be reformed through legislation alone, for in his judgment it was the only state young enough to gain by it (*Contrat*, II, 10). For the rest he warned, "After customs are established and prejudices become deeply set, it is a vain and dangerous enterprise to change them" (*ibid*, II, 8). And referring to changes of regime he admonished that "those changes are always dangerous . . . and one should never touch a government that is established except when it becomes incompatible with the common weal" (*ibid.*, III, 18).

63. One must discern at least three phases in the evolution of the idea of natural law. Until the Stoics the law of nature was not a juridic notion, but a term of comparison which denoted the uniformity and the normality of what is natural. With the Stoics, and the Romans above all, one can already speak of a theory of natural law. But the Roman conceptualization did not contain the idea of "personal rights" which is at the base of our idea of constitutional legality and which belongs to the third phase. (Cf. Chap. XIV, note 16 below.)

64. *Contrat social,* I, 8. Cf. also *ibid.*, I, 6.

65. *Ibid.*, III, 15.

66. One could quote at length, for this is a very firm point in Rousseau. Even

in the *Considérations sur le gouvernement de la Pologne,* that is to say in a context in which Rousseau has to soften and adjust his conception to a large State, he maintains that the "grandeur of nations, the extension of states" is the "first and principal source of human woes. . . . Almost all small states, whether republics or monarchies, prosper for the very reason that they are small, that all the citizens know each other. . . . All the large nations, crushed by their own masses, suffer whether . . . under a monarchy or under oppressors" (Chap. V). Also cf. *Contrat social:* "The larger a state becomes, the less freedom there is" (III, 1); "the larger the population, the greater the repressive forces" (III, 2).

67. *General Theory of Law and State* (New Haven, 1945), Part II, Chap. IV, B. a 2.

68. Hegelian idealism, to be precise. These infiltrations have been so deep that De Ruggiero's *Storia del liberalismo europeo* (trans. Collingwood, *History of European Liberalism* [London, 1927]) raises Hegel to the central figure of liberal thought and following the Kant-Hegel line reaches the conclusion, that "the State, the organ of compulsion par excellence, has become the highest expression of freedom" (p. 374, Italian ed.); this being, according to De Ruggiero, a typically liberal position, in fact the essential conquest of liberalism (cf. pp. 230-253 and pp. 372-374, Italian ed.). The reasons for my disagreement will be given in Chap. XV, below.

69. *Politics,* 1317 b (W. Ellis trans.)

70. For the difference between self-government, *Selbstverwaltung* (which German scholarship wrongly equated with self-government) and autarchy, cf. Giuseppino Treves, "Autarchia, autogoverno, autonomia," in *Studi in onore di G. M. De Francesco* (Milano, 1957), Vol. II pp. 579-594.

71. N. Bobbio, *Politica e cultura,* p. 176.

72. *Politica e cultura,* pp. 173, 272.

73. *On Liberty* (Oxford, 1947), pp. 67-68.

74. Cf. Chap. IV, 3, above.

75. Bruno Leoni, *Freedom and the Law* (New York, 1961), pp. 18, 19. Professor Leoni was kind enough to allow me to consult in advance the text of his lectures, and I am indebted to him for many of the issues discussed in the ff. Sect. 7.

76. There are also philosophers who maintain that freedom and law are mutually exclusive. This thesis does not apply, however, to the political problem of liberty, but to freedom understood as self-realization or self-perfection. I would go as far as saying that no author who has clearly isolated the problem of political freedom holds the view of "liberty against law," provided that some qualifications are made about what is meant by law. The thesis that

law infringes on individual liberty, held, e.g., by Hobbes, Bentham, and Mill, does not really contradict Locke's statement that "where there is no law there is no freedom." (*Two Treatises of Government*, Chap. VI, Sect. 27.) It is different either because they envisaged a different problem, or because they referred to the case of the unjust law (but in such a case that denial completes the sense of the thesis of liberty under law). Cf. note 20 above.

77. *Filosofia della pratica* (Bari, 1909, 4th ed. 1932), p. 333.

78. Cf. *L'Esprit des lois*, Bk. XXVI, Chap. XX: "Freedom consists above all in not being compelled to do something which is not prescribed by law; and we are in this situation only as we are governed by civil laws. Therefore we are free because we live under civil laws."

79. The Greek had no real equivalent of the Latin *ius*. The Greek *diké* and *dikaiosúne* render the moral but not the legal idea of justice: which means that they are not equivalent to the *iustum* (just) which derives from *ius*. On the meanings and etymology of *ius* as well as of the later term *directum* (from which come the Italian *diritto*, the French *droit*, the Spanish *derecho*, etc., which are not the same as the English "right," since the latter is concrete and/or appreciative whereas the former concepts are abstract and neutral nouns indicating the legal system as a whole), cf. Felice Battaglia, "Alcune osservazioni sulla struttura e sulla funzione del diritto" in *Rivista di diritto civile*, III (1955), esp. pp. 509-513; and W. Cesarini Sforza, *'Ius' e 'directum,'* Note sull'origine storica dell'idea di diritto (Bologna, 1930). From a strictly glottological point of view the origin of *ius* is not too clear. Let us just note that the associations of *ius* with *iubeo* (to order), *iuvo* (to benefit), *iungo* (to link), and *iustum* (just) all appear at a relatively late stage. Cf. G. Devoto, "Ius—Di là dalla grammatica," *Rivista italiana per le scienze giuridiche* (1948), pp. 414-418.

80. This is of course a very broad generalization. For a more detailed but swift historical analysis, cf. the survey of C. J. Friedrich, *The Philosophy of Law in Historical Perspective* (Chicago, 1958).

81. As can be easily gathered from the whole context of the book, I use "constitution" in the light of its political *telos* and *raison d'être*, and therefore in the perspective which conceives constitutional law—as Mirkine-Guetzévitch said—as a "technique of freedom" (cf. *Nouvelles tendances du droit constitutionnel* [Paris, 1931], pp. 81 f.) and defines a constitution as "the process by which governmental action is effectively restrained" (C. J. Friedrich, *Constitutional Government and Democracy*, p. 131). For the other loose meaning of constitution (but hardly of "constitutionalism" as a body of doctrine related to the constitutional function) see note 84, below.

82. I am of course referring to the original meaning: *Rechtsstaat* as a synonym of constitutional *garantisme* (cf. note 24 above). If the notion of state based on law is conceived in strictly formal terms it becomes—as Renato Treves has

rightly observed—purely tautologic: "If we start with the preconception that our point of view must be exclusively juridic, on what other basis could the State based on law be founded except on law? What else could the State realize except law? And what is the significance of saying that the State must find its limits in law, given the fact that law is in itself always a limit and a position of rights and duties which are reciprocally corresponding?" (R. Treves, "Stato di diritto e stati totalitari," in *Studi in onore di G. M. De Francesco* [Milano, 1957], p. 61).

83. As it is well known, for Kelsen any State is by definition a *Rechtsstaat,* since according to the "pure doctrine of law" all State activity is by definition a juridical activity which brings about an "order" which cannot be regarded as anything but juridical. Cf. his *General Theory of Law and State, passim.*

84. That is, simply to designate any "political form," or better any way of "giving form" to any State whatever. It is true that this loose meaning of constitution is not unprecedented (for example, the translators of Aristotle render *politéia* by "constitution"; erroneously to be sure, since *politéia* is the ethico-political system as a whole, not its higher law). However, today it has found a technical justification in the formal definition of law, which consecrates, willy-nilly, the existence of what Loewenstein calls "semantic constitutions," so called because their "reality is nothing but the formalization of the existing location of political power for the exclusive benefit of the actual power holders" (*Political Power and Governmental Process,* p. 149). Cf. Chap. XVII, note 57, below. As I have made clear in note 81 above, I never use "constitution" in this all-embracing sense, but to qualify a specific type of State.

85. I say "liberal constitutionalism" where American authors are inclined to say "democratic constitutionalism" on account of the peculiar meaning which "liberal" has acquired in the United States. (This question will be looked into in Chap. XV, 2 below.) The latter label, however, has two disadvantages: one is that it is historically incorrect, for it is difficult to understand in what sense English constitutionalism belongs in the orbit of the development of the idea of democracy; the other is that it is confusing in terms of the present-day constitutional debate as well, since the democratic component of our systems tends nowadays to erode liberal constitutions (as I shall point out in Chap. XV, 5, below).

86. Cf. Charles H. McIlwain, *Constitutionalism: Ancient and Modern* (Ithaca, 1940), Chap. IV. *Iurisdictio* and *gubernaculum* was the terminology used by Bracton towards the middle of the thirteenth century.

87. This misunderstanding has been well singled out by Bruno Leoni, *Freedom and the Law,* esp. Chap. III.

88. *Freedom and the Law,* pp. 147-149.

89. Cf. T. R. Adam in *Aspects of Human Equality,* p. 176.

90. B. Leoni, *op. cit.,* p. 79.

91. Cf. A. Passerin d'Entrèves, *Dottrina dello stato* (Torino, 1959), pp. 170-171.

92. Among the few notable exceptions see *The Public Philosophy* of Walter Lippmann (Boston, 1955), p. 179; and Charles Howard McIlwain, *Constitutionalism: Ancient and Modern,* which concludes with this pertinent appeal: "If the history of our constitutional past teaches anything, it seems to indicate that the mutual suspicions of reformers and constitutionalists . . . must be ended" (p. 148). In the same line of thinking, that is, in defense of the arguments for a *garantiste* constitutionalism, cf. also Giuseppe Maranini, *Miti e realtà della democrazia.*

93. Cf. Harold Laski, who was right in repeating an ancient but by no means antiquated truth: "Liberty . . . is a product of rights. . . . Without rights there cannot be liberty, because, without rights, men are the subjects of law unrelated to the needs of personality." (*A Grammar of Politics,* p. 142).

Chapter XIV

Equality

"It is precisely because the force of circumstances tends always to destroy equality that the force of legislation must always tend to maintain it."

—Rousseau†

1. A Protest-Ideal

IF WE KNOW how to proceed we need not get lost in the labyrinth of liberty, or rather liberties. But this is not the case for the labyrinth of equality—here we are still seeking Ariadne's thread. The literature dealing with equality is rather monotonous, often ingenuous and seldom, if ever, exhaustive. On the other hand the problem has so many facets and so many implications,[1] that after we have examined it from all angles we are left with the feeling of not having really mastered it. When we come to equality, Plato's remark about law comes to mind, "a perfectly simple principle can never be applied to a state of things which is the reverse of simple." [2]

Equality is the ideal which aims at the least natural of all political forms; we might say that it is the ideal which calls for the extreme denaturalization of the political order. To achieve inequality all we have to do is to let things take their course. Not action but inaction is required. But if we are to achieve equality we can never afford to relax. As Tawney wrote, echoing Rousseau, "While inequality is easy since it demands no more than to float with the current, equality is difficult for it involves swimming against it." [3] Tawney's image indicates the sense in which we might say that inequality is natural. It is a natural state of affairs, because it is a fact that men are not equal, either in regard to their mental and moral qualities or to their attitudes and abilities. But the problem of equality does not start from this point.

The demand for equality does not deny the existence of natural differences, or, shall we say, it loses much of its force and justification when it rejects such principles as "the right man in the right place," or "the best man in the highest place." However, this, too, is an ideal that is never realized, since in its stead what we find only too often is the privileged man in a privileged place. And this is where the demand for equality actually and rightly starts. The claim for equality is a protest against unjust, undeserved, and unjustified inequalities. For hierarchies of worth and ability never satisfactorily correspond to effective hierarchies of power.

When we act in the name of equality, then, we are going against the law of inertia governing human aggregations, which constantly tend to solidify and to perpetuate the existing vertical structures. This happens not only because fathers tend to perpetuate themselves through their descendants, but because the easiest way to manage the command-obedience relationship is by maintaining the *status quo ante*. It is much simpler to make society function in an orderly fashion by virtue of the belief that each man should live according to his station, and by means of routine, custom, and traditional social mechanisms, than by constantly raising questions about everything and everybody in the name of the principle that rank should correspond to merit. In this sense, therefore, the ideal of equality works against the force of gravity of politico-social organisms. By appealing initially to liberty, and subsequently—and more particularly—to equality, man asserts his wish to build a social order that is no longer subject to necessary forms of organization, to what might be called the natural functioning of the social machine. Equality is thus a *protest-ideal,* a symbol of man's revolt against chance, fortuitous disparity, unjust power, crystallized privilege.

However, this is only the negative side, or the polemic aspect of equality. And when we come to consider its constructive function and aspect, the concept becomes at once much less clear. First of all, what

327

is "rightful equality," the kind of equality to be considered just? Second, what means can we use to deal effectively with unjust inequalities? And this raises a third problem: to what extent is equality compatible with a free society, or, rather, under what conditions does it promote liberty and under what conditions does it suffocate it? Writers on the subject of equality are eloquent and persuasive as long as they give us a *cahier de doléances* denouncing the evils of inequality. But their arguments become thin and far less convincing as soon as they have to deal with the question of *how* the ideal of equality is to be realized. In this matter their outstanding characteristic seems to be ingenuousness. As an ideal expressing a protest, equality is intelligible and appealing; as an ideal expressing proposals —I mean as a constructive ideal—it is not. And here begin the puzzles, the questions that remain unanswered.

2. Justice and Sameness

Apparently, the notion of equality is much more intelligible than that of liberty. I cannot answer the question, "What is free?" with an ostensive definition, indicating an object or series of objects and saying: This.[4] Whereas I can reply to the question, "What is equal?" by pointing to billiard balls and saying: These are equal. The notion of equality, unlike the idea of freedom, lends itself easily to tangible illustration. But this is the very reason—and this is no paradox—that the concept of equality is still more ambiguous; for its meaning ranges from the extreme simplicity of the ostensive definition to the extreme complexity indicated by the idea of justice.

That is to say, the concept of equality has two basic meanings, which are at the same time heterogeneous and mutually conflicting. In one sense it is a moral ideal; in the other sense it is related to the notion of likeness. The argument can be developed in the sense that we seek justice, but also in the sense that we seek identity. If on the one hand the ideal of equality stems from the principle "To each his due," on the other it is fed by a distaste for variety, diversity, and unevenness. The two connotations diverge sharply. Nevertheless, it is not easy to separate them neatly. And even when we have succeeded in doing so, it is not at all certain that the second meaning gives way to the first.

The overlapping of equality-as-justice and equality-as-sameness can be traced to a semantic cause. I mean that behind the conceptual overlapping there is a semantic overlapping. The Italian *eguale,* the French *égal,* and the German *gleich* not only mean "equal" but also have exactly the meaning of the English word "same." To say in Italian, French, and German that two things are equal is to say that they are identical. In this respect English-speaking people are more fortunate, for in English usage it is unusual to say that two cars are equal when we wish to indicate that they are the same type of car. (Incidentally, this helps to explain why literal egalitarianism—the ideal of making men identical, if they are not assumed to be so already—never took root in Anglo-Saxon countries.) Nonetheless this overlapping has also appeared in English-speaking countries, for the association of the idea of equality with the idea of sameness was imported there by the translations into English of Continental authors, and also by way of the theory of natural law. In referring to the Declaration of Independence, Lincoln in his Springfield speech of 1857 explained that the "authors of that notable instrument did not intend to declare all men equal in all respects. They did not mean to say all were equal in color, size, intellect, moral developments or social capacity." [5] Now, it is clear that here Lincoln is referring to "equal" in the sense of "alike," and that his explanation would be superfluous if the two meanings had not mingled in English as well.

The extent and tenacity of this semantic ambiguity can be illustrated by the argument that men are entitled to equal rights and opportunities *because* they are, as such, equal, in the sense of being, at least in some respects, the same as each other. With all due respect to the illustrious thinkers who propound this view, the argument does not hold. There is no "because" about it. The moral quest for equality does not imply or require *de facto* equality. There is no necessary connection between the fact that men are or are not born alike, and the ethical principle that they ought to be treated equally. If it is true that equality is a moral principle, then we seek equality because we think it is just; not because men actually *are* alike, but because we feel that they should be treated *as if* they were (even though, in point of fact, they are not).[6] This is so true that, historically speaking, our most fundamental egalitarian principles have not been derived from

329

the premise that men are identical. If we have made them equal in respect to the law and to civil and political rights it is not because we have considered them all alike.

In short, the decision to grant equality is only motivated prima facie by the alleged reason that men are actually born equal. As soon as we clear up the confusion between equality in the moral sense and equality in the physical sense we realize that the very opposite is true: for we contend that it is *just* to promote certain equalities precisely to compensate for the fact that men are actually born different.

It is worth pointing out in this connection that ambiguity can hardly be avoided even if we start from the concept of justice rather than equality. For even the idea of justice conveys an idea of sameness. In a text written in the early Italian of the fourteenth century, Brunetto Latini reveals this connotation in all simplicity: "Just as justice is an equal thing, so injustice is unequal; and thus he who wants to establish justice tries to make equal the things that are unequal." [7] To be sure, the idea of justice is less crude than was suggested in this primitive text. Yet, underlying every discussion of justice there is the recurrent theme of identical treatment, of the same measure and proportion for all.[8] When we say, "To each his due," we mean that each should have a fair share, and a fair share means that, unless there is some justification for acting otherwise, shares should be approximately the same. Even if we repeat, with Aristotle, that equal things should be treated equally, but unequal things differently, even so we are asserting that justice demands the *same* treatment for the *same* differences. Now, I am by no means asserting that the idea of justice can be reduced to the physical or mathematical idea of sameness. Quite the contrary. I only wish to indicate how easy it is, even by taking this path, to mistake the moral meaning of equality for some sort of factual identity.

Up to this point I have dealt with a case of confusion. But where confusion stops, rivalry starts. I mean that it would be wrong to believe that, once we have isolated and identified the infiltrations of the idea of equality-as-sameness, we can brush the notion aside. For this meaning is not simply the product of semantic ambiguity, or of simple-mindedness. It has, on the contrary, an illustrious background.

Equality, wrote Hegel with his genius for synthesis, "is the abstract identity of the understanding." [9] Which means, in plain language, that the levelling and unifying connotation of equality reflects the very pattern of logical thinking, and specifically of scientific and mathematical thinking. And this is the reason why the idea (and ideal) of *Gleichmachung,* a uniform levelling, always finds new adherents. There is nothing necessarily primitive or ingenuous in thinking of equality as identity. Rather, this notion is another instance of the "power of reason," of its ability to reduce the heterogeneous to the homogeneous; that is, of the way in which our capacity for abstraction masters sense perception, and thereby the appearance of diversity, by reducing it to uniformity, regularity, and recurrence.

Therefore, we should not underestimate the appeal of the notion of sameness. Natural science proceeds by reducing the different to the identical. Why should the science of society not follow the same procedure? There is a subtle link between Newton and Rousseau, which has been acutely pointed out by Kant:

> Newton, before any one else, saw order and regularity united to a great simplicity where before him people saw nothing but disorder. . . . Rousseau, before any one else, discovered beneath the difference in the conventional forms of mankind, the nature of man.[10]

In effect, the science of society of the illuminists was frankly inspired by Newton's philosophy of nature and by the mathematical physics of the seventeenth century.[11] And modern political rationalism is fond of tracing its ancestry to that source. For if its calculations are to be certain and precise, if its projects are to be symmetrical and well-contrived, if everything is to fit properly, it must postulate the identity of men behind the veil of appearances. This amounts to saying that conceiving equality in terms of levelling and uniformity is congenial to the pattern of scientific thinking. Scientific training leads to a *Gestalt* which is apt to perceive the sameness of equality much more than "rightful equality."

The fact that the notion of equality goes back to two irreducible matrices, to two conflicting mental frameworks, helps us to understand why the relationship between equality and liberty is so troublesome. It explains why equality is understood as a way of enhancing individual freedom, but also as a reason for giving up individual freedom; why it can operate as a demand for more respect for each and every individual, but also as a way of repressing individuality and making individuals interchangeable; why it is apprehended as a dynamic ideal intended to promote social, economic, and political mobility, but also is denounced as a static and suffocating burden. Actually, in the name of equality two opposite solutions are favored: the one which asks for an equality that respects diversity, and the other which sees inequality in every diversity; the one which repudiates privileged differences in order to promote authentic ones, and the other which rejects any difference whatsoever. Clearly, under the heading "equality" we are speaking of *one* but are actually thinking of *two* equalities.

Our task is not yet over. Equality is not only theoretically two-headed but also practically Janus-faced. In actual operation also, the notion of equality is liable to much wider oscillations than that of liberty. The quest for equality may be more sincere than the quest for liberty, but it may also be less sincere; it may be purely disinterested, but it may also be far more interested.

Looking at things in a somewhat crude fashion, we may say that liberty acts for the advantage of the few (in the sense that it favors their greater force or ability), and, similarly, that equality acts as the force of the many, in the sense that it favors force of numbers. There is, however, an important difference between the two cases. In the name of liberty I cannot succeed in oppressing the many, at least in the sense that I cannot legitimize this behavior; whereas in the name of equality the many can easily succeed in legitimately tyrannizing over the few. However much we may want to accuse liberty of giving advantage to the strongest, we cannot extend our reproof to the point of saying that it gives advantage *only* to the strongest. For if this were so, why have the strongest always been much happier when they managed to get rid of liberty? It can correctly be argued, instead, that the principle of equality can be turned into a practice which gives advantage only to the weakest. The difference lies therefore in this, that while the principle of liberty cannot be turned in actual operation into its very opposite, the principle of equality can. Starting from a demand for justice, it can come to establish the most unjust inequalities by subjecting quality to sheer quantity. Equality is born as a moral vindication, but it may come to be a pure and simple form of promoting one's self-interest. As Georg Simmel remarked, for many people equality means only "equality with one's own superior," [12]—thereby resolving itself into a pure and simple means of overtaking, a device for pulling down those at the top and setting oneself in their place. From this point of view, Plato's irony when he wrote, in reference to the way in which democratic majorities wield their power, "I suspect that they are only too glad of equality," [13] was undoubtedly fitting.

Equality is indeed a moral ideal, but an ideal that is easily corrupted. It begins as the purest, sincerest vindication of justice, and can end as a hypocritical, insincere technique used by the worst to overthrow the best, by the *major pars* to overcome the *melior pars*. History has unfortunately always confirmed this degenerating trend.

In 431 B.C. Pericles said to the Athenians that "while the law secures equal justice to all alike in their private disputes, the claim of excellence is also recognized; and when a citizen is in any way distinguished he is preferred to the public service, not as a matter of privilege but as a reward of merit." [14] But at a century's distance Aristotle recorded a very different interpretation of the idea of equality, for democratic justice had become "the application of numerical, not proportionate equality; whence it follows that the majority must be supreme, and that whatever the majority approves must be the end and the just." [15] Aristotle's account recorded precisely the fact that the ideal of equality was rapidly transformed in the *polis* into a crude, arithmetical tyranny of the majority.

Clearly, if we wish to avoid losing sight of equality in this labyrinth we must always be on the alert, with regard to both the theoretical ambiguity and the practical corruptibility of the concept. Equality, as I said at the beginning, has on its side the not inconsiderable advantage of seeming a clear and simple notion. But in the long run this advantage is not an advantage. It explains the success of equality, but also its brief span of life. The more equality seems easy, the more it turns out to be unattainable and self-destructive.

3. Democratic and Other Equalities

We must now cease to speak of equality in the singular and proceed to deal with equalities in the plural. Let me stress again, as I have done in connection with the case of liberty, that we are not concerned with discovering the nature of true equality, or equality in the absolute. Here again we do not have to deal with a speculative problem, but with the empirical problem of those particular equalities that men have sought to establish in the course of their history. Just as liberty actually comes down to the struggle to achieve particular liberties, so equality is defined, historically speaking, as the repudiation of certain differences instead of others. And the discourse on equality must bring us to reply to a precise question: what is the specific equality which has precedence in democracy?

The question is relevant because there is a tendency to think in too summary a fashion that equality and democracy coincide. This is true only in a very general sense, namely, in the sense that the egalitarian ideal can be raised to the status of the symbol par excellence of the democratic idea. Tocqueville made the point very forcibly. Nonetheless this identification simply means that the demand for equality attains its greatest force and expansion within a democratic system. It does not mean that there are no equalities outside democracy, or that all equalities are a democratic achievement.

In the first place it must be recalled that, during the twenty-five centuries that separate the first appearance of the Greek word *isótes* from the meaning of "equality" nowadays, there has been a long process of elaboration and refinement carried out by jurisprudence, by Christianity, by moral philosophy—in short, by the whole tradition of Western thought. Democratic theory, as such, has contributed very little to this development. In the second place, we must not lose sight of the fact that with the wane of the Greek *polis* the idea of equality has become detached from that of democracy, and that it has traveled through history for more than two thousand years independent of the fortunes of the sovereign people. And this very fact suffices to point out how hasty is the conclusion that the idea of equality *sic et simpliciter* parallels that of democracy. Actually, many equalities have by no means sprung from democratic experience, and therefore not all, but only some species of equality belong to the democratic family as its legitimate descendants.

Equality before the law, *isonomía,* understood as we now understand it, namely, as equal protection of the laws, was only a short-lived experiment in the Greek democracies. The principle that every man is equal to every other in his intrinsic dignity and worth, is a Christian and ethical concept which was affirmed only after the wane of the ancient republics. Likewise, when we declare that all men, as such, have equal and inalienable rights, we are affirming an important egalitarian principle, but it was from the notion of natural law as implemented in the seventeenth century that it acquired its force.[16] Also, when we speak of *isogoría,* of equal freedom of speech and assembly, we refer to a kind of equality more closely associated with liberal liberty and constitutional protection than with ancient democratic practices.

What then is the specifically democratic contribution to the notion of equality? When we come to speak again, in modern times, of democracy, we see that the demand for equality involves three specific points: (i) *equal universal suffrage,* that is, extension of the right to vote to everybody as a completion of their political freedom; (ii) *social equality,* understood as equality of status, and thus implying absence of class or social barriers and discriminations; and (iii) *equality of opportunity,* in various meanings which we will discuss. Although these equalities have been affirmed in the context of liberal democracy, I would say that they are characteristic more of the democratic than of the liberal climate of opinion. For the liberal viewpoint has absorbed them to a different extent, or with other motivations.

The principle of *political* equality, understood in the sense that every man counts for one vote, and that one man's vote is the equivalent of the next man's, has for example been entirely accepted, even though liberal thought appears somewhat disenchanted in its reason for adhering to this principle (as when it asserts that it is better to count heads than to break them). The principle of *social* equality, instead, remains a characteristically democratic preoccupation. Liberalism does not reject it out of hand, but is not very sensitive about this problem. Its concern is primarily focused on political

335

freedom, not on social equality. As for the principle of equal *opportunities,* liberal thought in the twentieth century adopts it as its own, but on two conditions: that it be understood as a development of individual liberty, and that it be realized by means that do not conflict with that end.[17] And I would say that this is today the point under discussion between liberals and democrats within the liberal democracies. The issue of equality of opportunity separates liberals and democrats not because they do not share the same ideal, but because they often disagree on how to achieve it.

Equality of opportunity is not, however, the last equality to retain on our agenda. Economic equality is another egalitarian claim of our time, to be ascribed, however, to the context of socialism—or at any rate to the brand of *démocratisme* which paved the way to socialism—rather than to democracy. This is not to say that liberal democracy cannot appropriate many of the demands connected with the vindication of economic equality. For the principle of equalization of opportunities can also be developed in the direction of canceling out the unequal points of departure which are due to over-great disparity of wealth. Nevertheless there is a precise limit which distinguishes the formula of democratic economic equality from the economic equality which refers us, by association of ideas, to socialism of the Marxist type.

The equalities of liberalism end, ideally speaking, where the aim of safeguarding and strengthening individual liberty ends. Therefore democracy takes up the task of denaturalizing the social order where liberty leaves off. We now know that liberty, per se, does not equalize opportunities: this is an abandoned illusion of liberalism. Thus modern democracy seeks precisely that part of justice that does not follow spontaneously in the wake of freedom. To the extent that freedom produces or tolerates unjust disparities, the democrat supports just equality even at the expense of freedom. However, not at too great an expense of freedom. Democratic thought tries to balance freedom with equality, not to give up the former in order to attain the latter. If we take this ulterior step, then we arrive at socialism. This is not to say that socialists—and particularly all socialists—are indifferent to liberty. But their attention is so exclusively focused on

336

the problem of material or economic equality, that they are impelled to propose solutions, the cost of which—even though they are often not aware of it—is the loss of political freedom, and with it of many other important freedoms, if not of all. Of course, the boundary separating democracy from socialism is not clear-cut, any more than the boundary separating democracy from liberalism. The very existence of democratic socialism goes to show this. However, between a social democracy like American democracy, and a socialist democracy, there is a significant difference which is to be found in the difference between the values of equality esteemed by the first and second respectively.

In the United States equality means above all, as Bryce remarked, "equality of estimation"—an equality which goes back to the conviction that men are equal in their "ultimate value," and which therefore resolves itself into the equal value "which men set upon one another, whatever be the elements that come into this value." [18] For this reason American democracy has been characterized as a social democracy, as a way of life basically expressed in a general levelling of status, in equal treatment and respect for the next man, whoever he may be. The value of equality here is above all *isotimía,* equal respect, and is lived as an inter-subjective relationship between persons who do not consider themselves to be located in any scale of rank or class which might justify unequal recognition. The flavor of this equality has been well caught by the expression "freedom of irreverence." [19]

In a socialist democracy the atmosphere is very different. Since in this case the problem is economic equality (from which, eventually, social equality will automatically follow), this equality is not felt to be, or practiced as, an *ethos.* The difference lies, then, not only in the dissimilar natures of the respective values of equality, but also in the fact that while social democracy is *in primis* a way of life, socialist democracy is above all a way of governing, which is tantamount to saying that it is more the enforcement of a policy than a spontaneous force in social life, more legislation than custom. And this becomes a far-reaching difference as soon as we pass from democratic socialism to the socialism *tout court* which still clings to Marx.

4. Equalization of Circumstances

To arrive at a summary classification of the tangle of equalities under discussion, it is the traditional practice to distinguish between juridico-political equality, social equality, and economic equality.[20] This threefold partition has, however, the defect of being obsolete, in the sense that it groups, under the title of economic equality, solutions that are now very different from one another. I will therefore replace this latter class with the heading *equalization of circumstances,* to be subdivided into three groups: equality of opportunity in a formal sense, equality of opportunity in a material sense, and economic sameness. The classification then becomes the following:

1. Juridico-political equality.
2. Social equality.
3. Equalization of circumstances, understood as:

(i) Equality of opportunity in the formal sense of "equal access" to opportunities, as in the career-open-to-talent formula.

(ii) Equality of opportunity in the material sense of equalizing the starting-points, that is, creating by means of a relatively equal distribution of wealth the material conditions for equal access to opportunities.

(iii) Economic sameness: State ownership of all wealth.

In accordance with the criteria of justice which inspire these equalities and with the powers which correspond to them, our table can be rewritten thus:

a) To everyone the same legal and political rights, that is, the power to resist political power.

b) To everyone the same social importance, that is, the power to resist social discrimination (of status, of class, or any other).

c) To everyone the same opportunities to rise, that is, the power to put one's own merits to account.

d) To everyone the same starting-point, that is, an adequate initial power (in the sense of material conditions) to acquire the same rank and ability as everyone else.

e) To no one any (economic) power: everyone at zero level.

This classification makes it clear, I believe, that to speak *sic et simpliciter* of economic equality has become very deceptive. Until not

long ago, to equate economic equality with the socialist conception
was a precise account of a confused situation. But today it is a confused description of a situation that no longer exists. It is true that
the problem of equality of circumstances was restated and carried to
the forefront in the nineteenth century by socialism, and above all by
Marxist socialism; but it is no longer true that this problem finds its
solution only in socialism. On the contrary, it is highly doubtful
whether the Marxist solution is a solution, since the evidence offered
by the communist systems has confirmed *ad abundantiam* that to make
everyone a have-not does not satisfy the purposes in the name of which
Marx called for the extermination of the haves. If this is true, it follows that the modern formula for economic equality is no longer the
socialist. A conclusion—if we concentrate and think about it—which is
obvious enough. For the therapy suggested by Marxist socialism is,
in substance, a resurrection of the oldest of egalitarian medicines, the
one advocated by Plato and already criticized by Aristotle. And
present-day experience has again shown that it remains, despite all
exterior modernizations, the crudest, most primitive way of seeking
the ideal of equalization of circumstances; too crude and too simplistic
to succeed.[21]

Be that as it may, what matters most is that the difference between the democratic and the Marxist way of striving for equalization of circumstances be clearly perceived. This goal can be sought
for the sake of mobility or for the sake of sameness, for the sake of
freedom or for the sake of levelling. In both cases the intervention
of political power is required, but this intervention can be employed
for entirely different purposes: either with a view to giving to everyone enough power to offer him equal opportunities to rise, or with a
view to taking away all power from everyone for the sake of equality
in itself. And there is an abyss between the approach of granting
equal rights, opportunities, and starting-points on the basis of the
presupposition that the beneficiaries neither are nor must become
equal, and the approach of imposing sameness as an apriori, definitive
solution to the problem of these rights and opportunities.

If, therefore, we wish to continue using the expression "economic
equality," sanctified as it is by tradition, we must always be specific,

distinguishing between economic equality of the democratic type, and economic equality of the Marxist-socialist type, i.e., between equal power to rise, and enforcement of levelling. And if, for the sake of simplicity, the solution of democratic socialism (of the English or Scandinavian type) is incorporated in the democratic solution, our table of equalities can be presented again, and finally, thus:

1) Legal and political equality.
2) Social equality.
3) Equality of opportunity.
4) Democratic economic equality: fairly equal distribution of wealth.
5) Marxist economic equality: State ownership of all wealth.

Having arranged the list of equalities, we are confronted by three questions. In the first place, how can the aforesaid equalities be coordinated and integrated? That is, are they cumulative, or are they alternative? This interrogation is intimately connected with a second problem, the problem of means, of *how*. And this latter problem cannot be dissociated from a third question, namely, What about liberty? For the characteristic common to all equalizations of circumstances is the demand that a legislative hand intervene to correct or to replace the automatisms of a free-market political system.

5. The Maximization of Equality

The equalities under discussion have been presented in an order of succession which can be considered as corresponding to an ascending order of maximization of equality. But it is important to see exactly in what sense this is so.

It is customary to say that while the first equalities are of the formal type, the latter are of the material type. This assessment is correct when it is correctly understood. This, however, is seldom the case. For the distinction between formal and material equalities is often turned into one between apparent and real equalities. And to understand the distinction between formal and non-formal in this manner is to confuse the technical meaning of the term form with its

340

common meaning, or rather with the common practice of speaking of "form" as mere appearance, illusion, sham—or the like—which is a crude *quid pro quo*.

In a first sense, we speak of "juridical form," meaning by this the very requisite of a legal order. For the form of law and the formal nature of law constitute (at least *de jure condito*) the characteristics by virtue of which a law is a law. There is also a second, basically ethical sense of the notion of "form." By this it is maintained that it is only if norms have a formal formulation, that the addressee of the commands expressed by these norms is treated as a free subject. It is for this reason that Kant formulated his categorical imperatives in such a way as to indicate what ought to be the form of any moral action, and not *what* we must do. In other words, Kant refused to indicate the specific content of moral prescriptions, lest moral experience become a practice of submission to external norms (a heteronomous ethic), and not a matter of liberty, that is, the acceptance of rules imposed on us by ourselves (an autonomous ethic).

Now, juridical and political equality, as well as equality of opportunity, are *formal* equalities in these technical meanings of the term. To call them formal is not to say that they leave us defenseless in the face of inequality of privilege, or that we are dealing with semblances of equality. "Formal" is the method, not the result. It is therefore totally beside the mark to speak in a derogatory sense of the formal conditions (including the juridical and political ones) which promote equal opportunities, to say that these equalities are fictitious, or at any rate scarcely important. How great is their importance is open to question; but it is out of the question that their importance in comparison to the material equalities cannot be discussed in these terms, that is, by equivocation as to the meaning of "form."

We may now pose again the query: why is it that equalities are usually arranged in an order which goes from juridico-political equality to the economic equalities? In my opinion there is little sense in attempting to justify this sequence by bringing in a scale of values and by seeking to demonstrate in absolute terms that the last are more praiseworthy than the first. The truth is much simpler. And it is this: the order of succession which is given to the series of equalities does not reflect an increasing amount of objective importance, but an increasing intensity of desire. It is not a matter of axiological succession, but of psychological succession—which, by the way, is saying a great deal. Man reaches out towards what he does not have, and is soon tired of what he already possesses. In this sense, then, the order of arrangement followed in enumerating the list of equalities indicates a historical trend. But it is for this, and not for other sophisticated reasons, that the maximization of equality tends today towards the goal of economic equalities. Tawney not only explained the sense of this development, but also perceived its limit, when he observed, "Though the ideal of an equal distribution of material wealth may continue to elude us, it is necessary, nevertheless, to make haste towards it, not because such wealth is the most important of man's treasures, but to prove that it is not." [22]

Granted that some kind of equalization of economic circumstances is felt to be *the* goal of our time, this does not settle the question. To obtain, it is not enough merely to want. And to obtain what we want, or better the greatest possible amount of what we want, it is necessary to set aside wishful thinking and to have recourse to thoughtful knowledge. Hence the question is: how are we to understand the expression "more equality"? Three different theses can be put forward: 1) that there is one essential *major Equality* that includes all the others; 2) that greater equality is achieved by *adding* all the single or partial equalities together; 3) that increasing equality is attained by a better *balancing* of inequalities.

The first thesis has the greatest appeal, but is mistaken as well as destructive. Equality in the singular, and written with a capital letter, is only a deontological symbol, exactly like Liberty or Justice. It warms people's hearts, but provides no tangible benefits. To infer from it that there is a larger equality that includes all the small equalities is to invent another voracious Leviathan, a mythical "total Equality" that will swallow up the specific, concrete equalities. An essential, synthetic Equality does not exist. Actually, in the protecting shadow of this presumed all-embracing Equality we are just smuggling in a specific equality, the one which we cherish the most. But when a particular kind of equality—such as the Marxist economic equality—is passed off as the solution to the over-all problem of

Equality, we can be sure that this alleged final Equality will re-open the way to all the inequalities that it claims to have surpassed.[23]

The second thesis grants that there is no such thing as one essential Equality, and therefore holds that equality grows by addition. The thesis is that maximization of equality is achieved by adding together, one after another, all the separate kinds of equality. This approach is, to some extent, correct. Yet we must be very careful, because in historical arithmetic many additions have turned out to be subtractions. Although some qualities are cumulative, not all are. We must therefore proceed step by step, always calculating, before we make the next move, whether, by any chance, at the very moment at which we add a new equality to our column, we will not lose the previous one— and the one that upholds it.

To say the least, this warning is usually not taken seriously enough. On most occasions the problem is disposed of merely by saying: Given the fact that the formal equality of rights has been acquired, let us give it no more thought and proceed toward the further question of equality of wealth. Now, we cannot proceed so swiftly. We must proceed bearing in mind that the maximization of one variety implies, or at any rate can imply, the minimization of the others, and that in some cases two equalities may be mutually exclusive. The problem of equality, like that of political liberty, is a problem to be examined in terms of applicability. It is not enough to say: I prefer this equality to that. The point is to ascertain the order and the extent to which they are complementary and mutually compatible. To be sure, preferences can hardly be modified; but they can be kept under control by awareness of consequences, that is, by asking ourselves: what price are we disposed to pay to obtain the equalities which we desire, at the expense of those which we already enjoy? Equality of rights certainly does not bring, in itself, equality of possessions; but a drastic equalization of wealth apparently demands disparity of formal treatment. If equal rights do not imply equal power, on the other hand to give the State the power to equalize all power may well result not in increasing but in annihilating our powers of liberty.

Therefore the thesis that equality grows by addition does not provide an adequate model for the purpose of looking clearly into

343

the problem of maximizing equality. Since only some equalities sustain and integrate each other, this approach has a limited validity, while, on the other hand, it distracts our attention from what is really at stake. For we have reached a point at which it is no longer a question of making additions, but above all of making a choice about what position we wish to stand by, and of making this choice with our eyes open, being aware of what it implies. As our dissection of the generic formula "economic equality" shows, we are faced with a basic alternative: whether we wish to pursue economic equality of the democratic, or of the Marxist type. The addition model, so to speak, refers to a hypothesis as naïve as it is inexact, namely, that all inequalities can be progressively reduced, and little by little eliminated. But what is really meant by the phrase "maximization of equality" is something different.

In history, greater equality is never equality *in toto,* equality in every respect. What every age regards as progress towards greater equality reflects either an increased enactment of the same principle of justice, or an option for a different criterion of justice. In the first case, a society stands by the value of equality in which it believes, and therefore seeks maximization of it in terms of intensity. In the second, a society turns towards a different value of equality, and therefore what it considers a maximization actually is a change. In this hypothesis we do not have a greater equality which includes the types existing previously, but simply a new equality, which is preferred to the types that preceded it. In every case, we always eliminate *some* inequalities, not all. For in every society there are certain disparities that are resented, while other differences pass unnoticed and are accepted as a matter of course.

My own thesis is, therefore, the third thesis, namely that the proper focus is that of understanding equality as a problem of equilibrium. It is not a problem to be solved *pars pro toto* by pursuing a partial equality under the name of total Equality. It is not even a matter of adding together as many equalities as can make everybody equal in everything. The equality of which we are speaking has, as its raw material, man. This means that equality among men refers to the differences between men. Therefore equality cannot be other than a system of *reciprocal compensation* among inequalities. In other words, equality results from the interplay of a system of liberty-equalities that is so designed as to effectively balance one disparity with another.

It should be pointed out that while the addition model shows a final incompatibility between equality of the formal type and equality in the material sense, in a well-designed "system of counterbalances" contradictory equalitarian cross-pressures can well coexist; for in this configuration one form of equality is called upon to counterbalance another, and a situation of relative equality is produced by the reciprocal neutralization of single inequalities. Nor should it be thought that the formula "counterbalancing of inequalities" in some way precludes innovation. For a system of reciprocal compensation can be organized to act in relation to very different centers of gravity. The only condition is that any of these systems of equality be constructed according to a dynamic countervailing scheme.

6. Equality and Liberty

The difficulty with the problem of equality, as we have seen all along, lies in the complexity of its relationship to the problem of liberty. Equality is supposed to implement freedom, but it may destroy freedom: it presupposes it, but it can well overcome it.

In procedural terms it seems obvious enough that the demand for liberty comes first, since equality without freedom can hardly be asked for and may hardly seem worth having. An equality that preceded freedom would be only equality among slaves, who are, in fact, as equal as can be, but equal in having nothing and in counting for nothing, equal in being equally subjected. Therefore, just as political freedom, freedom *from,* is the preliminary condition for all the powers of liberty, of all the freedoms *to*—for the same reasons it is also the preliminary condition for all the powers of equality.

Yet, no sooner does a situation of liberty open the way to the appetite for equality than the ideal of liberty finds itself at a disadvantage and the appeal of equality proves stronger. This, we have seen, occurs for three reasons: first, because the idea of equality is more accessible, since equality can be given a tangible descriptive meaning (although a misleading one), whereas liberty cannot; second, because the ideal of equality is at an advantage on the psychological plane, in accordance with the rule that we want most what we have least; third, because the *Gestalt* of equality is somehow congenial to the scientific and rational mind (although in the ill-suited meaning of uniformity).

As little can be done to restore the balance in relation to the simplistic or psychological appeal of equality, it is all the more important to make clear that equality combines with freedom only when it is not understood as uniformity. For if we seek sameness we must dislike diversity, and if we dislike diversity we cannot praise freedom, except by being flagrantly inconsistent. This is tantamount to saying that equality combines with liberty only if it is understood as free and open circulation, as unchecked mobility. The liberal-democratic formula is not "unequal opportunities to become equal," but rather, "equal opportunities to become unequal." For we think that there is just as much injustice in enforcing arbitrary sameness on what is different, as there is in the acceptance of undeserved, established inequalities. In other words, to equalize artificially is to create a situation just as privileged as that of accepting artificial inequalities. The liberal-democratic criterion is that fictitious equalities must be opposed just as much, and for exactly the same reason, that unjustified inequalities must be fought.

Once it has been firmly established that equality, in history, has nothing to do with sameness, we still cannot relax. For it is by no means certain, even in this hypothesis, that equality and liberty are basically able to proceed together all the way. Once we enter upon the path of equalization of circumstances—even if it is with the purpose of creating equal opportunities for becoming unequal—it is by no means easy to stop at the right moment.

In the first place there is always the danger that in order to create the conditions for a satisfying material equality we may grow impatient with the fiscal or similar instruments, and therefore end up by having recourse to disparity of formal (i.e., juridical) treatment, thereby subjecting equality before the law and the principle of equal rights to a dangerous strain. F. A. Hayek maintains in this connection that even equalization of opportunities must necessarily be paid for, in the long run, by the loss of a juridical order based on general rules, since it implies "a return to the rule of status, a reversal of the 'movement of progressive societies,' which in the famous phrase of Sir Henry Maine 'has hitherto been a movement from status to contact.' " [24] That is, in short, a return to a sectional, discriminating legislation. Hayek's contention can be challenged, e.g., on the grounds that equality can be enforced by a law which says "no one is allowed any private property"—which is still a general law. Nevertheless, I feel that the danger pointed out by Hayek must not be underestimated. For a large part of today's legislation intended to create equalization of circumstances is in effect discriminatory legislation, and this trend, in the long run, may well lead us back towards the medieval conception of law. On the other hand, if a radical equalization brought about in one blow by means of general norms is a conceivable hypothesis, it is nonetheless true that with the passage of time the only way of preventing the re-creation of inequalities is continuous piecemeal intervention of the *gerechte Staat* (the just State) in the form of unequal laws.

There is, then, the solution that is attractive to socialists, even of the democratic type: resolving the problem of economic equality once and for all by means of public or State property. But as the State becomes progressively the major employer and the major controller of the means of production, premises are created for a truly formidable inequality of power. Be property private or public, it remains true in every case that "power over a man's subsistence is power over his will." [25] Today it is the State that keeps an eye on private property-owners; but tomorrow who will keep an eye on the property-owning State? Its employees? As Leon Trotsky forcibly put it in *The Revolution Betrayed,* in a communist State economy the only alternative for dissenters is death by starvation: for "he who does not obey does not eat." Even assuming a less drastic case, the fact is that when those who wield power possess everything and the power addressees nothing, the citizens are deprived of the very possibility of resisting the State's will on the grounds that they lack the economic self-sufficiency to do so. To say the least, in these conditions it is very doubtful whether the "controllers-being-controlled" circle can continue to work.

As anyone can see, questions arise which need very careful handling. If the State becomes all-powerful and gets out of control, it is by no means certain that it will be a benevolent State; on the contrary, it is highly probable that it will not. Equalities of the economic type are due to deliberate intervention from above, since it is agreed they are not attainable by means of the automatisms of freedom. But if we lose our freedom, the chances are that we also lose those equalities.

Clearly, then, the balance between liberty and equality is ever precarious. On this account, it is necessary to make an accurate distinction between the two problems, the problem of liberty and the problem of equality. The trend of our time, instead, is to intermingle them. Take, for instance, the much repeated sentence, "Equality is a form of freedom." Or take, still worse, the theses that equality is a "larger freedom," and a "higher freedom," if not resolutely the "real freedom." These slogans are, to say the least, largely misleading, for they confuse two issues which have to be dealt with separately.

To begin with, equality is a form of freedom only in the sense that it is a "condition to freedom." And to say that one thing is a condition of another is not to say that they are the same thing. Thus it can be maintained that an illiterate is probably in no condition to act like a free man, but it cannot be inferred from this that once he has learned to read and write he has become free. It depends. Similarly, granted that equality is a condition of freedom, it does not follow from this that by having been made equal we become *ipso facto* and for this very reason free. It depends: and above all it depends on what type of master has seen to making us equal. Let us note, also, that if equality is a condition of freedom, the opposite is even more true: namely, freedom is a condition of equality. Now, a Marxist would resist violently—and with reason—the argument of someone who wished to demonstrate that by reason of the fact that we are free we are also equal. But, then, by what logic does the Marxist pass on to maintain that if we are equal we are *ipso facto* free? It is wise, therefore, for us to stress that freedom is one thing and equality another, in order that we may avoid offering pretexts for the bad use of reason. Equality can be spoken of as a form of freedom only so long as it is clearly borne in mind that if our legs support our body (and are thereby a condition for our being able to walk) this does not mean in the least that our body amounts to a pair of legs.

If equality is only a condition of freedom, this is all the more reason for its not being a "larger" freedom, or even a "higher" freedom. These expressions have a psychological justification but no logical worth. As for the thesis that equality, and in particular economic equality, is "real" freedom, or even *the* real freedom, it is more than anything else a terminological trap intended to exploit the emotional appeal of the term freedom. And it should also be dismissed on the grounds that it encourages the belief in miracles, i.e., the belief that there exists a single simple solution for problems that have to be solved, patiently and laboriously, one by one.

This is not to deny that freedom and economic conditions are related. Actually the thesis that makes real freedom equivalent to economic equality is based on a premise which is sensible enough: namely, the problem of freedom begins at breakfast. I can well understand that someone suffering from hunger may call bread "liberty." However, this can only be an effective way—in the first instance—of asking for bread. And I say "in the first instance" because in illiberal systems the problem is not solved by giving more bread, but rather by taking away the right to ask for it. Granted that the problem of freedom begins with food, it does not end with food. It is not that we are free because we have full bellies. If it is true that political freedom does not solve the problem of bread, it is equally true that bread does not solve the problem of political freedom. At the beginning of the French Revolution Marat wrote to Desmoulins: "What good is political freedom for those who have no bread? It counts only for theorists and ambitious politicians." [26] The query was not unjustified, but the course of the Revolution would have shown that the reply was wholly inadequate. And one cannot help wondering whether Desmoulins himself, as he set out for the guillotine, did not see his way to discovering that political freedom has its uses, and that a very "unreal" freedom follows for those who call for equality confusing it with freedom, or who dismiss liberty as something less important than equality.[27]

NOTES

† *Contrat social*, II, 11.

1. See however the excellent symposium *Aspects of Human Equality*, eds. Bryson, Faust, Finkelstein, and MacIver (New York, 1956).

2. Plato, *Statesman*, 294 (trans. Jowett).

3. R. H. Tawney, *Equality*, 1st 1931 ed., Chap. I. The sentence has been modified in the 4th ed. (London, 1952). Cf. p. 47.

4. "Ostensive definition may be defined as 'any process by which a person is taught to understand a word otherwise than by the use of other words.' " Bertrand Russell, *Human Knowledge* (New York, 1948), p. 63. Cf. also R. Robinson, *Definition*, pp. 117-126.

5. *The Collected Works of A. Lincoln* (New Brunswick, 1953), Vol. II, pp. 406-407. For a historical survey and an analysis of Lincoln's position, cf., e.g., H. A. Myers, *Are Men Equal?*, Chap. IV, esp. pp. 89-94.

6. The objection to the ideal of equality founded on the argument that "men are, in fact, not equal" has been examined in Chap. IV, 1, above.

7. *Tesoro*, VI, 26.

8. Among the notable studies on the concept of justice, cf.: G. Del Vecchio, *La giustizia* (Roma, 3rd ed. 1946) with a very large bibliography and extensive quotations; Ch. Perelman, *De la justice* (Bruxelles, 1945); Hans Kelsen, *Was ist Gerechtigkeit?* (Wien, 1953); Norberto Bobbio, "La nozione della giustizia" in *Archivio giuridico*, fasc. 1-2 (1952), and "Giustizia" in *Dizionario di filosofia* (Milano, 1957); the issue on "La Justice" of the *Revue Internationale de Philosophie*, III (1957) (with contributions by R. McKeon, E. Garin, Ch. Perelman, *et al.*).

9. *Philosophie des Rechts*, par. 49.

10. *Observations on the Feeling of the Beautiful and Sublime*, cit. in Victor Delbos, *La Philosophie pratique de Kant* (Paris, 1905), p. 117.

11. Cf. Ernst Cassirer, *The Philosophy of the Enlightenment* (Princeton, 1951), Chaps. II and VI.

12. "Über und Unterordnung," trans. Kurt H. Wolff in his ed. of *The Sociology of Georg Simmel* (Glencoe, 1950), p. 275.

13. *Gorgias*, 483 (trans. Jowett).

14. Thucydides, *The History of the Peloponnesian War*, Bk. 11, par. 37.

15. *Politics*, 1317b.

16. The Stoics theorized a natural law, but not the "natural rights" which Grotius derived *ex principiis hominis internis* and are at the basis of the

modern idea of legality. Cf. A. Passerin d' Entrèves (*Natural Law*, pp. 59-61): "The *ius naturale* of the modern [seventeenth-eighteenth century] political philosopher is no longer the *lex naturalis* of the medieval moralist nor the *ius naturale* of the Roman lawyer." Cf. also E. Cassirer, *The Philosophy of the Enlightenment*, Chap. VI; and the still fundamental work of O. von Gierke, *J. Althusius und die Entwicklung der naturrechtlichen Staatstheorien* (trans., *The Development of Political Theory*, New York, 1939). Cf. above Chap. XII, note 26 and Chap. XIII, note 63.

17. This position has been stated very well by John Plamenatz, "Equality of Opportunity," in *Aspects of Human Equality*, p. 84: "The equality that matters in this world is equality of freedom, all other kinds of worldly equality being important only as means to it. There is equality of opportunity wherever any man has roughly as good a chance as any other of leading the kind of life he wants to lead." Cf. also *ibid.*, p. 94: "Our equality is rooted in freedom and is not to be understood apart from it. It is not equality of status but equality of opportunity, and the opportunity is to 'be oneself.' "

18. Cf. *The American Commonwealth* (New York, 1959), Vol. II, p. 514 f.

19. Naturally this does not mean that the United States has no social stratification and that status is not sought. Of course not. Yet even today a person coming to the United States from the Old World acquires the feeling of a previously unknown *isotimía*. Therefore the term "class" (even in the expression "open class system") as it is used by Americans is usually misunderstood by Europeans. For a development of these points see G. Sartori, "La democrazia americana di ieri e di oggi," in *Il pensiero americano contemporaneo*, pp. 308-310, 347-348. For a general survey and bibliography, cf. Milton M. Gordon, *Social Class in American Society* (Durham, 1958).

20. Bryce, along with many other authors, does not take up the merit of this last type of equality, remarking that since democracy "is merely a form of government, not a consideration of the purposes to which government may be turned [it] has nothing to do with Economic Equality. . . . Political Equality can exist either along with or apart from Equality in property." (*Modern Democracies*, I, p. 67). I agree on distinguishing between democracy in the political sense and in the social and economic sense, and in particular on the importance of the distinction between the "form" of a State and the "content" of its policy. Nevertheless how can one assert that political equality can coexist with economic equality without ascertaining that such is the case? Curiously enough, those who are concerned with material equality tend to solve—or rather not to solve—the political question in the very same way, applying to the political relevance of the proposed economic equalization the formula which Bryce had used for the opposite purpose: this controversy does not concern us.

21. This point can be made very simply by observing that Marx still argued the problem in terms of the (old) "substantive" notion of power, and that the "relational" nature of power has entirely escaped his attention.

22. *Equality* (New York, 1931), p. 48. This sentence no longer appears—significantly enough—in the 1952 ed.

23. To be sure, an all-inclusive equality may be conceived of as an open-ended formula, which is a different matter. For instance, Albert Hofstadter says that "equality of opportunity, in the broad sense of the career open to personality, is . . . the inclusive goal within which the partial goals of the special equalities have their significance" (*Aspects of Human Equality*, p. 137). Yet in practical terms I do not trust this approach, because a synthetic goal always tends to depreciate its components, no matter how much we take care to warn that they are essential.

24. Cf. F. A. Hayek, *The Road to Serfdom* (Chicago, 1944), p. 27, and Chap. VI, *passim*.

25. *The Federalist*, No. 79 (Hamilton).

26. Letter of June 24, 1790.

27. The subject will be referred to again in Chap. XV, 6, below.

Chapter XV

Liberalism and Democracy

"It is very easy to reject liberalism if it is identified with a theory or practice of freedom understood as power of the bourgeoisie, but it is much more difficult to reject it when it is considered as the theory and practice of limiting the State's power . . . for freedom as power to do something interests those fortunate enough to possess it, while freedom as non-restraint interests all men."

—Norberto Bobbio†

1. Overlaps

Liberalism and democracy, together with socialism and communism, are the labels which sum up the basic terms of the political contest of the nineteenth and twentieth centuries. Of these four labels only "communism" is clear, at any rate from 1918 onwards.[1] Nevertheless the break between socialists and communists has helped to make the term "socialism" less ambiguous, although socialism may lead two lives, since the differences between the Marxist and the Labor or Social-Democratic expressions of socialism are indeed considerable. Yet, by making some distinctions, we can make the meaning of socialism clear enough. The opposite has happened, instead, to the labels "liberalism" and "democracy." In the second half of the nineteenth century the liberal and the democratic ideal blended with each other, and in their blending became confused. The happy historical conjuncture which bound them together erased their respec-

353

tive boundaries and has therefore brought about varying attributions, depending on whether a writer is more concerned with keeping democracy in the orbit of liberalism, or with tracing the passing of liberalism into democracy. Many, beginning with Tocqueville, have made evident how extraneous freedom is to the internal logic of the idea of democracy;[2] but it would not be difficult to draw up a long list of authors who rank freedom as the first principle of democracy. Kelsen, among these, firmly asserts: "It is the value of freedom and not of equality that determines in the first place the idea of democracy." As for equality, its office is really modest: "Certainly," Kelsen grants, "the idea of equality also has its part, although . . . in an entirely negative, formal, and secondary sense. . . ."[3] At first glance it might appear that Tocqueville and Kelsen disagree profoundly. On the contrary they are, as a closer look reveals, of the same mind.

The misunderstandings spring from the fact that we say democracy sometimes to indicate "liberal democracy," and sometimes to indicate only "democracy." In the first case we are giving to democracy all the attributes of liberalism,[4] and the democratic ideal is therefore presented as an ideal of freedom; whereas in the second case liberalism and democracy are again separated, and consequently the democratic ideal goes back to being equality. It is not that one thesis is true and the other false, but rather that they light up two facets of the problem: maintaining that freedom is the requisite constituent element of liberal democracry—and at the same time remembering that it is by no means the requisite constituent element of democracy per se. When the western polity is made to revolve around the ideal of freedom, the thesis is to anchor democracy to liberalism. When on the other hand it is made to revolve around the ideal of equality, the hypothesis is that democracy may depart from liberalism.

If we can speak of a liberal democracy but also—at least hypothetically—of a non-liberal democracy, the implication is that to understand what democracy we want we must first establish what liberalism is. But there's the rub. In spite of the fact that the word liberalism is much used, when we come to examine how it is understood, we meet with the most extravagant interpretations. Very little agreement seems to exist about the basic meaning of liberalism; less,

I would say, than about any other label, even less than about democracy.

An initial complication is that, in becoming confused with the idea of democracy, the concept of liberalism is also promiscuously used in two senses: to indicate (i) only liberalism, or to indicate (ii) democratic liberalism. Thus we hear talk of "social liberalism," of "*étatiste* liberalism" (as Cranston calls it), of "welfare liberalism," and so forth. But clearly, when we speak of liberalism in these contexts we are considering the descent of liberalism, that is to say, a liberalism already combined with democracy—and these liberalisms of mixed parentage are of no use to us. I mean that if the concept of liberalism is to explain the concept of liberal-democracy, we must start with the *quid sui* of liberalism, with liberalism in its pure form. To examine a composite reality it is necessary to break it down into its single component elements. The first point to be made, then, is that we must concentrate on pure and simple liberalism.

A second complication is to be ascribed to the fact that "liberalism" can also be used (i) to designate a party (or a political program and movement), or (ii) in the historical meaning of the term. It may seem superfluous to call attention to this distinction, but in the case of liberalism it is not. For while a fairly definite connection can be traced between communism and a Communist (I give a capital letter to the party name or membership) and between socialism and a Socialist, in most cases there is only a very uncertain link, if any, between liberalism and a present-day Liberal.[5] For instance, an American Liberal would not be called a Liberal in any European country: we would call him a left-wing radical. Vice versa, an Italian Liberal in the United States would be labeled a Conservative. Thus an American Liberal is to an Italian Liberal as a left-wing progressive is to a right-wing conservative: the one is the opposite of the other. As for the English Liberal, he would stand halfway between his Italian and American homonyms without resembling either of them.

Now, it is no mere coincidence if in most cases there is no reliable connection between liberalism in the historical sense, and the party meaning of Liberalism. One of the reasons for this is that it is not easy to identify and isolate the historical features of liberalism.

355

And this starts a vicious circle: the uncertainty about "liberalism" results in "Liberalism" being used, in party parlance, in an entirely random and arbitrary fashion. On the other hand, if we do not know what the historical meaning of the term is, it is natural to take our bearings (as is done with Socialism and Communism) with reference to the party meaning. As a consequence, and in spite of all warnings, even authoritative writers come to overlap the two meanings, and thus to put forward, as liberalism, something that is not.

If party Liberalism, or rather Liberalisms, give us no clue to understanding liberalism, it is not much better to rely on the meaning of liberalism that T. P. Neill calls "ecumenical." For in this all-embracing meaning, which would include, according to Neill, "at least half of the human race," liberalism is simply the inborn attitude of a normal civilized Westerner towards life.[6] And Neill's generous estimate shows in itself that this cosmic meaning is much too vague to lead us anywhere. His approach is nonetheless interesting from another point of view, that is, for the distinction with respect to which he poses the problem. Neill writes: "It . . . seems proper and useful to distinguish between ecumenical liberalism and sectarian. The former refers to that liberalism which is identified with generosity of spirit or liberality of mind, the latter to a precisely defined and rigidly held body of doctrine. . . ."[7] Now, what strikes me about this distinction is that it eliminates liberalism. I mean that liberalism as the historical component of modern democracy is neither of the two. Neill offers us the alternative of flying in an ecumenical stratosphere, or of precipitating to the level of grass-roots politics. To follow either alternative is to lose sight of what liberalism is, and has been, as a historical accomplishment and body of doctrine.

Liberalism is certainly more definite and corporeal than a mere ecumenical feeling, and at the same time much less contingent and variable than the sectarian Liberalisms. It is true that liberalism is also an attitude, a mental pattern; however, unless we start from a definite historical significance of the concept, it is difficult to understand how we can speak with any propriety of a "liberal mind." The third point that I must make is, therefore, that only on condition that we have first established what liberalism has been in history, can we single out the liberal *forma mentis*.

I have pointed out that sometimes we use democracy as a short-hand term for "liberal democracy," while in other cases we mean only "democracy," and that, consequently, we should always make clear which path we are following. Let it be clearly understood, then, that in this chapter, as in other parts of the book, I take the latter approach. Why? To be sure, if the fusion of liberalism and democracy could be considered final, there would be no need to divide what is united. But the future seems to indicate that this union is ever more problematical. After their happy convergence in the last century, liberalism and democracy are coming again to diverge. And in this event it becomes essential to go back to distinguishing their respective functions and jurisdictions, in order to avoid working inadvertently for an illiberal democracy or losing democracy out of hatred for liberalism. Many people, and I dare say most people, would like liberty plus equality, or equality and also liberty. If we happen to lose both, it is no wild guess that this very often comes about by mistake, because we end by promoting something very different from what we expected.

2. An Unfortunate Word

While the *thing* liberalism has been—according to Harold Laski, an unimpeachable witness—the outstanding doctrine of the West for four centuries,[8] the *word* is much more recent. As a name, "liberalism" was first coined in Spain in 1810-11, more than two centuries later than the thing. This was unfortunate. Being born too late, the name has not had the time to take root. Moreover, for a number of other reasons it was born at the wrong moment, indeed at the worst possible moment. The history of the word is thus an interesting side of the story, and is worth telling. For, truly, few labels can compete with "liberalism" for having been born under an unlucky star.

The first misfortune was, as I said, being born too late. Too late not only because the term "liberalism" was coined after liberalism, as yet unnamed, had already produced its results if not the essential part of itself, but above all because at that moment history had begun to move fast, so fast that the liberals did not succeed in making up for the great amount of time that had ben lost between the clandestine birth and the official baptism. Now, that it was precisely at the moment when the name needed time to take hold and to establish its status that the rhythm of historical evolution became hectic—this was, it will be agreed, a rather unfortunate coincidence.

Thus, paradoxically, in some countries people began to speak of "liberalism" when they had ceased, or were ceasing, to be liberal—and this was notably the case with German liberalism. Elsewhere, especially in the United States, "liberal" never really arrived as a term loaded with historical substance, and—despite Vernon Parrington's history of the *Main Currents in American Thought*—it has not even managed to acquire a linguistic status. Liberalism in the European sense of the term has been, and still is, deeply rooted in American practice. Furthermore, the American Constitution—according to European standards—is the prototype of liberal constitutions in the precise sense of the word: that is, in its difference from constitutions of the democratic type. Yet no American would think of it as *the* typical "liberal" constitution. And this is because Liberal and Liberalism are used in the United States only in the sectarian sense. Inasmuch as the American tradition takes over and carries on the British tradition, Americans *are* liberals, but they do not *call* their behavior liberalism. The theory of their liberal practice is simply incorporated, *in toto,* in their theory of democracy.

In the summing up, while a nameless liberalism has constituted between the sixteenth and the twentieth centuries the most fundamental experience of European man, "liberalism" as a denomination *pleno iure* intended to epitomize that experience, has been successful (with the notable exception of English liberalism) only for a few decades. The case of France, in this connection, is indeed symptomatic. Here with Benjamin Constant and Tocqueville, liberalism had given birth to the highest and most refined intellectual evidence of itself; and yet, in France, the liberalism of Constant and his school had already been overthrown by the Revolution of 1848!

Why this premature decline, as a result of which liberals today exist *de facto* but hardly *de iure?* I mentioned that the second misfortune was that in the nineteenth century history began to move fast. It began to move so quickly that in the course of a few decades "liberalism" encountered two formidable competitors: the names "democracy" and "socialism." Now, political history hinges on elementary polarizations. Up to the fall of the Ancien Régime, that is, as long as the age of absolute monarchies lasted, the polarization was between monarchy and republic. Afterwards, once the republics had been achieved, or at any rate once the monarchy had been made harmless, the new ideal polarization, especially in the authors who had their mind on the experience of the French Revolution, was between liberalism and democracy. But soon enough the appearance of a third protagonist demanded a new alignment of the opposing fronts. This new protagonist was, in Europe, socialism.[9] And to the extent that socialism conveyed the workers' demands, the liberals and democrats were, and still are, reduced to working on the same electoral ground, and therefore, to converging.

Perhaps Tocqueville better than anyone else allows us to follow this development. In the first volume of *Democracy in America* published in 1835, democracy and liberalism appeared to him to be antithetical. One reason for this is that he was examining the United States while using, implicitly, a French frame of reference. And it must be remembered that in France (and, for that matter, in all of Europe) democracy was still an intellectual hypothesis built up on library reminiscences. Such was the democracy of Rousseau, and such it remained for those who drew their inspiration from it. Consequently, Tocqueville closely identified democracy with equality, and was led to stress the illiberal implications of democracy. In the second volume, which came out five years later, Tocqueville sounded the alarm even more, one of the reasons for this being that the English-inspired democracy which he had seen in America and which was more directly reflected in the first volume was one thing, and the democracy which he returned to see in France and which was more directly introduced into the compiling of the volume of 1840 was quite another. For the "democratic despotism" that Tocqueville had seen foreshadowed in the American scene was a much more threatening prospect in the light of the gospel of Saint-Simon's followers, or of the phalansteries of Fourier—that is, when reformulated by a rationalistic and simplistic radicalism.

But, suddenly, in 1848, democracy and liberalism are enemies no more: they join forces. His antithesis is no longer between liberalism and democracy, but between democracy and socialism. Attending the

Constituent Assembly (during the debate on the right to work), Tocqueville said: "Democracy and socialism are linked only by a word, equality; but the difference must be noted: democracy wants equality in freedom, and socialism wants equality in poverty and slavery." [10] Perhaps Tocqueville had changed his mind? Not at all. What happened was that at this point he abandoned the classical or pre-liberal meaning of the term democracy, and gave it the new, the modern meaning: his democracy was now liberal democracy. It was not his thought that changed—rather, it was the situation.

The Revolution of 1848 had clearly shown the strength of the new protagonist called "socialism." [11] And under the onslaught of those dramatic days, the alignment of political forces was quickly modified. Tocqueville, who in his visit to the United States had seen, after all, a truly liberal democracy, immediately sensed the meaning of the re-examination of conscience brought about by the 1848 events. Therefore, he divided his former concept of democracy into two parts. To socialism he attributed the illiberal part of democracy, democratic despotism;[12] whereas he associated its non-despotic part with liberalism. Liberty and equality were still contrasted to each other, but under new labels: the equality which is inimical to freedom was to be found in socialism, whereas the equality which is in harmony with freedom was to be found in anti-socialist democracy, in the democracy which accepts liberalism.

It must not be thought that these were mere verbal adjustments. Tocqueville, ever prophetic, made allowance in advance for what was to happen in the second half of the century. It is not that democracy drawn from memory was replaced in a flash, in 1848, by the liberal democracy which was the daughter of reality (and was already well under way beyond the Atlantic). What Tocqueville put on record was the birth of this alliance. It was only later, and gradually, that people became aware that what was being born from the seed of liberalism was a democracy quite different from that monolithic city whose fascination had been felt by European readers of Rousseau. The convergence betwen liberalism and democracy was undoubtedly a happy one, and on the whole the operation was successful. But it had to be paid for, and it is only today that we can judge how great was the price.

360

In substance it is liberalism which has prevailed, in the sense that liberalism has absorbed democracy far more than democracy has annexed liberalism. For democrats (with the exception of the radical, revolutionary wing which merges with socialism) have accepted the principle that freedom is the end and democracy the means. But judging from appearances it is democracy which has come out with flying colors. No sooner did the liberals find themselves a name than they had to change it. Partly because the label democracy had a freshness that the other lacked; partly because, semantically speaking, "democracy" is more tangible and palatable than "liberalism" (which has no appreciable descriptive meaning); and partly to avoid emphasizing cleavage, it was the liberals who ended by giving up their own identity and presenting themselves as democrats. Prima facie it was a modest concession to political convenience; but one destined to have, in the long run, far-reaching consequences. For what is not named, what remains unnamed, is no longer remembered. And thus the notion of liberalism today is associated in most people's minds with a typically nineteenth-century specimen, with something belonging to the past.

Naturally, the name liberalism has not taken second place only for the above reasons. There is, as I mentioned, still a third misfortune to add to the list. In those years the first industrial revolution, with all its strains, miseries, and cruelties, was taking place. And the industrial revolution was accomplished in the name of economic freedom. Today we know that industrialization—no matter under what banner it is brought about—exacts a heavy toll, and that in any case it is paid for by reducing consumption and exploiting the industrial proletariat. If ever socialist historiography exhausts the argument about the evils of capitalism in the nineteenth century, it will have to discover that the situation in the factories (and, for that matter, outside the factories too) has been no less inhuman in the twentieth century in the so-called socialist countries. Rather the opposite. Nevertheless, industrial progress in the West has come about under the auspices of free competition, of laissez faire, and of the gospel of the Manchester school.

Misfortune has thus brought it about that the name should be coined at a time when the novelty was not political "liberalism" but

361

economic "liberism." [13] As a consequence the label has come to have more an economic than a political association: liberalism was called "bourgeois" and "capitalist," and its prophets were thought to be Adam Smith, Ricardo, and Cobden. The association has remained so firm that even today many writers (especially those writing in English) still speak of classical liberalism as a laissez-faire liberalism—which is to say that they are still confusing liberalism with economic "liberism."

Now let me stress that this is very unfair to liberalism. Locke, Blackstone, Montesquieu, Constant—to mention a few of the real founding fathers of classical liberalism—were not the theorists of a laissez-faire economy. To them liberalism meant the rule of law and the constitutional State, and liberty was political freedom, not the economic principle of free trade or the law of survival of the fittest. And one might hazard the guess that if the term liberalism had been invented not in 1810-11, but a hundred years earlier or a hundred years later, this overlap would not have occurred. Had it not been for an unfortunate coincidence, it is likely that instead of using "liberalism" promiscuously to refer as much to the ideas of Montesquieu and Constant as to those of Adam Smith and Ricardo (how absurd, when we think of it!), we would be using two different names, devised to put the problem of political freedom in one context, and that of economic freedom in another.

This is still not the end of the story. The Spanish *liberales,* when they invented the name, had England in mind. But unfortunately in those years English philosophy had declined, with Bentham and James Mill, to a level of narrow utilitarianism and rather naïve hedonism. It is true that not James Mill but his son John Stuart Mill was the most typical representative of English liberalism in the nineteenth century. Yet John Stuart Mill always felt the influence of his father's ideas, and his intellectual stature was, on the whole, disproportionate to the role that he ended by assuming in the history of liberalism (which would have profited in a very different way by the translation into English of, for example, Constant). [14] This is shown by the fact that Mill's doctrine did not seem adequate even to his fellow-countrymen, since the following generation, men such as Thomas Hill Green, and Hobhouse, [15] sought inspiration from Hegel more than from Locke, and thus disseminated an idealistic version of liberalism, which, if it did not confuse the ideas of the English—who had a solid tradition behind them—certainly did confuse the ideas of the liberals throughout the Continent, and also in America.[16] Even in this respect, then, liberalism has not been fortunate. For certainly it was no help to it to be christened at the precise moment when English philosophy was in decline, and when even England was about to be introduced to an idealistic philosophy whose most direct and fortunate descendant has been, if anyone, Marx![17]

Corresponding to the (terminological) untimeliness of liberalism, there is also its ill fortune at the hands of the historians. Setting aside the quasi-silence on the part of American historians[18]—which is by itself a serious loophole—even Germany never produced histories of its own liberalism, even though it had provided no small number of contributions to Lockeian liberalism by way of the *Naturrechts* school, of Kant, of von Humboldt, and also, lastly, of the *Rechtsstaat* school (even if the latter only in part).[19] But when the great German historical school was flourishing, or at any rate when history came to be affirmed as the "history of ideas," German liberalism was either extinct or monopolized by the problem of national unity.

The historiographical gaps, added to the previously mentioned historical misadventures, have had this result: that when present-day scholars have set their hand to writing a history of liberalism, what has appeared has been, in the majority of cases, a history of liberalisms (in the plural). Guido de Ruggiero began with his truly outstanding *History of European Liberalism* of 1925. It is true that De Ruggiero concluded his analysis of liberalisms (English, French, German, and Italian) with a section intended to spell out the core of liberalism (in the singular). But De Ruggiero was a philosopher influenced in part by Benedetto Croce (who made liberalism into a highly abstract philosophical category);[20] and in part directly by Hegel. For both these reasons, the concluding section on liberalism as such is the least felicitous in his work, and the unitary concept of liberalism which he puts forward is singularly out of focus, in the sense that De Ruggiero makes liberalism into an *étatiste* liberalism of the Hegelian type.[21] De Ruggiero may not have succeeded in his synthesis, but in Cranston's *Freedom* his penetrating sketch of English,

363

French, German, and American liberalisms has no conclusion: Cranston altogether gives up any attempt to present a unitary idea. Even more, he allows his taste for multiplying liberalisms so much scope as to declare that only English liberalism is unambiguous, since even the French type should really be divided—according to Cranston —into two layers: the Lockeian, and that of *étatiste* liberalism. This, however, is an overstatement. In fact, the term *libéralisme* is just as unambiguous in French as it is in English. The supposed French *étatiste* liberalism does not exist *qua* liberalism. A State-loving variety of liberalism only appears with the second stage of the German tradition,[22] and it remains an open question to what extent this specimen may be properly classified as liberalism.

Must we come, then, to the conclusion that *a* liberalism does not exist but only *many* different liberalisms? And furthermore that these liberalisms must be sliced into a number of phases: the classical, the democratic, the social, the *étatiste,* the humanistic, the socialist, etc.? I think not. By the same token it could be maintained that not democracy but only many democracies exist, one for every nation, and further that each of these democracies changes from generation to generation. Yet on different grounds we may well speak of democracy in the singular, and it is perfectly admissible, correspondingly, to speak of liberalism in the singular—provided that the basic historical idea conveyed by this term is not confused with its local and sectarian varieties, or with its composite and ever changing stages.

3. Liberalism Defined

Very simply, liberalism is the theory and practice of individual liberty, juridical defense and the constitutional State. It will be noted that I say "constitutional State," and not—as is sometimes suggested —"minimal State." It is true that the constitutional State was born as a minimal State, since it was set up to uphold a liberty *against,* or *from* government. But if the liberal State was born as an expression of distrust of power, and therefore with the purpose of reducing rather than augmenting the functions of the State, one must not for this reason put the size of the liberal State ahead of its structure, that is, a contingent characteristic ahead of the essential. However much the constitutional State may have been conceived of as a small

364

State, and also as a do-nothing State, this does not prevent its becoming, if need be, a large State which does something, and even a great deal—on this essential condition: the more it ceases to be a minimal State, the more important it is that it remain a constitutional State.

It will also be noted that I am not concerned with distinguishing between classical liberalism, and new liberalism, as is often done by other authors. Of course, one can always make a distinction between old and new, and certainly twentieth-century liberalism is not something that has stood still since the age of Locke. But for the purposes of the inquiry, "What is liberalism?" the distinction between old and new phases, or forms, of liberalism does not seem to me to be helpful in clarifying the issue.

When we say "new liberalism," we often mean that the laissez faire formula of old liberalism has been dropped. But if this is so, then I consider the distinction both immaterial and misleading, since in this way we perpetuate the ambiguity which comes from mixing up a political with an economic problem, liberalism with liberism. Political liberalism existed long before economic liberism—and if it was able to do without laissez faire earlier, why should it not be able to continue to do so afterwards? This is not to say that the economic system is irrelevant to the political system, and that there is no connection between economic and political freedom. Of course there is. However, liberalism is not market economy, and I do not see why, when everyone distinguishes between democracy in the political and democracy in the economic sense, the same distinction is ignored in the case of liberalism.

The expression "new liberalism" can also indicate so-called welfare liberalism. But in this hypothesis we have gone on to consider the democratic development of liberalism, and, in particular, not so much what liberalism has given of itself to democracy, as what the idea of democracy has contributed to the liberal idea. New liberalism in this case is tantamount to saying democratic liberalism. There is no harm in it if we like to use the former instead of the latter label. No harm, provided that we know what liberalism without adjectives is. Otherwise we are in no position to establish to what extent so-called social or welfare liberalism remains liberalism.[23]

For instance, if the formula of the welfare State is understood as meaning that economic security is preferred to political freedom, this may well be a democratic development, but a development in which the economic appetite of the *demos* has consumed the liberal component: and in such a case to speak of a new liberalism is merely to descend to the sectarian level of abuses of the term. These and similar uses are "abuses" in that they in the final analysis have little other *raison d'être* than this: that liberalism is found to be, at a given moment, the best unappropriated label available on the market of political key-words. By legitimizing these uses we are hence adding to the confusion. And it is precisely because every ten years or so someone comes out with the idea of rejuvenating "liberalism," that we have come to the point of making it, as Max Lerner remarks, "perhaps the most disputed term of our generation" [24]—a concept so amorphous and changeable as to be left really at the mercy of arbitrary stipulations.

The retort to this may be that if no distinction is made between classical and new liberalism, a disservice is being done, in the end, to the liberal idea, since we are thus implicitly condemning it to being conceived of as an old idea. That is as may be. For not every innovation is progress and not every legacy of the past is worthless. There are old truths which are outworn, but there are also truths which express discoveries that defy the corrosion of time: and these are old truths in the sense that they are everlasting. So let us look more closely into this matter.

To begin with, this one point must be firmly established: there is a democracy older, and far more outworn, than liberalism. All those who understand democracy literally and who speak of it in the etymological sense are way behind the times. It is only if we speak of liberal democracy that we are speaking of a democracy which comes after liberalism, and which is younger than liberalism. But even in this contemporary reference it is not to be thought that the line of descent between the two is a clear-cut uni-directional line without variants. As a matter of fact the thesis that modern democracy is born from liberalism is at times contradicted. Panfilo Gentile, for example, writes that "it is commonly thought that first came liberalism and then *démocratisme,* as if . . . liberalism were only a timid predecessor. This opinion is by no means exact because . . . liberalism followed *démocratisme,* corrected it and went beyond it."[25] How do things stand then?

Here the complication lies in the fact that the English genealogy is different from the French. In the former case it was Lockeian liberalism which was transplanted to the New World and produced there the first modern democracy. But if we consider what happened in France (which also reacted on the neighboring countries), this genealogical line can be reversed, since the liberal element was imported, whereas the native element was democratic rationalism in the manner of Rousseau.[26] If the anglophile Montesquieu came before the anglophobe Rousseau, afterwards the roles were exchanged: Rousseau is older, Constant and Tocqueville are more modern. In effect, liberalism was accepted on the Continent and showed its best results after learning its lesson from the Jacobin democracy which preceded it.[27] This is what Panfilo Gentile meant to point out. So, while it is true— according to the main lines indicated by the original genealogy, the Anglo-Saxon one—that liberalism came first and democracy followed, it is equally true that in the nineteenth century liberalism was restated and refined on the basis of a previous unhappy democratic experiment. And these clarifications are of no small importance, because the world today is seething with people calling for a "post-liberal" democracy which is to supersede liberalism, without realizing that they are only working for a "pre-liberal" democracy which has long been superseded by liberalism.

In conclusion, if certain aspects of classical liberalism are dead, so be it. If the times have changed the liberal into a conservative, there is no harm in this: other people besides revolutionaries are needed in this world. If, finally, there is some part of liberalism that remains modern and belongs to the present, it is important that this part be understood. And that is the sum of the argument. In other words, I suggest that we should bother less about "new liberalism," and more about what is, and remains, new *in* liberalism.

4. Liberal Democracy

The framework of the basic relationship between liberalism and democracy can be outlined simply by referring to Tocqueville's classic distinction. To isolate liberalism from democracy, we say that liberalism calls for liberty and democracy for equality. To unite them, we say that it is the task of liberal-democratic systems to combine liberty with equality.

That liberty and equality can converge is shown by the very fact that our systems are both liberal and democratic. And how they can cooperate is just what we have been examining for some time. Actually it is not that liberalism is wholly a matter of liberty and democracy wholly a matter of equality. Rather, it is that there are freedoms which are not appreciated, or appreciated enough, by the democratic viewpoint, just as there are equalities which fall outside the range of liberal sensibility.[28] As I have already stressed, all the equalities are not democratic acquisitions, just as the over-all question of liberty cannot be reduced to its liberal formulation. If, then, liberty and equality mark the line of demarcation between liberalism and democracy it is because of a different underlying basic logic. And it is in this light that liberal democracy can be viewed as a skein with two ends. As long as the skein is not touched, all is well, but if we begin to pull the ends and unravel it, we see that it is made up of two different-colored threads.

If we pull the liberal thread, not every form of equality disappears; but liberal equality, as such, is above all intended to promote, by way of liberty, qualitative aristocracies.[29] Liberalism per se is wary of granting more than juridico-political equality because it distrusts and opposes any equality gratuitously bestowed from above. Croce gave us a concise picture of the liberal spirit in its purest form when he observed that for "liberalism, which is born and remains intrinsically anti-egalitarian, liberty, according to Gladstone's saying, is the way of producing and promoting not democracy but aristocracy." [30]

If, on the other hand, we start to pull on the democratic thread, we find an equality which neutralizes every spontaneous process of differentiation. As De Ruggiero remarked: "The art of stimulating from within the need to raise oneself is totally unknown to democracy, which contents itself with bestowing rights and benefits, which out of their being gratuitous are for this very reason depreciated and dissipated from the outset." In the words of De Ruggiero can be clearly seen the liberal's reproof. "It is a fact," he concluded, "that the rigid and unintelligent application of the principle of equality tends to cripple the efforts and the benefits of liberty, which of necessity are in the direction of differentiation and unevenness, and to spread, together with mediocre qualities, also the love of mediocrity." [31]

In the final analysis, equality has a horizontal urge whereas liberty has a vertical impetus. Democracy is concerned with social cohesion and levelling, liberalism esteems prominence and innovation. Equality desires to integrate and to attune, liberty is troubled, wasteful, and disordered. The fundamental difference is that liberalism pivots on the individual,[32] and democracy on society. De Ruggiero accurately caught the reversal which comes about in the two perspectives when he observed that democracy ends by turning upside down "the original relationship which the liberal mentality established between the individual and society: it is not the spontaneous cooperation of individuals' energies which creates the character and value of the whole, but it is the whole which determines and shapes its elements." [33] In one of his recent writings Bertrand Russell asks: "How can we combine that degree of *individual initiative* which is necessary for progress with the degree of *social cohesion* that is necessary for survival?" [34] This is an apt reformulation of Tocqueville's perplexity, and it is our ever-to-be-solved problem.

The relationship between liberalism and democracy must, however, also be considered on a more concrete level, coming down from the sphere of values and principles to that of specific political attitudes. In this respect liberalism is above all the technique of limiting the State's power, whereas democracy is the insertion of popular power into the State. Therefore, with the passage of time there comes to be created between the liberal and the democrat (whatever the party labels may be) a division of roles, as a result of which the former feels more the political concern, whereas the latter has more of a welfare concern.

Of course democracy has imparted something of itself to political liberalism, just as liberalism in its turn has imparted its own values to democratic sociality. Nevertheless, we may pass over this reciprocal *do ut des,* and make an approximate division of this sort: while the liberal is concerned with the form of the State, the democrat

369

is primarily interested in the content of the norms emanating from the State. In relation to the form of the State, the problem is to establish *how* the norms should be created; in relation to the concern about content, the problem is *what* must be established by the norms. The liberal is on the defensive on the social plane, but is active when it comes to supervising the method of creating the social order. The democrat is somewhat indifferent to method, is concerned above all with substance, and prefers exercising power (in the redistributive sense) to watching over it.

If we break down the component parts of liberal democracy in this way, the distinction between democracy in the *political* and democracy in the *social* (and economic) sense becomes clear. In the political sense there is no appreciable difference between the democratic and the liberal State: the former is, for the most part, the latter under a new name. When on the other hand we speak of democracy in the social sense, we are speaking of what is properly democracy and not liberalism.

"Social democracy," however, has acquired two different meanings. In a first meaning, which I would call primary, the label refers to an *ethos,* a custom, a *modus vivendi.* This is the meaning which we give to this expression when it refers, for instance, to the United States: to point—as Dicey has done—to a special and, so to speak, natural condition of society. But where democracy is imported, this meaning of "social democracy" hardly applies. Here the expression has taken on another meaning, which I will call secondary, according to which it does not point to a societal *modus essendi,* but rather to a way of governing society. And this is the social democracy which borders on economic democracy, and which can convert itself into a socialist democracy.

Clearly, the two things are very different. In the first case social democracy is the substratum and the extra-political foundation of political democracy. In the second it is a policy intended to create from above the circumstances which, in the judgment of the policy-makers, will produce a democratic society. Therefore, in the primary sense it is the antecedent fact of any policy, while in the secondary sense it is the product of a policy. Despite this difference, however, when we speak of *social* democracy we are using "democracy" legitimately in both cases; whereas when we say *political* democracy, for the sake of exactness we ought to say "liberalism."

In conclusion, the interplay between the liberal and democratic elements in our system can be summed up thus: the first is more concerned with the problems of political bondage, of individual initiative, and of the form of the State; whereas the second is sensitive about the problems of equality, of social cohesion, and of welfare policy. And I have wished to be meticulous in this analysis of the component parts of liberal democracy, because we are rapidly arriving at a point where we must choose, consciously if possible, between two things: between a democracy *within* liberalism, and a democracy *without* liberalism.

5. Democracy within Liberalism

Roughly speaking, in the nineteenth century it was the liberal element which prevailed over the democratic; in the twentieth century the pendulum has swung, and today it is the democratic component which prevails over the liberal. Tocqueville outlined the process in a masterly fashion when he wrote: "Our forefathers were ever prone to make an improper use of the notion that private rights ought to be respected; and we are naturally prone, on the other hand, to exaggerate the idea that the interest of a private individual ought always to bend to the interest of the many." [35] Yet, in spite of this latter "exaggeration," we are still seeking "more democracy." And I am not in disagreement with this attitude provided that what it implies be properly understood and that certain preliminary points be clearly affirmed.

In the first place, it should be understood that if our democracies are the product of liberalism plus democracy, it follows that they pose a problem of internal balance between their component parts. Consequently, we should not fail to realize that what is needed most, at the present stage, is a countervailing behavior, aimed at preventing one of the component parts of the system from ultimately overcoming the other. For we have reached the point where there is a need to make allowances for the "opposite danger." [36]

In the second place—I am still speaking in very general terms—we must take care not to confuse a chronological order, i.e., the *be-*

fore and the *after,* with an order of importance, i.e., the *less* and the *more.* If modern democracy is an *after* in relation to liberalism, this does not necessarily mean that it surpasses or supersedes liberalism, that is, that liberalism is *less,* less important. The association between what we obtain last (and least) and what ranks first in our order of preference is purely psychological, and often deceptive, in that what is desired most is not always what is most desirable. We must therefore never forget that what democracy adds to liberalism is at the same time a consequence of liberalism; and thus that to speak of democracy as something which "supersedes" liberalism—in the meaning of the German dialectical verb *aufheben*—may be very misleading.[37] Democracy is the completion, not the replacement, of liberalism.

If these points are kept in mind, then there is a sense in which "more democracy" is desirable and should be sought. For my warnings simply refer to the fact that we are often seeking a maximization of democracy in the wrong direction, that is, in the direction in which we destroy the liberal component of the system and receive nothing in exchange. The question is, then, to look for democracy where we can find it and obtain it—thereby paying special attention to the distinction between democracy in the social and economic sense on the one hand, and in the political sense on the other.

To maintain that democracy is *more* than liberalism is half true and half false. It is true if by this we mean that democracy is more than liberalism in the social sense. It is inexact if we mean that democracy is more than liberalism in the political sense. The so-called democratic State, if we go back to identifying it with its proper title, is the liberal-constitutional State; and this means that *political* democracy merges with liberalism and has been superseded by it. Therefore it is mistaken to call for a democratic take-over of the liberal-constitutional State. The slogan "democratize the State" is more than anything a bad substitute for the correct slogan "democratize society." This is shown by a number of Continental European democracies, which, on the basis of a social *ethos* that leaves much to be desired, have busied themselves with constructing a hyperdemocratic State, making and unmaking constitutions which are so "democratic" as to be of little use as constitutions.

372

"More democracy" thus means, when correctly understood, that democracy is not only a political form. It means, in the first place, that social equality and economic welfare are desirable. It also means that, at its roots, democratic life revolves around small groups, face-to-face relationships and "private government." [38] As Dahl and Lindblom well observe, "The nation-state can only provide the framework within which the good life is possible; it cannot fulfill the functions of the small groups. . . . To the extent that it attempts to do so, the nation-state must provide either an impoverished substitute for, or a grotesque perversion of, small group functions." [39]

Therefore more democracy does not mean less liberalism. To criticize the constitutional State in the name of, and for the sake of, democratic progress, or progressivism, is to look for the wrong thing in the wrong place. As a political form, our democracy cannot be much more than a juridical order geared to a cluster of techniques of liberty. However, this is no small thing, since it is the precondition of all the rest. That is to say that while liberalism is an instrument of democracy, democracy is not in itself a vehicle of liberalism. The formula of liberal-democracy is equality through liberty, by means of liberty, not liberty by means of equality. Logically the inversion is plausible, but empirically it is not.[40] It is exactly for this reason that democracy came back to life in the wake of liberalism. And for the same reason it is easy to predict that democracy will become once again a dead letter if liberal freedom is overthrown, and if the end of a greater equality is pursued to the detriment of the means which allow us to lay claim to it. We may praise equality more than liberty, but this does not change the order of the procedural *prius* and *postea,* it does not make what is first in order of preference also first in order of method.

The distinction between democracy in the social sense and democracy in the political sense results, then, in this conclusion: there is no contradiction in asking simultaneously for *more democracy* and *more liberalism*. And I feel that this is precisely what we ought to start doing.

It is well to remind ourselves in this connection that liberalism has depreciated as a result of its success. The constitutional State has succeeded so well in neutralizing power, that people have begun to notice economic much more than political constraints. Today most people still feel constrained very little by the State and very much by their employers. However, we should not fail to realize that this situation is being noticeably changed. No modern State is a minimal State any longer. With the passing of time the State itself has become more and more an employer. This has occurred not only through the dizzy increase in the number of bureaucrats, but also because many States have taken on the ownership of vast sections of economic life. Therefore, as Cranston rightly observes, "the constraints on which the liberal has concentrated have become *more* important; the constraints he has neglected *less* important. . . . It is therefore strange if it is true that liberalism has entered its 'decline as an ideology' just when this altered balance of social constraints makes the liberal analysis more timely and correct than it was when it flourished. . . ." [41]

Perhaps this is true but not strange. Hardly ever, at least in political matters, do we realize in time that the time has come to face the opposite danger. Yet, if it is true that liberalism has depreciated because of its success, it may yet regain its value as a result of its present lack of success. For those who believe in a democracy *within* liberalism, this is indeed a hope at which to grasp. For the time being, however, the fact is that many people believe that a democracy *without* liberalism would be much better.

6. Democracy without Liberalism

Now that the case for liberal democracy has been argued, it will be opportune to see how the opposite side argues the case against it. According to this latter approach, true democracy has yet to come, and it will be able to arise only through the destruction of the liberal State and of the corresponding so-called bourgeois freedoms. In short, the thesis here is that authentic democracy awaits us beyond liberalism.

How is this proved? The success of a demonstration depends, in the first instance, on the choice of the ground on which to do battle. It is not surprising, therefore, that the anti-liberal doctrine entirely reformulates the way of setting up the discourse. The relationship between liberalism and democracy is thus represented as a relationship between a chain of freedoms, the first link of which is a purely formal freedom, whereas the last link is the complete, real freedom. The advantages of such a presentation are obvious at a glance. First, it is immediately evident which is the minor and which the major term of the series and, secondly, a *continuum* is postulated such as to suggest in itself that the initial term turns into the final one without loss.

I lay stress on the approach since it is this which provides the conclusion, and, I might say, dispenses with the need to prove it. For if we call "freedom" what is otherwise called "equality," the rest of the argument follows very nicely. When the problem is discussed in relation to the concepts of liberty and equality, it is by no means self-evident that one term is less important than the other. If anything, the liberty-equality binomial conveys the evidence that the issue cannot be reduced to a problem of *Aufhebung,* of superseding, precisely because we have to deal with *two* distinct problems. But if I instead repeat the same word, taking care on the first occasion to present it negatively ("formal" liberty in this antithesis stands for apparent liberty) and on the second occasion positively (liberty in the "real" sense, meaning effective, true), the conclusion is as obvious as it is necessary: one freedom for another, the smaller is not worth as much as the larger, and if I have to reject the first in order to have the second, I choose "real" freedom.

As anyone can see, the argument hangs entirely on two terminological innovations, or manipulations: (i) the renaming of equality as "liberty," and (ii) the stress laid on the derogatory meaning of "formal" in representing politico-juridical freedom. According to the stipulative theory of definitions I suppose that one should merely try to ascertain whether these stipulations are useful, and someone may eventually end up by admitting that from a certain point of view (for the purpose of persuading an audience, for instance) they are indeed useful. According to my views, however, these stipulations are entirely arbitrary—and I take the term to mean unwarranted and mistaken.

To make two things verbally alike only makes them *verbally* alike. No matter how consistently we use "liberty" to denote equality, the fact remains that we are confusing different things. More precisely, in one instance (when we have our mind on the problem of

375

equality) we refer to a condition of liberty, while in the other instance (when we think of liberty) we no longer refer to a condition but to the thing itself. And this distinction is basic for a further reason: equality is a condition of liberty only on the precise condition that equality be desired for liberty's sake. If we have come to equate equality with liberty, this is only because we are accustomed to view equality in the context of a liberal civilization, and therefore in a framework in which a liberal *animus* happens to pervade our egalitarian claims. So not only equality cannot be identified with liberty because it is only a condition of liberty, but also even this link between the two is provisional and ever precarious.

Passing on to the second point, to call "formal" the freedom which we enjoy in liberal-democratic systems—when formal is used in the sense of "unreal"—is again to confuse the issue and to give the term a wholly arbitrary meaning. An unreal freedom is not a "formal" freedom, but—to begin with—a non-existent freedom, a freedom which is promised but not provided. Thus, no matter how often one may use the word "unreal" to denote our juridico-political liberties, the fact remains that these are so amply bestowed that they are even used for the purpose of denying them (to others). It follows from this that we cannot use "formal" in the sense of "non-real" in relation to freedoms that we do enjoy.

A distinction can be made between freedoms which are desired more and those which are desired less—and in this connection between a greater and a smaller freedom—but this does not detract from the fact that a freedom which is valued less is just as real as one which is valued more, if the latter requires the former in order to exist. Therefore political freedom is not less real, objectively speaking, than economic freedom, just as political and juridical equality are not less real than economic equality. And this is because if the freedoms and the equalities which procedurally come before, are lacking, then the others, those which procedurally come afterwards, become baseless.

It follows from this that when we recommend the rejection of politico-juridical rights and freedom on the grounds that they are false or at any rate insufficient, what we are in effect recommending —wittingly or unwittingly—is simply an arbitrary and discretional rather than a legally disciplined exercise of power. And what greater freedom—*vulgo* "real freedom"—can come out of this is indeed a well-kept secret. No one maintains that the subject of liberty is exhausted by the concept of freedom *from*. But while we cannot confine our attention to political freedom alone, it is certain that if we are restrained there is no further positive liberty which can be realized: eliminate the first freedom of the series, and the term "liberty" becomes devoid of meaning. There is an iron procedural *iter* which marks the expansion of liberty, and it is such that political freedom is the presupposition *sine qua non* of all the positive liberty-equalities.

The itinerary is not reversible, and there is no plausible argument in support of the thesis that real liberty follows from the achievement of material equality, that is, of economic equalization. How is it that equality of possessions, or, better, of lack of possessions, is held to imply real liberty? Those who hold this view evidently forget that man's power over man is not, or at any rate not only, a corporeal thing connected with property. Power is also a relational phenomenon. Therefore the elimination of the power deriving from ownership can only produce the consequence that all power takes on a relational form.

The suspicion gains ground, then, that those who reject liberalism have never really grasped what it is all about. However, while this is unfortunate, it is *de facto* immaterial. Many civilizations have already fallen, perhaps, because they were not understood and were no longer appreciated by their beneficiaries, and there is no reason to suppose that history must make an exception in favor of our present liberal civilization. I could not say whether it is probable, but certainly it is possible that liberalism will be supplanted, and there seem to be a good number of signs that the present-day liberal-democracies are departing from liberalism. But in that case there is something else awaiting us beyond the democracy that we know. What?

Since "democracy" has become a universally sanctified term apparently destined to keep us company whatever road we take, let us join in the game and reply: what awaits us is a totalitarian democracy. For a non-liberal democracy is a totalitarian democracy. If the expression has the effect of a *contradictio in adiecto* on us, it is because we have in mind liberal-democracy, the referent in relation to which it is really contradictory. But the label takes on a meaning which is by no means paradoxical if it is meant to indicate the point at which the democratic legitimation of power will arrive, assuming that it is detached from liberal beliefs and techniques. If we woke up one morning in fourth-century Athens, that democracy would give us the impression of a totalitarian democracy—with two differences: in the Greek world individuals' submission to their *polis* was, so to speak, spontaneous; and the democracy of the ancients was able to last as a democracy—albeit as a totalitarian democracy—because it was a Stateless democracy. But then to speak in our own case of totalitarian democracy is to speak of something that can survive, as a democracy, only for the space of a day. If the *polis* was a Stateless democracy, ours is one with a State. And this makes all the difference, since it leaves our popular power in a vacuum, entrusted to the *placet* of a distant central political power. And it is not only present-day demographic and geographic dimensions which tend in themselves to undermine effective popular sovereignty: it is also the very objectives of the modern State, ever more pressed as it is to provide for the needs and demands of society, and therefore ever more tempted to demand greater power as well as a power of rapid, unhampered decision-making.

Beyond liberal-democracy what one really glimpses is only the survival of the word, of the *name* democracy; that is, of a democracy for rhetorical consumption which, thanks to the *fictio* of some presumed popular support, is suitable for sanctioning the most despotic bondage. This means, in plain terms, that together with the demise of liberal-democracy, democracy dies too—regardless of whether we are referring to it in its modern or in its ancient form, whether it is a democracy based on freedom of the individual or one which only requires that power be exercised by the collective *plenum*.

NOTES

† *Politica e cultura*, p. 278.

1. In the years 1872-1918, i.e., during the period which runs between the break of the First International and the Russian Revolution, communism and socialism were used more or less interchangeably, but with a decided prevalence of the latter name. It is only with Lenin that "communism"

leaves the orbit of the broad Marxist interpretation of socialism. More exactly it was in March 1918 that the Bolsheviks left to the Mensheviks the label "Russian Party of the Social-Democratic Workers," adopting for themselves that of "Russian Communist Party."

2. One of the most penetrating formulations of this extraneity of background is given in this formula of Bruno Leoni: "Whenever majority rule is unnecessarily substituted for individual choice, democracy is in conflict with individual freedom." (*Freedom and the Law*, p. 133).

3. *Vom Wesen und Wert der Demokratie*, Chap. IX. In his *General Theory of Law and State* (Cambridge, Mass., 1945), p. 288, Kelsen is even more drastic: "democracy coincides with political . . . liberalism."

4. This is notably the case of the authors that tie the concept of democracy and that of "constitutional government" closely together by claiming that a democratic government is necessarily constitutional.

5. One might say that the same could hold for the link between "democracy" and "Democrat." Yet, within the Western world the meaning of Democrat is not as changeable as that of Liberal. Between an Italian and an American Democrat, for instance, there is far less distance than is found between the respective Liberals. On the other hand, the ambiguity in the use of "Democrat" in most cases derives from the ambiguity of "Liberal."

6. *The Rise and Decline of Liberalism* (Milwaukee, 1953), p. 25.

7. *Ibid.*, p. 23.

8. Cf. Harold Laski, *The Rise of European Liberalism* (London, 1936), p. 9.

9. The coining of the word "socialism" has been vindicated by Pierre Leroux, who used it for the first time in 1833. Actually Leroux was mistaken because the word had already appeared in France in 1831 (in an anonymous article attributed to Alexandre Vinet), and even before in England in the Owenist review *Cooperative Magazine* of 1827. Besides, Leroux used the word to deplore "the exaggeration of the idea of association or of society," and therefore in a critical sense which has not caught on. Let us just establish, then, that the word was already in the air around the years of the Revolution of 1830; that it was coined by cooperativist circles, and within the group of Saint-Simon in particular, as a term in opposition to "individualism"; and that for several decades it was used in a very loose manner, in associations that included doctrines as diverse as those of Saint-Simon, Fourier, and Proudhon. The works which attracted most attention to the label have been: the *Organisation du travail* of Louis Blanc (which came out in 1839), followed in 1848 by his *Le Socialisme: Droit au travail;* Prudhon's *Qu'est-ce que la proprieté* and his *Philosophie de la misère* (published in 1840 and 1846 respectively); and finally, the *Principes de socialisme* of Considerant (printed in 1847), the most important exponent of Fourier's doctrines.

10. It is the speech Tocqueville delivered on September 12, 1848.

11. It is true that in 1848 also the word "communism" clamorously came into the open with the *Communist Manifesto*. However, the communists were then a sectarian variety of socialism, and remained all along—despite Marx— a minor stream of the proletarian movement. As for the word, "communism" derives from the line Babeuf-Buonarroti, and began to be used in the secret revolutionary societies in Paris in the years 1835-40. It was made public by Blanqui, who in 1840 spread the idea of a communist revolutionary dictatorship. Marx did not come in contact with the term directly through the French, but through Moses Hess and Lorenz von Stein; and it was Engels who adopted it before Marx. See A. Cornu, *Karl Marx: L'Homme et l'oeuvre* (Paris, 1934) Chap. IV. Cf. the amplified ed. A. Cornu, *K. Marx, F. Engels, leur vie et leur oeuvre*, Vol. I (Paris, 1955).

12. In order to do justice to Tocqueville one should keep in mind that at the time "socialism" had a political rather than an economic implication and that it was meant to be a declaration of war against liberalism, a drastic vindication of the priority of the State over the individual.

13. To avoid misunderstandings I adopt the Italian common practice of using "liberism" and not "liberalism" to refer to the economic doctrine of laissez-faire.

14. I mention Constant because in a text as widely used as George H. Sabine's *A History of Political Theory* (New York, 1951) his name does not even appear; and the omission is altogether normal with English-speaking authors.

15. Cf. for all Hobhouse's influential *Liberalism* (1911).

16. As one can evince, e.g., from Sabine's *History of Political Theory* which presents Thomas Hill Green as a central figure of liberalism, and does not even mention Tocqueville and Lord Acton, let alone Constant. Clearly Sabine attributes a disproportionate importance to the "idealist revision of liberalism," which in reality is important only for the fact that (and on this point I agree with Sabine) "the philosophies of Mill and Spencer taken together left the theory of liberalism in a state of unintelligible confusion." (Chap. XXXII, p. 724.)

17. I mention the name of Marx to call attention to two facts: (i) that the philosophy of Hegel has found its most prominent historical incarnation in the Hegelian left (besides serving subsequently *pro tempore* as a support to Fascism and Nazism); and that (ii) the most genuine and coherent effort to utilize the idealistic speculation for laying down a basis for liberalism (which is that accomplished, *pace* Sabine, by Benedetto Croce) has above all demonstrated how badly the two things go together, and how necessary it is to maintain the link between liberalism and the empirical, matter-of-fact *forma mentis*. Cf. for this last point Norberto Bobbio, *Politica e cultura*, esp. pp. 238-268; and also G. Sartori, *Benedetto Croce, Filosofo della libertà*.

18. The fascinating history of Vernon Parrington, *Main Currents in American Thought,* illustrates, in the final analysis, only the evolution of the party or of the sectarian meanings of "liberalism" in the United States. I have already pointed out the omissions in Neill's *Rise and Decline of Liberalism* as well as the shortcomings of Sabine's presentation. Similar reservations could be made about Hallowell's *Decline of Liberalism as an Ideology* (Berkeley, 1943); and with even better reason (considering its informative purposes) on the perusal of J. Salwyn Schapiro, *Liberalism: Its Meaning and History* (New York, 1958), since his "elasticity of liberalism" is clearly the equivalent of the absence of a connecting thread. All in all, it is not without good reasons that the task of illustrating the word "liberalism" for the *Encyclopaedia of the Social Sciences* was given to Guido De Ruggiero (even though his synthesis was not too successful).

19. The German contribution has been somewhat overstated in Guido De Ruggiero's *Storia del liberalismo europeo.* But it is true that Humboldt's little book *Ideen zu einem Versuch die Grenzen der Wirksamheit des Staates zu bestimmen* (written in 1791, but published only in 1851) remains a classic example of the literature on liberalism.

20. Cf. Chap. III, 3, above.

21. Cf. Chap. XIII, note 68, above.

22. And, by reflection, of the Italian tradition. But even in Italy there are exceptions. If De Ruggiero is influenced by Croce and through him by the idealistic speculation, during the same years the English type of liberalism was authoritatively represented by Luigi Einaudi. The essentials of the long but courteous discussions on liberalism between Einaudi and Croce have been gathered in the anthological volume ed. by Paolo Solari, *Liberismo e liberalismo* (Napoli, 1957).

23. For welfare liberalism (of the English brand), cf. *The Unservile State, Essays in Liberty and Welfare,* ed. G. Watson (London, 1957).

24. Quoted in T. P. Neill *op. cit.,* p. 3.

25. *L'idea liberale* (Milano, 1955), pp. 5-6.

26. For the incomprehension of "English liberty" (which explains the superposition of Rousseau's influence over Montesquieu), cf. Joseph Dedieu, *Montesquieu et la tradition politique anglaise en France* (Paris, 1909), Chap. XII; and R. Derathé, "Montesquieu et J. J. Rousseau," *Revue internationale de philosophie,* III-IV (1955), pp. 367 ff., who notes: "It is only in the nineteenth century, at the time of the Restoration, that the *Esprit des Lois* acquired in France an undisputed prestige. . . . During the eighteenth century the book had not been taken too seriously."

27. It is precisely with reference to the French indigenous tradition that Talmon justly emphasizes that "diversity of views and interests was far from being

regarded as essential by the eighteenth-century fathers of democracy. Their original postulates were unity and unanimity. The affirmation of the principle of diversity came later, when the totalitarian implications of the principle of homogeneity had been demonstrated in Jacobin dictatorship" (*The Origins of Totalitarian Democracy,* p. 44).

28. Cf. Chap. XIV, 3, above.

29. One might say, in Bagehot's wording, that liberalism points to a "deferential" democracy, so named because "certain persons are by common consent agreed to be wiser than others, and their opinion is, by consent, to rank for much more than its numerical value." Cf. Walter Bagehot, *The English Constitution* (New York, 1893), p. 227. While the liberal *animus* would naturally tend to promote a "qualitative" democracy, the democratic logic as such aspires to an "equalitarian" democracy.

30. *Etica e politica,* pp. 288-289. Croce's polemics are directed against democracy also because he identified the latter with the abhorred philosophy of the Enlightenment. See, however, this more balanced judgment of 1936: "Liberalism is both friendly and inimical to democracy. A friend because its political class is an open class . . . which resolves itself in a government which in its very action educates the governed to the ability to govern. But it is an enemy of democracy when the latter tends to substitute quality by number and quantity, because it knows that in so doing democracy paves the way for demagogy, and without wishing to, for dictatorships and tyrannies, thereby destroying itself." (*Pagine sparse,* Napoli, 1948), Vol. II, p. 407.

31. *Storia del liberalismo europeo,* pp. 395 and 401. Whence the expression "mediocracy," which is becoming of current usage. Cf. E. M. Forster, *Two Cheers for Democracy* (London, 1951).

32. Meaning, as W. Lippmann well puts it, that "in the discipline of a free society it is the inviolability of all individuals which determines the social obligations." Lippmann points out forcibly that "it is here, on the nature of man, between those who would respect him as an autonomous person and those who would degrade him to a living instrument, that the issue is joined." *The Good Society* (New York, 1943), p. 387.

33. *Storia del liberalismo europeo,* p. 395.

34. *Authority and the Individual* (London, 1949), p. 11.

35. *La Démocratie en Amérique,* trans. Henry Reeve (New York, 1899), Vol. II, Bk. IV, Chap. VII, p. 343.

36. Cf. esp. Chap. IV, 5, above.

37. The importance and the role played by the key dialectical term *Aufhebung* will never be stressed enough. The verb *aufheben* conveys all in one three meanings: (i) to lift up "progressively," (ii) in the sense of "maintaining"

and/or (iii) in the sense of "annihilating." It follows that in German or in the languages (such as, unfortunately, Italian) which have an adequate equivalent for *aufheben*—phrases such as "democracy surpasses, or supersedes, or sublates liberalism" are overabused, and find everyone (apparently) in agreement in saying things which are (substantially) the opposite. English-speaking people should be grateful for the fact that *Aufhebung* is actually untranslatable in English. This is undoubtedly a handicap so far as the understanding of the idealistic philosophy goes, but on the other hand keeps the English-speaking people immune to that contagious dialectic acrobatism and miraculosity which plays such an important part in Marxism (cf. Chap. XVIII, note 32 below), and which helps to explain many of the political vicissitudes of Germany and Italy.

38. Cf. C. E. Merriam, *Public and Private Government* (New Haven, 1944). Private government to mean a self-government of voluntary associations outside of the government.

39. *Politics, Economics and Welfare*, p. 520.

40. The question whether liberty is the primary concept, or whether it can be deduced from equality has been a topic of great interest to Italian philosophy. For Benedetto Croce the "leading concept" is without question liberty: justice and equality are only "regulative concepts." The opposite view is held by the Marxist philosopher G. della Volpe, *Discorso sull'ineguaglianza* (Roma, 1943), and esp. in *La libertà comunista* (Messina, 1946). On the other hand Guido De Ruggiero, and Guido Calogero in particular, have emphasized the very close link between liberty and equality, and Calogero has resolutely equated liberty with equality-justice. The controversy has assumed a tone of great asperity. For Croce cf. esp. "Libertà e giustizia" in *Discorsi di varia filosofia* (Bari, 1945), Vol. 1, pp. 261-276. For Calogero see *Difesa del liberalsocialismo* (Roma, 1945), esp. his reply to Croce: "L'ircocervo, ovvero le due libertà," pp. 26-37. However, we must stress that this is a speculative dispute. On the basis of "pure concepts" (as Croce would say) it is possible to derive equality from liberty or, vice versa, liberty from equality: the demonstration can be made in either direction. But—and this is the point—the order and the connection of ideas is not necessarily an *ordo et connectio rerum*. I mean that the philosophic systemization of the relationship between the "categories" liberty and equality does not apply *eo ipso* to the relationship between liberalism and democracy: or rather, it applies only on condition that the problem is considered empirically as a procedural *consecutio* and not just as a logical and ideal deduction.

41. *Freedom*, p. 81.

42. Cf. Chap. XIV, 6, above.

Chapter XVI

Democracy, Planning and Technocracy

"The spirit of modern progress and of the political renewal of the European States is rooted in the following principle: the world is continuously remade through thought, and thanks to thought."

—Silvio Spaventa†

1. What Is Planning?

DEMOCRACY as we know it today has many more tasks and functions than it had, say, thirty or forty years ago. One can only acknowledge this fact. To a greater or lesser extent, varying from place to place, the democratic State is everywhere becoming a do-everything State. Whether this happens under the pressure of circumstances, or by virtue of a deliberate choice, our political systems appear to be more and more burdened with the weight of the social and economic life of the community. To be sure, in some manner and to some extent, the State has always intervened in economic processes. But the manner and the extent of its intervention today are unprecedented—so much so that the expressions "State regulation" or "State intervention" appear inadequate. Quantitatively inadequate first of all; but also qualitatively inadequate, that is, in view of the meaning and the intentions implied in this development.

There has been a great deal of discussion, especially in the

384

thirties, as to how the economic State should proceed, as well as regarding the most fitting label to use in this connection.[1] In the fifties, however, "planning" was generally acknowledged as the best-suited name (as a shorthand for State economic planning). Yet I would not say that the term planning, by reason of becoming so popular, has also contributed to clarifying thought. Being used, as one is actually wont to use it, to cover widely different phenomena, planning has become one of those terms which say both too much and too little. On the one hand, planning is set against the market system, and on the other one hears that such an antithesis does not make sense any more. The assertion is on the one hand that democracy and planning are incompatible, on the other that they are perfectly suited to one another. What these conflicting views actually show is that to make different things nominally alike does not make them actually alike, and therefore that we should try to talk of one thing at a time. We must distinguish at least three meanings of "planning":

1) planning as rational organization;
2) limited planning;
3) total planning.

In the first sense, we are not actually referring to a specific type of planning, but, rather, to one of the reasons why planning (either of the limited or total kind) may be advocated; or otherwise to a criterion by which one should assess the validity of any planning policy. This amounts to saying that the first meaning is not a technical meaning. The second and the third are technical meanings in the sense that they can be understood only in connection with the relationship occurring between the market and the non-market economy. However, only in the abstract can one discuss the problem of planning in politically neutral terms, merely as a matter of economic technique. For in reality it is always the State, a political agency, that is charged with the task of carrying out economic planning. From this viewpoint the above classification will have to be reformulated as follows:

1. Planning as an intellectual ideal.
2. Planning of the social-democratic type (democratic planning).

385

3. Planning of the communist type (totalitarian or collectivistic planning).

The latter classification brings out the purposes toward which a planning operation can be oriented. In the first meaning, planning appears somewhat as the policy of the party-less intellectuals, and, in general, of the politically uncommitted. Obviously this does not exclude the possibility that planning as a rational ideal may be found both in the democratic-laboristic view of planning and in the communist view. However, this meaning ought to be kept distinct, in the first place because it may well side with itself, and, in the second place, because it is important to realize that both the social-democratic type and the Soviet type of planning have another aim in view. Their aim is not only to rationalize the economic process but also, and just as much, to achieve social justice and/or economic equality. The advocacy of planning by both the democractic socialists and the Soviet Marxists reflects an anti-capitalistic ideology. Accordingly, it is a question of fact, to be answered a posteriori, to what extent the second and third types of planning actually satisfy the rational requirement put forward by the first approach. But let us take up these meanings in a more detailed fashion.

1) Planning as *rational organization*. Despite the fact that this is not a technical meaning of the term, we find it in use even in specialized literature, especially in the United States. Dahl and Lindblom, for instance, understand by planning "an attempt at rationally calculated action to achieve a goal." Furthermore, as if to leave no doubts as to the latitude of this definition, they state: "The attempt to achieve rational politico-economic action may . . . be described as economic planning whether the attempt employs the market or master mind." [2] Although many economists would not find this meaning useful, it is well to point out that Dahl's and Lindblom's approach is valuable in that it represents a fairly accurate description of the image most people have of planning. This is due also to the reason that the technical meanings and implications of planning can be grasped only by those who realize what a market system is, how it works, and what its purpose is—and obviously there are not many such people.

386

The definition in question is, clearly, a minimal definition: all it does is suggest the minimal requirement of the notion. By the same token it is also an all-embracing definition. Indeed, if all we mean by planning is a "rationally calculated action," then everything, or nearly everything, is planning, or at least attempts to be such. The most restrained and taken-for granted form of State regulation qualifies as planning, just as do the total plans of a master mind. In sum, vis-à-vis this definition of planning every organized society makes the grade, to some extent, as a "planned society." And if we define planning in this fashion, the question becomes very simple, for it boils down to the alternative: either we plan, or our behavior is bound to be irrational.

2) Planning as *limited planning*. The label I employ is meant to suggest a situation halfway between simple State regulation and total planning. That is, we find limited planning whenever the market and planning are found to co-exist in the same economic system. For this situation economists employ different terms: framework planning, indicative planning, planning by inducement, and many others. At any rate, whatever the labels, what matters is to determine where this loosely structured planning begins and where it ends.

Every government regulates the economic process, and of course every government does make plans. But this is not yet "planning." In the sense of the term we are now examining, planning is meant not only as a corrective of, but also as an antidote to, a market system. The term is used correctly only insofar as the system prevents the allocation of economic resources from taking place exclusively on the basis of the market price and of the expediency calculations of private agents. More precisely, planning is *more* than State intervention because the intervention it requires is no longer piecemeal, but, by definition, organic. Also, planning is not yet in existence when it is merely a matter of so-called automatic stabilizers of the economic system (credit measures, etc.). Finally, while one may well conceive of a State intervention meant to re-establish the conditions of a market economy (anti-trust laws, etc.), it would be improper to talk of planning as a means of re-establishing the market system, for planning owes its existence to the fact that it operates *against* the market. Under this type of planning the market functions as a

387

mechanism for price determination, and as the indicator of the consumers' preferences (and of producers' reactions): but the economic system as a whole is no longer governed by the laws of the market. It is piloted, instead, by a central agency, acting in response to goals such as social justice, distributive justice, full employment, development, or others (the goals will depend, at least as far as their priority goes, on the problems the specific country faces).

Actually the phenomena that take place in the market itself are so deeply affected by the presence and the operation of this planning agency, that it is maintained by some authors that in such a case we are no longer confronted with a market system. However, this assertion implicitly takes perfect competition as a frame of reference, and therefore takes on its proper meaning when completed as follows: ". . . if compared to the ideal-type of perfect liberism." It follows from this that if we establish a different term of comparison, that is, if we compare the market as it presents itself in this case with an ideal-type of perfect collectivism, then we would probably be led to conclude, once again, that despite everything limited planning is still a market system.

The breaking-point of the system is to be found where the planned sector has so expanded its area of operation and impact as to make the market more or less inoperative both as a system of price determination and as an indicator of consumers' preferences. On the other hand the democratic planner considers himself to be limited by the following requirements: to respect freedom in the choice of one's occupation, and in the choice of one's consumptions. This is why this type of planning is called "indicative planning" [3] to mean that it implies structural looseness, and also "planning by inducement" to focus attention on the limits at which the democratic planner must stop. [4]

A comprehensive definition of the middle-way formula could be the following: "planning" applies here to an *ex ante* coordinated project of rational utilization of the existing means in order to achieve goals which cannot, or would not, be attained through the free play of the market mechanisms. This is naturally a very broad definition, whose elements can be found operating to different degrees in different cases. It is adequate, however, for the purpose of bringing out the difference between what comes *before* limited planning, i.e., State regulation—and what would come *after* it, i.e., total planning. All in all, this is the non-Marxist sense of the term planning as it is usually employed in European literature (including British literature). And if we adopt this definition as a baseline, it will be easily seen that to the extent that American scholars tend to use planning in the meaning referred to as non-technical, much of what they call planning does not qualify as such.[5] That is to say that planning in the European sense involves *more,* indeed much more, than is meant by such scholars as Dahl and Lindblom.

3) *Total planning.* By this label I refer to those cases where a State-owned target economy suppresses the market system and substitutes a master mind for it. This is the Communist or Soviet meaning of planning, which is also indicated by such labels as collectivistic planning, totalitarian planning, and coercive planning or planning by coercion (in contrast to planning by inducement). The idea of what we today call "collectivistic planning" may be viewed as the joint outcome of the theories of Saint-Simon and Marx. The former preached the substitution of a centrally-led economy for the market system, whereas the latter demanded above all the demolition of private property. At first glance one may view the Marxist element as the key one in this solution, but in reality it is Saint-Simon's abolition of the free market which plays the crucial role.

To be sure, some students maintain that the Soviet system can work successfully only because the system's calculations are made possible by a disguised market system.[6] This may well be so. Nevertheless, collective planning does restrict freedom in the choice of one's occupation and of one's consumptions, and is carried out by dictating coercively and solely in view of the targets what the wages shall be and what the consumers must accept. Whatever the devices may be to which the Soviet planners have recourse in order to make the system work (as we would say) as economically as possible, these devices cannot obscure the borderline between limited and total planning. For in the Soviet case we are confronted with a target economy where the objectives are deliberated upon and imposed from above, whatever their economic and human cost. Total planning is the economy of an owner-and-seller State, not the economy of the consumers. And let it be noted that, historically speaking, this is the original, proper meaning of planning. In large substance, planning is a Russian invention.[7] Marx never envisaged the actual requirements of the system that he was broadly and implicitly advocating. And the West only started using the term planning in a technically precise sense, which is hardly related to its colloquial meaning, because of the Soviet challenge.[8]

We may now draw our conclusions. Given the fact that we have stipulated one label for three diverse referents, that is, given the fact that we have come to use "planning" to refer to at least three very different things, it is no wonder that the question of planning has become a maddeningly confused one in the course of just a few decades. There are indeed people who reject limited planning (definition two) because they confuse it with total planning (definition three). There are some, on the other hand, who accept total planning for reasons put forward to advocate planning as a rational ideal (definition one). Finally, there are others who demand planning as a rationalization of economic processes, are presented with forms of State intervention which are neither economic nor rational, and yet are happy all the same, because they behold the word and are unable to see into the thing. And I am not merely talking of the common man. Confusions of this type are frequent even among the experts.

2. The Grand Issues

A first *quid pro quo,* that is, a first kind of confusion, concerns the relationship between intellectuals and politicians, or, we might say, the man of science and the man of politics. It is no wild guess to assert that the popularity which planning enjoys among intellectual elites is due to their taking planning to mean a rational set-up of the economic process. Now, we ask: is this demand (planning as "rational organization") complied with? Or even: can it be complied with?

Obviously it is not easy to answer this question. Indeed all we can tangibly see and feel are nationalizations or socializations,[9] not "rationality." Now, may we assume that State ownership does in itself and by itself promote a more rational order? This seems to be one of those questions upon which one can argue *ad infinitum,* for we first ought to agree upon what is to be meant by economic rationality.

I believe, however, that whatever meaning one might attribute to rationality, there are good reasons for answering the question negatively.

Let us approach the problem from this angle: who are the planners? In a democratic system the main lines of an economic policy must be approved by parliament and deliberated upon by the government. This means that they fall within the province of politicians recruited through universal suffrage. The question then becomes the following: what are the chances that rational planning will issue from these hands? If we want to be sincere, we can only answer that the chances are pretty poor. The obvious reason for this is that a truly rational direction of the economic process would require leaders trained for this purpose and provided with adequate autonomy of decision plus the appropriate power of enforcement. The facts are, instead, that the recruitment of political personnel is more or less the same today as it was fifty years ago, when it was assumed that the best government was one which governed least; and that, consequently, today's politicians handle economic policy as they have always done, that is, with little competence, if any, and with frequent concessions to electoral and other contradictory cross-pressures. Hence what is very likely to happen is that from this kind of political personnel we may well obtain planning (if we ask for it), but of the second, or even third type. That is to say that the chances are that we will not obtain the rational type of planning we were seeking. For we will be presented with nationalizations or socializations which do not issue from a "rational" criterion, but rather from electoral concerns, and which respond largely to welfare, social, and egalitarian goals.

I am not implying that this outcome is bad. I am only saying that it is a different outcome, and that therefore many who enthusiastically approve every and any policy of nationalization as a victory of the light of reason over chaos and obscurantism are in danger of fooling themselves. Socialization, per se, has nothing rational about it. The State could well turn the whole productive system of a country into a public enterprise without thereby fostering any progress in the direction of a rationalization of the economic system. A policy of nationalization can be irrational as much as rational, just as the

State intervention with which we are familiar is sometimes rational and sometimes just planned chaos. Let this be reiterated: there is no necessary connection between planning and rationality, except in the banal sense that a primitive mind is unable to make plans. Actually, I do not even see why such a connection should be postulated and expected. After all the idea of planning has not been a discovery of the economists. It was put forth by the socialists, and this means that, historically, it constitutes a response to demands for distributive justice, not to the demands of reason, not to "reasons of reason."

Thus when we ask rational planning of our politicians, we are asking for the very thing that is hardest to obtain. This is not a reason for waiving the request, but it certainly is a reason for being clear-headed about it. Hence, it is important that we understand clearly in what sense and for what purpose one may speak of planning in the meaning number one, as "rationally calculated action."

In this meaning, planning is a normative, not a descriptive concept. In order to avoid misunderstandings, we must therefore distinguish between two different contexts. In the first of them we are faced with the following continuum: laissez faire, State regulation, limited planning, total planning. In the second context the continuum is instead: rational planning, social or welfare planning, and so forth. Limited planning and total planning both refer to a thing. Planning, as rational action, represents the normative assertion that planning, any planning, *ought to be* rational. It does not refer to a thing, but rather to one of the criteria on the basis of which planning may be carried out or assessed. And it must be stressed that it is only one such criterion, for it is not, indeed, the only one. Planning may also be assessed in terms of its social value, or in terms of just, or even literal equality: and each of these methods of assessment is perfectly legitimate. So it is important not only that we keep the descriptive meanings distinct from the normative use of planning, but also that we do not take rationality as *the* necessary standard of a planning policy. Otherwise, if we keep conferring a priori the halo of "rational progress" upon any form of planning, we will very likely end up by being deceived. Socialist poverty, as Peguy calls it, may be preferred to capitalist welfare, but there is nothing rational about this choice.

If there is often confusion and misunderstanding between the man of science and the man of politics, this is all the more true among the intellectual elites themselves. The polemics over the so-called grand alternatives, over which, roughly speaking, the scholarly generation of the fifties is arrayed against that of the thirties, provides ample evidence of this.

The generation of the thirties followed, in substance, the lead provided by Ludwig von Mises's criticism of a centrally directed economy in his *Die Gemeinwirtschaft*.[10] In the subsequent development of this line of criticism—which paralleled, let it be noted, the changes and developments in the Soviet experience of planning—three major points were raised. Roughly speaking, they were the following: (i) that centrally directed total planning is impracticable,[11] or (ii) that it can function economically only if operated according to marginal principles,[12] and (iii) that in any case collective planning requires a totalitarian dictatorship.[13] These views provoked, of course, considerable opposition;[14] but it cannot be denied, I believe, that the critics of the Mises-Hayek line took them seriously, and that a great deal of readjustment in the laborite and social-democratic conceptions of planning followed as a consequence of the neo-liberal warnings.[15]

The atmosphere of the fifties is quite different. The two basic problems discussed by the preceding generation, namely (i) whether one ought or ought not to plan, and (ii) whether democracy and planning can coexist, tend to be simply dismissed.[16] These are undoubtedly very broad generalizations, but I venture to say that in these last years the prevailing thesis has been that the "plan or no plan" dilemma is superseded, because it stands as a fact that every organized society requires planning. As to the query whether democracy and planning are compatible, it often receives the triumphant answer that, as anyone can see, the democracies have engaged in planning and no evils have followed. It seems to me, though, that both these arguments miss the point, at least to the extent that they are presented as a rejection of the Mises-Hayek theses; and that, furthermore, the present-day mood of dismissal revealed by these arguments is unhealthy and misleading.

To be sure, if one understands by "planning" merely a rationally preconceived decision-making process, then of course planning occurs, or at least is attempted everywhere. However, this was not the meaning attached to planning by the authors who were discussing the alternative "plan or no plan"; for they were concerned with planning as practiced in the USSR. Therefore, if it pleases us to use "planning" in a sense that is altogether different from the Leninist-Stalinist meaning of the term, we are just dealing with a different point. Likewise, to answer the query whether the loss of democracy is necessarily the price that must be paid in order to have planning by saying that this is a fictitious problem, since "from the middle of the nineteenth century onward the democratic nations became increasingly both . . . planned and unplanned," [17] is not to answer at all. For it was again the Soviet type of planning whose incompatibility with democracy was asserted by von Mises and von Hayek. If, by planning, one means something else, and in particular a mild kind of planning by inducement, then it is a different matter, and nobody would deny that the democracies can, in their own way, make plans. Here again, the victory in the argument is verbal, based on a *quid pro quo*.

It seems to me, therefore, that it is not the debate about the grand alternatives, but, rather, the debate against the grand alternatives that makes little sense. The two generations are not speaking of the same things. Basically, the "no plan" thesis has in mind the third hypothesis (total planning); the thesis unconditionally in favor of planning refers to the first hypothesis (rational decision-making); and the contention that planning and democracy can well co-exist holds, provided that we stop at the second hypothesis (indicative planning).[18] It follows from this that the pertinent question is: what is the proper context and scope of each definition?

The difference, and therefore the root of the misunderstanding between the two generations, lies in the fact that the first generation was envisaging long-range problems, whereas the following generation has short-range problems in its purview. In the former approach one covers a large horizon, but from a distance, with less perception of the details; in the latter, one sees the details but the horizon becomes small. It follows from this that those grand alternatives which are perceived and find their proper relief in the first outlook, fall outside the range of the second. And the reason why we have moved from a long-range to a short-range outlook is that the first generation had a conceptual problem in mind: it was intent upon understanding by means of a conceptual framework what was taking place—whereas the following generation is pragmatically oriented,[19] and thus its problem boils down to this: what really matters is *doing*, and hence what is required is a flexible criterion for action.

But if this is the way things are, then it is absurd to talk of "wrong approaches." For certain purposes one must gain insight into the world of ideas, whereas for others one must learn to move *hic et nunc* in the world of facts. There is no necessary conflict between a conceptual approach which determines the points of reference, and a pragmatic approach which is bent upon solving concrete day-to-day problems in a given setting—between assessing the principles, and ascertaining what one can do today, here, for tomorrow. Some want to *understand* in connection with the need of seeing afar; others want to *act* and are therefore concerned with seeing a-near. The first will probably show up badly in matters of action, as practitioners, and the second in matters of theory and with regard to long-range predictions. This is simply division of labor, and the only implication of this state of affairs is that we do not consult with theorists when we are faced with a practical problem, or with pragmatists when we are up against a conceptual problem.

When this division of roles is made clear, it appears that it is both incorrect and unnecessary to attack the "grand alternatives" and reject them as being unreal and metaphysical dilemmas. Metaphysical —we are told—because governments have in fact a limited range of choice and do not actually make "great global choices among grand alternatives." [20] This is true, but only as far as short-range predictions are concerned, and to the extent that only the governments which have already made their grand choice are taken into account. Obviously the argument did not apply to Russia in Lenin's time, or to China before Mao took over. Nor does it apply to those countries which hang in the balance between the Western and the Communist world. Actually it applies only to what goes on *within* our democracies, to the exclusion of what may happen *about* them. That is to say that the pragmatic approach helps us to travel through the United

States or some other stable democracy: but it is not sufficient, per se, to allow us to travel through the unstable democracies, and much less through the rest of the world.

Pragmatism solves the conceptual problems only insofar as it avoids them, or to the extent that they can be avoided. Actually to define planning as any "rational social action" [21] is merely expedient. Assuming that this word is fashionable and that we have to use it, the pragmatic mind suggests: then let us give it a simple, sensible, unprejudiced meaning. Nonetheless, the "rational social action" meaning of planning can hardly claim a theoretical status. On conceptual grounds this definition is open to a whole series of objections, starting from the classic rule that a necessary condition is not a sufficient condition. But I do not want to go into these objections. My purpose is not to criticize the pragmatic approach but only to point out that there is nothing to be gained by refuting the higher abstractions in order to claim an overriding status for the lower abstractions, while a great deal is to be gained if we take stock of the fact that both conceptual abstractions and operational tools are equally indispensable. A pragmatism with no theoretical background turns into a wishy-washy and parochial conceptualization, just as an overly conceptual approach with no pragmatic follow-up may lead to dogmatic stagnation. In truth, we need both—and there is room for everybody.

3. "Dirigiste" Democracy

So far, I have tried to draw a map and, *pari passu,* to lay to rest discussions which are both sterile and misleading. I would like now to ascertain exactly what our position is. Where do we stand? How far have we got? By way of a first approximation I would locate our present position as follows: we are looking forward to a more "rational" social and economic order,[22] and we are speaking a great deal about "democratic planning" as a necessity. However, it would be hasty to assert that we are making much progress either in the first or in the second direction. Actually, very few Western Societies can be correctly described as planned societies, whether we take as a baseline the criterion offered by definition number one (rationality), or the minimal requirements of definition number two (limited planning). In some instances we find a great deal of State ownership, and in most instances we see that State intervention becomes more and more massive. Indeed, we plan to plan, but the actual performance does not seem to measure up to the requirements it should meet in order for us to be entitled to call our democracies "planned democracies" proper.[23] Where is coordination? Where is the over-all project? And, if there is such a thing on paper, who is enforcing it?[24] We can build up a mountain by piling regulations, interventions, and socializations upon one another, but this mountain does not add up to a "plan" if the whole is not organically connected.

In effect, we are neither planned nor unplanned. We are located at a point which is not yet marked on our map,[25] and which I shall identify, until a better term turns up, by the term *dirigismo,* "dirigisme." [26] It may well be that (democratic) planning is a necessity; but so far it is not a fact. The fact is, rather, that ours are still market systems, partly corrected and partly tampered with. (And whether the improvement is greater than the damage remains an open question.)

Thus we find ourselves living in a *dirigiste* democracy. It is a hybrid, and an illegitimate hybrid at that—an unrecognized child. This is not, however, a sufficient reason for us to view *dirigiste* democracy with suspicion. History is full of hybrids, often queer ones, that have been regretted after their departure. On the other hand, it would be hasty to say that *dirigiste* democracy necessarily constitutes a transitional phase. If this were truly the case, we would not need to give our present position a name of its own; merely saying that we are "traveling toward" a planned set-up, would do. But *are* we traveling in that direction? I am not sure. For the only sure thing is that *dirigisme* will not turn into planning out of sheer inertia or by way of a natural metamorphosis.

Dirigiste democracy was born out of no pre-established plan, almost *rebus ipsis,* by virtue of the efforts of the "visible hand" to make up for the inadequacies of the "invisible hand." And as long as we proceed in the same way we shall only get bigger, reinforced doses of the same thing. This is tantamount to saying that if we wish to attain that other thing which is (democratic) planning, we must not continue this way. We shall have to make, instead, some structural changes, and, above all, we shall have to face with precise awareness

397

the problems involved. What is actually taking place, however, is very different, for we are confronted, with wishful thinking or sheer protest. I mean that most people either mistake the present state of things (*dirigisme*) for a situation (planning) which does not yet exist, or—passing to the other extreme—get so dissatisfied with the existing state of affairs that they are led to demand total planning, jumping, as it were, over democracy's head.

We ought not to dismiss lightly this last hypothesis, namely that we may take the step from *dirigisme,* not into democratic planning, but, if anywhere, into total and/or totalitarian planning. Indeed our ambitions are growing at such a pace that one really wonders how democracy's legs may keep up with them. For we are moving swiftly toward a technological world [27] whose ideals and requirements are bound to permeate and to reshape our very view of life. Over a century ago, Renan could write: "To organize humanity scientifically, this is modern science's ultimate word, this is its daring but legitimate claim." Renan was still speaking as a philosopher and in a prophetic style.[28] Today, however, the technological *forma mentis* is truly in the making, and this mental pattern envisions a perfectly pre-ordered and calculated society. The ideal, or, as I would rather say, the ambition, of a technological age materializes as a sort of engineering of history that strives toward the best of all possible worlds which scientific knowledge can and will design.

Now, let us be clear-headed about this. If democratic planning is judged by this standard, its respect for freedom in the choice of one's vocation (and for other freedoms as well) can only appear a form of disorder. Furthermore, it is materially impossible for democracy to attain the goal of a "scientific society" no matter how much we are willing to adapt its structure in view of the performance required of it. If this is the goal, limited planning, i.e., the kind of planning that is compatible with democracy, cannot be enough.

4. The Problem of Power

When we discuss laissez faire, or *dirigisme,* or planning (either limited or total), we should never forget that we are not discussing only an economic problem. Over and above the strictly technical and economic questions of minimizing costs and maximizing returns (and the like), the discussion involves a basic political question, namely, the problem of power—a power which is unceasingly strengthening and expanding itself. Weak and impotent as our democracies may often be, the fact remains that in the contemporary world the "power potential" has taken on dimensions which even our imagination, in its wildest flights, finds it difficult to envision. For a technological age supplies instruments which can multiply a thousand-fold the material force of man—and of a single man. We are witnessing a frightful increase in Power (I use a capital letter to allude to its potential), and this because its possibilities are practically beyond any physical limit.

The political problem, that is, the problem of the sovereign power, of State power, becomes by the same token more acute, more vital than ever. We must therefore ask ourselves: What is the democratic position on the problem of power? Better put, what is the liberal-democratic solution of the problem of power? Prima facie it would appear that there is no unequivocal answer to this query, since two opposite views are held.

The first view is that Continental democracies have—historically speaking—carried forward the work of the absolute monarchies, by acting as supreme levelling powers which have destroyed all inter-mediate powers.[29] Democracy, in this view, has meant a menacing concentration of power in the State; for once the intermediate *loci* of power between the citizens and the State have been demolished, all that is left is a boundless plain of subjects which can be easily dominated from the only extant summit. But while some authors view with apprehension the disruption of all the peripheral and autono-mous centers of power which could somehow counteract the demo-cratically legitimate central power, other authors seem to hold an opposite view. For the present-day democracies are being denounced for tolerating—under the cover of formal equality—the growth of economic inequalities, and indeed for permitting the formation of gigantic financial and capitalistic power holdings which often appear to be stronger than the State itself.

These two diagnoses appear diametrically opposed to one an-other. According to the first, democracy levels everyone down into impotence. According to the second, democracy is itself impotent

399

because it is overpowered by economic powers. In the first case it is said: by its equalizing action democracy makes everyone powerless before the Leviathan. In the second case it is argued: democracy does not equalize at all—indeed it is itself deprived of its power by *de facto* potentates. Thus, while the first thesis demands that concentrated power be decentralized, the second advocates a strengthening of the central power, and, in view of this, the entrusting of economic power no less than political power to the State.

We should not fail to see, however, that these two diagnoses refer to different problems. Those who stress the danger of an enormous concentration of power in the State view the problem in a political framework, whereas those who demand more power for the State are motivated by a concern for socio-economic justice. But if this is the case, we need not discuss which of these two views is valid. Once we have discounted the exaggerations of either approach (but especially of the second, since there is some fantasy in the image of an octopus-like all-powerful Capitalism depicted by socialist literature), we may well admit that both views are correct, each in its own context.

Thus the politically-minded observer may well feel that democratic equalization creates a vacuum of power in social life; and he may rightly lay stress on the fact that if we distributed the same minimal amount of power equally among all the members of the society, no one would be endowed with a sufficient amount of it: so that the whole operation would amount to a mere pulverization of these powers. As a consequence, the politically-minded rightly favor pluralistic solutions, the existence of innumerable active and autonomous centers of power which the State is strong enough to discipline but not to destroy.[30] On the other hand, those who view the problem of power in an economic framework are well entitled to be concerned over the existence of power imbalances which betray the spirit of democracy and belie its seeming equality. For their attention is focused primarily not on the citizen-State relationship, but rather on the relationship between employers and employees.

The foregoing does not mean that when we are asked, "What is the democratic solution to the problem of power?" we have to answer: There are two mutually exclusive ones. For the answer issuing from a concern over economic power relationships comes *after* the one issuing from a concern over political power relationships. Even if we assume that political democracy is less important than so-called economic democracy, the order of procedural priorities still indicates that we cannot put economic democracy ahead of political democracy. One cannot solve the so-called social question simply by putting the problem of the State into brackets, for the solution of the socio-economic problem is demanded of the State. Therefore the problem of power becomes relevant to the employer-employee relationship only *postea*. It is relevant *antea,* in terms of procedure, to the citizen-State relationship. And as regards the political problem of power, it is not two solutions that are available, but just one.

Empirically speaking, the people and the State are two very distinct entities.[31] To put it more precisely, the referent of the word "people" is not the referent of the word "State." We may speak, if we wish to do so, of the democratic State as a "people's State." Nevertheless, this image only indicates that a bridge is now connecting the two banks—and a bridge does not replace the banks, it presupposes them. So no matter how much we toy with the sentence "the people are the State," it is the bridge, not the banks, that is precarious and ephemeral. Leaving metaphors aside, the State is not *the* people, but only some (actually *few*) people who are seated in a particular *locus* called State. It follows from this that the power which materially belongs to the State does not belong to the people, and vice versa that the people's power is not the State's. Therefore, the more power is vested in the State, the less stays with the people. Conversely, an authentic "State of the people" would be one where, at the limit, the *demos* took away all the State's power.

Two consequences follow: (i) all that can be done concretely from the outside consists in limiting and controlling the State's power, and (ii) this requires power to be adequately spread and distributed. In regard to the means, the technique for neutralizing power is not to allow too powerful powers to exist: i.e., the device is to allow the existence of counter-powers. In regard to the end, which is the democratization of power, the requirement is that these counter-powers be, to a large extent, of a democratic kind, that power becomes diffuse, that it be made to flow over the whole of social life,

401

and that it be vested in innumerable voluntary associations, in private governments. And we know of no solution other than this.[32]

Not only is this the democratic solution to the problem of power, it is also the *porro unum* of democracy—and we could also say, going back in time, the core of the political tradition of the West. For the whole of Western tradition has been endlessly concerned with this basic demand: that power be depersonalized, that impersonal power be substituted for personal power, that the person-in-office be absorbed into the office. The first answer to the query, "Why democracy?" is then the following: democracy is still the only political formula we know of which can solve the problem of man's power over man. In other words, the very *raison d'être* of democracy lies in this fact: that it provides a solution for the *problem-of-the-persons* to whom power is to be entrusted. But democracy succeeds, on the whole, in exorcizing arbitrary and personal power precisely because it is a mechanism purposely created to this end. It works with this task in view. It is effective to the extent that it serves this purpose. What about other purposes? In particular, is democracy an adequate instrument in view of the ambitions of a technological age, of an age that looks forward to the "planning of history"?

If we manage to control power, this is largely because democracy works, in practice, as a device for slowing down, filtering, and decanting the processes of power. From the standpoint of the speed at which it works, democracy entails a rather slow and halting process of decision-making; and from the standpoint of its scope of action, democracy implies the restriction of the range of decisions to a somewhat limited area. We cannot avoid paying a price and accepting certain limitations if we want to tame power. The price is a kind of temporizing inertia, often a lack of resolution, and, what is more, a remarkable waste of effort. And the main limitation lies in this: the very purpose of neutralizing the power of those in command sets the boundaries of the area that can be covered by policies acting through democratic channels. It follows from this that if we demand of democracy a stepped-up process of transformation acting with marked decision over a wide area, we are bound to wreck the system. Nor is it difficult to understand why.

A democratic system does not require nor presuppose a qualifica-

402

tion for politics. In a democracy, even the professional political leader is hardly an expert (I mean somebody having an *ad hoc* training and background). And there is nothing absurd about this, provided the system is not asked to extend its action beyond the limits within which its premises hold: that is, provided that the policies enacted by parliaments and by democratic governments be confined within the area where the expert and expertise are not needed. For it is not true in principle that politics, as such, does not require specific knowledge and competence. It is only true that a *certain kind* of politics can do without the expert: specifically the "small politics" whose primary concern is to guarantee man from despotic domination. In other words, the democratic postulate that politics does not involve special qualification is valid insofar as democratic politics remains, we might say, a middle-range politics. If a political system is grounded on the assumption that everybody is able, by birthright, to handle political affairs, then it must comply with its own assumption, and thereby recognize that certain boundaries are not to be crossed: namely, that the range of the political decision-making allowed by the system must exclude the sectors and types of intervention which would require a qualified and specialized leadership.

This means, in plain terms, that to the extent that democracy is based on lack of expertise it does not provide a foundation from which to launch into the building-up of a society of reason—that is, from which to enter into the "grand politics" of an engineering of history. If we want democracy, we must be content with what it provides. Otherwise, if we want a rational society, then we shall have to call upon the experts and entrust ourselves to them unreservedly. For it is absurd to fire the engineers and then expect any bricklayer to do their work. An operation requires a surgeon, and if we do not want the surgeon we shall have to do without the operation. Do we partake of the ideal "represented by the man whose . . . ambition is to turn the world . . . into an enormous machine, every part of which, on his pressing a button, moves according to his design"? [33] Fine. But the price to be paid for this clockwork world is democracy.

I am not concerned with arguing whether the ideal of a future meticulously calculated and worked out in advance by a supermind be a palatable one. We must realize, however, that democracy is not only an inadequate *instrument* for achieving that goal, but also that the ideals of a clockwork world on the one hand, and of a liberal-democratic society on the other, are directly opposed to each other *as ideals*. On the basis of our conception of life, it makes no sense that someone should be in charge of predetermining and calculating how we should achieve happiness, what we should want, and what we should value. We have been brought up to believe that everybody has his own wants for his own reasons. In this *Weltanschauung,* to objectivize the world of preferences, of happiness, of goals, amounts to an ultimate form of bondage, since it means that we are treating man as an "object" and thus depriving him of the very reason for his existence. In the democratic conception of life in particular, the people's interest can be determined only by the people's will. This does not only mean that there is no other way of making sure that it is the interest of the people that shall be attended to. It also means that man is interested in what *he himself wants,* not in what someone else wants for him.

We may grant, by way of hypothesis, that sometime in the future our know-how may make possible such a science of society as could really master the world of man. Even in such a situation, however, our conception of life would demand that the expert not be in charge of deciding for the non-experts what is the good life. The social engineer would not be asked to tell us what we should want and which goals we should seek. He would be in charge, rather, of warning us in advance about our mistakes, and of telling us ahead of time what we might run into if we chose to launch upon a given venture.[34]

5. Inconsistencies

At the midpoint of the twentieth century we find ourselves half-way between these two extremes: a government of the non-experts over the experts, or a government planned out by the experts without democracy. The democratic postulate of "no qualification" had its purest expression in the *polis,* where officials were appointed by lot. Today we apply it to a lesser extent, since, after all, elections are expected to sort out some "elected" people, that is, to make a selection. In the framework of a democracy intent upon planning, that postulate will have to find a still more restricted application.

And beyond this point, it simply will not be applied at all: when total planning is sought, then the democratic incompetence must yield before technocratic competence.

One of the most striking features of the present time is an ever-growing gap between the know-how acquired by some people who are not entitled to make decisions (economists, political scientists, etc.), and the amateurism of the actual decision-makers. And unless democracy is rapidly to become a very old-fashioned—and inefficient—political form, we shall have to reduce this imbalance between, let us say, a powerless knowledge and an all-powerful ignorance. That is, we shall have to surrender, in the long run, to the need for proceeding swiftly in the direction of a democracy which, without being governed by experts, relies openly on their advice. Actually, despite all the talk to the contrary, we are moving toward *less* power of the people. The obvious reason for this is that a maximum of popular power is possible only in simple societies whose leadership-tasks are relatively elementary. As the mechanisms of social and economic life become more and more complex, interlocking, and pre-ordained, the expert's opinion must acquire a much greater weight than his vote as an elector. Even though electoral or similar reasons may lead the politician to disregard the specialist's advice, already today the "power of initiative" tends to shift from the parliament and the executive toward brain trusts and the research and reference services.

These facts must be clearly perceived and acknowledged, because if we want democracy to survive it must work, and in order for it to work we have to realize that we must put our house in order. That is to say, that if we want our State to become an "economic State," then we must ensure that it be made to function; that the notion of democracy be understood in accordance with the recognition of the role of the expert; and, at the same time, that the boundaries of the latter's intervention be well defined and firmly established.[35]

If these conditions are complied with, I feel that we can envisage with confidence the possibility of a planned democracy proper, even if in this case the area of operation of democratic mechanisms will have to suffer, in comparison with a *dirigiste* democracy, further restrictions. This fact should not alarm us, for a democracy survives as long as what is essential—and therefore *must* be controlled—is kept within the area of democratic control. Bureaucracy, for example, is not organized in accordance with democratic criteria; yet we are not dismayed by this. This is still more the case with the military establishments (and it is worthwhile to point out that even in Greek democracy the choice of the *strategoi,* the military commanders, was an exception to the rule of appointment by lot). Actually we can observe, in general, that most of the organisms at work within a democratic regime do not have a democratic structure. So we may well contend that the introduction of planning need not pose insoluble problems—on one condition, however: that we give them careful thought, and that, to begin with, we become aware of the fact that we *are* confronted with problems to be solved.[36] Instead most people seem to live deep in a sort of dreamland, that is, deep in contradiction: for they would like to play half-back on the field and at the same time lead the cheers.

When John Stuart Mill argued that men and women must have political rights "not in order that they may govern, but in order that they may not be misgoverned," [37] he conceived of democracy in a way that is suited to the requirements of a democracy intent upon planning. But if we think, instead, that men and women ought actively to govern, then it is absurd to advocate planning, since the latter requires that the non-expert be subordinated to the expert, and will thus have to become, more and more, a *governed* rather than a *governing* democracy. It is all the more absurd to want, at the same time, a world where the good life is to be chosen *subjectively,* and a world where a technological sophocracy is charged with choosing the *objective* good life. Nor does it make any sense to develop on the one hand a political mechanism meant to work through a minimal expertise and within the limits of a *generic reasonableness*—that is, on the basis of common sense—and to claim on the other hand that the same mechanism meet the demands of a specialized, *scientific reason.*

Our democracies—from a functional standpoint—are at a disadvantage because we keep requiring that increasingly technical problems be solved by just anyone. Yet many people, and most politicians, act as if the slogan "ever more democracy" were a remedy for the ill doings of unskillfullness. And since at the same time the same people ask for "ever more planning," all of this goes to show that we are afflicted by schizophrenia, that our intelligence is losing control over the facts, and that it is high time that we clarified our thinking and made our choices. For we cannot *have* both, namely more democracy (i.e., a maximum of popular power) and more planning (i.e., more power for the planners). We may only *ask* for both: and this means that our head will be proceeding in one direction while our steps will be going in another. Do we need to be told the rest of the story? That is, do we need to be told that by going along with our eyes turned to the left and our legs moving toward the right, we shall finally stumble—and in a final way?

6. The Government of Science

I have no business preaching goals, and it is not my task to show which value preferences we ought to pursue. I am simply saying: whatever goal we choose let us be consistent, and in particular let us make no mistakes in regard to the means. And I am laying the emphasis on the problem of how the desired goals can be attained, because I am under the impression that the drift we have been following implies a very basic mistake as far as the calculation of the means is concerned.

In making its estimates, reason is often tempted to forget that, when all is said and done, it is not *reasons* but *persons*—not disembodied ideas but incarnate ideas—who are to govern us even in a world governed by reason, as it were. This is, of course, a very tempting omission. Thus Marx and Engels found a solution to all difficulties by predicting that in the future the "government of things" would take the place of the "government of men." [38] And today a similar simple fiction makes us envision in a rose-colored light all of tomorrow's problems, by suggesting that a government of science will take care of them all—the assumption being, as A. Downs well points out, "that governments are not institutions run by men, but are depersonalized frictionless machines which operate according to mathematical rules. . . . Being machines, they have no private motives. Being frictionless, their particular processes of operation do not affect their outputs." [39]

Certainly, if we place the impersonal majesty of Science and

407

Reason where the more prosaic reality of persons should be, then everything fits beautifully and turns out smoothly—in theory. However, not in history, that is, not when the real actors replace the fictitious ones. Government will always be of men, never of things, and, furthermore, no government is a frictionless machine made up of perfect altruists.

But let us look more closely into the matter. For instance, what exactly does the expression "government of science" mean? If we understand by it that technicians and scientists will replace politicians, that is, that the future politician will be recruited among technicians and/or scientists, this is not only a very hazardous prediction, but also a solution which would not settle the problem at all. Even assuming that the role of the politicians will be taken on by scientists, this does not settle the question whether they will act, in their political capacity, as scientists. I mean that a government of scientists may well have little in common with a government of science, except in the displeasing sense that the "scientific politician," so to speak, will use his technical know-how as a very effective *instrumentum regni,* as a perfect instrument of domination. However, that politicians will be replaced by scientists is indeed a very unlikely hypothesis. What is likely, on the contrary, is that the scientist will be put to use by the politician, and that the technical skill of the former will prove very useful to those who know how to master not knowledge, but men.[40]

Therefore, the idea of a government of science can arouse pleasant and hopeful associations only to the extent that it hinges on the idea of a phantomatic, disembodied "government of Reason." But in this case we are heading toward endless and severe delusions. That the politics of the future will become merely a matter of deciding how to get at scientifically established goals through scientifically calculated means, or that it will consist simply in choosing the best among the projects put together by the experts—these are nice fairy tales which will be followed, if we let them lull us to sleep, by a bitter awakening. The depersonalization of power has indeed been a task to which Western man has devoted all of his political ingenuity. Yet it would be reckless to say that we have succeeded in making the politician into a mere administrator of the public interest whose sole motivation is discharge of a social function providing benefits to other men. But if the conversion of politics into administration is a myth, how much more will this be the case with regard to a conversion of policy-making into a science at the expense (let us not forget it) of a system of "control over persons"? To be sure, "If men were good these counsels would not be good"; or, as an author of the *Federalist* wrote, somewhat echoing Machiavelli, "If men were angels there would be no need for government." [41] But men are not angels, and although we need not give up the ultimate hope of making man good, I find it indeed hard to understand how any positive result can be achieved by forgetting about his existence, that is, by excluding the variable "human beings" from our calculations and pretending that they are not there. The problem is precisely that they *are* there!

Too many of our contemporaries—spoiled by the effortless enjoyment of a freedom which they did nothing to establish—are behaving as if the problem of power had been solved once and for all. Since their fathers handed down to them a domesticated power, their sole concern has become the planning of rational and functional societies *sub specie* of wholly depoliticalized societies. This is the reason why, in designing the best of all possible worlds, they leave gaping holes through which despotic, uncontrolled power is bound to re-enter. For the hard reality of politics takes its revenge upon those who neglect it,[42] and indeed will take advantage of such careless inattention. The technician, the specialist, the engineer, the manager, all the new protagonists of a polytechnical age are—for the same reasons that this used to be the case with regard to the philosopher—the natural allies of despotism. It is not that they wish to be the midwives of totalitarian tyranny. It is simply that the solutions they propose lead to this outcome, whether they are aware of it or not.

Hölderlin wrote: "What has always made the State into a hell on earth has been precisely man's attempt to make it into his heaven." [43] Yet Hölderlin could not even imagine the Moloch which today's State threatens to become. Talk about Leviathan! Technology multiplies ad infinitum the potential impact and reach of the secular arm. Hardly any material impossibility curtails the power of power today. At this stage, power can indeed become virtually limitless. In view of these perspectives, I am inclined to think that an excess of prudence would be better than making false moves. And, as it is our ambition to master the world—man's world, not just nature's—through the mind, I confess that I concur fully with what Hayek has recently written: "Not the least important task for human reason [is] rationally to comprehend its own limitations." [44] I know that reason is a good servant, but I am afraid of those who serve it. I employ it because I cannot do otherwise; but I do not worship it, because I know how fallible it can be.

NOTES

† Silvio Spaventa, *La politica della destra* (Bari, 1910), p. 473.

1. The French proposed many: "directed economy" on the one hand, and on the other the more bland formulae of a "concerted," "controlled," or "organized" economy; but the most characteristic label was the first one, set forth by Bertrand de Jouvenel, in *L'Économie dirigée* (Paris, 1928). The Italians adopted the label *economia programmatica* (programmed economy), while the Germans used *Planwirtschaft*. The sense of this search for an *ad hoc* denomination was twofold: to indicate the end of the "spectator State" while differentiating this new Western trend from the Soviet collectivistic economy. For an extensive survey, cf. *La crisi del capitalismo* (Firenze, 1933) with contributions by Pirou, Sombart, Durbin, Patterson, Spirito; and esp. *L'economia programmatica* (Firenze, 1933), with contributions by Brocard, Landauer, J. A. Hobson, Lorwin, Dobbert, Spirito. Both volumes have an extensive bibliography by G. Bruguier.

2. *Politics, Economics and Welfare,* p. 20. Cf. *passim* Chaps. I-III.

3. It is the label suggested by Ugo G. Papi in the collective volume *Pianificazione economica in regime democratico* (Roma, 1953).

4. Cf. in general the joint work *Pianificazione economica in regime democratico;* and *La pianificazione economica e i diritti della persona umana* (Roma, 1955), esp. the contribution of G. Di Nardi, pp. 55-72.

5. Ruth Glass, e.g., notes: "The Americans, therefore, talk of the need to 'co-ordinate planning,' while to the European planning implies co-ordination (though it may not be effective)." *International Social Science Journal,* Vol. XI (1959), No. 3, p. 406. This difference in itself implies many others.

6. Cf. in particular M. Polanyi in *Colloques de Rheinfelden,* pp. 122-141, and the following discussions. For an earlier assessment cf. Robert Mossé, *L'Économie collectiviste* (Paris, 1939), Part II.

7. For a sympathetic exposition cf. Ch. Bettelheim, *Les Problèmes théoriques et*

pratiques de la planification (Paris, 1946). As for the principles of Marxist political economy, cf. for all Paul M. Sweezy, *The Theory of Capitalist Development* (New York, 1942).

8. Somewhat emphatically but exactly E. H. Carr states: "The economic impact of the Soviet Union on the rest of the world may be summed up in the single word 'planning.'" *The Soviet Impact on the Western World* (New York, 1949), p. 20.

9. Technically, and juridically, nationalization and socialization are not the same, and can also be distinguished from State ownership (*statalizzazione*) and collectivization. But for the purpose of this discussion these distinctions are not relevant.

10. First published in 1922, and then revised and translated into English in 1936 with the title *Socialism* (London, 1936).

11. This was Mises's initial thesis. But one should remember that at the time it was formulated his referent was the "War Communism" of 1921-1922. For a more precise formulation of this thesis—which maintains that in the absence of a market resources cannot be rationally allocated—see the fine symposium by Hayek, Mises, N. G. Pierson, and Halm, *Collectivist Economic Planning* (London, 1935). On the problem of economic calculations in a planned system, cf. finally T. J. B. Hoff, *Economic Calculation in the Socialist Society* (London, 1949).

12. This view was stated by F. H. Knight in "The Place of Marginal Economics in a Collectivist System," *American Economic Review*, March 1936, Suppl. The first anticipations on how a socialist economy could be operated are, however, to be found in Pierson, Pareto and Enrico Barone.

13. This is the thesis which has been particularly stressed by Friedrich A. von Hayek, esp. in *The Road to Serfdom*. However this view is shared, although in a less dramatic form, by all the aforementioned critics.

14. Reaching highly emotional tones in Finer's excessive reply to Hayek. Cf. Herman Finer, *Road to Reaction* (New York, 1945).

15. In fact, beginning from 1933 a large part of the supporters of a socialist economy readmits the market as an indispensable instrument for allocating resources, either in the form of a publicly owned marketing economy, or at any rate as an accounting method for prices analogous to market competition. Cf. Oskar Lange in O. Lange, F. M. Taylor, *On the Economic Theory of Socialism* (Minneapolis, 1938); A. P. Lerner, *Economics of Control* (New York, 1944); and H. D. Dickinson, *Economics of Socialism* (Oxford, 1939).

16. Thus John Friedmann, editor of the issue of the *International Social Science Journal* (UNESCO), dedicated to the "Study and Practice of Planning" (Vol. XI (1959), No. 3, p. 327) comes out with this bold assertion: "For perhaps

two decades the great debate about planning has raged. Now it is over. The question has been resolved. The great protagonists . . . are silent. The field has been taken over by other men. We no longer ask: Is planning possible? Can planning be reconciled with a democratic ideology? But: How may existing planning practice be improved? The problem of planning has become a problem of procedure and method." I quote this passage for its testimonial value of a climate of opinion.

17. R. A. Dahl, in *Research Frontiers in Politics and Government*, p. 46.

18. The implication of these specifications with reference to the neo-liberal theses is that Mises and Hayek can be accused of having exaggerated as regards the hypothesis of a "limited indicative planning" (and up to this point we can accept Barbara Wooton's reply, *Freedom under Planning* [London, 1945], and with it many others of a similar tenor). But I do not think that Mises and Hayek are wrong as regards the hypothesis of "total collective planning": in this connection none of the confutations seem convincing. Cf., however, for a defense of the Communist thesis, Maurice Dobb, *Political Economy and Capitalism* (London, rev. ed. 1940), Chap. VIII.

19. Considered in this light I have nothing to object to the statement made by Dahl and Lindblom: "Plan or no plan is no choice at all; the pertinent questions turn on particular techniques: who shall plan, for what purposes, in what conditions, and by what devices?" (*Politics, Economics and Welfare*, p. 5). Very true, but for the United States.

20. In *Research Frontiers*, etc., p. 46. Cf. also in *Politics, Economics and Welfare*, p. 5, where Dahl and Lindblom speak of "tyranny of the *isms*" and assert: "the great issues are no longer the great issues, if ever they were."

21. Dahl and Lindblom, *op. cit.*, p. 300. Cf. also Dahl in *International Social Science Journal*, Vol. XI (1959), No. 3, p. 340: ". . . now planning is more and more regarded as equivalent to rational social action, that is, as a social process for reaching a rational decision."

22. At least in the "functional" sense of rationality (coordination between means and ends) indicated by Mannheim. Cf. *Man and Society in an Age of Reconstruction*, pp. 52-60.

23. Perhaps the only satisfactory case in this connection is the Swedish one. Cf. Gunnar Hecksher, "Pluralist Democracy—The Swedish Experience," *Social Research* (Dec. 1948), pp. 418-461.

24. The following testimony by a former English minister describes a situation which is certainly not any better in the parliamentary systems on the continent, and which holds true also for the United States: "The one thing that is hardly ever discussed is general policy. . . . There are only departmental policies. . . . The whole system is one of mutual friction and delay with at best some partial measures of mutual adjustment between unrelated policies.

It is quite incompatible with any coherent planning of policy as a whole or with the effective execution of such a policy." (Cit. in S. E. Finer, *A Primer of Public Administration* [London, 1950], p. 51.)

25. For locating this point in descriptive terms, cf. the over-all comparative review of government economic planning in Gunnar Myrdal, *Beyond the Welfare State* (New Haven, 1960).

26. I have been uncertain whether to translate literally the Italian term or to substitute for it, for example, the label "Amphibial State," coined in 1948 by Schumpeter. However, in Schumpeter's meaning the amphibial State covers the entire span which runs between capitalism and full-fledged socialist planning, whereas I am concerned with distinguishing an amphibian solution located between market and democratic planning (indicated by the term "dirigisme") from the following (hypothetical) amphibian solution located between democratic planning and totalitarian planning. On the other hand, and semantically speaking, "dirigisme" conveys the idea that I wish to convey, i.e., of a system which is "directed" but, on the whole, directed without "plan."

27. So swiftly that after twenty-seven years Aldous Huxley was able to write a second counter-utopia, *Brave New World Revisited* (New York, 1958), introduced with these words: "In 1931 when *Brave New World* was being written I was convinced that there was still plenty of time. . . . The prophecies made in 1931 are coming true much sooner than I thought they would" (pp. 3-4).

28. *L'Avenir de la science* (Paris, 1890), p. 37. Reran's was the language of Condorcet and Saint-Simon. "The science which will govern the world," he wrote in the same passage "will not be politics . . . but philosophy." Cf. G. La Ferla, *Renan politico* (Torino, 1953), *passim*.

29. This is notably the thesis set forth in Tocqueville's *L'Ancien Régime et la révolution*.

30. It is maintained that social pluralism is the equivalent of the constitutional separation of powers. I agree on this parallelism, as long as it remains understood that a social pluralism lacking constitutional protection is of itself ineffective: i.e., it cannot replace but only implement what could be called "constitutional pluralism."

31. This elementary observation is often obscured by the fact that jurists try to reconcile the sovereignty of the people with that of the State. But one must not confuse the political theory of (democratic) sovereignty with the juridic theory of (state) sovereignty. The first is intended to legitimize or disclaim the legitimacy of a government, while the second is intended to make the government possible.

32. The outcome of the "democratic centralism" advocated by Lenin is the

most convincing proof *a contrario*. The parable of that experience is well followed by E. H. Carr. *The Bolshevik Revolution*, Vol. I, pp. 184-232.

33. Cf. F. A. Hayek, *The Counter-Revolution of Science: Studies on the Abuse of Reason* (Glencoe, 1952), pp. 101-102.

34. The limit could be stated in this summary fashion: that a government of experts may be admitted in regards to "means" but not to "ends."

35. This warning applies also to Mannheim's suggestions concerning an "indirect planning," i.e., a social science manipulation of the environment from which to obtain spontaneously from the individuals the desired behavior. Cf. "Planned Society and the Problem of Human Personality" in *Essays on Sociology and Social Psychology* (New York, 1953) Part IV; and *Freedom, Power and Democratic Planning* (New York, 1950), *passim*. Mannheim's "planning for freedom" may be a solution, but there is a point in which a planning which operates on the "nature" of man raises this question: Is not the power of the conditioners over the conditioned the same as leaving the latter at the mercy of the former, of the change agent? Mannheim himself was aware of this danger. Answering to the question "Who plans those who do the planning?" he avowed: "The longer I reflect on this question, the more it haunts me." (*Man and Society*, etc., p. 74). As C. S. Lewis aptly puts it, in the final analysis "the power of Man to make himself what he pleases means . . . the power of some men to make other men what *they* please." *The Abolition of Man* (New York, 1947), p. 37. Cf. also section 6, below.

36. Paradoxically, the problem of reconciling democracy with a government of experts was faced with more awareness and attention in the past than in the present. The classic project is still Sidney and Beatrice Webb, *A Constitution for the Socialist Commonwealth of Great Britain* (London, 1920), which in substance proposes to allow Parliament the right to discuss but not to decide, except for approving the reports made by the experts. But the solution offered by the Webbs had its starting points in *Considerations on Representative Government* (cf. esp. Chap. V) by J. S. Mill, who had in turn felt the influence of the Benthamist Edwin Chadwick. Among the relatively few contemporary authors who have been preoccupied with this problem, cf. H. Laski's *Fabian Tract* n. 235 (1931).

37. *Representative Government* (New York, 1951), p. 391.

38. So affirmed Engels in *Antidüring*, Pt. III, Chap. II. For the sake of accuracy one should note that the substitution of the administration of things for the government of persons is a thesis advanced by Saint-Simon. For this reason Röpke has rightly called "eternal Saint-Simonism" the ideal of a technocracy of social engineers. See his chapter "Ewiger Saint-Simonismus," *Civitas humana*, (Erlenbach-Zürich, 1949), pp. 133 f.

414

39. Anthony Downs, *An Economic Theory of Democracy* (New York, 1957), pp. 285-286. And cf. *passim* Chap. XV, "A Comment on Economic Theories of Government Behavior" for a number of penetrating remarks.

40. For a criticism of the "technocratic ideology," cf., finally, Jean Meynaud, *Technocratie et politique* (Lausanne, 1960), Part II.

41. *The Federalist*, No. 51. The authorship of this paper is not certain, but it is probably Madison's.

42. The entire course of the Soviet experience with respect to the ideals which inspired the Revolution of 1918 should be considered from this very point of view: how the Marxist economic therapy of political problems has been reversed in actual operation in the absolute subordination of every aspect of human life to the most integral "reason of State." Today all the Soviet ideology is at the service of politics; and this happens exactly because Marx had forgotten about the political dimension of his economic solutions. Cf. Henri Chambre, *Le Marxisme en Union Soviétique* (Paris, 1955), "Final Remarks."

43. *Hyperion*, Vol. I, Bk. I.

44. *The Counter-Revolution of Science*, p. 92.

Chapter XVII

Another Democracy?

"It is not a question of accepting our time without discussion. Quite the reverse. Every 'our time' carries with it its norm and its abnormality, its commandments and its falsifications. . . . The more seriously one accepts 'his time,' the more vigorously one should not compromise with its frauds."

—Ortega y Gasset†

1. "Democracy" in Marx and Lenin

It is understood in this book that to say "democracy" is the same thing as to say "Western-type democracy." I should not like to be accused of forgetfulness on this account. If I have not considered other types, the omission is, so to speak, necessary, because a theory of democracy has to *define* democracy. I know that some people speak of popular and progressive democracies; but to speak of them does not mean or prove that they exist. Discourses about "another democracy" create, at the most, a presumption. Nobody questions the fact that the USSR, for example, exists as a State; but this does not imply that it exists as a democracy, i.e., that the Soviet political system belongs to the type in which the power of the people is in some way operative.

Anyone intending to make definitory investigation must set out to decide *what is* democracy; and this demands that one should determine what democracy *is not*. Of course, my definition can be wrong.

416

It remains true, nevertheless, that *omnis determinatio est negatio,* that any determination involves a negation, so that anyone taking the trouble to define excludes, by this very act, what is defined inversely. What remains to be seen is whether or not my definition is exact. And from my point of view it will be a question of justifying the exclusion, that is, explaining why I think that the discussion of Western-type democracy is all the discussion to be had about democracy.

Let us distinguish, for convenience of analysis, between the word (with which I shall be concerned in this section), the doctrine, and the facts. And let us begin from the beginning, that is, with Marx and Engels. Marx declared and thought himself a democrat. He used the name democracy, and ended by stating clearly enough what he meant by it. In the *Communist Manifesto* of 1848 Marx had limited himself to asserting that it was the task of the proletariat as a dominating class to "arrive victoriously at democracy" —a democracy referred to as "an association in which the free development of each is the condition for the free development of all." [1] And up to 1870-71 (that is to say, up to the writings on the Paris Commune collected under the title *The Civil War in France*), Marx had not been more specific. He knew what he wanted, but had not concerned himself with how to get it.

The goal was revealed, concretely, by this series of demands, all but one economic in character: 1) expropriation of landed property, 2) heavily graduated income tax, 3) the abolition of all right of inheritance, 4) the confiscation of emigrants' and rebels' property, 5) the centralization of credit in the hands of the State, 6) centralized control of the means of communication and transportation, 7) increase in number of State-owned factories, 8) equal liability of all to labor, 9) combination of agriculture with manufacturing industries, 10) free public education.[2] It appears from this enumeration that the "communist democracy" as it was understood by Marx in its essentials—since for him the economy was the essential—amounted to the measures which would have instituted a classless society, the economic equality of a workers' society.

It was the experience of the Paris Commune which recalled his attention from the *what* to the *how,* from economics to politics, and

in particular to the method of steering the revolution of the proletariat. In his writings of 1871 the political form of his economic democracy materialized by means of the following measures: suppression of the standing army, police, and bureaucracy; universal suffrage; brief duration and revocability of appointments; elective judges
—and even these subject to recall.[3] These measures of the Commune
furnished, according to Marx, "the foundations of true democratic
institutions." [4] However much Marx may have expressed reservations
about the men of the Commune and their tactical ability, he had no
reservation whatever as to the exemplary value of that experience,
which in his opinion had shown "the tendency of a government of
the people on the part of the people." [5] The secret of the Commune,
wrote Marx, "was this: it was essentially a working-class government,
. . . the political form at last discovered under which to work out
the economic emancipation of labor." [6]

As anyone can see, Marx's ideal was the simplest literal democracy, a self-government of the producers so simple and so literal that
Marx reduced the political problem to the elimination of the State
and to the provisions which would have got rid of it for ever.[7] It
may be objected that there is something else; that I have forgotten the
dictatorship of the proletariat. Actually, I have not forgotten it, since
the dictatorship of the proletariat, for Marx, consisted of the measures
of the Paris Commune described above. In 1891 Engels concluded his
Introduction to the new edition of Marx's *The Civil War in France*
with these words: "The German philistine has later been thrown once
again into wholesome paroxysms by the expression 'dictatorship of
the proletariat.' Well, gentle sirs, would you like to know how this
dictatorship looks? Then look at the Paris Commune. That was the
dictatorship of the proletariat." [8]

If Marx allowed this truculent expression to slip from his pen,[9]
his dictatorship of the proletariat was not the establishment of a State-
dictatorship, but the destruction of the State by means of the
proletariat-as-dictator. Dictatorship, for Marx, was simply another
word for "revolution," it only meant the use of force. And he used
the phrase "dictatorship of the proletariat" literally: not to mean dictatorship *in favor* of the proletariat, but to mean direct exercise of force
on the part of the proletariat under arms. Proletariat, in other words,

is the subject of the phrase. Therefore the dictatorship of the proletariat was for Marx the actual revolution of the proletariat, nothing other than "the proletariat organized as the dominating class" [10] which used its own force to dissolve the State and defeat its enemies (not to remake another State to which to give himself again).

One may cavil about Marx's time schedule, and about the difference between the State to be "destroyed" (*zerbrechen*) immediately, at one stroke (the bourgeois State), and the State which-is-not-a-State (one should not forget that Marx was thinking dialectically, in the Hegelian manner) which is the dictatorship of the proletariat, and which should instead "wither away" of its own accord. But in any case, there is no doubt that for Marx the revolution of the proletariat should destroy not only the bourgeois State, but the State in itself; and that the two operations should proceed hand in hand, in a parallel fashion, without the proletariat re-forming a new State, even if it were a proletarian State.[11] The peculiarity or, if one prefers, the anomaly of the dictatorship of the proletariat is precisely that of being a Stateless dictatorship. "The Commune," Engels pointed out in a letter to Bebel, "was no longer a State in the proper sense of the word." [12] And Lenin commented and confirmed in 1917: "The Commune ceased to be a State . . . in the place of a special repressive force, the whole population itself came onto the scene. All this is a departure from the State in its proper sense. And had the Commune asserted itself as a lasting power, remnants of the State would of themselves have 'withered away' within it. . . ." [13]

Clearly, then, the dictatorship of the proletariat is in Marx the emergency self-government (for the period of overt class war) of the proletariat itself, and nothing more.[14] And his democracy is a Stateless democracy, the spontaneous offspring of the happy economic harmony of a society of equals, and nothing more.

If Marx is perfectly clear, in the sense that the simplicity of his conception leaves no doubts, Lenin is very much less so, and indeed becomes extremely obscure. In writing *State and Revolution* Lenin's purpose was, apparently, only to establish the authentic interpretation of Marx's ideas on democracy, the State, and the dictatorship of the proletariat. But it is exactly this which complicates matters. For

419

Lenin introduced, without seeming to, a major variation into the Holy Scriptures, since he considered the relationship between democracy and State in a way that Marx did not. This alters everything, whereas Lenin wished to show that he had changed nothing, that Marx was always with him, or better that he was always with Marx. Moreover Lenin was writing *State and Revolution* when the October Revolution was on the way (the volume bears the date August 1917). He did not have to draw *ex post* the conclusions from a concluded revolution, like Marx in 1871. Lenin was in a hurry, and he had in mind to unleash a revolution. It makes a difference.

The question of democracy is examined by Lenin in relation to three phases of development: the capitalist, the socialist (inferior or incomplete communist phase), and the communist. This tripartite division must not, however, make one believe that the discussion proceeds in an orderly fashion, and that Lenin illustrates three notions of democracy, one for each context. Quite on the contrary, the discussion proceeds haphazardly, and in order to unravel the tangle so as to find the thread of it, it is necessary to distinguish between a basic idea and a series of minor strands.

Basically, the idea of democracy was associated in Lenin with the existence of the State. Democracy, he wrote, "is a form of the State, one of its varieties." [15] Which form? Which variety? To Lenin it did not matter. To him the State, any State, was "an organization of violence for the suppression of some class," it was a "special apparatus for compulsion," or a "special machine for repression." [16] This amounts to saying that to Lenin any State was solely and simply a dictatorship. But if this is so, then "democracy" does not qualify any specific type of State: all States are alike, they all oppress the *demos,* they all are anti-democratic. It should follow from this—logically—that in this connection it is useless to concern oneself with the concept of democracy. If the notion of democracy still retains a meaning, evidently one must seek it elsewhere, outside the realm of the State. But no: to Lenin the equation democracy=State was the primary association, the one on which he laid by far the greatest stress. And the reason for this is not hard to discover: what interested Lenin most of all was to bring charges against democracy. His *leitmotif* was: since the State is bad, democracy is bad too. From the premise that democracy "is a form of the State, one of its varieties" Lenin drew without delay the conclusion "consequently it, like every State, represents . . . the organized, systematic use of violence against persons." [17] Therefore—this was the gist of Lenin's argument—democracy is to be destroyed by the same token by which the State is to be destroyed.[18]

The significant point about this demonstration is that Lenin never made it clear that in speaking of democracy-as-State, and thus of democracy as something to be rejected wholesale, he was alluding to bourgeois democracy. Lenin admitted in a subordinate hypothesis that democracy is also something else. But he did not say that his criticism of democracy qua State system ended where the capitalist conception of democracy ends. He spoke of democracy as the "organized systematic use of violence" in the absolute, as if to say: this is an intrinsic characteristic. We shall see why. At the moment it is of interest to emphasize that if Lenin had been coherent his approach should have brought him to a swift, clear-cut conclusion: to declare openly that he repudiates democracy, that communism has nothing to do with democracy, and that whatever there is in common between democracy and the dictatorship of the proletariat (which should be, according to his definition, the "systematic use of violence"), is only a deplorable transitory necessity.

But when Lenin came to the second phase, to the dictatorship of the proletariat, he changed his tune. He maintained that the dictatorship of the proletariat is "more democratic" than bourgeois democracy. If he meant that in this case the exercise of violence is even more systematic than before, one cannot object: his logic would be faultless. But instead he now used "democracy" in an approbatory sense. In a capitalist society—argued Lenin—democracy is democracy for a minute minority; whereas the dictatorship of the proletariat is democracy for the vast majority, and is dictatorship only as regards a minority of oppressors. The text goes thus: "The dictatorship of the proletariat, i.e., the organization of the vanguard of the oppressed as the ruling class for the purpose of suppressing the oppressors, cannot result merely in an expansion of democracy. *Simultaneously* with an immense expansion of democracy, *which for the first time* becomes democracy for the poor, democracy for the people, and not democracy for the money bags, the dictatorship of the proletariat imposes a series of restrictions on the freedom of the oppressors, the exploiters, the capitalists. We must suppress them . . . their resistance must be crushed by force; and it is clear that where there is suppression, where there is violence, there is no freedom and no democracy." [19]

The passage is interesting for two reasons. The first is that the emphasis tends to be more on the non-democratic than on the democratic aspect of the dictatorship of the proletariat. And the second is that now Lenin means by democracy the opposite of what he did before: in effect, he says quite definitely that the use of repression, the use of violence, is not democracy. What is then his second interpretation—the laudatory one—of democracy? The passage quoted shows that now Lenin is using democracy in its literal sense of "power of the people," and that democracy is associated with liberty. And if we search the entire volume carefully, we shall find here and there, incidentally, those features of the concept which are familiar to us: that democracy is equality, that it is subjugation of the minority to the majority, and even the proposition that "we cannot imagine democracy, even proletarian democracy, without representative institutions." [20] All this, it is true, is conceded in passing, somewhat reluctantly, and always surrounded by evasions and reservations.[21] The fact remains, however, that we find in Lenin a positive meaning of democracy to the extent that he associates the term with its traditional bourgeois connotations. We may put it thus: either Lenin clings to the equation democracy=State, or he is unable to step out of the framework of our concept of democracy. And so we have arrived at this paradoxical conclusion: that to the democracies of the Western type, Lenin applies the characteristics of dictatorship (restriction of liberty and use of force); whereas to the dictatorship of the proletariat he attributes the characteristics of what we call democracy (liberty for the vast majority).

One might object that it is not a paradox because, even if Lenin's exposition is hard to follow, the substance is this: that ours claim to be democracies and are not—whereas in socialism our falsehoods begin to be transplanted into reality, since in the dictatorship of the proletariat the vast majority has the power and the liberty. We need not ascertain whether these are the facts. For the fact is that this was not at all Lenin's logic. If it were, then in the third phase, that of communism, Lenin should have said that with the withering away of the dictatorship of the proletariat, true and complete democracy would be achieved. Period. But he did not say so. Lenin scarcely puts his foot into the realm of the future before he shuffles the cards again.

This passage is revealing: "Only in communist society, only then 'the State ceases to exist,' and it 'becomes possible to speak of freedom.' Only then will there become possible and be realized a truly complete democracy, democracy without any exceptions whatever. And only then *will democracy begin to wither away.* . . . Communism alone is capable of giving really complete democracy, and the more complete it is, the more quickly will it become unnecessary, and wither away of itself." [22] So the thesis is now that communism will cause even the truly complete democracy to wither away. Clearly, here Lenin is returning to the primary association, that is, to the thesis that the existence of democracy is tied to the existence of the State. And that is why Lenin, when he repudiated democracy-as-a-State, was very careful not to place this meaning in the context of bourgeois democracy.

At this point, however, Lenin has to dismiss a democracy about which he had shortly before (with reference to the dictatorship of the proletariat) spoken favorably. Therefore he mitigates his tone, mixing together the basic No with a Yes dictated by circumstances. Prima facie, Lenin says and gainsays. But in substance he supports the No. Lenin's ultimate ideal is a suppression of the State which, by reason of his *idée fixe* that democracy=State=oppression, is the elimination of democracy as well. He warned: "It is constantly forgotten that the abolition of the State means also the abolition of democracy; that the withering away of the State means the withering away of democracy." [23] Now Lenin has to liquidate democracy diplomatically: but he wants to liquidate it. He insisted: "The more complete the democracy, the nearer the moment when it begins to be unnecessary." [24] And in the dialectical vagueness of this and other similar passages, there is, I believe, a basic consistency.

Communism is "true democracy" because Marx said so, and

Lenin had to say what Marx said. But Lenin is not convinced. He sensed, one suspects, that he had succeeded in identifying this true democracy in a positive fashion only insofar as he had used the same criteria as are valid for bourgeois knowledge. For his part, Marxism offered him only criteria for refuting democracy. Therefore Lenin rebels, in the final analysis, at the idea of bringing communism back to democracy, even to true democracy. Communism, to Lenin, was another thing, it had to be something more: in it even the most perfect and literal democracy no longer had any meaning, it was extinguished. To Lenin the word democracy recalled a contaminated and compromised reality, a despicable bourgeois invention. If he could, Lenin would have said so overtly. He could not because the sacred texts did not allow it. And therefore he said it under his breath, between the lines. But he said it, there is no doubt about it.

In the context of bourgeois democracy, democracy *does not exist,* by definition; in the context of the dictatorship of the proletariat there is more democracy than before (which is not a large concession, since before there was none at all), but all the same real democracy still *cannot exist;* and in the context of communism democracy *should not exist* because it is superfluous. While in Marx the idea of democracy can be pinned down, in Lenin it always evades one's grasp; it bounces from one phase to the next phase, and when one reaches the final stage one is told that there is no further point in bothering with it. And this comes about because Lenin reverses Marx's opinion on a major point. For Marx, democracy as such is a Stateless society; for Lenin democracy is irremediably a State, and therefore a Stateless society cannot be a democracy.

As the foregoing analysis shows, Lenin's text is, to say the least, very confusing. In the first place we meet with the other-worldly and wholly gratuitous definition that democracy is the "organized, systematic use of violence"; then with a transitory definition to be used only to explain why it is that the dictatorship of the proletariat is more democratic than the democracy of the bourgeoisie; and, finally, with a missing definition, so to speak, for we discover that the third definition, the one which ought to tell us what true democracy is, is not there. Basically, democracy means to Lenin exactly the same thing as dictatorship (exercise of force and repressive violence); in the context of socialism, democracy means what it means for the capitalists; and in the context of communism, it means nothing.[25]

In practice, Lenin's pyrotechnic display serves to show that the Marxist-Leninist is always, automatically, democratic, whereas all the others are always, automatically, non-democratic. But the truth is, very simply, that Lenin understood neither the democracy which he rejected nor the reality which he was bringing about. And the point to be made is this: that to the extent to which "democracy" in Lenin has a constructive, usable meaning, it is the same meaning as is given to it in the West. Otherwise, insofar as Lenin tries to give democracy a *sui generis* meaning, a communist meaning, it has none.

This being the case, I believe that further investigation of the communist meaning of "democracy" is not worth the trouble. I say again: there is none in Lenin, and that is all the more reason why there is none after him.[26] For as the line of Holy Scriptures gradually lengthens, while, on the other hand, the actual facts depart more and more from the forecasts of the prophets, there is nothing left for the Soviet apologist to do but to entrench himself in dogmatism and Byzantinism: in dogmatism to shut his eyes to reality, and in Byzantine exegesis to show that reality develops according to his faith. We may therefore put to one side the inquiry about the name, and pass on to consider the over-all doctrine.

2. The Theory of Democratic Dictatorship

Today, systems of the Soviet type are called "popular democracies."[27] Evidently this is a pleonastic expression. Democracy already means popular power so that this expression comes out, in full, as "popular power of the people," or, if one wants to be facetious, "bi-popular power." Marx observed that "it is not by linking the word people and the word State in a thousand ways that one will make the solution of the problem a hair's breadth nearer."[28] Similarly, it is not by saying "popular democracy," or eventually—why not?—even "popular democracy of the people," that the problem will be changed by a hair's breadth. The last expression would be doubly tautological, but would not for this reason indicate a differentiating characteristic of tri-popular power with respect to the point of departure, that is, to the pure and simple concept of democracy. Therefore, if the label "popular democracy" is to have a meaning, it must refer to the idea of direct democracy. This—let it be noted—is not an inference of my own. It was Marx's thesis (and also Lenin's) that true democracy could only be direct democracy. That was their test. It is only right, therefore, to apply it to the democracies which in the name of Marx and Lenin are called popular democracies to mean that they are authentic ones. Granted that a direct democracy stands closer to the people, and is, in this sense, more popular than a representative democracy, the question is: are systems of the Soviet type democracies of the direct type?

The reply is, clearly, No. That the presumptive democracies of the Eastern kind are systems in which there is no longer any bureaucracy, or police, or standing army, but only the armed proletariat which administers itself (this being, I recall, the formula of Marx and Lenin for the proletarian democracy within a dictatorship of the proletariat), is a factually false statement. And even if one makes shift, as is done, with the thesis that, although they are not yet direct democracies, such is the trend and such will be their point of arrival, it must be said again that this thesis is false. For this is not at all the direction in which the so-called popular democracies are proceeding, either in the political or in the economic domain. Their objective, if they have not already achieved it, is total planning. And total planning and direct democracy are mutually exclusive.[29] Direct democracy postulates that the functions of government are of so limited and elementary a nature that anyone is capable of doing whatever there is to do—and while progress towards direct democracy requires that the domains reserved for the experts alone should be eliminated, progress towards over-all planning requires that everything should be directed peremptorily from above by a technocratic vanguard.

In effect, if communist doctrine continues to refer to a direct democracy of the self-governing proletariat, it does so above all for outside consumption.[30] The doctrine of "self-management of the workers," as one says today,[31] is advertised abroad, but very little at home. It is advertised abroad because it is an invaluable instrument of revolutionary propaganda. The revolutionary of our times starts

426

at a disadvantage, since he no longer finds before him a rigid body, such as the autocratic State, which can only be broken by force, but rather a plastic body, the democratic State, which nothing prevents from reforming. To justify *within* democracy the revolt *against* democracy one must therefore raise the stake by demanding a hyper-democracy. Since the actual democracies are indirect, it is convenient to invoke direct democracy; since they confine themselves to controlling power, one should require the direct seizure of power; and since popular power is not literally put into effect, it is expedient to demand that it be made literal. And as long as it is a question not of building a new democracy but of dismantling those which exist, these arguments have an unquestionable appeal. So one can very well explain why communism keeps alive the ideal of direct self-management by the political and economic community. Nonetheless, to the extent that Soviet doctrine speaks of direct democracy, it is speaking of a dogmatic legacy of the sacred texts blatantly and increasingly contradicted by the facts.

The expression "popular democracy" does not indicate, then, any existing or foreseeable characteristic of the system. If anything it indicates the feature which is most foreign to the Soviet system. It is somewhat astonishing, therefore, that this label was put into circulation when it had become clear that the ideal of Marx and Lenin which could have justified it was nothing more than an anachronistic utopia. Or better, it is not at all astonishing: rather it confirms the fact that in the communist lexicon the word "democracy"—whether by itself or in various associations—is used because it is expedient, not because it is tied to some definite, intelligible meaning, not because it designates something. However that may be, for the purpose of identifying the so-called democracies of the Eastern type we shall have to set aside any underlying assumption of direct democracy. The characteristics of the system are indicated not by the assertion that one is dealing with popular democracies, but by the assertion that one is dealing with dictatorships of the proletariat based on one-party systems. If they are democracies, then, they are indirect democracies like ours, but differing from ours because they are (i) dictatorial and (ii) one-party.

The first characteristic is, therefore, the dictatorship of the pro-

letariat: a dictatorship which is democratic—thus runs the argument
—because it is *of* the proletariat. Actually this was the hope, or better, the expectation, of Marx and Lenin. But they wanted (let us not
forget this) not a State-dictatorship, not the State-as-dictator, but the
proletariat-as-dictator. The *sine qua non* condition for a dictatorship
of the proletariat is that there should no longer be a dictatorship *of
the State*.[32] As long as there is a State, Marx would say, by coupling
in a thousand ways the words State and proletariat the situation will
not be modified by a hair's breadth. It follows from this that, according to Marx and Lenin, what at present exists in the USSR is not,
definitely not, a democratic dictatorship. Given the fact that there is
a State which, instead of withering away, during the last forty years
has become ever more all-powerful and gigantic, the meaning of this
development is—according to the texts which are relevant to the
case—that what actually exists in Russia is a dictatorship *over* the
proletariat, i.e., a dictatorship pure and simple.

The argument, as anyone can see, rebounds on the heads of its
present-day propounders. And this is the reason why it is often popu-
larized in a vaguer and less barefaced form, by maintaining that,
dictatorship for dictatorship, the dictatorship of the proletariat is
nevertheless more democratic than the dictatorship of the bourgeoisie.[33] But the credit which is given to such demonstrations simply
shows that—at least in politics—people understand very little of what
they are saying. For the term "dictatorship" stands for a *form of State*
(even for Marx and Lenin, as long as the State is not abolished).[34]
More precisely, dictatorship denotes a system of government *legibus
solutus*, exempt from controls and limitations, in which all the power
is concentrated in the *locus imperii*. It follows from this that expressions of the type "dictatorship of the proletariat" or "dictatorship of
the bourgeoisie" are simply historical and logical nonsense, since dictatorship is—by definition—*personal power*, and hence power which
is solely "of the dictator," of the dictator in person and his inner
circle, and of nobody else. No sooner is a government so contrived as
to be controllable, and is in fact controlled, than dictatorship is out
of the question. Therefore the problem is not to whom a dictatorship
belongs—this one already knows—but whether the State under con-

sideration is a dictatorship or not. And if it is a dictatorship, then it is not a democracy.

Hence, in the first place, one cannot make the comparison between the so-called capitalist States and the so-called proletarian States by saying "dictatorship for dictatorship." For the former are States of non-dictatorial structure, whereas the latter happen to be States of dictatorial structure. Once this very basic difference is established, one can go on to discuss the question of the "hegemonic class," [35] that is, to what extent it is true that within bourgeois democracies the hegemonic class is the bourgeoisie, and also whether it is true that within the Soviet dictatorship, the proletariat is really the hegemonic class. Provided that it remains clear that this discussion changes nothing with regard to the form of the State, which remains as it is. The question of whether there is a dominant "pressure-class" *qua* class, and of the social extraction of those who exert the greater influence on the State *ab externo,* may be a very important question, but it is another question.

Therefore, when present-day Marxists say that for them dictatorship is the "hegemony of a class," they are wrong. They forget that this would be so *if* the State were no longer in existence. Until that far distant moment, their definition of dictatorship contradicts the sacred texts (which in this case do refer "dictatorship" to the State), and remains quite irrelevant to the actual circumstances of their world no less than of ours. In short, the communist definition of dictatorship is not a definition of "dictatorship." The argument of the hegemonic class can make us believe that the question of the form of the State is not important, but it does not allow us to say that the bourgeois democracies are not democracies, or that the Soviet dictatorship is not a dictatorship. In particular, it cannot prove that there is no difference, or little difference, between a State in which the power is controlled and shared, and a State in which it is uncontrolled and concentrated; and it can prove even less that the second is more democratic than the first.

Two points are, I think, established. First, it cannot be maintained that the Soviet dictatorship is a dictatorship *of* the proletariat: at the most it can be maintained that it is a dictatorship *for* the proletariat. Second, it cannot even be maintained that it *is* a democratic dictatorship: at the most it can be maintained that that dictatorship *will become* a democracy sometimes in the future. And the latter was, in substance, the fundamental thesis of the founding fathers.[36] For they were the first to admit that a dictatorship of the proletariat was a means, not a solution. It is for this reason that they insisted so much on its transitoriness and brevity.[37] The society of the future will be free and democratic, they maintained, *after* the phase of the dictatorship of the proletariat. And it is the provisional nature of the dictatorship of the proletariat which guarantees the happy outcome. The key point of the whole doctrine, then, boils down to this: that communism will convert itself into a democracy because the dictatorship of the proletariat is entrusted with the task of destroying the classes and the State, so that once this task has been completed, the dictatorship too will be finished. In substance the entire construction stands on a *promise:* the promise that the dictatorship of the proletariat will be "transitory," because it promises that its purpose will be to create a Stateless society. Unfortunately it is an assurance completely lacking in credibility and probability.

To begin with, how a State on which everything depends and to which everything is entrusted, truly the most mastodontic, totalitarian, and monolithic State ever to exist, can set out on the road to extinction is, I confess, beyond my understanding—as well as against all the evidence, for it has consistently developed in the very opposite direction.[38] In the second place, if there is a State which promises not to desire its suicide, it is par excellence the dictatorial State. Present-day Marxists maintain that if the bourgeois State is not converted into a dictatorship, the State as such cannot perish. In substance this is the old thesis in accordance with which a despot is needed to put and end to despotism. But this argument can only lead—as Rosa Luxemburg pointed out—to a "capitalist State in reverse." [39] Actually all the evidence supports the forecast that when a limited State (the constitutional State) is replaced by the "strong State," what is likely to happen is not that the latter will perish but that it will desire to live and need to expand more forcibly than ever, precisely because it is a dictatorship.

Be that as it may, the point is that with regard to a dictatorship there is no sense in furnishing assurances, assigning limits, and giving promises: for any assurance is void *ex hypothesi*. Since a dictatorship allows a discretionary, uncontrollable power, this very fact excludes *a limine* every possibility of assigning it a temporal limit and mortgaging its development. Promising a liberty which must first pass through the grasp of a dictatorship is like saying that we must break the jar to make sure that its contents will be saved for posterity. The thesis of the "provisional nature" of the dictatorship of the proletariat has the same credibility as the promise of someone who issues a blank draft giving verbal assurances that some incognito will fill it in the future in the proper manner, and that another unknown third party will honor it when it falls due.

As the Italian saying goes, we are just left with "fried air." Or we might say that we are left to wonder at the absurd contradiction of a doctrine which, on the one hand, demands the utmost maximization of personal and concentrated power (dictatorship), and on the other hand, demands that it be exercised by an impersonal collective entity (the proletariat) according to the requirements of a maximal decentralization of power. In truth, the only possible way out is to fall back on the promise that the dictatorship in question will be a dictatorship *for* the proletariat. And this thesis, of course, can always be defended.

In terms of strict logic everything is possible. In calculating probabilities, there is even a probability that an illiterate confronted with a typewriter will strike the keys in such a way as to produce a novel. It is, however, highly unlikely, just as it is improbable that in a totalitarian and professedly anti-liberal State the subjects will be treated as masters, thanks to a benevolent despot wholly dedicated to altruism. The connection between dictatorship and philanthropy is only a risky conjecture. And in politics we are not interested in possibilities hanging by the slender thread of hope, or of miracles, but in those probable possibilities which are provided with all the required safety devices. For, as Guicciardini said: "Quelle sicurtà che sono fondate in sulla volontà e discrezione di altri sono fallaci." [40] Bertrand Russell, ever brilliant if often controversial, has written that while our definition of democracy "is that it consists in the *rule* of the majority, the Russian view is that it consists in the *interests* of

431

the majority." [41] I do not know whether Russell intended to be malicious; but how can one forget that from Plato onwards this has always been the argument in favor of the autocrat? Not government *of* the people, since the people do not know enough to recognize their real interest; but instead government *over* the people, despite the people, in the *interest* of the people: this is the justification of every monocracy—a justification which is opposed by the argument that if there is an invariable rule, in life as in politics, it is that no interest is ever protected if the interested party cannot express his interest. Those who are absent are always wrong.

To complete the argument, there remains to be considered the other characteristic, namely, that the Soviet system is based on a single party and consequently only allows voting on a single list. In this connection it is maintained that a multi-party system corresponds to a society of classes, and that therefore—once classes are abolished —everyone comes to be of the same opinion and true democracy is one-party. [42] I note that here we are dealing with a sequence of unverifiable and scarcely credible assertions; and that every time it is possible to check them, they are found to be false. Kelsen has formulated the objection excellently by observing that if, as Stalin asserts, "a political party were nothing but 'a part of a class,' and if more than one party could only exist where antagonistic classes exist, there would be no reason not to grant complete freedom to political parties in Soviet Russia." [43] It is also pertinent to point out how this theory mirrors the ever returning ideal of a monochrome world which is characteristic of absolute regimes, and how a return has thereby been made to the old position that variety is incompatible with authority, so that only unanimity, and not dissent, can be the basis of the State.

All in all, the one sensible observation in all the monotonous, endless apologetic literature on communist systems is that in Russia, as in other countries in similar situations, a dictatorship and a single party were and are "necessary." This may be so—but if it is, where does democracy come into it? For to maintain that in a certain situation it is necessary to have recourse to dictatorship is tantamount to maintaining that in that situation democracy is impossible.

The foregoing analysis suffices to show, I dare suggest, that the theory of a dictatorial, one-party democracy in itself makes it superfluous to carry on the inquiry from the doctrine to the facts, from what *is said* to what *is*.[44] I mean that the communist doctrine as such supports *ad abundantiam* the conclusion that the "other democracy" is little other than a phantom alternative.[45] This results, it will be noted, from judging it by its own criteria, by Marx's and Lenin's criteria. The dictatorship of the proletariat has not withered away, it still exists. We are therefore still in the phase of imperfect communism, with reference to which the Leninist thesis is that the dictatorship of the proletariat is "more democratic" in relation to the very criteria which are valid for judging bourgeois democracy. But this is not so. This can be proved to be unequivocally false. Therefore, if I have spoken only of democracy of the Western type it is because it does not appear to me that any others exist; in other words, because I do not believe that a *name* suffices to give reality to a democracy. *Ab esse ad posse valet illatio, a posse ad esse non valet*—we can draw inferences from "being" to "being possible" but not from "being possible" to "being."

3. Words Have Consequences

It is nonetheless a fact that the "phantom alternative" is believed in, that many people give credit to "another democracy." I could retort that this is hardly probatory, since credulity has little to do with credibility. Moreover, belief in phantoms ought to astonish those who profess a materialistic philosophy and follow a "bucket theory of mind,"[46] that is to say, the thesis that thought is simply a passive copy of reality, a "reflection of matter" (as Stalin maintained);[47] not those who hold that man is a symbolic animal living a mental life, and for whom it is the *intellectus* which attributes existence to the *res*. But these answers are a meagre satisfaction if, at the settling of accounts, credulity overcomes credibility and people end by believing the unbelievable. Therefore we must give this side of the problem the attention it deserves.

After all, credulity has its causes. And in this connection it is well to call to attention that those who have really understood the importance of the manipulation of symbols are the Marxist-Leninists. For no political proselytism is more subtle in manipulating language and more intent on fighting—in spite of the fact that historical materialism is an *Unterbau* philosophy, a philosophy of the subsoil—at the level of the most rarified *Oberbau,* that of words. Instead, paradoxically, we who believe in ideas forget the importance of the language which expresses them, to such a degree as to accept almost en bloc the phraseology of our opponents. That is, to the point of leaving to our adversary the advantage, indeed the great advantage, of terminological initiative.

Take, for example, the antithesis consecrated by linguistic usage, and still more by our own ingenuousness, between "Western" and "progressive" democracy. On one side is a neutral connotation: the West—while on the other there is an approbatory word: progress. Syntactically, I can consider it a two-way alternative; but pragmatically it is a ready-made choice.[48] If a democracy is *called* progressive, for an *animal loquax* it *is* progressive. To accept that terminology is equivalent to suggesting that matters are so; at least as long as the factual evidence is not available. But how many Westerners are in a position to really know the facts concerning an Eastern experience? Similar remarks apply to the antithesis between "liberal democracy" and "popular democracy," which is also much less innocent than it seems. Here too the semantics elicits a response in favor of the latter. For, of the two, the term "popular" is apt to be the more appealing. "Popular democracy" is on the brink of saying: This is *your* democracy—whereas "liberal democracy" would be, in this contrast, that pertaining to others, a non-popular type.

Again, "ideology" is—as is well known—a term advertised and marketed by Marxism for derogatory purposes, a term which most people associate, however confusedly, with Marx's theses.[49] Yet we use the expression "democratic ideology" as a matter of course, as if to say that every discourse on democracy can only be an ideological discourse. In particular, a large number of political scientists are only too glad to concede that to say "philosophy" of democracy is the same as saying "ideology" of democracy. A fine present to the Marxist technique of liquidating with one phonetic stroke the ideals and the doctrine of democracy as the by-products of a false class conscience, of "bourgeois ideologism"! This is not, of course, the intention of the non-Marxists who use the word. But good intentions count for little

434

when a word has been tied for more than a century, by means of a powerful propaganda machine, to very different intentions.

It is indeed strange. Anyone who does not accept the theory of economic factors is called by the Marxists an "idealist," as though to say that he is a wool-gatherer who, forgetful of reality, sees nothing beyond the *logos* and the mere dialog. But then the so-called idealist reveals himself in the test of debate, i.e., right on his own ground, that of dialog, as a poor debater. Instead, those who call themselves "materialists" are shown to be very cunning in the art which we call persuasion and the ancients called rhetoric. Actually the penetration of the Marxist Word has not revealed any necessary connection with the evolution of material factors, of the forces and forms of production; rather the Word has penetrated in a way diametrically opposed to Marx's expectations. And this goes to show that the real "idealists"—I mean the efficient ones—are the Marxists, and that we are very mistaken in underplaying the power of the Word, I mean of the word as such. Whatever may be the destiny assigned to us by the *historia abdita,* the history which is yet unknown to us, one thing is certain: that if we lose the war of words, the logical corollary is that the "other democracy" will be believed in. And I fear that we are indeed on the verge of losing the war of words.

It has become a commonplace, even among the most sophisticated Western scholars, to indulge in assertions of this type (I am quoting Karl Popper): "We need not quarrel about words, and about such pseudo-problems as the true or essential meaning of the word democracy. *You can choose whatever name you like* . . . [as] this is not a quarrel about words. . . ." [50] Of course, the real quarrel is not *about* words. And I wholeheartedly agree with the point that Popper is trying to make. But Popper, as well as many other distinguished scholars, commits an error, I believe, when he passes lightly over the fact that the quarrel does go on *by means* of words. To be sure, if people followed the concept, or the idea, whatever the word might be, then it would be pedantic and irrelevant to quarrel about words. But if people follow the word and lose sight of the concept—as is far more often the case—then I fear that I cannot concede, as if it were an irrelevant matter, that one can choose whatever name one likes. Words are an intrinsic part of our quarrels, and to "win a word" is in itself to win a great deal.

We say that ideas have consequences. True, but words also have consequences. As Thomas Aquinas would have said, words have an "inclination." A certain idea is conveyed by a certain word. And to name a thing in a certain way is the same as to determine in advance the way of interpreting that thing. Words are blinders which lead us to see this, and not that, to look here, and not there. Also, some words have emotive properties. Therefore when thought does not control words, or remains indifferent to the use which is made of them, then it is the words which get the better of thought and corrupt it. Anyone who has read with the attention it deserves the Appendix of Orwell's *1984* will admit that he exemplifies very effectively the extent to which words condition thought and can sterilize and distort it. It follows from this that it is a grave error to undervalue the terminological element of the political struggle. The terminological weapon, in a world which is ever more pervaded and dominated by the blare of mass media, no longer allows one to say (albeit wrongly) that words are unimportant.

4. Terminological Housecleaning

Up to now I have indicated, on the whole, some rather complicated ways of approaching the problem democracy. But there are also simple ways, and if elaborate arguments are required for intellectual consumption, it is a great pity—in democracy—to forget about the non-intellectuals. The simple argument can be summed up in this recommendation: never accept incorrect and mystifying words. That is, let us not participate in the stipulative game of attributing arbitrary names to things. As R. Robinson (although himself a stipulator) so aptly warns us: "We should make sure that our stipulation is not a deception and will not deceive." [51]

It may be said that my recommendation appears simple, but that to apply it is very difficult. What is the "proper" meaning of a linguistic term? I am ready to agree that the question is awkward: but only if we take it as a philosophical question, that is, only if I have to explain to a meeting of philosophers what is the ultimate nature and essence of language. For the degree of approximation necessary and sufficient in the context of the ordinary language with which I am concerned now, the objection is immaterial, and actually provides another instance of what I have called the "microscope fallacy." [52] When, in using a word, I relate it to something quite different from what the listener has in mind, that is, when I give it a meaning which is misunderstood and is bound to be misinterpreted, this is an improper use: improper because it is mystifying. That is all—and I insist in saying that it is a very simple rule.

In the war of words, epithet is used for argument, and reasoned discourse is ousted by the use of emotive symbols with a positive charge for oneself and a negative charge for the opponents.[53] The purpose of this is to induce the audience to react emotionally, unthinkingly, without stopping to reflect, on the basis of sheer signal reactions, as happens when a conditioned reflex is touched off. Thus everybody insists on saying "democracy" because this has become a signal which arouses a favorable reaction in the addressee, even if the actual referent of the word has become totally different from that which justified the rise of the affective association. Actually, at this stage the heuristic validity and the informative connotation of the word democracy no longer have any relevance. Speaking in general, the optimum is, rather, that a given linguistic symbol should have no verifiable meaning.[54] Let us be under no illusions. All that interests the parties who are engaged in the war of words is that a given word should touch on phobias and philias which are deeply embedded in our subconscious.[55]

In short, the terminological war, as I call it, is fought by having recourse to loaded words that appeal to emotional bias or prejudice.[56] And if this is the case, then it is of the utmost importance that terminological muddling be opposed by terminological housecleaning. Just as it is useful for the pseudo-Democrat to say "democracy," it is well for the real Democrat not to say it with regard to a pseudo-democracy. And if we are too timid to put the right word in place of the deceptive one, at least let us demand a fair statement of alternatives—such as: Western democracy versus Eastern democracy.

I suggest this antithesis rather than that between liberal democracy and communist democracy, because liberalism and communism are doctrines which the public at large shows no sign of grasping. It is better therefore to go back to the pure and simple geographical identification, which points at the same time to the safest way of weighing the alternative in question. For anyone who is cautioned that behind these geographical labels there are two very different historical backgrounds of civility and culture, is in a position to understand that to opt for the "other democracy" means—to get down to essentials—to opt for "another history" or, more precisely, for the values of another civilization.

As long as we could allow ourselves the luxury of ignoring the non-Western world, it was sensible enough that, in order to gauge the difference between countries emerging from a common civilization, it was sufficient to look at their constitutions. But today we are confronted with a larger world, and even constitutions (at least new ones) are taking on a deceptive function: even "constitution" is used at times as a trap-word.[57] And these are two good reasons for getting rid of the lazy habit of gauging a democracy by the standard of its formal exterior, of what the letter of its written constitution says. However much I may firmly believe that constitutions are an essential part of democracy, I do not believe in the least that they can produce a democracy. Our constitutions are a consequence, not a cause. Their meaning is tied to the *telos* of safeguarding and expressing the value beliefs of the West: the principles of legality, individual liberty, and respect for man as a person. Therefore in order to know whether we are dealing with a democracy or not, the essential point is to ascertain what a given society thinks about these fundamental values. Adherence to the so-called Eastern democracy means therefore, *tout court,* the repudiation of the values of Western civilization. Let us not confuse a language which is familiar to us (that of Marx), with what his words come to mean in another cultural setting.[58]

Of course, it is impossible to impose the use of correct antitheses; it is always possible, however, to neutralize biased ones. Either we all use neutral terms, or, if the adversary uses approbatory labels (for himself), we in turn must use approbatory expressions (for ourselves). What matters is to give the listener as little chance as possible of deciding on the basis of automatic responses to a mere word: that is, we must make it necessary for him, somehow, to *enquire about*

438

the thing. However displeasing it may be, this is the *dura lex* of the war of labels.

It is mortifying, I agree, to have to bother with such trivialities; but credulity follows trivial paths and it is necessary to combat it on its own ground. On the other hand, we need not blush when a little linguistic hygiene is recommended, when it is urged (i) that every word should be used in the sense in which the addressee understands it, and (ii) that the alternatives between which we are called upon to choose should be semantically and pragmatically balanced. The war of words is a war between noble and ignoble names, and it is such that the nicknames stick and the demonstrations (even assuming that they were followed and grasped) are forgotten. The contemptuous epithets of "bourgeois," "capitalist," and "reactionary" democracy weigh more heavily on the destiny of our time than all Marx's volumes, and however many battles are won in confuting his utopia, the slants maintain, by themselves, the mirage of an escape towards "another democracy."

5. Neutral Science and Marxism

Political science lives under the incubus of being accused of partiality. Having asserted itself in a world in which the word "democracy" is contended for between Marxists and non-Marxists, and thereby comes to mean two opposite things, the political scientist is tempted to preserve his neutrality by saying: It is a question of definitions. In full, this sentence can be rendered as follows: To anyone who defines democracy with reference to its Western exemplars, the "other democracy" is a counterfeit; but to anyone who defines democracy in the Eastern manner, it is our democracy which fails to pass the test. But if this is supposed to be a solution, then it calls to mind the epigram about Monsieur de La Palisse—a quarter of an hour before his death the man was still alive.

Clearly, if we say that some matter is a "question of definitions," the statement cannot close a discussion: if anything, it is bound to open a discussion. Unless we are looking for a mechanical formula for neatly dodging all problems, the statement implies that we must go into the matter fully and requires, to begin with, that these wretched definitions be examined. And no sooner do we leave the realm of the vague and enter that of the precise, than we discover that the so-called Eastern definition is something like the Arabian phoenix of which Metastasio sang: "Everyone says that it exists somewhere, but no one knows where." [59]

For the sake of the argument I am prepared to concede everything—to grant that liberty and respect for each individual person are irrelevant to a democracy,[60] and to admit that "popular power" is all that is required. But I do not see how one can go as far as to discard even the basic semantic and etymological "inclination" of the term, and stipulate for example a definition which states: democracy is a system of decision-making in which the people must be activated and mobilized so as to carry out without hesitation every order given them by power-holders appointed through autocratic coöptation. This is not, in my opinion, an admissible definition of the term democracy even though it may be considered a sufficiently accurate description of what goes on in Soviet practice.[61] Assuming that in a dictatorial one-party system the people wish to make their opinion heard, how are they to do it? The Soviet doctrine in itself indicates that all the means are lacking which would permit some articulate popular pressure on the summit, and that the very right of non-agreement is not recognized as a legitimate claim. Now to manifest one's dissent, to transfer one's vote from one party to another, and to select freely one's governors may be considered unimportant claims, but are precisely the claims conveyed by the use of the word democracy. I mean that if they are considered irrelevant, neither the *demos* nor its *kratos* are any longer in the picture.

Definitions are important, but they are not all-powerful, for they are bound to linguistic terms, and more specifically are curbed by (i) the degree of flexibility and magnitude of a given root within the linguistic system as a whole, and by (ii) the historical record, or content, of the word which one is concerned with defining. Therefore we cannot resolve every controversy by having recourse to the formula "everything depends on definition." I would say that *much* depends on definitions; but if one says everything, then I would reverse the argument by saying: everything depends on *not defining*. In the specific case, the alternative of another democracy does not

seem to be sustained by another definition, but rather by the fact
that we avoid defining it. Our difficulties and our present situation of
democratic confusion are not due so much to conflicting definitions,
as to non-definitions—literally speaking, to indefiniteness.

In the inquiry undertaken by UNESCO in 1948 on the ideological conflicts of our time, one of the questions was whether the term
democracy should be used in a narrow or a broad sense.[62] The question was harmless because, clearly, for certain purposes one uses the
concept in a narrow sense (meaning, by this, political democracy)
and for other purposes in a broad sense (social and economic as well
as political democracy): the important thing is not to confuse them.
Nevertheless, some respondents resented the question itself. Among
others, I. M. Bochenski curtly answered: "All questions asking how
a word *ought to be* used are without scientific meaning and cannot
be answered. All that can be said is how *in fact* a term is being used
by a (logical) class of men k." [63] Setting aside the consideration that
in the questionnaire the "should" was quite innocently used, Bochenski's reply is characteristic because it shows how, in the very name
of scientific objectivity, we may come to sanctify the technique of
non-defining, and thereby the art of being elusive. This scientific
covering-up is, however, scientifically indefensible.

In relation to the requisites of scientific knowledge, it is an
incontrovertible fact that progress of knowledge in general follows
the rule that it is useful to substitute a more precise for a less precise
term, and that whenever it is possible it is well to reduce the margin
of ambiguity in words. There is no decalogue which tells us how to
proceed in these operations, it is certainly not possible to attribute a
single meaning to every linguistic symbol, and for my part I do not
even believe that we should attempt to freeze the vocabulary beyond a
certain point. However, scientific knowledge advances because when
we accept or refuse the received definitions of a term, this is done with
reason, and not simply because a particular term is "in fact" being
used thus "by a (logical) class of men k." Science does not follow
the majority, and if Lavoisier had not swept away the linguistic approach consecrated by the alchemists, chemistry would never have
been born.

Furthermore, the rule put forward by Bochenski is quite absurd

441

from the point of view of communication, since the purpose of language is that men should understand and not misunderstand each other. Words are an instrument of communication to the extent that they are more or less received in the same sense as that in which they are pronounced. And if men come to understand each other somewhat, it is because parents to children, schools to pupils, writers to readers, and, in general, more influential to less influential adults—all without ceasing—lay down norms about the meaning of words, and thereby seek to attribute to them a sufficiently unambiguous meaning. We spend our whole lives saying: This word must, or should, be understood thus. Now, if a child points to his father and says "house," I presume that one may continue to correct him. But if an adult looks at the moon and says "sun," then the rule suggested by Bochenski would require this comment: some people call the sun "moon," and others call the moon "sun," and this is the reason why for some people day is night, and for others night is day, etc. But I assume that it is not the task of science to take us back to the time of the tower of Babel.

We may agree on these preliminary points, but—the question will still arise—what about the neutrality of science? This is, to be sure, a relevant question. But I wonder whether, by accepting a somewhat mysterious Eastern meaning of the word democracy because of the mere reason, or rather the mere *fact,* that it is in use (and, let it be noted, in use not by way of spontaneous linguistic development but in the way that compulsory currency is), we are really serving the neutrality of science, or whether we are actually paving the way to the shipwreck of science in silence and solipsism. For the attitude of someone who accepts indiscriminately everything that *is said,* instead of finding out what *is*—i.e., the truth-value of what he is being told— is more similar to the path of Pontius Pilate than to the behavior of Galileo.

Actually, I am under the impression that the problem of the neutrality of science is not focussed properly. It is correct to say that science cannot choose between the Western and Eastern conceptions of democracy—but on one condition: that this is really the case— that this is a correct alternative. This is precisely what the political scientist, no less than the political theorist, has to find out. Otherwise,

442

for the sake of being neutral (in the manner of Pontius Pilate) he no longer seeks knowledge and simply ceases to be a scientist. And assuming that he finds out that the choice in question does not exist as a choice *between democracies*, it is precisely his business to state the correct set of alternatives. Granted that in doing so he will displease Marxists, it remains more important, at least in my opinion, not to displease truth. *Magis amica veritas*.

Being neutral does not mean conceding that everyone is right, but means weighing up everyone's right. And let us not miss the point. What is under discussion here is by no means the preferability of one democracy in relation to another, but whether it is proper to write "democracy" where, in order to make people understand as much in the West as in the East what is being dealt with, we should write "dictatorship." This is not taking sides, or, if it is, it is taking sides for science against deception.

Let us suppose that an author writes a treatise on monarchy, in which a head of State elected periodically by universal suffrage is spoken of. Would it be anti-scientific and indicative of ideological bias to object that this author is confusing a monarchy with a republic? Our imaginary author may reply with the statement that he does not accept the accepted meaning of the term monarchy, and that he means it in its literal, etymological significance of "government of the one." All well and good. But if, as I continue to peruse his treatise, I then notice that his monarchy is explained as a government *of* the people, is it not my strict duty to object that his use of the term monarchy can denote only a government *over* the people exercised by one person through the agency of a few?

Changing but one name, this is exactly my argument against the so-called Eastern type of democracy. And let this point be clear: there is no necessary connection between the denial of the "other democracy" and the belief in our democracy. Nothing would be changed in my argument if my own opinion were that no democracy is a valuable goal. In other words, I do not hold in the least that it is obligatory to revere democracy. What I do hold is that it is obligatory to use the word "democracy" in strict relation to its historical and semantic connotation, and in a way that will not deceive. And I consider that this is a scientific duty, a rule with which the political scientist must comply—at least, if he wants his science to exist *qua* science.

NOTES

† *Obras* (Madrid, 1936), p. 742.

1. *Manifesto*, II.

2. *Ibid.*

3. *The Civil War in France*, Address II (1871). (Quoted in *Capital and Other Writings of Karl Marx*, trans. Max Eastman [New York, 1932], pp. 403-405.) Lenin summed up the essence of these measures in his first *Letter on Tactics* (April 1917)—exactly with reference to the dictatorship of the proletariat—as follows: "I . . . uphold the necessity of the State in this period, but, in accordance with Marx and the experience of the Paris Commune, not of an ordinary bourgeois parliamentary State, but of a State without standing army, without police opposed to the people, without bureaucracy placed above the people."

4. *The Civil War in France*, in *Capital and Other Writings*, p. 407.

5. *Ibid.*, p. 412.

6. *Ibid.*, p. 407.

7. One should keep in mind that for Marx the Paris Commune was to "serve as a model to all the great industrial centers of France. The Communal regime once established . . . , the old centralized Government would in the provinces, too, have to give way to the self-government of the producers." (*ibid.*, p. 404) As one can see, the "size of the States," a problem which did concern Rousseau, is resolved very simply by Marx with the fragmentation of the national State into a series of proletarian *polis*.

8. Introduction, *The Civil War in France*, in *Capital and Other Writings*, p. 381. The Institute Marx-Lenin of Moscow has substituted "the social-democratic philistine" for "the German philistine." I have kept the usual text because it seems to fit better in the general sense of Engels' Introduction, which refers to the "superstitious faith in the state" which is characteristic of the Germans in general, and not only of the social-democratic philistine.

9. I put it thus because it seems that the expression was used by Marx only three times, and in texts of minor importance: *The Class Struggles in France* (1850); a letter to Weydemeyer of March 5, 1852; and the *Critique of the Gotha Programme* (1875). Cf. Lucien Laurat, *Le Marxisme en faillite?* (Paris, 1939), pp. 41 ff.

444

10. It is a phrase in the *Manifesto* which Lenin underlines with particular emphasis in the following statement: "Here we have a formulation of one of the most remarkable and most important ideas of Marxism on the subject of the State, namely, the idea of the 'dictatorship of the proletariat.' " *State and Revolution* (New York, 1932), II, 7.

11. In connection with this ideal, Engels wrote to Bebel on March 18, 1875 proposing "to replace the word 'State' wherever it was mentioned by *Gemeinwesen*" (community). And Lenin's testimony to this effect is unequivocal. In *State and Revolution* he wrote: "In the first place, the proletariat, according to Marx, needs only a State which is withering away, i.e., a State which is so constituted that it begins to wither away immediately, and cannot but wither away" (II, I). A little later he added: "Once the majority of the people *itself* supresses its oppressors, a 'special force' for suppression is *no longer necessary*. In this sense the State *begins to wither away*. Instead of the special institutions of a privileged minority . . . the majority can itself directly fulfill all these functions; and the more the discharge of the functions of State power devolves upon the people generally, the less need is there for the existence of this power" (III, 2).

12. Letter to Bebel, March 18, 1875.

13. Lenin, *State and Revolution*, IV, 3.

14. No one perhaps has expressed Marx's idea so clearly as Rosa Luxemburg: "Dictatorship, yes, yes! But this dictatorship consists *in the way democracy is applied*, not in its abolition. . . . This dictatorship must be the work *of the class* and not of a small minority which rules in its name." *La rivoluzione russa* [1918] (Italian trans. Roma, 1959), IV, pp. 117-118.

15. *State and Revolution*, V, 4.

16. Cf. *ibid*. II, 1, and V, 2.

17. *Ibid.*, V, 4.

18. Lenin affirms it insistently: "Democracy is *also* a State, and . . . consequently democracy will *also* disappear when the State disappears" (*Ibid.*, I, 4). Again: "Democracy is . . . the organization of violence systematically applied" and therefore the "suppression of the State is at the same time the suppression of democracy" (IV, 6).

19. *Ibid.*, V, 2.

20. *Ibid.*, III, 3. This latter admission by Lenin, however, is nothing more than the echo of a very obscure statement made by Marx in *The Civil War in France*, where he had written: "The Commune was to be a working, not a parliamentary, body. . . ." (*Capital and Other Writings*, p. 404). Lenin comments: "The way out of parliamentarism is to be found, of course, not in the abolition of the representative institutions and the elective principle,

but in the conversion of the representative institutions from mere 'talking shops' into working bodies. 'The Commune was to be a working, not a parliamentary body, executive and legislative at the same time.' 'A working, not a parliamentary body' [Lenin exclaims triumphantly]—this hits the vital spot of present-day parliamentarians. . . ." (*State and Revolution*, III, 3). What this is supposed to mean in practice is what Lenin does not tell us. It is worth noting that Marx's judgment and above all Engels' judgment with respect to representative institutions was not always negative. In Engels' letter of June 15, 1885 to J. P. Becker, one finds this bold admission: "From 1848 the English Parliament has been without a doubt the most revolutionary organism in the world."

21. Cf. Chap. V, 4, the twisted treatment of the notion of equality; and Chap. IV, 6, the specious distinction with respect to the relationship between majority and minority, where Lenin exclaims: "No, democracy is *not* identical with the subordination of the minority to the majority. Democracy is a *State* recognizing the subordination of the minority to the majority, i.e., the organization for the systematic use of *violence* by one class against the other. . . ." etc. Thus Lenin deviates towards his favored argument without concluding on the topic in question.

22. *State and Revolution*, V, 2. The two phrases Lenin quotes are from Engels.

23. *Ibid.*, IV, 6.

24. *Ibid.*, V, 4.

25. Note this apt comment by Kelsen: "All these absurd contradictions are the inevitable consequence of the fact that the dictatorship of the proletariat is just what it calls itself: a dictatorship, not a democracy, and the fact that it must be interpreted to be democracy, since it is called so by Marx and Engels." *The Political Theory of Bolshevism* (Berkeley, 1948), p. 51.

26. For additional evidence, and for making sure, cf., e.g., Stalin, *Principles of Leninism*, 2 vols. (London, 1933), *passim*.

27. To be exact this label dates back to 1945, and is applied specifically to the satellite States, or to forms of government which imitate the Soviet system, not to the Soviet system itself. This for two reasons: (i) the Soviet system already had its denomination consecrated by the Stalinist Constitution of 1936, and (ii) because its declared function of "guiding State" does not permit a homonymy with the "guided States." But since communist propaganda has adopted the label of popular democracy without recalling these subtleties, and since popular democracies proper are still "copies" (in the Platonic sense) of the "idea" realized in the Soviet democracy, I follow the extensive use of this label. From the structural point of view as well, the differences between popular democracies and the Soviet democracy are not appreciable. Cf. Michel-Henry Fabre, *Théorie des démocraties populaires* (Paris, 1950).

28. *Critique of the Gotha Programme.* The passage is also quoted by Lenin in *State and Revolution,* V, 1.

29. Cf. Chap. XVI, 4, 5, above.

30. It is symptomatic that in the Soviet *Petit dictionnaire philosophique* (French trans., "Éditions en langues étrangères," Moscou, 1955), the expression "direct democracy" is not even listed. There are instead twelve columns devoted to "popular democracy." This in spite of the fact that Lenin had spoken of direct democracy often enough as the corrective and the antidote to bureaucratization.

31. The current Italian expression is *autogestione dei lavoratori.*

32. In other words an external dictatorship (which uses violence against the minority of the former oppressors) may coexist with an internal democracy (of the proletariat) only on this condition: as long as a self-governing proletariat exercises the dictatorial power *as a class.*

33. In addition to the passages already quoted from Chap. VI of *State and Revolution,* cf. also *passim* Lenin's pamphlet publ. in 1918, *The Proletarian Revolution and Renegade Kautzky.*

34. The older meanings of dictatorship (cf. Chap. VII, 5, above) have no significant bearing on this discussion, for it is clear (it can also be unequivocally evinced from the Soviet Constitution of 1936) that both for us and for the communists, dictatorship of the proletariat refers to the Soviet state in existence.

35. This is the terminology used by the outstanding communist theorist in Italy, Antonio Gramsci.

36. Cf. Engels' letter to Bebel (March 18, 1875): "It is pure nonsense to talk of a 'free people's State'; so long as the proletariat still uses the *State* it does not use it in the interest of freedom but in order to hold down its adversaries, and as soon as it becomes possible to speak of freedom the State as such ceases to exist." *Karl Marx and Friedrich Engels—Correspondence 1846-1895* (New York, n.d.), p. 337. Lenin is implicitly referring to this passage when he remarks: "While the State exists there is no freedom. When there is freedom there will be no State." (*State and Revolution,* V, 4). And again: "Every State is a 'special repressive force' for the suppression of the oppressed class. Consequently, *no* State is either free or a 'people's state.' " (*Ibid.,* I, 4.) Also recall the passage already cited where, in speaking about the dictatorship of the proletariat, Lenin affirms with force: "It is clear that where there is suppression, where there is violence, there is no freedom and no democracy." (V, 2).

37. On the eve of the Revolution Lenin declared sharply: "The proletarian State will begin to wither away immediately after its victory" (*State and Revolution,* II, 2). And one could keep on quoting at length.

38. It is well to emphasize in this connection that Lenin pictured the process of the extinction of the State, regardless of its duration, as a continuous one. This is not only the conception of *State and Revolution* and of the *April Theses,* but also the sense of all of Lenin's subsequent anathemas against bureaucratization. Even when the principle of "socialism in a single country" and the experience of power induced Lenin to postpone the dismantling of the State, he did not change his mind on the continuity of the process, nor did he give any reason to suppose that the historical period required to make the transition to communism should be prolonged *ad infinitum.* In 1918 Lenin said this period would be about ten years. In his speech of May 1, 1919 he declared that the majority of the people between thirty and thirty-five years of age would see the dawn of communism. Eventually he went as far as conceding that "Ten or twenty years sooner or later make no difference when measured by the scale of world history"; but this was the maximum lapse of time he envisaged. Cf. E. H. Carr, *The Bolshevik Revolution,* Vol. I, p. 241.

39. Cf. Rosa Luxemburg, *La rivoluzione russa,* IV, p. 108: "Lenin says that the bourgeois State is an instrument for the oppression of the working class, the socialist State an instrument for the oppression of the bourgeoisie. The latter then would be nothing more than a capitalistic State somewhat in reverse with its head down." From a Marxist point of view one can hardly conceive a more drastic criticism.

40. "Those safeties which are based on the will and discretion of others are deceptive." Guicciardini, *Ricordi,* 27.

41. *What Is Democracy?* (London, 1946), p. 14.

42. Cf. Stalin, *Leninism, Selected Writings* (New York, 1942), p. 395.

43. Hans Kelsen, *The Political Theory of Bolshevism,* p. 57.

44. The query would be: Do the ideals stressed by Marx still have any bearing on the course of development of the Soviet experiment? For it is evident that the relationship between what *should be* and what *is* cannot be loosened to such an extent as to imply that a deontology may have no impact whatever on reality. The impression is that the other democracy—with respect to the deontology which has generated it—is simply a fact which has escaped control.

45. Cf. J. Barents, *Democracy, an Unagonized Reappraisal,* pp. 28-29: "Our conclusion can only be . . . that the idea of a people's democracy can be no contribution to a new theory of democracy, or to supplementing the older theory of democracy." Cf. *contra* Georges Vedel, *Manuel élémentaire de droit constitutionnel* (Paris, 1949), esp. pp. 240-253. Vedel justifies the Soviet theory as a second conception of democracy, basing his arguments on Rousseau —evidently disregarding the (limited) dimensional context to which Rousseau attached the validity of his ideal City (cf. Chap. XIII, 4, 5, above).

46. This felicitous metaphor is in K. R. Popper, *The Open Society and Its Enemies,* Vol. II, p. 214.

47. Cf. the official *History of the Communist Party of the Soviet Union* (New York, 1939), Chap. IV, 2. The text in question was published later separately under Stalin's name with the title *Dialectical Materialism and Historical Materialism.*

48. I use "pragmatically" according to Charles W. Morris' framework, i.e., with reference to the classification of the general field of semantics in: words considered (i) in relation to other words (syntax), (ii) in relation to the objects that they denote or designate (semantics, proper), (iii) in relation to the subjects who use them or who are influenced by them (pragmatics). Cf. *Foundations of the Theory of Signs,* in *International Encyclopedia of Unified Science,* Vol. I, 2 (Chicago, 1938).

49. Cf. Chap. XVIII, 2, below.

50. Cit. in M. Cranston, *Freedom,* p. 112 [the italics are mine]. Cranston too, says: "I see nothing to be gained from insisting that they [the communists] ought *not* to call their totalitarian republics 'democracies' . . ." (*Ibid.,* p. 110).

51. *Definition,* p. 82. For my criticism of the stipulative theory of language, cf. Chap. X, above.

52. Cf. Chap. VIII, 6, above.

53. Cf. the emotive use of language, concerning which see, e.g., Charles L. Stevenson, *Ethics and Language* (New Haven, 1945).

54. In Max Lerner's wording the *optimum* is not the "instrumental" but the "manipulative" use of ideas: to mean that the validity of the ideas is irrelevant, since the end in view is all that matters. Cf. *Ideas are Weapons* (New York, 1939).

55. A study which strongly stresses this element with reference to Pavlov's theory of conditional reflexes is: S. Chakhotin (or Tchakhotine, as in the 1939 French ed.), *The Rape of the Masses* (London, 1940).

56. A number of pertinent examples may be drawn from, e.g., R. N. Carew-Hunt, *Guide to Communist Jargon* (London, 1957). Studies on propaganda, especially on war or totalitarian propaganda, may also be usefully consulted, even if such studies rarely examine the problem directly or primarily from the angle of semantic mystification.

57. I have reference to the constitutions which Karl Loewenstein labels "semantic constitutions" (cf. Chap. XIII, note 84, above). And let us keep in mind that "already two-fifths of the world population are living under semantic constitutions" (*Political Power and the Governmental Process,* p. 162; cf. also pp. 144-145 and 148-150). On the Soviet constitution in particular, see the last

449

volume by Henri Chambre, *Le Pouvoir sovietique: Introduction à l'étude de ses institutions* (Paris, 1959), which sets forth in detailed evidence how the Soviet theory of the State and the corresponding constitutional practice is characterized by an unmitigated primacy of fact and arbitrary action on law.

58. Cf. Ortega y Gasset, who as early as 1925 wrote: "From the time bolshevism appeared I have maintained that this movement is completely separate from European politics and particularly Russian, that is, to the extent that Russia is not Europe, and where European culture exists only as a repertoire of theories, or better yet terminologies." "Sobre el fascismo," *Obras*, Vol. II, (Madrid, 1946), pp. 493-494.

59. Metastasio, *Demetrio*, II, 3: "Che ci sia ciascun lo dice, dove sia nessun lo sa."

60. Although Rosa Luxemburg would not have granted this. Cf. this eloquent testimony of hers: "Freedom which is reserved only for those who adhere to the government, for the members of a party, no matter how numerous they may be, is not freedom. Freedom is always the freedom of those who think differently; and not because of any fanatical attachment to 'justice,' but simply because everything that is educational, beneficial and purifying in political freedom depends on this and loses its effectiveness when 'freedom' becomes a privilege." *La Rivoluzione russa*, IV, p. 109.

61. "The essence of Soviet 'democracy' "—as David Granick well puts it— "consists of participation in everything except basic decision-making." Cf. *The Red Executive* (New York, 1960), p. 196.

62. Cf. *Democracy in a World of Tensions*, pp. 516-517.

63. *Ibid.*, p. 477.

Chapter XVIII

Conclusions

*"Practical men, who believe themselves to be
quite exempt from any intellectual influence,
are usually the slaves of some defunct economist. . . . The power of vested interests is
vastly exaggerated compared with the gradual
encroachment of ideas. . . . Sooner or later,
it is ideas, not vested interests, which are
dangerous for good or evil."*

—J. M. Keynes†

1. The Confused Society

THE HEDONISTIC VALUE attributed to goods is directly proportional to their rarity. *Mutatis mutandis* this rule could be applied to
the historical fluctuation of value principles. Western man has enough
liberty and is tempted by the glow of prosperity: consequently he
attaches a decreasing value to individual liberty and an ever growing
value to economic welfare and security. His ideal becomes *sécurisme,*
the cult of security. He is less aware of the importance of a constitutional State which guarantees his liberties, and increasingly desires a
protective State which will take care of his needs. And it will be a
huge, ever growing protective State, since the spiral of needs has
virtually no limit: for in the end, as Hegel said, "it is no longer
need [the necessity], but opinion [the desire] which has to be satisfied."[1]

451

Technological progress is per se a powerful concomitant to this transformation of ideals. Together with the flood of plenty which it brings along, it is producing a soft society characterized by the psychological outlook of the spoiled child. Technology, however, also opens the way to an age of overpopulation and super-organization in which the individual is reduced to a mere cipher and feels increasingly powerless and stifled. And as a society is gradually overburdened by demographic pressure, and is *pari passu* enmeshed in a huge organizational net, it tends to be less and less hospitable to a liberal conception of life. For there is no doubt that the ideal of liberty is better adapted to a society which is not saturated, which affords opportunities and leaves sufficient room to allow individuals a certain amount of mobility.

On the other hand, history has tried us severely, perhaps too much. We are weary, maladjusted, anxious, and, let us admit it, frightened. The religion of progress has turned—in the happy phrase of Kingsley Martin—"into a gospel of acceleration." Since the time of the French Revolution and the first industrial revolution we have been in a rush; and rapid, incessant change gives no time to regain a stable equilibrium. Furthermore, a "rapid movement was exhilarating and men forgot . . . to ask in what direction they were hurrying." [2] On top of all this, we have been grievously exhausted by the carnage of two world wars, which have in many cases been followed by painful experiences of civil terror, or at any rate by profound class tensions. And we have emerged not long ago from a state of war, real warfare, only to be plunged straightaway into the wearing atmosphere of the cold war. Our nervous systems are shaken, we live in fear of the morrow, and of a terrifying morrow in which the prospect of man's self-destruction is certainly not mere science-fiction.

Hobbes's *Leviathan* came out in 1651 after the bloodshed of a cruel civil war. To Hobbes and many of his contemporaries the supreme goal seemed to be social peace: and to attain it Hobbes theorized the omnipotence of the State. After making due allowances, there are a number of analogies which could also apply to our situation. We too, in our exhausted state, want peace at all costs. And as the gospel of acceleration has brought us not moral but material progress, we clutch desperately at this tangible benefit. Cost what it may, we ask for a secure job, an assured salary and a protected existence; and in order to achieve these benefits we may well be once again disposed, as were Hobbes's contemporaries, to entrust our fates to whoever promises to take care of us.

It may be that, in the final analysis, this is the meaning of our time and the ultimate reason for the crisis of liberal democracy. But if this were so, all the fuss which is being made about the "real" democracy which takes over formal democracy, about the "concrete" liberty which takes the place of abstract liberty, about "true" justice as opposed to legal justice, and so forth, would be mere nonsense, mere fireworks. It is not real liberty which concerns us, it is simply that we no longer appreciate liberty as such. It is not true democracy which matters to us, it is simply that democracy in itself no longer appeals to us. We are tired of liberty and democracy, because we are soft, we are spoiled, we are weary, and, on top of all this, *noti nulla cupido,* we are bored with the familiar.

However, I am not at all sure that this is the correct diagnosis. I mean that I am not at all sure that a deliberate choice in favor of *other values* is actually taking place. It seems to me, rather, that if we are making a choice of the kind, we are making it unwittingly. That so much is being said about "true" liberty and "true" democracy seems to suggest that the ultimate values and fundamental beliefs of Western civilization are, and remain, deeply rooted, and justifies the suspicion that we are not being confronted so much with a purposeful shift as with an outflanking of these values. And in that case the crisis of liberal democracy turns out to be in large part the fruit of our mistakes, of the confusion of ideas in which we are wandering.

An intellectualistic interpretation of history? If by this it is meant that I do not believe in the approach of historical determinism or materialism, that is correct. Not that I underestimate the impact of material change, and of the situation of demographic saturation and of super-organization in which we will increasingly find ourselves living. But the last word can only come from the word. I mean that man is an *animal loquax* who does not react directly to things and facts, but to a certain interpretation of things, to a certain appraisal of facts. As all his history shows, he is capable of responding to his environment in many ways. In Schelling's wording, man has the power of "determining determinations." And this is not because we cling to the postulate that man is endowed with an ultimate freedom of the will. Even if this metaphysical issue remains undecided, man is not a sheer reflection of his environment, and he escapes predetermination, for the plain, worldly reason that he lives a mental life, that he is a symbolic animal. But if this is true, then it becomes very difficult, if not virtually impossible, to separate—in regard to man—what is objective from what is subjective. And if this much is conceded, it is enough for me. For my approach comes down simply to this argument: in order to arrive at "objective" causes, "subjective" disturbances and variables must be disposed of.

It is futile, to say the least, to explain our present plight by invoking the inexorable march of events and other such remote and convenient alibis, when there are more proximate and much more identifiable responsibilities. The sea has its nature, but if we are shipwrecked because we lack a pilot and we are not looking at the compass, we are not entitled to say that it is the sea's fault. Even if our crisis is brought about by deep-seated, formidable forces, these forces are not independent, mute facts operating outside of our mental perception of them. Therefore, once we have granted that there are many reasons for the crisis into which we are drifting, one of these—and certainly not the least—is surely to be found in our errors in calculation and forecasting, and in our inability to maintain a proportion between ambitions and means.

It is also futile, on the other hand, to develop a defeatist neurosis and a complex of decadence. Why not, instead, examine calmly and in a less sweeping fashion what part of the so-called inevitable is actually evitable? For example, confusion of ideas is one of our direct responsibilities, one of those "causes "which are by no means beyond our control. So, why not regain control over this matter? As Orwell judiciously observed, "One ought to recognize the fact that the present political chaos is connected with the decay of language, and that one can probably bring about some improvement by starting at the verbal end." [3] Certainly this is not the cure for all ills, but it is a constructive suggestion which becomes all the more important, the more the work of terminological repair is neglected.

To be sure, it is only a beginning, but it is a beginning on the right side, putting the horse before the cart, and not—as is done by those who start from "objective causes"—the cart before the horse.

2. Democracy, Ideology and "Ideocracy"

It took Mannheim, a writer who can hardly be credited with idealistic softness, to coin the pregnant expression "idea-struck age," and to note that liberal democracy is the typical product of it.[4] Democracy, we could say, is the fruit of an *ideocracy,* meaning by this that no historical venture of man has depended in so pronounced and hazardous a manner on the force of ideas, and therefore on our capacity for employing them and on our ability to master the symbolic world.[5] It is no wonder, then, if democracy suffers more than any other ethico-political formula from that deadly disease— mental confusion. If we no longer believe in the value of ideas, or if the ideas which feed the democratic ideocracy approach the vanishing point, it is hard to see how a democratic reality can survive. And the prospects, it must be admitted, are not comforting.

The sphere of critical knowledge itself—which is, in the final analysis, the kitchen in which the menus of the future are being prepared—is deeply affected, almost to the point of paralysis, by a suspicion of ideas, or an indictment against ideas, set in motion by that modern version of witch-hunting which is the denunciation of an "ideological bias." [6] And the extent and pervasive quality of the atmosphere of suspicion generated first by Marx and then by Mannheim,[7] is revealed by the frequency with which people today write "ideology" where before they wrote "idea."

It is true that there is a substantial difference between the respective positions of Marx and Mannheim, and also between Mannheim and those who use the word "ideology" simply because they find it in use, and hence with a meaning which they declare to be harmless. However, if it were really harmless they should find no difficulty in using "ideology" to describe their own ideas, whereas this actually happens very seldom. We are most generous in dealing the label out to third parties, but very careful, in most cases, to avoid applying it to ourselves. And I am afraid that the reason for this is that everyone senses that when an idea, a doctrine, or a theory is called an ideology, the implications are not complimentary. If there is a difference between idea and ideology—as the creation of the latter term implies—then this difference can only be that ideology is, even in the so-called neutral interpretations, a contaminated idea of an inferior class.

Let us therefore not evade the issue. When ideologies are in question, the problem is no longer one of judging an assertion with respect to its *validity*, but of judging it in relation to the *motives* for which it is uttered. The inquiry "Is this assertion true?" is replaced by: "Why is he making it?" As Robert K. Merton has well noted in his examination of Mannheim's sociology of knowledge, in this approach "one no longer inquires into the content of beliefs and assertions to determine whether they are valid or not, one no longer confronts the assertions with relevant evidence, but introduces an entirely new question: how does it happen that these views are maintained? Thought becomes functionalized; it is interpreted in terms of its psychological or economic or social or racial sources and functions. . . ." [8] To be sure, the question: Why does he say what he is saying? is not new. But up to now it was used to explain error, whereas today it is used to devalue every assertion to the level and purpose of ideological function. Thus an impersonal world of knowledge which looks forward to the possibility of a common understanding is replaced by a fragmented multiplicity of individuals who—being simply the echoes of their own existential situation—defend (according to Mannheim) their particular ideology within the framework of their "total" ideology.

In this atmosphere of distrust, on account of which everyone feels exposed to judgment in the light of hidden motives which impel him to speak, the potential defendants ask themselves: How can I put myself on firm ground? In other words, what kind of assertions can be trusted? What *is not* ideology? Since an ideology is admittedly not a scientific truth, the reply comes almost automatically: to preserve ourselves from ideological bias we must stick to science. An expensive salvage operation—it must be stressed—because, to begin with, in this way we have implicitly, when not explicitly, agreed to sacrifice the bulk of the Western cultural heritage: philosophy. Millennia of earnest, patient, devotion to "love of knowledge"

456

are being yielded en bloc to the accusers with a cursory syllogism of this type: science is not ideology—philosophy is not science—therefore philosophy is ideology.

Mors tua vita mea, your death is my life, one might say. It is not so, however, because the salvage operation saves little, if anything at all. For the sciences of man can be saved in their turn from the charge of ideological bias to the extent that they are *wertfrei,* value-free. And this is easier said than done, for the basic reason that language as such embodies value outlooks and attitudes, an inclination to perceive and not to perceive, to prefer and not to prefer.[9] Consequently, the bulk of social science itself, if not all of it, can always be liquidated—should anyone wish—as being bourgeois science, as being science which is still, and inescapably, impregnated with the class values of the capitalist world.

Let us be under no illusion. However much we run away, we cannot escape. The weapon wielded by Marx will ever threaten us— for we can escape it only if we stop running away. But, precisely, why are we running away? Let me phrase the question thus: what is there to be gained in replacing the *theory* of knowledge with a *sociology* of knowledge? I would say: a vicious circle. For the meaning of an ideologically focussed discussion can be reduced, in substance, to this kind of argument: one person says of another, "He has bad sight because he was born with only two eyes"—and the accused replies: "Why, how many have you?" Thus, it does not take much to foresee that this brand of witch-hunting can only lead— if we consent to join the game—to a "reinforced dogmatism"[10] on one side, and to an "intellectual nihilism"[11] on the other.

As F. A. Hayek has aptly pointed out, recourse to the sociologico-Marxist explanation of thought is based on a super-rationalism which prepares the ground for a thorough irrationalism. In the first respect, one must postulate a privileged super-mind, an infallible, unconditioned mind which represents an exception—for reasons which will ever remain mysterious—to the rule of ideological conditioning: and so we arrive at reinforced *dogmatism.* And in the second respect, "if truth is no longer discovered by observation, reasoning, and argument, but by uncovering hidden causes which, unknown to the thinker, have determined his conclusions, if whether a statement is true or false is no longer decided by logical argument and empirical tests, but by examining the social position of the person who made it . . . reason has been finally driven out"—and so we arrive at mental and intellectual *nihilism*.[12]

This does not mean that I think antechamber explanations have no worth. They have, but on condition that they are kept in their place and that their limit is accurately affirmed: that is, on condition that a sociology of knowledge (or psychoanalysis, to mention another instance) is not used to replace a theory of knowledge, but only to supplement it. This is tantamount to saying that those who explore the anteroom—i.e., the stage which precedes the actual formation of thought—have to remain in their anteroom, without claiming to explain beforehand what happens *afterwards,* in the other room. In relation to the creativity or inventiveness of thought, the sociology of knowledge is little more than a caveat, a warning. Once we have been urged to examine our conscience and to make a self-analysis of our intellectual earnestness and integrity, the jurisdiction of the theory of existential and social conditioning of thought ends. Given a need, a situation and an interest, the creative mental response that will follow is not given. No sociology of knowledge can explain Marx or Mannheim: it can only explain the success of Marx and Mannheim.

Those who fall prey to the fascination of the sociologico-Marxist explanation of thought forget the very important distinction between receiver and inventor of culture, between passive and creative thought, and thus between the spreading of thought and its formation. And yet this is the hub of the matter. The sociology of knowledge believes, or deludes itself into believing, that it can resolve problems regarding the genesis of mental products. Actually, what Maquet calls "Mannheim's law" is valid for quite another purpose: that is, to explain by what criterion the receivers of culture choose between the mental products submitted to them. In other words, the sociology of knowledge is neither an epistemology nor a logic. It cannot tell us either whence the creativity of thought springs, or how to judge the correctness of thought. It shows us instead for what motives the non-thinkers or the non-thinking (at any rate those whose profession is not that of thinking), adhere to other people's thought. One could

perhaps say that the sociology of knowledge does not apply to thinking (the output), but to persuasion (the input). It provides a criterion
for foreseeing the success of an already-created thought: not for
thinking it.

If this is true, then there is no reason for paralyzing the sphere
of critical thought with the devices of Marx and Mannheim (and
even Freud). On the contrary, there are plenty of reasons for rejecting the intrusion of the concept of ideology in a sphere and at a
level where it does not belong.[13] There is no sense in speaking of
philosophy as ideology, or in giving science itself an ideological taint.
Philosophy and science can, and do, assume the form of ideology
with respect to the way in which they are retranscribed, simplified,
and emotionally slanted at the level of common discourse. In short,
they are disseminated as ideologies.[14] But if they are such on arrival,
they are not on departure, that is to say, *qua philosophia* and *qua
scientia*.

It will be conceded that there is a difference, indeed a very great
difference, between the way a worker or a peasant understands
Marx, and what Marx actually had in mind when he was attacking
and overturning Hegelian philosophy. And if the word ideology
is suitable for the first case, for grass-roots Marxism, it cannot be
suitable for the second, for Marx as a thinker and philosopher. In
point of principle, if ideology serves to denote the fall or popularization of thought, it cannot be applied to the opposite process, the
emergence or creation of thought. If it is used in connection with
a quest for "certainty," [15] then it cannot be used to refer to the
quest for "truth." Therefore, as long as we remain at the level of
knowledge proper, there is nothing to gain and everything to lose
by using a word whose underlying implication—whether we like it
or not—is that ideas and ideals are only a specious justification, and
whose aim is to distract our attention from the substance of thought
to what is prior to and behind thought. This is to enter a blind
alley blocked by the peremptory objection that "if we knew how
our present knowledge is conditioned or determined, it would no
longer be our present knowledge. To assert that we can explain our
own knowledge is to assert that we know more than we do know,
a statement which is nonsense in the strict meaning of the term." [16]

459

It requires little effort to understand why the game of unmasking ideas as ideologies is, and is destined to be, successful. By this token anyone can reject any argument without arguments. How convenient! This is all the more reason for those who *have* arguments not to join the game, and for refusing to accept the word which introduces it and legitimizes it. This is not, of course, merely a matter of tactics. At least as far as I am concerned, I persist in believing that ideas (of philosophers no less than of scientists) are to be understood and not unmasked, and that our first task remains to inquire whether they are true or false, verifiable or unverifiable, consistent or contradictory. I may seem naïve, but I would like to recall that "whether we like it or not, we swim in a sea of ingenuousness, and the most ingenuous are those who think that they have avoided it." [17] And I wonder whether the most naïve will not turn out to be those who reduce knowledge to a concern with knowing whether thought is bourgeois or not bourgeois, capitalist or not capitalist. Once it is agreed that the color which suits one doctrine is red, and that the color suited to the others is, say, black, our knowledge remains where it started, or rather takes a step backwards. For to make of thought a matter of discussing whether it is progressive or conservative is for the most part a way of concealing bad thinking and of cheating with good thinking. [18] And such a way of reasoning is indeed a sinister omen, as much for the fate of culture as for that of an experiment in reasonableness such as democracy.

Let this be clearly understood: liberal democracy ends the very moment an "idea-struck age" passes away, killed (be it noted) not by material factors but by a cultural pattern of distrust and suspicion of ideas. [19] Once we have sacrificed ideas and ideals on the altar of ideology, nothing can await us but a sheer "outburst of energies," to use once again a telling expression of Mannheim's. It will not be a chiliastic, ecstatic, and orgiastic kind of outburst as were the Peasant Wars; [20] rather, I imagine, it will be an outburst of activist modes of response, well-channeled and kept under iron control. But this difference, I confess, is small consolation to me.

3. Liberal Democracy or What?

If someone were to observe without malice that these pages reflect a liberal-democratic point of view, I would have no difficulty in agreeing that it is so, and also in explaining the reasons why: namely, that it is not my purpose to talk about something that does not exist, and that I am unable to judge what exists by using a yardstick which in its turn does not exist. In other words, my point of view is liberal-democratic because the opposite point of view is only a point of non-view. And this is not a daring assertion, since I have yet to meet with an author whose ideal is a freedom-less democracy. If we run through the writings of all the relevant students of modern democracy, we notice that, albeit in various ways and to varying extents, they are fundamentally in agreement in concluding that, without liberty, democracy has no meaning. Without exceptions. The fact is, therefore, that *there is no other point of view:* and this is a fact to which perhaps insufficient attention has been paid.

Rousseau? No, Rousseau does not represent another point of view. It is sufficient for this purpose to recall how he posed the problem of his ideal city: "to find a form of association which will *defend* and *protect* every member belonging to it, and in which the *individual,* while uniting himself with all the others, will obey only *himself* and remain *free* as before." [21] The concepts that I have stressed by italics—defence, protection, individual, freedom, obedience to oneself—are the most basic and familiar themes of the liberal conception of life. Again, when in the *Social Contract* Rousseau put to himself the question, "In what precisely does the greatest of all benefits consist, such that it should be the object of all legislation?" his reply was: "It reduces itself to two principal objectives, liberty and equality." And for Rousseau the latter objective was an implication of the first: one should pursue equality—he said—"because liberty cannot exist without it." [22]

If Rousseau has been interpreted as the prophet of totalitarian democracy, it is because the outcome of his solution belies his intentions,[23] because the results went beyond his expectations. This is the same as saying that when we consider Rousseau as the theorist of an illiberal democracy, we are actually considering the failure of his theory.[24] Of his own accord Rousseau put democracy where Montesquieu put the constitution; indeed two very different solutions, but aimed at the same end, the end of protecting the liberty of the individual from oppression.[25] More precisely, Rousseau wanted direct democracy to take the place of liberal *garantisme,* and this because he

believed the former solution to be safer—from the standpoint of preserving liberty—than the latter. So that, once it is established that
direct democracy is impossible, the argument is once again that it is
liberal *garantisme* which safeguards democracy.

Marx? No, in substance not even Marx offers another point of
view. He was a philosopher of strict Hegelian descent; and when
Marx decided to abandon philosophy to the "gnawing criticism of
mice" he leaped with one bound over to economy, leaving to the
chefs of the future the task of devising the political solutions to the
problems which he had opened up. In this vacuum, that is, in the
vacuum separating the problems of Hegel from those of Adam
Smith and Ricardo, Marx as a political theorist mainly confined himself to forecasting the natural extinction of politics. He was convinced that, once his grandiose operation of economic surgery had
been accomplished, humanity's recovery from all the ills with which
it had been afflicted would be automatic. His expectation was that
"when . . . class distinctions have disappeared, and all production
has been concentrated in the hands of a vast association of the whole
nation, *the public power will lose its political character.*" [26] One can
say that as far as competence and mastery of the problems of politics
are concerned, Marx was indeed naïve. Nevertheless, and I would say
for this very reason, Marx's ideal was the purest and most literal
democracy: so pure and literal as to be *sic et simpliciter* a "self-
government of labor." He looked towards a Stateless democracy,
without vertical structures, without power problems, without cleavage
or conflict of any sort: in a word, towards the most primitive,
simplistic, idyllic administration in common of the communal life.[27]
And the point is that in Marx this democratic primitivism was visu-
alized in the service of liberty, of the most complete, absolute liberty.

In the *German Ideology* of 1845-46, the young Marx pictured
the world of the future with disarming libertarian candor. He wrote:
"In communist society, where nobody has one exclusive sphere of
activity but each can become accomplished in any branch he wishes,
society regulates the general production and thus makes it possible
for me to do one thing today and another tomorrow, to hunt in the
morning, fish in the afternoon, rear cattle in the evening, criticize
after dinner, just as I have a mind, without ever becoming hunter,

fisherman, shepherd, or critic." [28] People will say that this is the naïveté of youth. Yet, in conformity with this idea, Marx and Engels rejected the principle of division of labor to the last.[29] And let us remember the motto to be inscribed by the communist society—according to Marx—on its banners: "From each according to his abilities, to each according to his needs." [30] Now, it is a fact that the so-called individualistic ethic has never been carried so far as to say: "to each according to his needs." And this means that we must be very careful before assuming indiscriminately that Marx's concept of liberty was simply part and parcel of his anthropological collectivism.

Marx the political theorist, the man who flirted (*kokettieren*) with Hegelian philosophy, dissolved the individual in the community just as Hegel merged him with the State. That is to say, Marx as philosopher freed himself with a single philosophico-dialectic stroke from all the concrete problems of his political society of the future, by postulating a "generico-social" man, we might say a disindividualized man who no longer has an *ego* which can be contrasted to the *alter*.[31] In this context Marx was an extreme collectivist. But if we pass on to Marx the student of economy, undertaking to resolve the problems of humanity in an economic key, his outlook changes, and I would say that it acually reverses itself.

Marx's *idée fixe,* in *Das Kapital,* was unpaid work for the worker. And this was because the economic process was considered from the point of view of he who works and not of consumption, from the angle of the intrinsic value of the labor-force, and not of the value for use of goods. All well and good. But such a way of posing the problem can come to mind only to the extent that our preoccupation is with the single individual, with men considered separately. This is tantamount to saying that Marx's cry of protest against the "inhumanity" of the capitalist economy implies an individualistic ethic. If the individual were really called upon by Marx to sacrifice himself to mankind and to dissolve in the community, *Das Kapital* would hardly make sense. From the point of view of a collectivist conception of man, a market system may be criticized for not being a radical solution, but it certainly does not justify any indignation, since the characteristic of the market is precisely to establish the price of goods by leaving out of consideration their individual cost, that is, the work actually expended by the person who made them. To put it another way, the characteristic of a market economy is to consider the objective utility of a good—namely its utility for a "generalized other," for consumption—with a total disregard for the subjective effort, namely for the *quantum* of work which it represents for those who produced it. Yet Marx cries out at this scandal, he finds the system inhuman. He may be right. But clearly to put the criterion of the "value-of-work" in the place of the value-of-trade and the value-of-consumption, means to re-assert the value and the rights of the individual *as such,* that is, to take the part of the single person whom the market mechanisms sacrifice to the interests of an anonymous, merciless collectivity of consumers.

That this implication should have escaped Marx was only to be expected, since he was wholly absorbed in his crusade to exterminate the capitalists. But this does not alter the fact that his "philosophic collectivism," once it is put to the test on the ground of concrete remedies and suggestions, melts away like snow in the sun. Marx was for a man conceived of as a "generic being," as *Gattungswesen,* as long as this anthropology helped him to explain what otherwise remains unexplainable, namely how a society can function without a State and without hierarchies. But no sooner is this problem coped with, than his ideal of "economic liberation" of man takes on the features of an intransigent ideal of individualistic justice.[32] For the rule of a collectivist anthropology should be: To each what brings benefit to the whole—and cannot be: To each the full reward for his work.

It is not important here to inquire why his therapeutics—in the political as much as in the economic sphere—has worked in a very different way. What matters is that we realize that Marx rejected representative democracy because he wanted *more* democracy, liberalism because he wanted *more* liberty, and laissez-faire because he wanted an economic system which would attain perfect retributive justice. In short, Marx was anti-everything because he was a thorough-going extreme libertarian. It is the grievous gaps in his doctrine and the total lack of foresight in his political thought which have turned Marxism into quite another thing. But, for his own part, Marx did not suggest to us a counter-ideal, but the *same ideal* in its most extreme, utopian, and perfectionist form.[33]

I ask again: what is the alternative solution? What authors and what confirmation can speak in favor of a "freedom-less" conception of democracy? To be sure, a number of pamphlet writers, mob orators and the like, do dismiss political freedom and preach the extermination of liberal civility and civilization. However, their job is the manipulation of symbols and their purpose is mass mobilization—not knowledge and thinking. They can bear no witness. It is quite true that it is the simplifiers and the popularizers who mold the image of "true democracy" for the public at large. And I am well aware of the fact that ordinary political discourse comes down to expressing emotions rather than knowledge, subconscious longings and desires rather than responsibly assessed goals. Therefore I see very well that knowledge can point down one path, and history set out on another. But to have to deal with an unreasoning world is not a reason for giving up reasoning. If readers may misunderstand what they read, that is no justification for starting with bad understanding from the very beginning—when the problem is to understand.

To someone who accused him of taking sides, the placid Abbot Galiani once replied drily, and irritably: "Je ne suis pour rien. Je suis pour qu'on ne déraisonne" [34]—I am in favor of nothing. I am against people talking nonsense. If I may borrow from Galiani, I am for liberal democracy because I am against incompetence and cheaters. Actually, I am not taking sides *for,* but *against* the inconsistency of the many who refuse with one hand what they demand with the other, who refuse the means and yet want the ends.

4. Apprehensions

Every generation wants to be new, to be original; it feels that it has to say something not yet said and contradict what has already been said. If this were not so, life would seem purposeless to us, and history would lack dynamism. But it is not easy to be original. Many people think themselves original just because they are ignorant. Thus, unwittingly, they often discover what has already been discovered, invent what has already been invented, and attempt what has already been attempted, thereby repeating old mistakes and perennially unsuccessful undertakings.

Then there are those who seek originality in extremism. But the extremist—as Ortega y Gasset said—is a "born falsifier," someone who substitutes exaggeration for creation and innovation. And exaggeration, Ortega stressed, "is the opposite of creation, it is the definition of inertia. The immoderates are always the inert of their age. The creative man . . . knows the limits of original truth and, for this very reason, is on the alert, ready to abandon it the moment it begins to turn into untruth." [35] The extremist, instead, lives by stealing the ideas of others and by presenting their distortion as an innovation. Thus, his originality lies mainly in noise, in using inflated words—an immoderate vocabulary whose repercussions, as the extremist himself discovers only too late, have actually gone beyond his intentions.

I make these observations because the ease and frequency with which political dilettantism flows into, and joins forces with extremism has been, for a not inconsiderable period of recent European intellectual history, rather striking. The figure of the revolutionary intellectual, of the intellectual in revolt who joins the ranks of the intelligentsia, is relatively new; for our intelligentsias certainly cannot be compared to the Encyclopedists, the amiable *philosophes* of the Age of Enlightenment. The latter devoted themselves to Cartesian truth, to clear, distinct ideas: their mission was to enlighten by spreading knowledge. Quite a different thing, then, from the attitude of the intelligentsias which originate from the historicism of the Hegelian Left, whose urge is to rush headlong into action because they have to be "historical at all costs": meaning by this that one should always be abreast of the future, on the high tide of time, that one should frantically anticipate the movement of history. To listen to them, one would think it necessary "to act," only to act, always to act. In effect, theirs is not so much spasmodic action as spasmodic talk made out of words which are out of control.[36] Thus, for about a century we have exaggerated in exaggerating. We urgently need, therefore, to take stock of the situation, and the time has come, I believe, for some meditative seclusion (which does not mean that we should exaggerate in the opposite way by shifting from over-talking to quasi-silence).

Certainly we must go forward—not stand still or, even worse, go back. But "forward" and "backwards" with respect to what point of reference? History is the myth of Sisyphus, every generation has to start anew. None of us is born civilized: our real birth certificate should bear the year zero. Our historical maturity of men of "our time" must always be reconquered: and each time we have to cover a longer distance. My question, and I should say my fear, is: has the line of Western tradition become too long? Do we still have the energy to travel its full length? From time to time I am struck by the suspicion that the house is more civilized than its inmates, and that civilizations crumble because they end by being more advanced than their tenants. Are we really pregnant with the future, or are we in effect unable to keep pace with our time?

Someone opens the way to the years to come, but I fear that many of those who claim to be already living in the future are actually a rearguard which has long since lost touch with the present. And if going forward means going ever further away from liberal democracy until one loses it, I willingly number myself among those who pursue it, that is, among those who are concerned with distinguishing between verbal advances and failures of achievement. "Faites vôtre devoir et laissez faire aux Dieux"—says a hero of Corneille[37]. Do your duty and leave the rest to the gods. I feel that this is the best we can do.

NOTES

† *General Theory* (New York, 1935), pp. 383-384.

1. *Philosophie des Rechts,* par. 190 appendix.

2. Kingsley Martin, *French Liberal Thought in the Eighteenth Century* (London, rev. ed. 1954), p. 278. The passage refers to the Age of Enlightenment, but the author evidently is referring also to us.

3. "Politics and the English Language," in *Selected Essays,* p. 157.

4. Cf. *Ideology and Utopia,* p. 192, and Chap. IV, 3 *passim.*

5. As results implicitly from the text I am using "ideocracy" also as a sub-stitute for the literal meaning of ideology, that is, for "discourse on ideas," and therefore not in Lasswell's and Kaplan's meaning, i.e., in reference to "symbol specialists" and to denote "any body politic in which the predominant forms of power are those resting on the manipulation of symbols" (*Power and Society,* pp. 212-213). In this manner, after *ideology* we make useless for a positive connotation *ideocracy* as well. My point is that it is exactly because we are living in an age of "disrespect to ideas" that the safeguarding of a term that alludes to the respect of ideas becomes essential.

6. "Ideology" was coined by Destutt de Tracy in 1796 to indicate the science of the study of ideas. But already Napoleon gave it a negative meaning, saying "ideologists" to allude to hare-brain speculations based on nothing concrete. Marx gave ideology an opposite negative sense, that is, not of ideas existing in a vacuum but of ideas rooted in class interests. Lenin contradicted Marx on the question of the superfluity of ideologies, for he defended the necessity of a "socialist ideology," without modifying, however, Marxian gnosiology, and thereby keeping for the label "bourgeois ideology" the value of anathema which Marx gave it. It is worth adding that also in Hitler's powerful propa-ganda machine (second to the Communist only in terms of duration) ide-ology was used in a disparaging sense with exclusive reference to capitalistic and democratic ideologies. Therefore the obstinacy with which most diction-aries continue to record the word "ideology" in its original literal meaning is rather surprising.

7. On the Marxist notion of ideology from Marx to Lenin, cf., e.g., Henry Chambre, *Le Marxisme en Union Soviétique,* Introduction. On Mannheim, cf. esp. Jean Maquet, *La sociologie de la connaissance* (Louvain, 1949), and Robert K. Merton, *Social Theory and Social Structure* (Glencoe, rev. ed. 1957) Chap. XII and esp. XIII.

8. R. K. Merton, *op. cit.,* p. 457.

9. Cf. Chap. IX, 1, notes 11 and 12, above.

10. Cf. K. R. Popper, *The Open Society,* p. 215.

11. R. K. Merton, *op. cit.,* p. 503.

12. Cf. F. A. Hayek, *The Counter-Revolution of Science,* p. 90. In sum, the alternative of this gnosiology is either blind trust of some infallible super-thinking, or silence and non-thinking.

13. The ideological indictment has spread like an oil stain because we have been so unreflecting and unprecise as to confuse the question raised by Marx with that of *Wertfreiheit,* thus treating ideological objectivity and axiological objectivity as though they were one and the same thing. This is exactly why we must not encourage this *quid pro quo* by admitting that the presence of

value judgments in philosophical and in scientific language is equivalent to rendering it ideological.

14. In this connection W. Weidlè has hit upon an excellent definition: "Ideology is a system of ideas about which no one thinks any longer." ("Sur le concept d'idéologie," *Le Contrat social* [1959], II, p. 77.)

15. For this aspect of the concept of ideology, cf. Chap. IX, 5, above.

16. F. A. Hayek, *op. cit.,* p. 89.

17. Ortega y Gasset, *Kant 1794-1924 (Reflexiones de centenario)* par. II.

18. When Aristotle illustrated his ideal of *politéia* and the virtue, or *dikaiosúne* (justice), upon which it would have to be built, he was undoubtedly speaking of something that had already been outdated by the "progress of time." Therefore Aristotle's thought would have been (according to the classifications which we have devised today) conservative, if not reactionary. The fact remains that the "retrograde" Aristotle is still alive and modern after more than two thousand years, whereas there is no trace left of the "progressives" of the time. In the long run, as Lord Keynes put it, we are all dead. What survives us is what we have had to say, not the progressivism or the conservatism of what we have said.

19. And, let it be added in passing, by the consequent mistrust of "value ideals." An intellectual élite which accepts the equation "values = ideology" produces a culture which cannot be concerned, for instance about liberty (liberty as a value). It is pertinent to wonder, then, how a free society can survive if its "ideocrats" hold that freedom should be the concern of somebody else; that is, in which those who know do not speak, and those who speak do not know. The usual answer is that the philosopher, the social scientist and the jurist are concerned with freedom when they vote, i.e., as citizens. However, some very elementary mathematics shows that, in voting terms, a "silent knowledge" amounts to nothing.

20. Although Mannheim recognized that "many of the elements constituting the chiliastic attitude were transmuted into and took refuge in syndicalism and Bolshevism." Cf. *Ideology and Utopia,* p. 223, and Chap. IV, 3 *a, d.*

21. *Contrat social,* I, 6 [my italics].

22. *Contrat social,* II, 11. See also Rousseau's Second *Discours.* That Rousseau spoke in the language of individualism has been emphasized by numberless authors. Cf., e.g., Leo Strauss, *Natural Right and History* (Chicago, 1953), Cobban's *Rousseau and the Modern State,* and Derathé's previously mentioned books.

23. And this was due to perfectionist concerns. Cf. Talmon's general conclusion: "Totalitarian democracy early evolved into a pattern of coercion and centralization not because it rejected the values of eighteenth-century liberal indi-

vidualism, but because it had originally a too perfectionist attitude towards them. . . . Man was not merely to be freed from restraints. All the existing traditions, established institutions, and social arrangements were to be overthrown and remade, with the sole purpose of securing to man the totality of his rights and freedoms, and liberating him from all dependence." (*The Origins of Totalitarian Democracy,* p. 249.)

24. But also, to some extent, the failure of his interpreters in interpreting him. For Rousseau was well aware of the *"polis* size" limitation, so to speak, of his ideal. (Cf. Chap. XIII, 4, and 5, above.) In the last analysis it is we who, after two centuries, have amplified the weak points of Rousseau's system by projecting in a historical vacuum principles and techniques which Rousseau applied to a small homogeneous community.

25. It is not therefore a paradox to observe, with Kelsen, that "his attack against the English parliament shows to what degree freedom was for him the foundation of his political system." *Vom Wesen und Wert der Demokratie,* Chap. I.

26. *Communist Manifesto,* II. Cf. also Marx's reply to Proudhon: "The working class will substitute . . . for the old bourgeois order an association which will exclude classes and their antagonism, and there will no longer be political power, properly speaking, since political power is simply the official form of the antagonism in bourgeois society." *The Poverty of Philosophy* (1847), Part II, 5.

27. That this was a "primitive" ideal of democracy was stated by Lenin himself. Polemizing against Bernstein, who had criticized Marx's ideal as a "primitive stage of democracy," Lenin replied: "Under Socialism much of the 'primitive' democracy is inevitably revived, since for the first time in the history of civilized society, the mass of the population rises to independent participation, not only in voting and elections, but also *in the every-day administration of affairs.* Under Socialism, *all will take a turn in management* [government], and will soon become accustomed to the idea of no managers at all. . . . Socialism will . . . create such conditions for the majority of the population as to enable *everybody,* without exception, to perform State functions. . . ." (*State and Revolution,* VI, 3. My italics.) Cf. also the *Party's Program* of 1919, in which Lenin insisted on the need of having every member of the Soviets participate in turn and always in different capacities to the administration, so that finally the entire population be included in the State-no-longer-State.

29. Cf. the *Critique of the Gotha Programme* (New York, 1938), where Marx says: "In a higher phase of communist society . . . the enslaving subordination of individuals under division of labor, and therewith also the antithesis between mental and physical labour, has vanished" (p. 10). As anyone can

see, in 1875 the thesis of the *German Ideology* remains unchanged, even if revived in a less picturesque language.

30. It is the famous passage of the *Critique of the Gotha Programme.*

31. Cf. Karl Löwith, *Von Hegel bis Nietzsche,* Part II, Chap. IV, 3; and also, in apologetic key, G. della Volpe, *La libertà comunista,* esp. Chap. III.

32. This is easily explained, since Marx treats the relationship between individual and society dialectically, and using the verb *aufheben.* Thus his "philosophic collectivism" is related to an individual who is *aufgehoben* in the community in the sense of being "annihilated"; whereas his "economic individualism" is founded on an individual who is *aufgehoben* positively, that is, "lifted up" in the community in the sense of being "maintained" within the whole. Cf. Chap. XV, note 37, above.

33. In the last analysis the problem posed by Marx to his interpreters is the same as Luther's, who as a religious writer is considered a libertarian, and as a political writer an absolutist. Actually, as has been shown by S. S. Wolin, "Politics and Religion: Luther's Simplistic Imperative," *American Political Science Review,* I (1956), pp. 24-42, every political simplicism and primitivism transforms an extreme ideal of liberty into a practical acceptance of despotism: these being the two sides of a same "simplistic imperative."

34. Galiani, in *Mélanges d'économie politique* (Paris, 1848), p. 13.

35. Ortega y Gasset, *Obras* (Madrid, 1936), p. 742.

36. Cf. G. Sartori, "Intellettuali e intelligentzia," *Studi politici,* I-II (1953), pp. 29-53.

37. *Horace,* 710.

Index of Names

Abel, Theodore, 153
Acton, (Lord) J. E., 240, 248, 278, 380
Adam, Thomas R., 310
Adams, Maynard E., 178
Adler, Mortimer J., 314, 315, 316
Adorno, Theodor W., 153
Alain, 132
Almond, Gabriel, 155, 203
Anshen, Ruth Nanda, 276, 314
Aquinas, Thomas, 274, 436
Arendt, Hannay, 27, 137, 153
Aristotle, 32, 61, 188, 253-254, 255, 260, 279, 300, 316, 324, 330, 333, 339, 469
Arnold, Thurman, 93, 177
Aron, Raymond, 176, 180, 190-191
Austin, John, 307-308
Ayer, Alfred J., 177, 186

Babeuf, (Gracchus), 380
Bagehot, Walter, 7, 93, 382
Baker, (sir) Ernest, 270
Bakunin, Michael, 122
Balladore Pallieri, Giorgio, 269
Barbeyrac, J., 268
Barents, Jan, 16, 448
Barone, Enrico, 411
Bartolo da Sassoferrato, 148
Barton, Allen H., 92
Basso, Lelio, 247

Battaglia, Felice, 29, 269, 323
Bay, Christian, 129
Bebel, August, 419, 445, 447
Becker, J. P., 446
Bell, Daniel, 202, 203
Benney, Mark, 92
Bentham, Jeremy, 15, 323, 362
Bentley, Arthur F., 179, 199, 270
Berelson, Bernard R., 77, 92, 130
Berger, Morroe, 153
Bernstein, Eduard, 470
Bettelheim, Charles, 410
Bierstedt, Robert, 153
Blackstone, (sir) William, 362
Blaisdell, Donald C., 199
Blanc, Louis, 379
Blanqui, Auguste, 156, 380
Bluntschli, Johann Kaspar, 31, 271
Bobbio, Norberto, 29, 48, 49, 70, 111, 271, 301, 350, 353, 380
Bochenski, I. M., 441, 442
Böckh, August, 272
Boorstin, Daniel J., 247
Bracton, (de) Henry, 324
Braga, Giorgio, 203, 204
Brecht, Arnold, 177, 178, 182, 200
Bridel, Marcel, 271
Brocard, Lucien, 410
Brodbeck, Arthur J., 92
Brown, Roger W., 28
Bruguier, Giuseppe, 410

473